Rethinking J.S. Bach's *The Art of Fugue*

The enigmatic character of *The Art of Fugue* became apparent as early as in its first edition, printed more than a year after the composer's death. Carl Philipp Emanuel Bach, who published both the first and second editions, raised several unsolved questions regarding this opus. Anatoly P. Milka presents a consistent and coherent solution to the unresolved questions about the history, structure and appearance of J.S. Bach's *The Art of Fugue*, opening new perspectives for further exploration of this musical masterpiece. Milka challenges the present scholarly consensus that there are two different versions of *The Art of Fugue* (the Autograph and the Original Edition) and argues that Bach had considered four versions, of which only two are apparent and have been discussed so far. Only Bach's illness and death prevented him from fulfilling his plan and publishing a fourth, conclusive version of his opus.

Anatoly P. Milka is Professor and Dr Habil of Musicology at the St Petersburg Conservatory and the St Petersburg State University, Russia. His publications in Russian include *Theoretical Foundations of Functionality in Music* (St Petersburg, 1982); *Bach's Musical Offering: Toward Reconstruction and Interpretation* (Moscow, 1999); *Intriguing Bachiana* (with Tatiana Shabalina; St Petersburg, 1997, 2001); a facsimile edition of *L'A.B.C. Musical von Gottfried Kirchhoff* (St Petersburg, 2004), and Bach's The Art of Fugue: *Toward Reconstruction and Interpretation* (St Petersburg, 2009). This is his first book appearing in English.

Marina Ritzarev is Professor and Dr Habil of Musicology. She was a student and scholar in St Petersburg and Moscow before moving to Israel in 1990, where she teaches at Bar-Ilan University. She has authored books in Russian on Dmitry Bortniansky (1979, 2015), Maxim Berezovsky (1983, 2013), Sergei Slonimsky (1991) and the Russian Sacred Concerto (2006). Her two books in English – *Eighteenth-Century Russian Music* (2006) and *Tchaikovsky's 'Pathétique' and Russian Culture* (2014) – were published by Ashgate.

Esti Sheinberg is Associate Professor of Practice in Music History at the Glenn Korff School of Music, University of Nebraska-Lincoln, USA (BA in musicology at the University of Tel-Aviv, Israel; PhD in music at the University of Edinburgh, UK). She has authored *Irony, Satire, Parody and the Grotesque in the Music of Shostakovich* (Ashgate, 2000) and edited *Music Semiotics: A Network of Significations – in Honour and Memory of Raymond Monelle* (Ashgate, 2012).

Rethinking J.S. Bach's
The Art of Fugue

Anatoly P. Milka

Translated from Russian by Marina Ritzarev

Edited by Esti Sheinberg

LONDON AND NEW YORK

First published 2017
by Routledge
2 Park Square, Milton Park, Abingdon, Oxon OX14 4RN

and by Routledge
711 Third Avenue, New York, NY 10017

Routledge is an imprint of the Taylor & Francis Group, an informa business

© 2017 Anatoly Milka

The right of Anatoly Milka to be identified as author of this work has been asserted by him in accordance with sections 77 and 78 of the Copyright, Designs and Patents Act 1988.

All rights reserved. No part of this book may be reprinted or reproduced or utilised in any form or by any electronic, mechanical, or other means, now known or hereafter invented, including photocopying and recording, or in any information storage or retrieval system, without permission in writing from the publishers.

Trademark notice: Product or corporate names may be trademarks or registered trademarks, and are used only for identification and explanation without intent to infringe.

British Library Cataloguing in Publication Data
A catalogue record for this book is available from the British Library

Library of Congress Cataloging in Publication Data
Names: Milka, A., 1939 (Anatoly Pavlovich) | Ritzarev, Marina, 1946 translator | Sheinberg, Esti, 1954 editor
Title: Rethinking J.S. Bach's the Art of fugue / by Anatoly P. Milka; translated by Marina Ritzarev; edited by Esti Sheinberg.
Other titles: "Iskusstvo fugi" I.S. Bakha. English Description: 2016. | Includes bibliographical references and index.
Identifiers: LCCN 2015045559 (print) | LCCN 2015046922 (ebook) | ISBN 9781472458865 (hardcover: alk. paper) | ISBN 9781315606095 (ebook) | ISBN 9781472458889 (epub)
Subjects: LCSH: Bach, Johann Sebastian, 1685–1750. Kunst der Fuge.
Classification: LCC ML410.B13 M5313 2016 (print) | LCC ML410.B13 (ebook) | DDC 786/.1872—dc23
LC record available at http://lccn.loc.gov/2015045559

ISBN: 9781472458865 (hbk)
ISBN: 9781315606095 (ebk)

Bach musicological font developed by © Yo Tomita

Typeset in Perpetua
by codeMantra

For the blessed memory of my friend Valery Maisky

Contents

List of figures ... ix
List of schemes ... xi
List of tables ... xiii
List of music examples ... xv
List of abbreviations ... xvii
Preliminary notes concerning the figures ... xix
Preface ... xxi

Introduction ... 1

PART I
Toward the history of the conception ... 3

1 The last decade ... 5
2 On the conception of *The Art of Fugue* ... 18
3 Bach's illness and the changes in his handwriting ... 24

PART II
The principal documents: The Autograph and the Original Edition ... 35

4 The Autograph ... 37
5 The Original Edition ... 56

PART III
J.S. Bach's work on *The Art of Fugue* ... 67

6 The versions in Bach's music ... 69
7 The First Version of *The Art of Fugue* ... 79

8	The Second Version	88
9	Toward the Third Version	102
10	The Third Version	110
11	The Fourth Version	129

PART IV
Carl Philipp Emanuel Bach's work toward the publication of *The Art of Fugue* — 145

12	Settings, attitudes and circumstances	147
13	Sequencing and titles in the Original Edition	162
14	The history of the 1752 edition	169

PART V
Toward a new interpretation of *The Art of Fugue* — 173

15	The title page as a 'letters and numbers game' and the question of authorship	175
16	*Contrapunctur 5*	189
17	Myths about the Canon in Augmentation	197
18	The autograph of the last fugue: An unfinished copy?	209
19	'Over this fugue …'	235
20	Revelation (instead of an Epilogue)	240

Bibliography	249
Index	257

Figures

Unless otherwise specified, all figures listed here are defined as public domain.

1.1	Athanasius Kircher, *Musurgia Universalis*, frontpiece	12
2.1a	J.J. Fux: Fugue in *Gradus ad Parnassum*, Latin edition, p. 169	20
2.1b	Same fugue in Mizler's German edition of *Gradus ad Parnassum*, Tab. XXIII (2nd system, f. 2)	20
3.1	BWV 210, (D-B Mus. Ms. Bach St 76), title page	26
4.1	The Autograph P 200: the title page	38
4.2a–d	Examples of pagination numbers in the Autograph	43
4.3	Numeration of the first four fugues in P 200, misinterpreted by Friedländer as page spread numbers	43
4.4	P 200, fifth spread, left: the fifth fugue's original serial number appears where the fugue starts, at the middle of the page; Friedländer added a digit '5', at the top of the same page	44
4.5a	Erroneous 'correction': P 200, page 14. The fugue's serial number '6' is deleted, and the digit '7' is marked instead	45
4.5b	Page 16 of the Autograph: the original serial numbering of fugue 7	45
4.6	Four different numerations: P 200, 10th spread	46
4.7	P 200: inscription at the bottom of the title page	46
4.8	P 200: *Canon in Hypodiapason*	50
8.1	The first mirror fugue (P 200, pp. 33–5, marked XIII)	88
8.2	The second mirror fugue (P 200, pp. 36–8, marked XIV)	89
8.3a	The opening of the canon (P 200, p. 32, marked XII)	90
8.3b	The opening of the second canon (P 200, p. 38, marked XV)	90
8.4	Beginning of the canon (P 200, p. 33, marked XII)	91
8.5	Beginning of the canon, proposta (bars 3–4) and risposta (bars 7–8) encircled	91
8.6	P 200, canon XII, bar 21 and canon XV, bar 26	93
8.7	P 200, ornamental changes in canon XV, bars 1–9	94
8.8	P 200, canon XV, corrections in bar 11	96
8.9	P 200, canon XV, corrections in bars 34–38	96
8.10	P 200, canon XV, bars 11, 23–24, 49–50: corrections discontinued	97
9.1	P 200, canon XV, written over the spread of pages 38–9; crammed writing on the left page, clear and flowing on the right one	103

x *Figures*

11.1	Subsidiary pagination of the Canon in Augmentation (P 200/1–1)	134
13.1	The titles of the two mirror fugues, Original Edition, DK–Kk mu 6406.2030	164
15.1	P 200: the title page of *The Art of Fugue*	175
15.2	P 200/1: the title page on the supplements folder	176
15.3	The title of the 1751 Original Edition, DK–Kk mu 6406.2030	176
15.4	Numerical alphabet and paragram in Harsdörfer's *Poetischer Trichter*	178
15.5	'SigC' from the title page of P 200, and 'GrafC' from J.C.F. Bach's letter, courtesy of the Niedersächs Staatsarchiv, Bückeburg, shelfmark: F2 Nr. 2642	181
16.1	The page spread of fugue IV in P 200	190
16.2	P 200, fugue IV, bar 41/41 has 14 notes; the four notes in the treble spell B-A-C-H	191
16.3	P 200, fugue IV: the theme, presented in all parts, consists of 14 notes	192
16.4	The page spread of *Contrapunctur 5*, Original Edition, DK–Kk mu 6406.2030	193
17.1	P 200/1–1: the engraver copy of the Canon in Augmentation, first page	198
17.2	*Canon per Augmentationem in Contrario Motu*: page 48, Original Edition, DK–Kk mu 6406.2030	199
17.3	Canon in Augmentation, bars 23–25 and 31–33; comparison of the first page of P 200/1–1 and page 48, Original Edition, DK–Kk mu 6406.2030	201
17.4	P 200: first bars in canons XII and XV	204
18.1	C.P.E. Bach's notice on the verso of the Original Edition's title page (DK–Kk mu 6406.2030)	210
18.2	The paragraph in the obituary describing *The Art of Fugue*	212
18.3	Mirror fugue XIII, beginning, P 200	215
18.4	P 200/1–3: the last page of the 'unfinished' fugue (bars 227–239)	222
18.5	P 200/1–3: the first page of the 'unfinished' fugue (bars 1–68)	223
18.6	P 200/1–3, second page: bars 113–114 crossed out, correction inserted at the bottom of the page	225
18.7	P 200/1–3: bars 109–115 (top system) and their correction (bottom page margin, below the bottom system)	226
19.1	P 200/1–3: C.P.E. Bach's inscription on the last page	235
20.1	The Astronomical Clock in Marienkirche, Lübeck	243
20.2	Adam Gumpelzhaimer, Canon *Clama ne cesses* from the *Compendium musicae* (Augsburg, 1611)	245

Schemes

4.1	The disposition of music sheets in the main body of P 200	42
4.2	P 200: last three bifolios (Bögen) prior to its acquisition by Poelchau	48
4.3	P 200: organization of sheets at the time of their deposit in the Royal Library	48
4.4	Bach's 'six-sheet' group model	52
5.1	Ordering changes between the Autograph and the Original Edition	60
6.1	The first version of *Clavierübung III*	70
6.2	The second version of *Clavierübung III*	71
6.3	The third and fourth versions of *Clavierübung III*	74
7.1	Structure of the First Version of *The Art of Fugue*	84
7.2	Structure of the First Version, showing paper types	85
8.1	Structure of the Second Version of *The Art of Fugue*	98
8.2	Sheet structure of the Second Version of *The Art of Fugue*	99
9.1	A hypothetical additional binio allows the inclusion of new pair of mirror fugues for two claviers	104
9.2	Hypothetical unrealised plan of the entire Second Version	105
9.3	Hypothetical structure before the creation of the Third Version	106
9.4	Proposed hypothetical structure of *The Art of Fugue* (without the 'draft' canons)	107
9.5	A hypothetical interpretation of the phrase 'einen andern Grund Plan', scribbled on the verso of the last page of P 200/1–3	108
10.1	The Third Version of *The Art of Fugue*: structural options and solutions	110
10.2	The first set of four fugues	112
10.3	The order of pieces in the Third Version	123
11.1	The early subsidiary pagination of the group of canons	136
11.2	The second subsidiary pagination of the group of canons	137
11.3	The plan of the second half, before the insertion of Cp[14F]	138
11.4	The plan to insert Cp[14F] to the second half	140
11.5	The layout of the cycle's second half after the insertion of the engraver copy of Cp[14F]	141
15.1	Paragrammatic correspondence between number of bars and the hypothetical title page	185
20.1	The numerical structure of *The Art of Fugue*	240

Tables

4.1	Numerations and content plan of the Autograph, main body (P 200)	40
4.2	Rastration in the Autograph, main body (P 200)	51
5.1	Order of pieces in the Original Edition	61
5.2	Rhythm and metre changes from the Autograph to the Original Edition	63
10.1	The first set of four fugues in the Third Version	112
10.2	The first set of three fugues in the Third Version	113
10.3	The first appearance of the theme in diminution in fugues VII and VIII	114
10.4	The first appearance of the theme in augmentation in fugues VII and VIII	114
10.5	The second set of four, based on double fugues	114
10.6	The mirror fugues defined by theme presentation	117
10.7	The second set of three: mirror fugues (initial variant)	118
10.8	The second variant of the set of three mirror fugues	118
10.9	Ordering of canons in the Third Version (first variant)	120
10.10	Organisation of the canons by an increasing entry interval	120
10.11	Final organisation of the canons in the Third Version	121
11.1	Cp12 and Cp[13] in the Third Version, before the introduction of Cp[14]	129
11.2	The mirror fugues after the introduction of Cp[14]	130
11.3	The mirror fugues after the first reordering	130
11.4	The mirror fugues after the replacement of Cp[14] with Cp[14F]	131
11.5	Probable repositioning of the mirror fugues, avoiding juxtaposition of similar tempi, topics and presentation of themes	131
11.6	Comparison of Wiemer's and Butler's subsidiary paginations	133
13.1	Plan of the Original Edition	163
15.1	Reorganisation and resizing of the first set of four pieces	185
16.1	The 'natural' numerological system	194
16.2	The 'trigonal' numerological system	194
16.3	Value of 'contrapunctur' according to the natural numerological system	195
16.4	Numerological interpretation of the fifth fugue's title	195
16.5	Value of 'contrapunctur' in the trigonal numerological system	195
17.1	Score sizes of the Canon in Augmentation in P 200/1–1 and in the Original Edition	202
18.1	Text comparison: the advertisement, the notice on the first edition and the preface to the second edition	213

Music examples

6.1	Possible variants for bars 100–103 of fugue BWV 552₂	75
6.2	Possible variants for bars 113–17 of fugue BWV 552₂	76
7.1	The themes of fugues I and II	79
7.2	The themes of fugues III and IV	80
7.3	Themes and countersubjects of fugues V and VI	81
7.4	Stretto theme entries in fugues VII and VIII	81
7.5	Thematic materials of fugues X and XI	82
8.1	The themes of the two *rectae* mirror fugues XIII and XIV	89
8.2	The themes of the two *inversae* mirror fugues XIII and XIV	89
9.1	P 200, canons XV and *XVIII*, motivic comparison	106
10.1	Beginning of Contrapunctus 4 in the Original Edition	111
10.2	The first bars of fugues VII and VIII	113
17.1	Canon in Augmentation, variants of the first countersubject	205
17.2	Canon in Augmentation XII and XV, comparison of bars 10–12	206
18.1	Nottebohm's combination of themes	216
18.2	Combination of themes using the 14-note version of the main theme	217
18.3	The hypothetical *fuga inversa*	217
18.4	P 200/1–3, the 'unfinished' fugue: corrections	226

Abbreviations

BD   *Bach-Dokumente*, Hrsg. v. Bach-Archive Leipzig (Supplement zu: Johann Sebastian Bach Neue Ausgabe sämtlicher Werke):

      BD I   *Schriftstücke von der Hand Johann Sebastian Bachs. Kritische Gesamtausgabe*, eds. Werner Neumann and Hans-Joachim Schulze (Kassel: Bärenreiter; Leipzig: VEB Deutscher Verlag für Musik, 1963)

      BD II   *Fremdschriftliche und gedruckte Dokumente zur Lebensgeschichte Johann Sebastian Bachs 1685–1750. Kritische Gesamtausgabe*, eds. Werner Neumann and Hans-Joachim Schulze (Kassel: Bärenreiter; Leipzig: VEB Deutscher Verlag für Musik, 1969)

      BD III   *Dokumente zum Nachwirken Johann Sebastian Bachs, 1750–1800*, ed. Hans-Joachim Schulze (Kassel: Bärenreiter; Leipzig: VEB Deutscher Verlag für Musik, 1972)

      BD V   *Dokumente zu Leben, Werk, Nachwirken Johann Sebastian Bachs, 1685–1800*, eds. Hans-Joachim Schulze and Andreas Glöckner (Kassel: Bärenreiter, 2007).

BJ   *Bach-Jahrbuch* (1904–)

BWV   Alfred Dürr, Yoshitake Kobayashi and Kirsten Beißwenger (eds.), *Bach-Werke-Verzeichnis: Kleine Ausgabe (BWV^{2a}), nach der von Wolfgang Schmieder vorgelegten 2. Ausgabe* (Wiesbaden, 1998)

Cp   Contrapunctus [a fugue as designated in the Original Edition] followed by its serial number. As the Original Edition does not give the serial number after 12, numbers 13 and 14 are in square brackets. The fugue for two claviers and the final piece (*Fuga a 3 Soggetti*) are distinguished as Cp[14] and Cp[14F] respectively

KB   *Kritischer Bericht* (Critical commentary volumes) accompanying *NBA*:

      II/1   Friedrich Smend, *Missa; Symbolum Nicenum; Sanctus; Ossana, Benedictus, Agnus Dei et Dona Nobis Pacem (später genannt 'Messe in h-Moll')* (Kassel, 1956)

      IV/2   Hans Klotz, *Die Orgelchoräle aus der Leipziger Originalhandschrift* (Kassel, 1957)

      IV/4   Manfred Tessmer, *Dritter Teil der Klavierübung* (Kassel, 1974)

      VIII/1   Christoph Wolff, *Kanons, Musikalisches Opfer* (Kassel, 1976)

      VIII/2   Klaus Hofmann, *Die Kunst der Fuge* (Kassel, 1996)

MMB   [Mizler's *Musikalische Bibliothek*] Lorenz Christoph Mizler von Kolof, *Neu eröffnete musikalische Bibliothek, oder Gründliche Nachricht nebst unpartheyischem Urtheil von musikalischen Schriften und Büchern* (Leipzig, 1736–1754)

NBA	[*Neue Bach-Ausgabe*: Complete edition of Bach's works] *Johann Sebastian Bach, Neue Ausgabe sämtlicher Werke* (Kassel, 1954–2008)
NBR	*The New Bach Reader: A Life of Johann Sebastian Bach in Letters and Documents*, edited by Hans T. David and Arthur Mendel, revised and enlarged by Christoph Wolff (New York, 1998)
P 200	Shelfmark of the Autograph of *The Art of Fugue*
	P 200/1 Shelfmark of the folder with the supplements of the Autograph
	P 200/1–1 Shelfmark of Supplement 1 to the Autograph
	P 200/1–2 Shelfmark of Supplement 2 to the Autograph
	P 200/1–3 Shelfmark of Supplement 3 to the Autograph
WZ	Wasserzeichen (watermark). The number refers to the catalogue entry in: Wisso Weiss and Yoshitake Kobayashi, *Katalog der Wasserzeichen in Bachs Originalhandschriften*, *NBA* IX/1–2 (Kassel, 1985)

Preliminary notes concerning the figures

The two main sources used in this book are:

(1) The Autograph manuscript of *The Art of Fugue*. The original document, kept as D–B Mus. ms. Bach P 200 and P 200/1 (the latter is the folder holding the three supplements to the main body of the Autograph) in the Staatsbibliothek zu Berlin—Preußischer Kulturbesitz, is scanned in full in the *Bach-Digital Project* (www.bach-digital.de), and marked as public domain. Excerpts from these scans are taken from P 200[1]; P 200/1–1[2]; P 200/1–2[3] and P 200/1–3[4].

(2) The Original Edition of *The Art of Fugue* (1751). The original document, shelfmark DK–Kk mu 6406.2030 in the Royal Library of Copenhagen, is scanned in full (img.kb.dk/ma/uklav/bach_kdf-m.pdf). Excerpts from these scans are printed here with the kind permission of the music collection of the Royal Library in Copenhagen, Denmark, and are listed in the following list as DK–Kk mu 6406.2030.

Notes

1 www.bach-digital.de/receive/BachDigitalSource_source_00001071
2 www.bach-digital.de/receive/BachDigitalSource_source_00001072
3 www.bach-digital.de/receive/BachDigitalSource_source_00001073
4 www.bach-digital.de/receive/BachDigitalSource_source_00001074

Preface

From the author

Valery Maisky, an extraordinary musician, mentor and scholar, was the one who acquainted me with this great composition that Bach entitled *The Art of Fugue*. I still remember this event, so many years ago, and that date for the strong impression, from both the composition itself (which I then heard as a whole for the first time in my life) and its interpretation. Valery performed Bach as a great master when he was still in his student years. As yet I cannot define the magic in his performance that literally penetrated one's soul and remained unforgettable.

It was Maisky who organised then a student community for the study of Johann Sebastian's music at the conservatory. We proudly called it among ourselves the *Bach-Gesellschaft*, realising, of course, that it had no relation to the world famous organisation. It was Maisky who took several of us to the renowned organist Isaya Alexandrovich Braudo, to learn the art of performance and receive invaluable knowledge. Valery himself taught us when the maître was busy. Since then, many musicologists combine their studies with taking organ classes.

Valery revealed for us how diverse are the analytical and performing views and interpretations of the cycle, pointing out that the answers can be found in Bach's Autograph.

The Autograph is kept in the Music Department of the Staatsbibliothek zu Berlin—Preußischer Kulturbesitz, Musikabteilung mit Mendelssohn-Archiv, shelfmark: Mus. ms. Bach P 200. My deep gratitude to the personnel of the archive and especially its director in the early 2000s, Dr Helmuth Hell, who granted me the privilege to work at length with the original Autograph of *The Art of Fugue* and the two Original Editions.

I am greatly indebted to Dr Ute Nawroth for kindly sharing with me information from the history of the library, its custodians and curators, starting from Siegfried Dehn, as well as the important information on the history of *The Art of Fugue* Autograph's restoration. My cordial thanks for valuable consultations and discussions of questions related to *The Art of Fugue* go to Professors Dr Hans-Joachim Schulze, Dr Christoph Wolff and Dr Peter Wollny. Special thanks to Frau Viera Lippold, the assistant librarian of Leipzig Bach-Archiv for her help in searching for additional materials. Finally, I would like to acknowledge St Petersburg State University for their generous research grant 30.38.159.2013.

In the process of my work on this study, I had to reconsider many principles and sometimes even uneasy questions about the theory of fugue and counterpoint, their interpretation in Bach times as well as peculiarities of polyphonic technique as it was practiced in eighteenth-century

Germany, including by Bach himself. As some studies show, it is easy to arrive at mistaken conclusions through incorrect interpretation and without an adequate understanding of these questions. I am greatly indebted to my St Petersburg colleagues. Dr Professor Kira Iosifovna Yuzhak, my constant interlocutor, critic, helper and editor, with whom we closely collaborated. Prof. Alla Irmenovna Yankus granted me fruitful discussions of complex questions of the theory of fugue and canon, as well as most valuable consultations on the lives and works of Bach's sons.

While all the above work resulted in the Russian edition (St Petersburg: Compozitor, 2009), this book has undergone a second birth. It was most rewarding that two scholars, Prof. Marina Ritzarev and Dr Esti Sheinberg contributed their time to translate and edit that first version. Looking back at this five-year project, through which each one of us was incredibly busy with jobs, deadlines, conferences and our own books—I admire their patience and creative efforts. I am very grateful to Marina Ritzarev for her initiative, coordination of the project and the translation; all this—beyond our professional fraternity in eighteenth-century studies and my respect to her inspiring skills in making a fascinating story from a learned musicological narration.

My special and deepest gratitude goes to Esti Sheinberg for her meticulous and uncompromising editing. Amazingly, her academic discipline and rigour did not suppress her scholarly intuition and most creative relation to my ideas. Finally, what was not taken for granted—Esti Sheinberg tactfully managed to smooth a subtle but perceptible difference between Russian and Western scholarly conventions. Without this rare and happy combination of her professional qualities—this new book would be simply impossible.

I greatly appreciate the decision of Ashgate Publishing to undertake this edition and personally the Senior Commissioning Editor Laura Macy for her kind support of this not-so-easy project.

Anatoly Milka
St Petersburg, Russia, 2015

From the translator

Perhaps, if I stayed in St Petersburg, where I studied with Anatoly Milka and Valery Maisky and where I attended this Bach circle (Bakhovsky kruzhok) on Sunday afternoons in the empty building of our Conservatory, I would never think of sending this study across Russian boundaries. The great distance, however, made me feel a certain responsibility, maybe similar to what Roman Jakobson felt when he initiated the translation of Vladimir Propp's *Morphology of the Folktale*.

I strongly felt this book is special, and that it should reach a wider, international audience. It did not only tell the story of *The Art of Fugue* but went beyond it; it is a deeply caring, human document of Bach's surroundings, his sons, friends and colleagues. Anatoly Milka brought to life the Leipzig of mid-eighteenth century, the court of Frederick the Great and the general European intellectual milieu of that period. In this environment, a work was being born, and a great mind was engaged in intense self-struggle and professional, intellectual and spiritual doubts, decisions and deliberations, all followed after and described in a meticulous academic methodology.

It was a precious and exciting privilege to work on this book and collaborate with my two colleagues, separated by three continents and cultures, but united by love and reverence for Bach, for scholarship and for the universal guide in the complex counterpoint of this project—the sense of humour.

Marina Ritzarev
Tel-Aviv, Israel, 2015

From the editor

When Marina Ritzarev suggested that we translate 'a thought-provoking book about Bach's *Art of Fugue*', I thought she was joking. My Russian is poor and my knowledge of Bach's work is not a specialist's one. However, she did not joke, and I, struck by an inexplicable hubris attack, said yes. Five years later, I feel deeply grateful for this learning experience. I am indebted to both Prof. Anatoly Milka and Marina for their trust in me, their teachings and their saintly patience during our hours–long trilingual Skype sessions in which I insisted on (and was granted!) detailed explanations about every possible aspect of the text and for countless hours of editorial work with Marina, whose help, encouragement and support proved cardinal for the completion of this enterprise.

This was a complex editorial project, that posed many and various challenges. Both Marina and I are very grateful to the experienced and supportive group of editors we have worked with: Laura Macy, Emma Gallon and Barbara Pretty, who accompanied the project in its various stages and offered priceless professional assistance.

I am grateful to the Library services of the University of Nebraska–Lincoln and particularly to the friendly staff at its Music Library, to their efficient interlibrary loan service and their electronic books and journals collections. I am also greatly indebted to our reviewers for their good advice and to the countless people who, privately or within academic and other institutions, are transforming the Internet into a cornucopia of historical documents. I would never be able—while sitting by my computer in Virginia, Nebraska or Israel—to access centuries-old manuscripts and books or look at art works from all over Europe, without the generosity of the Bach-Digital project, the Internet archive of historical documents, the International Music Score Library Project, Wikimedia, Wikisource and, yes, the Google search engine and Wikipedia. When contemplating these wonderful virtual cathedrals, built by so many anonymous Others who are, too, simply fascinated by sheer learning, I begin to wonder if maybe, just maybe, World Peace is not such an absolutely impossible dream....

Esti Sheinberg
Lincoln, Nebraska, USA, 2015

Introduction

Seemingly, no composition by J.S. Bach has been honoured with as many monographs and articles as *The Art of Fugue*, not many Bach scholars could resist the magnetic power of this masterpiece, devoting to it countless pages of study. This is due not only to the puzzling trajectory of its composition and publication, but also to the fact that there is still no scholarly consensus about its ever been completed.

Undoubtedly, this is the central and most intriguing question associated with *The Art of Fugue*. Certain scholars, grounding their claims on primary resources such as preserved scores and documents, avow that the composer did not finish it. Others, no less persuasively, insist that the composition is completed, corroborating their claim with indirect evidence, circumstantial particulars and the fact that many materials of *The Art of Fugue* were lost after the composer's death. Each side sticks to its own truth, leaving the question unresolved.

This book proposes a solution that combines both primary and circumstantial data into a meaningful complex. The hypothesis presented here goes beyond the preserved documentation that is directly related to the creation and publication of *The Art of Fugue*, suggesting interpretations that interweave various contexts of Bach's biography such as his social circumstances, his contacts with family members and—strangely perhaps—even with his illness and death. Further, it points at possible correlations between the contrapuncti and canons of *The Art of Fugue* and contemporary theories about counterpoint and fugue composition. All this is cardinal to the examination of the work's completion. Particularities of the composition process are discussed as well as specific inscription techniques, paper types and note corrections. Within this broader context, both the manuscript autograph and the first printed edition of the work, respectively referred to as 'The Autograph' and 'The Original Edition',[1] offer a wealth of relevant scholarly information formerly left unaccounted. In order to warrant a proper understanding of Bach's ways of operation throughout the composition process, these two surviving documents are meticulously detailed in Part II of this book. The Autograph and the Original Edition differ significantly in content and internal order.[2] However, as facts show and as most scholars agree, no existing source reflects Bach's conclusive conception of the work, and in particular the internal ordering of the fugues.

The author closely inspects both the Autograph and the Original Edition and reveals in them traces reflecting Bach's creative process. In Part III of this book, these two sources are combined with additional information, concluding in the proposal of four different versions of *The Art of Fugue*, consecutively envisaged by Bach. The first two versions are implied in the

Autograph, and the other two—deduced from a combination of the Original Edition with information from the Autograph's supplements. In Chapter 11, entitled 'The Fourth Version,' we propose a new perspective, suggesting Bach's vision of a final, albeit never-materialised version of the work and describing its likely structure and features.

While deeply indebted to other reconstruction attempts, each with its own valuable insights, this book differs from former studies in its interdisciplinary approach. The purport of Baroque music included visual and conceptual elements, such as outlines created by the musical graphic notation, resulting in certain visual figurations, and that contributed to its signification. Symbolisation was a main device of Baroque musical expression, combining rational and emotional aspects of music into an interaction that exceeded their separate effects. An appropriate interpretation of Bach's compositional choices must take such features into account, particularly in the many cases when his procedures may otherwise seem inexplicable, strange or even nonsensical.

Equally, a proper understanding of the Original Edition's structure requires not only J.S. Bach's actions, but also a careful account of the steps taken by Carl Philipp Emanuel Bach during the publication of his father's work. Consequently, descriptions of circumstances and individuals that contributed to and even guided both Johann Sebastian's and Philipp Emanuel's actions and ways of operation are provided, including listings of names, professional occupations, relocations and contacts and various additional data deemed relevant. A careful consideration of the theory of fugue composition and of some paradoxes associated with certain types of fugue, as well as of canon composition methods during Bach's lifetime, may shed light on certain peculiarities of the Autograph (for example, the fact that some sections had to be written prior to others). Several explanations of additional terms are provided in notes, where a correct understanding of the eighteenth-century idiomatic use of musical terminology is needed to follow the logic of our argumentation.

Notes

1 This is the standard name for the first edition of *The Art of Fugue* published by Carl Philipp Emanuel Bach after his father's death.
2 'Order' here means the sequencing of pieces (and their engraving) in *The Art of Fugue*, which actually leads to a reconstruction of the composer's idea. See Gregory Butler, 'Ordering problems in J.S. Bach's *Art of Fugue* resolved', *The Musical Quarterly*, 69/1 (1983): pp. 44–61. Later, Butler revised some of the principal ideas of this paper and presented his new view in 'Scribes, Engravers and Notational Styles: The Final Disposition of Bach's *Art of Fugue*', in *About Bach*, Gregory G. Butler, George B. Stauffer and Mary Dalton Greer (eds) (Urbana and Chicago, 2008), pp. 111–23.

Part I

Toward the history of the conception

1   The last decade

Scholars often highlight the last years of Bach's life as 'the last decade'.[1] This emphasis goes beyond the sheer chronological facts, since during these years the composer's views, preferences and creative strategies were substantially modified. These changes were so dramatic that several contemporary testimonies, by people who were not in contact with the composer during these last years,[2] literally contradict the facts of his activity. This deep change in Bach's intellectual world was influenced in more than one way by the milieu in which he lived and worked.

Church and University

When Bach left Cöthen and moved to Leipzig in 1723, after 15 years of service as the court musician, he encountered a creative atmosphere that was utterly different from the one he knew. Leipzig's educated society was divided into two factions. Bach's colleagues in the Thomaskirche and Thomasschule were related to the Church, while the philosophers, mathematicians, historians and philologists at the University formed a separate group. While the Church and the Thomasschule were among the most conservative institutions of Saxony (and possibly of all Germany), the University of Leipzig was one of the most progressive and freethinking strongholds of contemporary science. The two institutions opposed each other in a constant bitter feud, in which the Thomaskirche authorities held that all evil subversions were generated within the University walls. This state of affairs had affected the character of several Leipzig churches. For example, the University Church of Saint Paul was distinguished by its more relaxed ways, including its accommodating some fashionable musical styles. Its operatic tone, for instance, not only raised eyebrows within the Thomaskirche administration, but also upset Johann Kuhnau, Bach's colleague and predecessor in the Thomasschule. Bach had some limited duties at the University Church but no real influence on its policies concerning music performance. Consequently, the contract that Bach signed with the Thomaskirche included two curious clauses: one demanding that the music he composed should bear no resemblance whatsoever to operatic styles[3] and the other requiring a formal consent from the Thomasschule administration for any service engagement with the University.[4] Bach agreed to these stipulations and signed the contract that, in a way, functioned as a voucher for his duties and commitments.

Strange as it may seem, this institutional glaring prevailed, although only individuals holding a university degree were allowed to lead an establishment such as the Thomasschule.

Graduates of the Leipzig University comprised the majority of the school's top management, and Johann Kuhnau had a PhD.[5] Conversely, the University employed several of the School's teachers, although eventually the extremely conservative atmosphere of the Thomasschule prompted most to resign and remain employed just by the University. A list enumerating all the members of the Thomasschule staff during Bach's employment there illustrates this tendency:[6]

- Johann Heinrich Ernesti, rector of Thomasschule since 1684, died in 1729. Bach served under his supervision during his first five years, approximately.
- Christian Ludovici, conrector, and from 1697—rector. In 1724 he left the School for the University of Leipzig.
- Johann Christian Hebenstreit, conrector from 1725.[7] In 1731 left the School for the University of Leipzig.
- Johann Matthias Gesner, rector since 1730. Served in this position for four years. In 1734 left the School for the University of Göttingen.
- Johann August Ernesti, conrector from 1731 and rector from 1734. In 1759 he left the School for the University of Leipzig.
- Johann Heinrich Winckler, from 1731 a teacher at the Thomasschule (*collega quartus*). In 1739 he left the School for the University of Leipzig.

Several of these persons were connected to Bach's family, mostly through christening ceremonies for his children. For example, Johann Heinrich Ernesti's wife, Regina Maria, was the godmother of Gottfried Heinrich Bach, born in 1724; Johann Christian Hebenstreit's wife, Christina Dorothea, was the godmother of Christina Dorothea Bach, born in 1731; Johann Matthias Gesner's wife, Elizabeth Karitas, was the godmother of Johann August Abraham Bach, born in 1733, and whose godfather was Johann Heinrich Ernesti. Occasionally, though not often, one of them would contribute toward Bach's music, too. For example, Winckler wrote the texts for cantata BWV Anh.18 (*Froher Tag, verlangte Stunden*), composed for the inauguration ceremony of the newly rebuilt Thomasschule, in 1732. Several individuals from the Thomaskirche clergy were also connected with the University in one way or another. At least four of them served, beyond their church obligations, as professors of theology and history of the church:

- Urban Gottfried Siber served as a minister in the Thomaskirche from 1714 until his death in 1741.
- Romanus Teller, a minister in both the Thomaskirche and the Peterskirche (1737–40).
- Christian Weiss the younger, a minister in the Nikolaikirche (1731–37).
- Christoph Wolle, a graduate of the Thomasschule (where he studied under Kuhnau) and a minister at the Thomaskirche (1739–?).

All these, just like the University professors mentioned above, were connected to Bach's life in similar ways. For example, Urban Gottfried Siber baptised three of Bach's sons—Gottfried Heinrich (1724), Johann August Abraham (1733) and Johann Christian (1737); Christian Weiss the Younger was godfather to Bach's daughter Johanna Karolina (1737); his father, Christian

Weiss the Elder, was Bach's confessor from 1723 to 1736; Subsequently, his confessors were Romanus Teller (1737–40) and Christoph Wolle (1741–50).

Among Bach's friends at the University of Leipzig were those who had no affiliation with the Thomaskirche or its school. At least seven of them are known today:

- Johann Jacob Maskov, professor of constitutional law and history, was the author of books about the history of the Great Roman Empire.
- Andreas Florens Rivinus was professor of law and *rector magnificus* of the University in the years 1729–30 and 1735–36.
- August Friedrich Müller was professor of philosophy and law and rector during the years 1733–34 and 1743–44.
- Johann Friedrich Menz,[8] professor of logic, poetics and physics, served as rector twice: in 1735–36 and 1743.
- Gottfried Leonhard Baudis was professor of law and served as rector in the years 1736–37.
- Johann Christoph Gottsched was professor of logic, poetics and metaphysics; he served as rector throughout 1738–43 and then again in 1749, and authored numerous books on literature, linguistics, rhetoric, poetics and more.
- Gottlieb Kortte was professor of law and author of many historical and legal works.

The involvement of these individuals in Bach's life included christening honours, too. For example, Baudis's wife, Magdalena Sybilla, was the godmother of Bach's son, Ernestus Andreas (1727), and Andreas Florens Rivinus was godfather of Bach's son Ernestus Andreas, while his brother Johann Florens Rivinus was Johann Christian Bach's godfather (1735). However, the impact of these university professors on the composer's life went beyond honorifics and into more practical roles in his professional career. For example, Johann Jacob Maskov and Gottfried Leonhard Baudis were members of the council that elected the cantor for the Thomasschule, and they voted for Bach; several of Bach's cantatas (BWV 198, Anh. 13b and Anh. 196) were set to poetic texts by Johann Christoph Gottsched, who often had expressed publicly his admiration for Bach's music.[9] Johann Friedrich Menz possessed a unique sixteenth-century manuscript with a mysteriously cryptic canon by Teodoro Riccio, and asked Bach to decode it. After resolving the puzzle, Bach copied it onto a separate sheet, which Menz then added to his own album.

The governor of Leipzig, General Count Joachim Friedrich von Flemming, was in charge of all the city's administrations: municipality, church and university. He kept regular contact with Bach, with whom he had been acquainted since the composer's employment by Duke Wilhelm Ernst in Weimar. Apparently it was Count von Flemming who schemed, together with Louis Marchand, the famous competition (that in fact had never occurred) between the two outstanding clavecinists in his Dresden palace.[10] It is clear that von Flemming held Bach in high esteem, since he patronised, supported and commissioned new works from the composer. Bach was in charge of music performances at municipal ceremonies honouring visits of the Royal family members, quite often also composing the music for these events. In this regard, the University of Leipzig students and professors fulfilled important roles, performing masses, processions, and even torchlight parades. When in Leipzig, Bach wrote several musical works honouring von Flemming, presenting him as one of the prominent figures connecting the composer with the University.

All the above representatives of the University establishment and people closely associated with this institution took part in Bach's life events in one way or another, whether by reviewing his work in the press, writing poetry for his works, or as patrons and dedicatees of his musical works. For example, Gesner praised Bach several times, most remarkably in his annotated edition of Quintilianus' *The Institutione Oratoria*.[11]

Two of the four versions of Bach's Cantata BWV 36 (36, 36a, 36b and 36c) are associated with Bach's academic contacts: BWV 36b (*Die Freude reget sich*) is dedicated to Andreas Florens Rivinus (or a member of his family) on his birthday, and BWV 36c (*Schwingt freudig euch empor*), originally composed in 1725 congratulating 'a teacher' on his birthday, was reused in 1731 for the birthday of Johann Matthias Gesner. The Cantata BWV 207 (*Vereinigte Zwietracht der wechselnden Saiten*) was composed in honour of Gottlieb Kortte's appointment as professor at the University in December 1726. The name day of August Friedrich Müller, the future Rector of the University, was marked with the performance of Cantata BWV 205 (*Der zufriedengestellte Aeolus. Dramma per musica*) on August 3, 1725.

Several of Bach's students were University scholars as well. Best known among them are Christoph Nichelmann, Lorenz Christoph Mizler, Johann Friedrich Agricola, Johann Philipp Kirnberger and Johann Christoph Altnickol. Christoph Nichelmann (1717–62) was the author of the treatise *Die Melodie nach ihrem Wesen sowohl, als nach ihren Eigenschaften*, written 'in response to the controversy over the merits of the French and Italian styles'.[12] Lorenz Christoph Mizler von Kolof (1711–78) studied at the University in 1731–34, culminating his education with the defence of his thesis: 'Dissertatio quod musica ars sit pars eruditionis philosophicae'.[13] From 1737 he lectured at the University on mathematics, philosophy and—for the first time in German universities—music. During his life in Leipzig, Mizler was Bach's student, and in his journal, the *Musikalische Bibliothek*, he referred to Bach as his good friend and patron.[14] Johann Friedrich Agricola (1720–74) studied at the University of Leipzig during the years 1738–41. He is known for his annotated translation of Pier Francesco Tosi's treatise *Opinioni de' cantori antichi e moderni*.[15] Its German translation was published as *Anleitung zur Singekunst*.[16] Johann Philipp Kirnberger (1721–83) studied during the same years as Agricola. His main work appeared in the two volumes of *Die Kunst des reinen Satzes in der Musik, aus sicheren Grundsätzen hergeleitet und mit deutlichen Beyspielen erläutert*.[17]

Bach's sons, too, had links within the University's community. In 1729, Wilhelm Friedemann, after graduating from the Thomasschule, enrolled at the University, where he read mathematics, philosophy and law for more than four years.[18] Philipp Emanuel was a university student for more than seven years (1731–38), three of which he stayed in Leipzig.[19] It is clear, therefore, that despite his church employment, Bach's connections and contacts with the University included professors, poets and scholars with whom he constantly communicated.

The University of Leipzig

Leipzig's intellectuals, who were involved in both pietistic and rationalist circles, stood in opposition to the city council's and the Thomaskirche's traditionalist administrations who perceived the University's activities as seditious. The academic alleged subversions started long before Bach's arrival to Leipzig. Years before he was even born, the city was renowned as a centre of non-orthodox scholarly publications. Prominent among these were non-canonical interpretations of the Holy Scriptures and studies of Kabbalah, such as Johannes Olearius' controversial interpretation of the Bible[20] and Johann Henning's *Cabbalologia*.[21] The first theological periodical, *Unschuldige Nachrichten von Alten und Neuen Theologischen Sachen* was founded in Leipzig, 1717, by Valentine Ernst Löscher.[22] Scholarly studies of Kabbalah had an impact on paragrammatic poetry, a tradition rooted in Kabbalistic writings,[23] such as Riemer's *Über-Reicher Schatz-Meister Aller hohen Standes und Burgerlichen Freud- und Leid-Complimente*.[24] Picander, too, introduced paragrammatic poems in his five-volume *Ernst-Schertzhafte und satyrische Gedichte*.[25] Thus, the scope of interests was by no means limited to religious studies but expanded to general philosophy, literature, poetry, history, education and even ethnography. For example, Caspar Knittel's *Via Regia Ad Omnes Scientias et Artes*[26] and Christian Weise's *Curieuse Fragen über die Logica*[27] dealt with a wider philosophical scope, while August Bohse's *Letzte Liebes- und Heldengedichte* enhanced publications of contemporary literature.[28] Two textbooks published by Johann Christoph Mieth: *Das ABC* and *Das Einmahl Eins*[29] answered the increasing demand for general education among the growing middle class, while Johann Gottfried Mittag's *Leben und Thaten Friedrich August III*[30] and Johann Jacob Schudt's four volumes of *Judische Merckwürdigkeiten*[31] presented new approaches to historical and ethnographical scholarship. Last but not least, the Latin version of *Monadology*, by Leipzig University alumnus Gottfried Wilhelm Leibniz, was published in 1721 (under the title *Principia philosophiae*), in the Leipzig academic journal *Acta Eruditorum*. Needless to say, the philosopher's concepts of *monads* and *universal language* did not earn him and his ideas the Church's sympathy, let alone any support.[32]

As already mentioned, Bach's rapport with the university's academics was limited to specific individuals and activities: working, social and personal contacts, ranging from their accompanying his children's christening ceremonies to his socialising with them in various events and entertainments that included music. It is impossible to imagine that in such close personal and professional connections Bach could remain absolutely unaware of the main scientific ideas that circulated among his university acquaintances. Further, Bach strived to compensate for his lack of a university degree by becoming an autodidact, conscious of keeping up with the state of the arts concerning the issues that engaged the enlightened minds of his milieu.

Bach's broad intellectual interests are reflected in his large personal library. He had an impressive collection of theological literature, first and foremost Martin Luther's books. However, it also featured works of quite different leanings, such as studies that explored and discussed questions of Kabbalah. One should keep in mind that building a private library, in Bach's times, was quite an expensive hobby. The acquisition of a new book was a marked event, instigated by a substantial need. During Bach's later years, his library was enriched by music treatises.[33] He also owned studies on canonical and non-canonical interpretations of the Holy Scriptures, investigations about numerical interpretations of biblical events and specific publications discussing possible applications of Kabbalah.[34]

It is not a coincidence that the knowledge encompassed in these literary sources interested Bach mainly during his last decade. The impact of the intellectual elite of Leipzig University, which so noticeably influenced the entire European worldview, could not leave Leipzig's own society unmarked. It is unsurprising, thus, that the university milieu, general academic atmosphere and the smaller circle of Bach's friends and acquaintances in particular, played a vital role in fashioning his intellectual aspirations. In this context, Bach's cooperation with the Society of Musical Sciences played a decisive role.

The Society of Musical Sciences

Lorenz Mizler, Bach's student and friend, founded in 1738 a unique musicians' association, called the Society of Musical Sciences. Mizler's initiative reflected a popular fashion of numerous societies, related to various areas of life, which mushroomed throughout Europe during that period. This group of musicians ascribed great importance to enhance the perception of music as a science. Uncharacteristically, this particular society operated by correspondence rather than by personal meetings, because the society's members resided far from each other, in various European cities.

The mail service was absolutely reliable. Periodically, a 'packet' containing miscellaneous data and materials, such as current information and compositions by its members would be sent around.[35] For example, Mizler's letter of September 1, 1747, sent from Końskie (Poland) to the Society's member Meinrad Spieß in the Irsee Abbey near Kaufbeuren, says:

> Auf meiner Rückreise über Leipzig habe Herrn Capellm. Bach gesprochen, welcher mir seine Berlinische Reise u. Geschicht von der Fuge, die er vor dem König gespielt, erzählt, welche nächstens in Kupfer wird gestochen werden, u. in dem Packet der Soc. ein Exemplar zum Vorschein kommen. Ich habe den Anfang schon davon gesehen.[36]

> [On my return by way of Leipzig I spoke with Herr Capellmeister Bach, who told me of his Berlin journey and the story about the fugue he played for the king, which will shortly be engraved in copper and appear in the Society's packet. I have already seen its beginning.]

In a later letter to Spieß (October 23, 1747) Mizler wrote:

> Das letzte Packet aber, so den 29 May d. J. schon abgelaufen ist noch nicht zurücke, u. weiß noch nicht, wo es so lange ausgeruht. Sie werden es von Herrn Bach erhalten u. von meinem hochzuehrenden Herrn Collegen kommt es an mich, der ich bitte solche ie eher ie lieber zu befördern, wenn es eingelaufen. (*BD* II/559, p. 438)

> [But the last packet, which was sent out on May 29 of this year, still has not returned, and I do not know where it rests for so long. You will receive it from Herr Bach, and it will then come to me from my honorable Herr colleague, whom I ask to send it at his earlier convenience.]

In addition to the 'packet', the Society had an official publication, the *Musikalische Bibliothek* journal.[37] It supplied information about musical life in Germany[38] and about the new scholarly works and musical compositions that deserved special attention. The compositions themselves were published, too, in whole or in part.

The main interests of the Society, which fully coincided with typical Enlightenment European trends, were reflected in its constitution. One of these was the expressed interest in the culture of past centuries—from classic antiquity to more recent styles, historically and/or nationally defined, and in knowledge that was lost or forgotten in the course of history.

The Society's constitution stated that each of its members should commit to promote and assert the greatness of ancient music. This emphasis should be highlighted, since the fashionable style (especially of the Prussian King's court, which was the most active and influential in Germany) was dominated by newly composed music.[39]

Bach's interest in studying old musical works and past compositional techniques reflects the Society's stated preferences. In this context, he copied and performed music by former masters, mainly Italian. Thus, for example, extant manuscripts show that in the years 1742–47 he copied and arranged for performance (adding orchestral instruments) Giovanni Palestrina's masses *Ecce sacerdos magnus* and *Missa sine nomine*[40] and Frescobaldi's works, including his *Fiori musicali* collection.[41] He studied the old masters' contrapuntal techniques not just by copying and arranging their compositions, but also by reading old theoretical treatises and manuals. Christoph Wolff and Kirsten Beißwenger list the studies registered in Bach's personal library.[42] Among them are treatises by Angelo Berardi (*Documenti armonici*, 1687) and Johann Joseph Fux (*Gradus ad Parnassum*, 1725, of which Bach owned both the Latin original and Mizler's German translation of 1742); Friedrich Erhardt Niedt (*Musicalische Handleitung*, 1700);[43] Johann Gottfried Walther (*Musicalisches Lexicon*, 1732), and Andreas Werckmeister (*Orgel-Probe*, 1698).[44] Further, the autographs at the *Singakademie* collection in Berlin suggest that the composer may have examined treatises by other authors too,[45] such as *Le istitutioni harmoniche* by Gioseffo Zarlino (1558) and *Melopoeia* by Sethus Calvisius (1592). But even without these two last publications the total scope of these examples provides clear evidence to Bach's growing interest in earlier compositional techniques during the 1740s.

Being involved in the Society of Musical Sciences' activities enhanced Bach's interest in mathematics and its connections with music and symbolic systems. The Society's enthusiasm for this field follows views inherited from Antiquity, which considered music as an aspect of mathematics. This approach, typical to the Pythagoreans, permeates the publications of Mizler's Society and his own work. For example, at the time of doctoral defence, his dissertation was titled *Quod musica ars sit pars eruditionis philosophicae*,[46] but upon publication its title was corrected to *Quod musica scientia sit pars eruditionis philosophicae*,[47] *musica ars* being replaced by *musica scientia*. While indeed the Latin word *ars* means both *science* and *art*, it was important for Mizler to replace the word with *scientia*, highlighting his understanding of music as a science.

The *Musikalische Bibliothek* often referred to ideas of great scholars, from Pythagoras to his disciples and followers. Special attention was given to both ancient and current interdisciplinary studies, which included mathematics. Here were published treatises on music by the Byzantine philosopher Michael Psellus (in both Greek and German on facing columns)[48] and by the outstanding mathematician Leonhard Euler.[49]

Two ideas related to Pythagoras should be marked as fundamental to the Society of Musical Sciences. The first sees numbers at the basis of all that exists, be it idea or matter. This is the source of the well-known proposition stating that any field of knowledge can be a science as long as it can be expressed and explained mathematically. The second idea sees the real meaning of the Divine Word as hidden from the uninitiated and the key to its understanding as lying within the language of symbols.[50]

The special role of numbers in music as science and in the Society's ideology is expressed not only in Mizler's works (first and foremost in his dissertation) and in the publications of the *Musikalische Bibliothek*, but also in the medal that was issued to mark the founding of this organisation. At the centre of the medal is engraved a sequence of the first six digits: 1, 2, 3, 4, 5 and 6. According to Pythagorean theories, this particular part of the numerical series and its structure explain the material foundations of the world. This idea was developed in Johannes Kepler's *Harmonices mundi*,[51] in Athanasius Kircher's works, especially in his *Musurgia*

12 Part I: Toward the history of the conception

universalis (1650). On the front plate of this work appears Pythagoras, shown at the bottom left corner of the plate, presenting his mathematical theory as a foundation of music and of the universe (see Figure 1.1), where music is explained as a universe,[52] and in the studies of Gottfried Wilhelm Leibniz, particularly in his dissertation *De arte combinatoria*.

Figure 1.1 Athanasius Kircher, *Musurgia Universalis*, frontpiece.

These studies, which presented a syncretic unity of mathematics, music and mystical symbol systems, enjoyed great popularity within the Society. The *Musikalische Bibliothek* briefly explains the image on the medal:

> Nemlich das nackende Kind so gegen Morgen zu hoch flieget, auf den Kopf einen klarleuchtenden Stern und in der rechten Hand eine umgekehrte brennende Fackel hat, neben welcher eine Schwalbe flieget, zeiget das Anbrechen der Tages in der Music an. Der Cirkel der durch die drei Winckel eines gleichseitigen Dreiecks gehet und die musikalischen Zahlen 1.2.3.4.5.6. in sich hält, und um welchen Bienen fliege, ist das Siegel der Societät der musicalischen Wissenschafften, welches der Flies der Societät, die Musik durch die Mathematic und Weltweiszheit zu verbessern, vorstellet.[53]

[A naked child flies toward the dawn, a shining star on his head and an inverted torch in his hand, accompanied by a swallow announcing the new day. The circle cuts through the corners of an equilateral triangle, in which the musical digits 1, 2, 3, 4, 5 and 6 are enclosed, and around which bees fly. This is the hallmark of the Society of Musical Sciences, in which diligence establishes the perfection of music through mathematics and philosophy.]

Symbolism was present not only on the medal of the Society of Musical Sciences, but also in its publications. Beyond being connected with numbers, thus related to ancient Middle Eastern cultures, it also relates to visual images and shapes, which brings them closer to the classical mindset, where knowledge is associated with measurement.[54]

Like members of many secret societies, the members of Mizler's society protected their true identities by pseudonyms using names of famous ancient scholars and musicians. The names Aristotle, Archimedes, Pythagoras, Socrates and Terpander relate to just a few members.[55] They indicate how members of the Society characterised each individual affiliate, given name and symbolic pseudonym forming a kind of paragrammatic pair, in which both elements mutually commented on each other.

Bach's newly acquired knowledge about music of past periods is reflected, in one way or another, in his last decade's oeuvre where an increasing number of *stile antico* indications can be found.[56]

This can be substantiated mainly by works composed during the last decade, such as sections of the Mass in B minor, the six-part Ricercar from the *Musical Offering*, several pieces of *The Art of Fugue*, and even some fugues in the second volume of *The Well-Tempered Clavier*, as well as other works for clavier and for the organ. Bach's study of the old masters' contrapuntal techniques is also apparent in his interest in deciphering and creating canons. Indeed, the vast majority of works that Bach named as canons were composed during his last decade. Then, far more than in previous periods, his compositions are characterised by the use of symbol systems of various kinds—whether based on gematria or on other principles. The principle of paragram and paragrammatic composition significantly influenced different aspects of Bach's works, such as the Mass in B minor and most of his Leipzig cantatas.

His interest—and then membership—in the Society of Musical Sciences enhanced Bach's attention to practical composition and to methodical textbooks for both professional or amateur organists and clavecinists. Notwithstanding their didactic purposes, this group of works, to which *The Art of Fugue* undoubtedly belongs, is considered musical masterpieces of the highest artistic value. Many features of the described social context, in which this work was fashioned, may shed light on the factors that brought Bach to its composition.

Notes

1 Christoph Wolff, 'Toward a Definition of the Last Period of Bach's Work,' in C. Wolff, *Bach: Essays on his Life and Music* (Cambridge, 1991), pp. 359–67.
2 Even his son Carl Philipp Emanuel, who left for good the parental home in 1734, comments in his letter from January 13, 1775, to Johann Nicolaus Forkel, in answer to the latter's questions about his father's taste and pedagogical principles: 'In der Composition gieng er gleich an das Nützliche mit seinen Scholaren, mit Hinweglaßung aller der trockenen Arten von Contrapuncten, wie sie in Fuxen u. andern stehen.' [In composition he went right to the practical with his pupil, with

14   Part I: Toward the history of the conception

omission of all the *dry species* of counterpoint, as they appear in Fux and others.] *Bach-Dokumente* [*BD*] III/803, p. 289. English translation by Stephen L. Clark, *The Letters of C.P.E. Bach* (Oxford, 1997), p. 73, emphasis only in the translation. While this perception was true about the past with which C.P.E. was familiar, it did not correspond with the realities of Bach's activity in his last decade.

3   This cautionary appears twice. First, on April 22, 1723, during the procedure of Bach's election: 'hätte er solche *Compositiones* zu machen, die nicht *theatralisch* wären' [he should create such *compositions*, that would not be too *theatrical*] *BD* II/129, p. 94, emphases in the original. The second time was on May 5 of the same year when, signing the indemnity agreement with the Thomasschule Rector, Bach was requested 'zu Beybehaltung guter Ordnung in denen Kirchen, die *Music* dergestalt einrichten, daß sie nicht zu lang währen, auch also beschaffen seyn möge, damit sie nicht *opernhafftig* herauskommen, sondern die Zuhörer vielmehr zur Andacht aufmuntere' [to keep the good order in the churches, to set the *music* so that it will not last too long, and also create it in such a way that it will not give an operatic impression, but rather encourage the listeners to succumb to worship.] *BD* I/92, p. 177, emphases in the original.

4   'Und bey der *Universität* kein *officium*, ohne E.E. Hochweisen Raths *Consens* annehmen solle und wolle' [and not accept or want any *office* at the *University* without the *consent* of the Honorable and Learned Council.] *BD* I/92, p. 178, emphases in the original.

5   Johann Kuhnau graduated from the University of Leipzig, where he defended his doctoral dissertation 'De juribus circa musicos ecclesiasticos' [On the legal aspects of church music].

6   Christoph Wolff, who meticulously studied Bach's connections with the University of Leipzig, provides a detailed account on these personalia. Christoph Wolff, *Johann Sebastian Bach: The Learned Musician* (Oxford, 2000) pp. 305–39.

7   Wolff states 1724 (ibid. p. 321). However, the University of Leipzig website states 1725. http://www.uni-leipzig.de/unigeschichte/professorenkatalog/leipzig/Hebenstreit_1279/ (accessed January 18, 2015.)

8   Wolff spells Mentz; the University of Leipzig's list of rectors spells Menz.

9   *BD* I/249, p. 184; II/309, p. 223; II/483, p. 387.

10 For a thorough discussion of this anecdote see Peter Williams, *The Life of Bach* (Cambridge, 2003), pp. 117–21.

11 *M. Fabii Quinctiliani De Institutione Oratoria. Libri duodecim collatione codicis Gothani et Iensonianae editionis aliorumque librorum ac perpetuo commentario illustrati a Io. Matthia Gesnero* (Gottingae, 1738), book I, Chapter 12, p. 61, note 3. Translated to English in *The New Bach Reader: A Life of Johann Sebastian Bach in Letters and Documents*, Hans T. David and Arthur Mendel (eds.), revised and enlarged by Christoph Wolff (New York, 1998) [*NBR*], no. 328, quoted in Wolff, *Johann Sebastian Bach: The Learned Musician*, pp. 322–3.

12 [Melody: its essence and properties] (Danzig, 1755). See Douglas A. Lee, 'Nichelmann, Christoph' in *Grove Music Online. Oxford Music Online*, http://www.oxfordmusiconline.com/subscriber/article/grove/music/19862 (accessed January 17, 2015).

13 [Arguing that musical science relates to philosophical scholarship] (Leipzig, 1734).

14 '… Capellmeisters Bach, den ich unter meine guten Freunde und Gönner zu zehlen die Ehre habe' [Kapellmeister Bach, whom I have the honor of counting as one of my good friends and patrons]. Lorenz Christoph Mizler von Kolof, *Neu eröffente musikalische Bibliothek oder Gründliche Nachricht nebst unpartheyischem Urtheil musikalischen Schriften und Büchern* [*MMB*]. Available online at the Bayerische Bibliothek digital website: http://www.mizler.de/, accessed January 18, 2015. (Leipzig, 1738), I/4, p. 61; reproduced in *BD* II/420, p. 322.

15 [Reviews of Ancient and Modern Singers] (Bologna, 1723)

16 [Introduction to the Art of Singing] (Berlin, 1757)

17 [The Art of Pure Setting of Music, Derived from Trusted and Clear Principles and with Illuminated Examples]. Volume i (Berlin, 1771), with a new title page (Berlin and Königsberg, 1774), and

volume ii (Berlin and Königsberg 1776–79). The two volumes were translated to English by David Beach and Jurgen Thym as *The Art of Strict Musical Composition* (New Haven and London, 1982).

18 While studying at the University of Leipzig, Friedemann actively assisted Bach by copying his works, helping through rehearsals and teaching his private students, including Christoph Nichelmann. In 1733, Friedemann moved to Dresden where he effortlessly won the position of organist at the Frauenkirche.

19 Philipp Emanuel was admitted to Department of Law at the University of Leipzig on October 1, 1731. On September 9, 1734, he transferred his law studies to the University of Frankfurt-an-der-Oder, moving there at the beginning of the academic year 1738.

20 Johannes Olearius, *Biblische Erklärung darinnen nechst dem allgemeinen Haupt-Schlüssel der gantzen heiligen Schrifft* [Biblical clarification, with a general key to the Holy Scriptures] (Leipzig, 1678–1681). All five volumes appear in the inventory of Bach's private library.

21 Johann Henning, *Cabbalologia, i.e. Brevis Institutio de Cabbala cum Veterum Rabbinorum judaica, tum Poetarum Paragrammatica, Artis Cabbalistic-Poeticce* [Cabbalologia, that is, a short introduction to Kabbalah, according to the ancient rabbinical Jewish tradition, and paragrammatic poetry, the art of the Kabbalistic poets] (Leipzig, 1683).

22 [Virtuous messages of old and new theological matters].

23 See Ruth Tatlow, 'J.S. Bach and the Baroque Paragram: A Reappraisal of Friedrich Smend's Number Alphabet Theory', *Music and Letters*, 70/2 (1989): p. 202.

24 [The newest art to achieve pure and galant poetry] (Leipzig, 1681).

25 [Serious, jocular and satirical poems] (Leipzig, 1727–51). Picander was the pseudonym of the writer and poet Christian Friedrich Henrici.

26 (Leipzig, 1687). Full title: *Via Regia ad Omnes Scientias et Artes, hoc est Art universalis, Scientiarum omnium Artium arcana facilius penetrandi, et de quocunque proposito Themate expeditious disserendi, practice, clare, succinte, curioso ac studioso Lectori* [The royal road to all arts and sciences, that is, to the universal art, offering an expeditious method to easily penetrate the secrets of all the sciences of art, presenting it in a practical, clear and succint outline for the curious and studious reader].

27 (Leipzig, 1696). Full title: *Curieuse Fragen über die Logica, welcher gestalt die unvergleichliche Disciplin von allen Liebhabern der Gelehrsamkeit sonderlich aber von einem Politico deutlich und nützlich soll erkennet werden: in Zweien Theilen, der anfänglichen Theorie, und der nachfolgenden Praxi zum Besten durch gnugsame Regeln, und sonderliche Exempel ausgeführet* [Unusual questions on logic, which shape the unique discipline of all lovers of learning, but especially needed and clearly useful to a public officer: in two parts, the first (presenting) the theory, and the following (presenting) the best practice with sufficient common rules, and demonstration of specific examples].

28 [Latest love and heroic stories] (Leipzig, 1706).

29 (Leipzig, 1695 and 1703, respectively). Full titles: *Das ABC: cum notis variorum* and *Das Einmahl Eins: cum notis variorum* [The Alphabet, with various notes; and The Basics, with various notes].

30 [The life and deeds of Friedrich August III] (Leipzig, 1737).

31 [Jewish notable features] (Leipzig, 1714–17).

32 It is highly unlikely that Bach ever met Leibniz, who left Leipzig in 1667 and died in Hanover, 1716, but the philosopher's Leipzig works, the *Disputatio Metaphysica de Principio Individui* [metaphysical disputation about the individuation principle] (1664) and his *Dissertatio de arte combinatoria* [On the Art of Combinations] (1666), both submitted during his student years, were thoroughly studied by the first lecturers of the Department of Psychology at the University of Leipzig and, together with works by Christian Thomassius and Christian Wolff, became major sources for the department's early curriculum and a source of pride for the University of Leipzig. (See the website of the University of Leipzig, Department of Psychology: http://www.uni-leipzig.de/~psycho/hist_eng.html, accessed January 18, 2015).

33 Musical treatises were included in his score collection. Unfortunately, this part of his library was not registered in the inventory of his property. Although hard work has been devoted to

16   Part I: Toward the history of the conception

the reconstruction of Bach's library, the collection has not yet been restored in its entirety. Still, existing evidence, mainly related to the last decade of Bach's life, points at the great interest the composer had in theoretical works. See: Kirsten Beißwenger, *Johann Sebastian Bachs Notenbibliothek* (Kassel, 1992).

34 For example, the chapter 'Ob die Christen mit gutem Gewissen zugeben können daß man die Cabbalam ohne ihnen gebraucht?' [Whether Christians can in good conscience admit that one used the Kabbalah without them?] in Müller's *Judaismus*, where the author discusses the possibility of applying Kabbalah to Christian exegesis. See Johann Müller *Judaismus Oder Jüdenthumb: Das ist: Ausführlicher Bericht, Von Des Jüdischen Volcks Unglauben, Blindheit und Verstockung, Darinne Sie Wider Die Prophetischen Weissagungen, Von Der Zukunfft, Person und Ampt Messiæ, Insonderheit Wieder Des Herrn Jesu Von Nazareth Wahre Gottheit, Gebuhrt Von Einer Jungfrauen, Geschlecht und Geschlecht-Register, Lehre, Wunderwercken, Weissagungen, Leben, Wider Die H. Dreyfaltigkeit, Absonderlich Wider Das Neue Testament mit Grostem Ernst und Eifer Streiten* (Hamburg, 1644). For reference and commentary see Robin A. Leaver, *Bachs theologische Bibliothek* (Stuttgart, 1983).

35 The content of each packet was printed in the *Musikalische Bibliothek*, the Society's publication (in the section 'Nachricht von der Societät der musikalischen Wissenschaften in Deutschland von 1746 biß 1752'), as well as preliminary notices of the upcoming issues. Thus, in volume IV, after a brief characterisation of the eighth and ninth 'packets', follows a list of 31 records reflecting the intentions of the heads of the Society to include relevant works in the future. *MMB* IV/1 (1754): pp. 119–29.

36 *BD* II/557, p. 437; translation based on *NBR*, no. 247, p. 228.

37 *MMB* I–IV (Leipzig, 1739–54).

38 The sections 'Musikalischen Neuigkeiten' and 'Nachricht von der Societät der musikalischen Wissenschaften in Deutschland' ['Musical News' and 'A Message from the Society of Musical Sciences in Germany', respectively].

39 Ernest Eugene Helm, *Music at the Court of Frederick the Great* (Norman, 1960), pp. xviii–xx.

40 Barbara Wiermann, 'Bach und Palestrina – einige praktische Probleme II', *Bach Jahrbuch [BJ]* 89 (2003): pp. 225–7.

41 Wiermann, ibid.

42 Wolff, *Johann Sebastian Bach: The Learned Musician*, pp. 333–4; Kirsten Beißwenger, *Johann Sebastian Bachs Notenbibliothek* (Kassel, 1992), pp. 226–400.

43 Beißwenger points out that Bach's library contained its 1700 edition (ibid. p. 366).

44 There is no reference to Andreas Werckmeister's treatise in Kirsten Beißwenger's study.

45 The research of this collection, which is still in progress, cannot exclude these sources from the potential list of publications owned by Bach.

46 [Why does musical art relate to philosophical scholarship?, 1734].

47 [Why is musical science related to philosophical scholarship?, 1740].

48 Michael Psellus, 'Des Psellus vollständiger kurzer Inbegriff der Musik,' *MMB* III/2 (1746): pp. 171–200.

49 Leonhard Euler, 'Tentamen novae theoriae musicae ex certissimis harmoniae principiis dilucide expositae. Auctore Leonhardo Eulero. Petropoli, ex typographia academiae scientiarum, […]. Das ist, Versuch einer neuen Theorie der Musik aus den richtigsten Gründen der Harmonie deutlich vorgetragen von Leonhard Euler. (Petersburg, 1739). *MMB* III/1 (1746): pp. 61–136; III/2 (1746): pp. 305–46; III/3 (1747): pp. 539–58, and IV/1 (1754): pp. 69–103.

50 The German translation of *De Vita Pythagorica liber* by Iamblichus from Cochide (c.250–330), a neo-Platonian philosopher and follower of Pythagoras, uses the expression 'Verabredeter Zeichen' [prearranged symbols]. The work recounts a number of Pythagoras' ideas (Iamblichus. *De vita Pythagorica liber*. Translated by Michael von Albrecht, Zurich, 1963).

51 [Harmonies of the World, 1619].

52 Athanasius Kircher, *Musurgia universalis sive ars magna consoni et dissoni in X. libros digesta*. (Romae : Ex typographia Haeredum Francisci. Corbelletti, 1650).

53 *MMB* IV/1 (1754): pp. 106–7.
54 This distinction is quite limited and only points at a tendency; more often than not, both aspects of symbolism are simultaneously present in one way or another.
55 The attempts to identify all the members (including Bach) did not succeed so far. The pseudonym of Aristotle was given to Telemann, Socrates – to Heinrich Bokemeyer, Archimedes – to Georg Heinrich Bümler, Terpander – to Christoph Gottlieb Schröter. Naturally, the pseudonym of Pythagoras was given to Mizler, the founder of the Society of Musical Sciences.
56 See Christoph Wolff, *Der stile antico in der Musik J.S. Bachs* (Stuttgart, 1968), where this phenomenon is convincingly discussed.

2 On the conception of *The Art of Fugue*

To this day, no definitive answer has been offered to the question concerning the purpose for which *The Art of Fugue* was conceived and composed. Several hypotheses, each with its own supporting arguments, were proposed. Of these, two have gained popularity: the first sees *The Art of Fugue* as Bach's intended contribution to the Society of Musical Sciences, of which he was a member; the second regards the cycle as part of Bach's pedagogical constructions, as were the *Auffrichtige Anleitung*[1] collection of inventions and sinfonias, and *The Well-Tempered Clavier*.

Hans Gunter Hoke unequivocally supports the first hypothesis.[2] His conviction is based on two arguments: first, *The Art of Fugue* meets all the requirements for such a contribution; second, in 1750, when the work was nearing its publication, Bach approached the age of 65, which marked a milestone for the members of the Society of Musical Sciences.

According to its constitution, the Society's fellows had to submit an annual contribution for publication. This could be a musical composition, a manual or an essay, which should comply with the basic principles and aspirations of the Society. For example, Paragraph Eight of the constitution required that each member submit at least one manual or essay of practical usefulness,[3] endorsing the renaissance of 'die Majestät der alten Musik'.[4]

At the age of 65, members moved into a new, honorary status and were exempt from the annual contribution. It would only be natural for Bach to establish his reputation and mastership with a particularly praiseworthy work. *The Art of Fugue* was just such a composition, thus making Hoke's hypothesis quite plausible.

However, later research shows that *The Art of Fugue* was conceived much earlier, probably sometime between 1739 and 1742.[5] It seems improbable that Bach designed his *last* contribution approximately 10 years before the due date, and, moreover, five to eight years prior to his joining the Society.

According to the second hypothesis, Bach created *The Art of Fugue* in the same vein as his inventions, sinfonias, and *The Well-Tempered Clavier*, for educational purposes: to teach clavier playing and composition techniques of forms based on imitations. Christoph Wolff notes that 'the various movements make up a practical textbook on fugue in five chapters: simple fugues, counterfugues, multiple-theme fugues, mirror fugues and canons—remarkably predating any theoretical textbook on the subject.'[6]

This hypothesis is concurrent with remarks made by Carl Philipp Emanuel Bach, Friedrich Wilhelm Marpurg and Johann Mattheson about *The Art of Fugue*.[7] It also corresponds with the principles and interests that were characteristic of the Society of Musical Sciences' pursuits.

Although officially becoming a member as late as June 1747, Bach followed closely the Society's activities from its very beginning, 10 years earlier. He kept contact with its members and was regularly updated about its ongoing issues, difficulties and creative aspirations.

This constant flow of information and interchange of ideas expanded the composer's views on music creativity. Indeed, during his last decade, Bach was focused on traditional strict counterpoint and its compositional techniques.[8] He was fascinated by the mathematical aspects of music, which were the subject of animated debates among the Society's members.[9] Barbara Wiermann, analysing lists of books and score collections in Bach's library, notes:

> ... [die] zusammengetragenen Materialen zeigen, wie Bachs—über die Jahre wechselnde—musikalische Interessen nicht nur in seinen eigenen kompositorischen Vorhaben oder dienstlichen Aufgaben zum Ausdruck kommen, sondern sich gleichermaßen in seinem Notenbestand an Werken anderer Komponisten spiegeln.[10]
>
> ... [(the) materials gathered show how Bach's musical interests—which changed over the years—were expressed not only in his own compositional projects, whether undertaken for himself or as part of his official duties, but were similarly reflected in his collection of other composers' works.]

Another indication of Bach's active interest in the state-of-the-art research of music theory, as well as of its practice, is the translation of Fux's *Gradus ad Parnassum* from Latin to German that Mizler published in 1742.[11] It is known that Bach owned both Latin and German versions of this treatise.[12] A work that inspects contrapuntal techniques is, therefore, in full accord with the trends and tastes that characterised the Society during all the time of its existence.

A comparison between the printed publications of the Latin original and its German translation reveals a notable peculiarity. In the Latin version, the musical examples are inserted in the body of the text, where they are discussed. In Mizler's published annotated translation, however, the examples are grouped as a musical supplement at the end of the book, following the custom of contemporary German publications (compare Figures 2.1a and 2.1b).

This editorial decision could, perhaps, point at a vein of thought that may have led to the conception of *The Art of Fugue*. The bulk of musical examples in the German edition looks like a collection of counterpoints, in which one section of short fugues (Tables XXIII to XXXV) stands apart. Written in score layout and in vocal clefs, almost all these fugues are based on just five themes, three of which are variants of each other, thus suggesting a tendency toward monothematicism. The first fugue of this section is based on the *Gradus*'s most prevalent theme. All the fugues on this theme are written in the first church mode (Dorian on D) and ordered in ascending degrees of complexity: first, the number of parts is increased from two to three and then four; then, the themes themselves are elaborated with added sophistication in the relations among the parts. Such organisation resembles that of *The Art of Fugue* in its early versions.

Both Bach's and Fux's fugue themes share their metre and order of voice introduction—alto, soprano, bass and tenor—which are more characteristic of strict choral style than of baroque instrumental music. Even the themes themselves could be related, Bach's theme seemingly an elaboration of Fux's. Bach's countersubjects, with their gradual progression into quarter notes and syncopations after a leap, are, too, conversant with the style of *Gradus*. It is thus hard to

Exercitii V. Lectio IV. de Fugis quatuor partium. 169

cujus est indagare, quo modo concentui, aut plus Harmoniæ, aut gratiæ aut varietatis accessurum sit; plerumque tamen usu receptum est, ut Tenor Cantum, Bassus Altum intrando sequatur. Cæterùm crescente partium copiâ, haud exigua tibi cura sit, ne partibus nimis infarcitis, & in angustum contractis ab una alteri liberè vagandi facultas admittatur. Quemadmodum enim per confertam turbam transeunti à dextra, sinistrâque, & à fronte impingere contingit; ideoque transitus aut omninò non, aut difficulter succedit : ita pari modo fit in Compositione, quando pars parti obsitans liberum incedendi campum non habet, belléque concinendi facultas tollitur. Quapropter summopere adnitendum est, ut hunc scopulum evadas.

Joseph. Quid verò remedii, quando preter opinionem tale quid contingeret?

Aloys. Aut mutandum modulationis consilium erit, aut parti, cui, nonnisi intrudendæ locus est, adminiculo pausæ silentium impones, usque dum reingrediendi cum subjecto spatium aperiatur. Satius tamen est, prævidendo, meditandoque partes ita disponere, ne consilii cæpti pauló post te pœniteat: præstat enim jura intacta relinquere, quàm post vulneratam causam remedium quærere. Opus igitur est, ut, dum uni parti vacas, cæteræ ne memoriâ excidant, neque partibus aliquibus tantum tribuas, ut superstiti nihil aut spatii ad gradiendum, aut concinnitatis ad cantandum remaneat. Exemplar tibi considerandum, imitandumque subjiciam, servato primæ trium partium Fugæ themate, aliisque ad quartæ partis introitum.

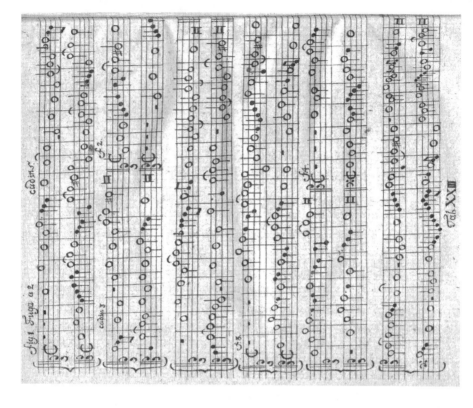

Figure 2.1b Same fugue in Mizler's German edition of *Gradus ad Parnassum*, Tab. XXIII (2nd system, f. 2).

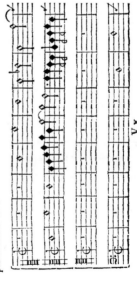

Figure 2.1a J.J. Fux: Fugue in *Gradus ad Parnassum*, Latin edition, p. 169.

avoid detecting an intentional attempt to signal that no earlier scholarly treatise, not even the best—and undoubtedly *Gradus ad Parnassum* was a work of that rank—had ever manifested such mastership in displaying the richest potentials of fugal writing. *The Art of Fugue* would establish Bach's unique offering of the truly artistic illustration of fugue.

This is exactly the tenor in which Carl Philipp Emanuel Bach presented *The Art of Fugue* in his announcement of the publication, in May 1751:

> Durch den Mangel an wohlansgearbeiteten Exempeln ist das Geheimniß der Fuge zeithero sehr sparsam fortgepflanzet worden. Viele große Meister hielten oft aus Eifersucht damit zurucke. Diejenigen, die einen Trieb hatten, einige Einsicht darinne zu erlangen, musten es ihnen gleichsam abhören. Wenn die Regeln, die man uns dazu ertheilte, auch gut und hinlänglich waren, so fehlte es dabey an nöthigen Exempeln. Man weiß aber, wie fruchtloß ein Unterricht ohne Exempel ist, und die Erfahrung zeiget, was man für einen ungleich größern Vortheil aus practischen Ausarbeitungen, als aus magern theoretischen Anweisungen ziehet. Gegenwärtiges Werck, welches wir dem Publico ankündigen, ist durchaus practisch.[13]

> [Due to the shortage in elaborate examples, the mystery of the fugue has been hitherto scantily explained. Often, many great masters jealously held [these secrets] back. Anyone interested in attaining an insight [of them], must, as it were, hear them. While the rules imparted to us are good and adequate, too, the need for good examples is still felt. One only knows how fruitless is a lesson without an example, and experience shows that the advantage one draws from practical elaboration is incomparably greater than [that gained] from mere theoretical statements. The present work, which we now present to the public, is practical throughout.]

Five years later, when he decided to offer the copper plates of the *The Art of Fugue* for sale ('at a reasonable price'), Emanuel wrote a similar description, highlighting the practical worth of this composition when combined with a theoretical guide:

> So viel wird mir davon anzumerken erlaubt sein, daß es das vollkommenste practische [sic] Fugenwerk ist und daß jeder Schüler der Kunst, mit Zuziehung einer guten theoretischen Anweisung, dergleichen die Marpurgische ist, nothwendig [sic] daraus lernen muß, eine gute Fuge zu Machen.[14]

> [May I note that this is the perfect practical fugue-composition and that, in combination with a good theoretical instruction, such as Marpurg's, any student of the arts should learn how to compose a good fugue.]

It seems that all these facts support the second hypothesis, according to which *The Art of Fugue* was composed as a comprehensive artistic illustration of the theory of fugue, or even as a practical instruction manual of fugue writing. Further, in all available contemporary sources, treatises and textbooks, there is no discussion of several types of fugue that Bach used (for example, the 'mirror' technique) nor even of their theoretical rationale. Even in Marpurg's treatise, which was the most comprehensive theoretical study of fugue, published soon after Bach's death, these types are not mentioned.[15]

However, both hypotheses could be reconciled given Bach's inclination to re-use his own and other composers' works. For instance, he used the triple canon, registered in Wolfgang Schmieder's catalogue as BWV 1076 and as BWV 1087/13 at three different times and in three situations. The canon first appeared in Elias Gottlieb Hausmann's portrait of Bach, painted in 1746; a year later, Bach submitted this canon as his annual contribution to the Society of Musical Sciences. Both instances are marked as BWV 1076. The third time occurred no earlier than October 1747, when the canon was included in the cycle of the *Fourteen Canons on the First Eight Notes of the Aria Ground from the Goldberg Variations* (BWV 1087/13).[16] Further, Bach composed another canon—a double—on the same bass, and used it at least twice, in two variants; the first is marked BWV 1077 (presented as a gift, in Johann Gottfried Fulde's album) and the second as yet another piece in the *Fourteen Canons* cycle, marked BWV 1087/11.

In this perspective of Bach's biography and his character, as described by his contemporaries, it is quite possible that Bach felt free to 'feed two birds with one seed'[17] and achieve a double purpose with one work. The first hypothesis is thus feasible, too. The year 1750 that marked Bach's 65th anniversary was approaching, and it is quite likely that *The Art of Fugue* began to be thought of by its composer not just as a user's manual (and, respectively, as an artistic treatise of fugue forms and techniques), but also as his final creative contribution to the Society of Musical Sciences, particularly since the composition fully complied with the requirements of the Society's constitution.

It is well known that J.S. Bach's idea to compose and publish *The Art of Fugue* was not fully realised by the composer himself. Presently, two main sources of *The Art of Fugue* are available for scholarly study. The first is the Autograph of the work, kept in Berlin and often nicknamed the Berlin Autograph.[18] The second source is the edition published by Carl Philipp Emanuel Bach, which was printed twice: at the end of September 1751 and six months later, at the beginning of April 1752. In the scholarly literature, the two latter publications are titled 'the Original Edition.' These sources will be discussed in Part II of this book (Chapters 4 and 5, respectively). First, however, we will examine the changes in Bach's handwriting throughout the year 1749.

Notes

1 [Honest Guidance]. See Anatoly Milka, 'Inventsiya — tak chto zhe eto takoe?' [An Invention — what is it, then?], in Anatoly Milka and Tatiana Shabalina, (eds.) *Zanimatel'naya Bakhiana* [Intriguing Bachiana], vol. 1 (St Petersburg, 2001), pp. 87–116.
2 Hans Gunter Hoke, *Zu Johann Sebastian Bachs Die Kunst der Fuge* (Leipzig, 1979), pp. 14–15.
3 *MMB* III/2 (1746): p. 350 (paragraph 8).
4 [the majesty of ancient music]. Ibid. p. 354 (paragraph 25).
5 Yoshitake Kobayashi, 'Zur Chronologie der Spätwerke Johann Sebastian Bachs: Kompositions- und Aufführungs-tätigkeit von 1736 bis 1750', *BJ* 74 (1988): pp. 49–51. Wolff, *Johann Sebastian Bach: The Learned Musician*, pp. 433–35.
6 Wolff, ibid. p. 436.
7 See, for example, C.P.E. Bach's offer to sell the copper plates of *The Art of Fugue* in Marpurg's Berlin journal *Historisch-Kritische Beyträge zur Aufnahme der Musik*, on September 14, 1756 (vol. 2, pp. 575–76; reprinted in *Dokumente zum Nachwirken Johann Sebastian Bachs*, *BD* III/683, pp. 113–14); Johann Mattheson's handwritten annotation in his own copy of the *Philologisches Tresespiel* (Hamburg, 1752), p. 98, and Friedrich Wilhelm Marpurg's preface for the 1752 edition of *The Art of Fugue* (reprinted in *BD* III/648, pp. 14–16). All three examples are translated to English in *NBR*, nos. 375 and 376, pp. 377–8, and no. 374, pp. 375–7, respectively.

8 See Walter Werbeck, 'Bach und der Kontrapunkt—Neue Manuskript-Funde', *BJ* 89 (2003): pp. 67–95; Daniel R. Melamed, 'Bach und Palestrina—Einige praktische Probleme I' (short contribution); *BJ* 89 (2003): pp. 221–4; Barbara Wiermann, 'Bach und Palestrina—Neue Quellen aus Johann Sebastian Bachs Notenbibliothek', *BJ* 88 (2002): pp. 9–25.
9 For example, Mizler provided a German translation, with an introduction and commentary, of the first four chapters from the *Tentamen novae theoriae musicae*, a treatise by Leonhard Euler, the Swiss mathematician who sought to incorporate music theory into the mathematical sciences (St Petersburg, 1739). The German translation appeared in installments in four consecutive issues of the *MMB* (see note 38 to Chapter 1). The translation was preceded by Mizler's extensive review of Euler's treatise: 'Tentamen novae theoriae musicae, das ist: Versuch einer neuen theoretischen Music [sic], aus untrüglichen Gründen der Harmonie deutlich vorgetragen von Leonhard Euler, Petersburg 1739', published in the *Zuverlässige Nachrichten von dem gegenwärtigen Zustande, Veränderung und Wachstum der Wissenschaften*, Leipzig 1741, pp. 722–51. Both the review and the translation are significant indications of the central role this topic occupied in the Society's discussions.
10 Barbara Wiermann, 'Bach und Palestrina …' p. 9.
11 Johann Joseph Fux, *Gradus ad Parnassum, sive manuductio ad compositionem musicae regularem*. Viennae, 1725. Translated to German by Mizler as [Fux, J.J.] *Gradvs ad Parnassvm oder Anführung zur Regelmäßigen Musikalischen Composition* (Leipzig, 1742).
12 Bach's annotated Latin copy of Fux's work has been registered: see Kirsten Beißwenger's *Johann Sebastian Bachs Notenbibliothek (Catalogus musicus)* (Bärenreiter, 1992). It is quite obvious that Bach was familiar with Mizler's German translation, since it probably was on his advice and under his supervision that Mizler undertook this project. Bach's ownership of this German edition was confirmed by Wolff, *Johann Sebastian Bach: The Learned Musician*, pp. 333–4.
13 Thomas Wilhelmi, 'Carl Philipp Emanuel Bachs *Avertissement* über den Druck der *Kunst der Fuge*,' *BJ* 78 (1992): pp. 101–2.
14 *Historisch-Kritische Beyträge zur Aufnahme der Musik*, on September 14, 1756 (vol. 2, pp. 575–6). *BD* III/683, p. 113.
15 Friedrich Wilhelm Marpurg, *Abhandlung von der Fuge nach dem Grundsätzen und Exempeln der besten deutschen und ausländischen Meister* (Berlin, 1753–1754).
16 According to context, these canons may appear under two different titles: Bach's autograph, found inside the back cover of the composer's copy of his Goldberg Variations, carries the title *Verschiedene Canones über die ersteren acht Fundamental-Noten vorheriger Arie von J.S. Bach* (translated by Christoph Wolff as *Diverse canons on the first eight notes of the ground of the preceding aria by J.S. Bach*). However, the first publication of these canons, edited by Wolff (Kassel, 1976) carries the title *Johann Sebastian Bach, Vierzehn Kanons über die ersten acht Fundamentalnoten der Aria aus den 'Goldberg-Variationen' BWV 1087* (*Fourteen Canons on the First Eight Notes of the Aria Ground from the 'Goldberg-Variations'*), a logical change given that here the canons appear by themselves, with no 'former aria', therefore requiring reference to the original theme by name. See Christoph Wolff, 'the Handexemplar of the Goldberg Variations' in *Bach: Essays on his Life and Music*, pp. 162–77, formerly published in *The Journal of the American Musicological Society*, 29/ii (1976): pp. 224–41.
17 The editor feels reluctant to use the 'kill two birds with one stone' expression. A quick search online brought up the above creative suggestion (http://www.ticklebugs.com/pages/contests.htm, accessed January 18, 2015).
18 Deutsche Staatsbibliothek Berlin (since 1992: Staatsbibliothek zu Berlin—Preußischer Kuturbesitz), Mus. ms. autogr. Bach P 200.

3 Bach's illness and the changes in his handwriting

There is a consensus among Bach's scholars concerning his fatal illness: it started with a cataract, developed from age related (type 2) diabetes, complicated by his myopia (short-sightedness).

Some scholars mention possible glaucoma (an increased intraocular pressure).[1] Such a combination of pathological conditions requires surgical intervention. Bach did endure eye surgery, and it was assumed that he died because 'his whole system, which was otherwise thoroughly healthy, was completely overthrown by the operation and by the addition of harmful medicaments and other things.'[2] It is also considered that one of the illness's symptoms was the noticeable changes in his handwriting during the years 1748–49. The connection between his ophthalmological disease and the changes in his handwriting was accepted as obvious. However, there is a reason to challenge this opinion.

Forensic examinations of handwriting discuss changes in handwriting caused by various diseases and particular circumstances.[3] These analyses suggest that the deterioration of Bach's handwriting during his last two years was unrelated to the weakening of his eyesight.[4] Numerous analytical graphology examinations confirm this notion.[5] Bach's handwriting in his letters and his music autographs from 1749, as well as text inserts in his scores, do not show signs caused by any of the eye diseases that afflicted him.[6]

However, certain signs in the composer's manuscripts from these years suggest a decline in blood supply to the cerebral cortex, which is a gerontological phenomenon rather than an ophthalmological problem.

Under this condition the handwriting changes gradually. One of the first signs is that the linking of letters and their components is impaired. As the disease progresses, sensing the contact between the pen and the paper is disrupted, leading to increased pressure on the pen. In a later stage there appears a variation in the angles of letters.[7] Finally, the smooth cursive writing becomes angular, and the letters are placed in various positions relative to the paper's lines.

Unlike such diseases as diabetes, hypertension, ulcers and many others, which develop intermittently, with alternating periods of aggravation and remission, the disruptions of blood supply to the cerebral cortex, if untreated, advance at an exponential rate without any remissions. At the early stages, the disease develops slowly, with almost unnoticeable effect. At a later stage, though, it becomes aggressive, and the changes in handwriting follow its dynamics. There is no documented evidence that Bach underwent any treatment, and therefore it is very likely that his disease developed exponentially and without remissions.

Other factors influence one's handwriting, too. Excitement, stress and anger are usually associated with an accelerated writing motion, while an attempt to write calligraphically or to forge someone's handwriting would result in a slower speed. Other issues might affect script, such as unsuitable surfaces, uncomfortable hand positions or the need to write on the edge or the lower margin of the paper sheet.

Typically, a transition from the old German script[8] to Latin (in Italian, French and English words) influences the handwriting, too. In such cases, text written in Latin script is usually marked, either by increased letter size,[9] disjointed writing or both.

A general feature of German handwritten documents is that in switching from Kurrent to Latin script within one document, the latter script's letters are less linked to each other. This can be seen in Bach's autographs—both early and late. For example, the receipt from May 26, 1706, shows that the level of connectedness in the Latin part of the text is about 50 percent,[10] while in German the rate was 80 percent. In the recommendation letter for Johann Nathanael Bammler, from April 12, 1749, the ratio is approximately 50 percent and 66 percent respectively.[11] The level of connectedness in the titles and in pure Latin texts (with no German script) is even lower. For example, the inscription on the title page of the Cantata BWV 210 (1741 or 1744) shows a level of connectedness of 38 percent (Figure 3.1).

Disregarding such considerations might hinder the accuracy of a manuscript analysis. Thus, Reinhard Ludewig, in his interesting book, analysed peculiarities of J.S. Bach's handwriting in two of his letters,[12] observing that 'during this time occurred a serious collapse in Bach's vitality'[13] in one case and 'as if the life power is ebbing' in the other.[14]

Indeed, the first letter (from October 6, 1748), when compared to its reference, looks less attractive from an *aesthetic* point of view. However, the dynamics of hand motions, as reflected in the handwriting, is nevertheless quite confident and does not indicate any signs of strength loss. Instead, it bears all the signs of haste: reduced components of letters, augmented intervals between the words and so on).[15] Bach himself comments about the time pressure that caused this haste, opening his letter with the phrase 'Ich werde wegen Kürtze der Zeit mit wenigem viel sagen …'.[16]

Unlike that first letter, the second one (from April 12, 1749) displays signs that previously had not been observed. We will mention only three: (1) unsure command of hand motion is evident in the pen pressure; (2) various instances of the same letters being written in different angles and (3) letters are positioned at different heights relative to the horizontal line of writing. Earlier documents do not carry these characteristics. This means that Bach was gradually losing control over the contact of pen to paper, which in its turn means that his progressive disease, disrupting his cerebral blood supply, had moved to its next stage. This circumstance confirms Ludewig's thesis that the second letter indicates 'ebbing of vitality'.[17]

Describing the characteristics of Bach's handwriting during his last years, Georg von Dadelsen correctly notes the decreasing level of connectedness between letters within words.[18] Clearly, this is one of the symptoms of Bach's illness that affected his handwriting. As an example Dadelsen brings the Canon BWV 1077 from October 15, 1747. The level of connectedness in its text is quite low—17 percent. However, this evidence cannot be accepted as a valid indicator of Bach's characteristic handwriting for several reasons, mainly because the inscriptions on this autograph are in Latin and Italian, both using non-German script.

26 Part I: Toward the history of the conception

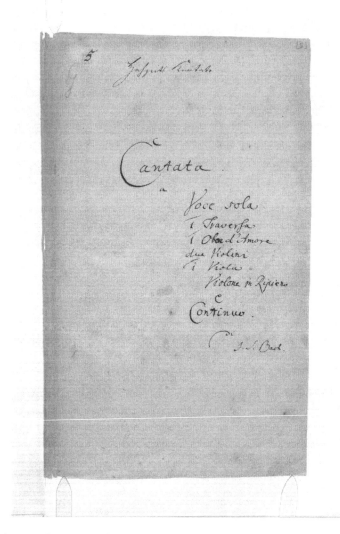

Figure 3.1 Title page of BWV 210, showing 38 percent level of letter connectedness.

As marked above, the inscriptions performed in Latin often have a significantly lower level of connectedness than those in Old German. Besides, and regardless of other considerations, sometimes the text function affects script connectedness more than age and/or illness do. For example, Bach's intention to highlight the significance of every word in the text of the Canon BWV 1077, which is satiated with symbols, wrought the low level of connectedness. This was enhanced by the choice of the marked Latin language for the inscriptions, as well as by his effort to achieve the highest calligraphy, slowing down the writing speed, which, in its turn, further affected letter connectedness.

The special circumstances in which a text was written should also be taken into account in analysing Bach's autographs from his last years (especially from the beginning of 1749). Alfred

Dürr correctly dates the handwritten additions to the performers' parts of *Dem Gerechten muss das Licht* (BWV 195) and the St John Passion (BWV 245) as the very last instances of Bach's handwriting: "Nirgends findet sich jene zittrig-klobige Spätschrift, wie sie an Kantate 195, an den spätesten Eintragungen zur Johannes-Passion und gelegentlich auch an den spätesten Teilen der h-Moll-Messe zu beobachten sind."[19] The handwritten additions to the parts of the cantata *Lobe den Herrn, meine Seele* (BWV 69) could be added to this list.

Indeed, these script insertions bear many traits of Bach's "trembling-clumsy" late handwriting.[20] Interestingly though, the handwriting in these particular insertions is still relatively proportional, and in most cases the components of each letter have similar orientation (straight and slightly to the right).

The handwriting in the Mass in B minor (*Symbolum Nicenum*) is more disproportional, making "trembling and clumsy" a fitting description. The letters and their components differ in size and in slant (straight, slightly to the left and slightly to the right). The handwritten insertions of this type can be seen also in the last additions to Cantatas BWV 69, BWV 195 and the St John Passion (BWV 245); for example, in the Passion, the inscription *Finis 1. Partis* on page 7 of the first violin part, after the transposed choral. This is also evident in the inscription *Lipsiae, d. 15. Octobr: 1747.* at the bottom of the page in the manuscript of Canon BWV 1077. These particular inscription characteristics, however, should not be related to the peculiarities of Bach's writing of that period, because they are positioned in spots that were awkward for writing: on the very bottom of the sheet or in one of the bottom corners.[21] The conditions worsen when the inscription is made in an album (*Stammbuch*), over a paper stack or in a book margin.

However, the inscriptions made by Johann Sebastian on the title page of the choir parts and on the insertions into the instrumental parts of the double-chorus motet *Lieber Herr Gott, weck uns auf* by Johann Christoph Bach (1642–1703), a family relative who worked as organist from Eisenach, are different.[22] Christoph Wolff notes that 'they also reveal that the ailing old man clearly had trouble writing: the lettering is unwieldy—uneven, stiff, disproportionately large, and disjunctive.'[23]

Other insertions in the performing materials of BWV 69, 195, 245 and the above-mentioned motet *Lieber Herr Gott, weck uns auf* clearly belong to the same period,[24] probably after completing the Mass in B minor. However, Bach's handwriting in the motet shows further changes. Here we find the falling level of connectedness not only between the individual letters but also between their components. Thus, the letter B in the words *Bach* (on the title page) and *Basson* (in the title of the bassoon part) was drawn in three separate motions, as a combination of three separate components. A similar case is the drawing of the digit *8*, with three separate movements as well. Letters *O, g, a* in the word *Organo* (the title of the organ part) have been performed in two separate movements. These changes of Bach's handwriting in the motet suggest that Bach wrote these inscriptions after the Cantatas BWV 69, 195 and the St John Passion.

Unfortunately, examples of Bach's latest handwriting, which are usually associated with the second half of December 1749 and the beginning of 1750 (such as those described above), can be dated through circumstantial evidence only, and are based, as a rule, on handwriting analysis and information about Bach's biography. The easiest procedure to trace the evolution of his handwriting would be to compare as many as possible of Bach's dated signatures, where the visual appearance of the writing is the only variable, while its content remains the same. Reinhard Ludewig, in his insightful book, presents facsimiles and discusses several of these signatures showing the general deterioration of the composer's handwriting during the years 1748–49.[25] Five documents that Bach signed between July 31, 1748, and December 11, 1749, clearly exhibit the process:

- Letter to Christian Friedrich Schaller (July 31, 1748)[26]
- Letter to Johann Elias Bach (November 2, 1748)[27]
- Letter of recommendation to Johann Nathanael Bammler (April 12, 1749)[28]
- Receipt of purchasing Piano et Forte (May 6, 1749)[29]
- Letter of recommendation to Johann Nathanael Bammler (December 11, 1749)[30]

While it is true that all five autographs were drawn under different conditions, in various speeds and with quills of various qualities, they convincingly show the main changes in Bach's handwriting during these years.

The signature from July 31, 1748, shows that Bach had no difficulties in writing until as late as summer 1748. It displays full control over the pressure on the quill and over its contact with the paper; the drawing of curves and hook-like elements is smooth.[31] The last signature, however, exhibits a much slower pace of writing; the control over the contact of quill and paper is weakened, creating an increased pressure and sharp angulation in curved letters, such as 's', 'o', 'e' or 'a'.

In the two letters from 1748 the letter 'B' (in 'Bach') is written with a single stroke of the quill. In the recommendation letter from April 12, 1749, however, this letter is drawn with two strokes, while its writing in the other recommendation letter, from December 11, 1749, seems to have required three separate strokes (as in the motet *Lieber Herr Gott, weck uns auf*, mentioned above).

By that time, the imbalance between the flexor and extensor writing motions was increased, causing difficulties with writing hook-like curves, such as the one needed for the combination 'ft', which Bach completely avoids in his signature from May 6, 1749, substituting it with the graphically simpler variant 'st'. It is interesting to compare this last signature with another inscription drawn by the composer: *Duo Voces Articuli 2*, written while finalising the Mass in B minor.[32]

A comparison between this inscription and the signature on the recommendation letter for Bammler, dated December 11, 1749, shows the same kind of changes in the speed of writing, level of connectedness, pen pressure and curved letters outlines. Since by the second half of 1749 Bach's handwriting remained stable only for short periods, it is feasible that both autographs are chronologically close to each other.

However, until the surgery, the above changes in Bach's handwriting were more gradual, and it is unlikely that he would suddenly lose the ability to control the quill.

The five signatures display the changes in Bach's handwriting from the end of July 1748 to the end of 1749, that is, until about seven months before the composer's death. The time-span between each two adjacent examples ranges from one to seven months. This indicates that the changes in handwriting during the composer's last period were progressive in nature as was the deterioration of blood supply to the cerebral cortex.

An inspection of manuscripts written by Christoph Willibald Gluck in his last years (1786–1787) substantiates this view. The changes in his handwriting are very similar to those of Bach's last manuscripts. It is known, though, that Gluck died as a result of a stroke, and that unlike Bach, he did not suffer from any impediments in his vision.[33]

October 1749—the final point?

The most important question for our study is finding out as accurately as possible the last date on which Bach was still able to read and write. Where should we draw that fatal line defining the day on which he could no longer control his quill?

Yoshitake Kobayashi provides an unambiguous answer:

> Spätestens ab Ende Oktober 1749, als Bach eine Quittung im Zusammenhang mit dem Nathanischem Legat von seinem Sohn Johann Christian schreiben ließ … vermutlich bedingt die Behinderung des Sehvermögens, keine Schreibarbeit mehr.
>
> [At the very latest by the end of October 1749, when Bach's receipt concerning the Nathan Bequest (Nathanischen Legat) was written by his son Johann Christian … most likely, due to deterioration of vision, he could no more perform any work for which writing was required.][34]

A few years after Kobayashi's publication, the newly discovered document challenged his conclusion. However, only the first part of the Nathan Bequest is extant, a fact that led Robert Lewis Marshall to argue that, 'with the exception of the date, Christian set out to copy the 1748 receipt literally. It was almost certainly completed on the following leaf. Whether or not Johann Sebastian Bach signed it himself is not known.'[35]

Both views present sensible reasoning, and therefore it cannot be confirmed whether the document was not only written by but also signed by Christian. It seems more probable that it was J.S. Bach's signature that finalised it (or else it would not be legal), in the same way he did it in another document of the same year, written two months later.

This document is Bach's letter of recommendation for his student, Nathanael Bammler, dated December 11, 1749.[36] Like the Nathan Bequest receipt, this letter was signed by Sebastian Bach but not written by him. Wollny notes that there were documents that Bach could still write after October:

> Das zweite Eilenburger Zeugnis für Bammler dokumentiert nun jedoch, daß Bach auch nach Oktober 1749 noch selbst schrieb … Hieraus folgt, daß das späteste Stadium der Handschrift Bachs bis mindestens Mitte Dezember 1749 ausgedehnt werden muß.[37]
>
> [The second Eulenburg reference for Bammler proves that Bach could still write after October 1749 … It follows that the latest stage of Bach's handwriting should be extended at least until mid December 1749.]

Christoph Wolff, too, suggests a date later than October 1749: 'We may then surmise that the last musical scores to stem from Bach's hand—parts II–IV of the Mass in B minor and the unfinished quadruple fugue from *The Art of the Fugue*—were written no later than the first weeks of 1750.'[38] The scholar relates the Et incarnatus from BWV 232 to the very latest examples of Bach's oeuvre.[39] The letter from December 11, 1749, discovered by Wollny, is significant because it is the latest known dated sample of J.S. Bach's handwriting. Thus, the thesis that proposed the date of October 1749 as a boundary line, beyond which Bach could not use pen and paper, remains unconfirmed. Further, it is inconsistent with evidence found in surviving documents (produced by C.P.E. Bach), such as the announcement of the subscription, notification and preface. Moreover, it contradicts facts in Bach's biography during this period.

Actually, nothing changed in his life during this time. He continued to teach, to organise and present new and repeated performances of his and other composers' works. Sometimes he rewrote texts or applied new figured bass lines. He was involved in the polemics with Christoph Gottlieb Schröter (answering him in writing!), reacted to ongoing musical events in Germany, etc. All this suggests that October 1749 was not the decisive point after which, as Kobayashi states, Bach could not write anymore and led the life of a blind man. This does not mean that Bach did not experience serious discomfort with his vision, which undoubtedly was deteriorating. Nevertheless, this was not a sudden event. This conclusion is substantiated by other facts, too, albeit indirectly. It becomes particularly convincing when the circumstances of the surgery are clarified.

The surgery

None of Bach's letters includes any hint of complaints regarding his vision or of a possible surgical intervention. It is possible, therefore, that he did not plan such a radical treatment at all and that the decision to undergo surgery was spontaneous and circumstantial. The trigger was the visit of a British celebrity—the oculist John Taylor—in Leipzig, which, as a popular newspaper's report suggests, became a focus of interest:

> Am verwichenen Sonnabende und gestern abends hat der Herr Ritter Taylor auf dem Concertsaale, in Gegenwart einer ansehnlichen Gesellschaft von Gelehrten und anderer Personen von Stande, öffentliche Vorlesungen gehalten.[40]

> [Last Saturday night and yesterday evening Sir Taylor gave public lectures at the concert hall in the presence of a considerable assembly of scholars and other persons of rank].

The newspaper also noted the general public reactions that went beyond sheer curiosity: "Es ist erstaunlicher Zulauf von Leuten bey ihm, welche seine Hülfe suchen." [The concourse of people who seek his aid is astonishing.][41] Bach, however, did not seem to be in such a hopeless condition that would require seeking help through surgery. The Obituary tells that the composer went to surgery 'partly on the advice of several of his friends, who placed great confidence in an oculist who had recently arrived in Leipzig.'[42] This is an important piece of information: Bach's decision to undergo surgery was not his own initiative, but rather the result of persuasion. The report suggests that Bach lost his eyesight as a result of the operation, and that until that moment he still could see. This observation is cardinal to our discussion, because it means that by the end of March 1750 Bach could read a musical text and use pen and paper. He could continue his work, in one way or another, on something that was still unfinished. Even though he probably endured discomfort and a limited ability to see, he could continue working on *The Art of Fugue*, and in particular on the last fugue.

There are yet additional facts to substantiate this claim, albeit indirectly: the rearrangement of the canons after Christoph Friedrich had left for Bückeburg and several particularities of Bach's handwriting: different positions of digits in relation to the staves; increased pressure; clumsy outline of curves, performing the hook-shaped elements of the digits with several motions and so on. These characteristics appear in the digits that retain the permutation, indicating that the composer continued to work on this composition into 1750. These digits, so it seems, are the very last element that Bach had written on manuscript paper. A comparison between the character of their outline and his handwriting in the autograph of the 'unfinished' fugue (August 1748 / October 1749) would clearly show, even without a graphology analysis, that the time gap between them was significant and that they could have been written much later.[43]

If the work on *The Art of Fugue* continued into the year 1750, and if Bach could read and write with relatively manageable difficulties during most of the season 1749/1750, conclusions concerning the date of composition of *The Art of Fugue* may be significantly affected. Since no less than six months (calculating from October 1749) or even a year and a half (calculating from August 1748) remained until the surgery, it would follow that Bach left the last fugue unfinished for quite a long time, while its completion required very little work. With such a grandiose project as *The Art of Fugue*, such a conclusion sounds almost unbelievable!

Notes

1 Detlev Kranemann, 'Johann Sebastian Bachs Krankheit und Todesursache: Versuch einer Deutung,' *BJ* 76 (1990): pp. 53–64. Reinhardt Ludewig, *Johann Sebastian Bach im Spiegel der Medizin: Persönlichkeit, Krankheiten, Operationen, Ärzte, Tod, Reliquien, Denkmäler und Ruhestätten des Thomaskantors* (Leipzig, 2000), pp. 13–20. Richard H.C. Zegers, 'The Eyes of Johann Sebastian Bach,' *Archives of Ophthalmology*, 123/10 (2005): pp. 1427–30.

2 *BD* III/666, p. 85. '… im übrigen überaus gesunder Cörper (sic), wurde auch zugleich dadurch, und durch hinzugefügte schädliche Medicamente, und Nebendinge, gänzlich über den Haufen geworfen …' originally published in the Obituary by Carl Philipp Emanuel Bach and Johann Friedrich Agricola (1750), published in *MMB* IV/1 (1754): p. 167. English translation in *NBR*, no. 306, p. 303.

3 Michael P. Caligiuri and Linton A. Mohammed, *The Neuroscience of Handwriting: Applications for Forensic Document Examination* (Boca Raton, 2012). See particularly Chapters 4 and 6.

4 Roswitha Klaiber and Reinhard Ludewig, 'Zur schriftpsychologischen und medizinischen Interpretation der Autographen von Johann Sebastian Bach', *Zeitschrift für Schriftpsychologie und Schriftvergleichung*, 1, (2000): pp. 2–21.

5 Gabriele Schmidt, Ingrid Kästner and Reinhard Ludewig, 'Medizinisch-graphologischer Beitrag zum Einfluß der visuellen und kinästhetischen Kontrolle auf die Schreibhandlung', *Zeitschrift für Menschenkunde*, 60/1 (1995): pp. 219–44; Thomas Perrez, 'Graphologische Aspekte der morbiden und prämorbiden Parkinsonschrift', *Zeitschrift für Menschenkunde*, 60/1 (1995): pp. 245–56; Reinhard Ludewig, 'Zur Interpretation ausgewählter Schriftveränderungen', *Zeitschrift für Menschenkunde*, 63/2 (1999): pp. 2–16.

6 Ludewig, *Johann Sebastian Bach im Spiegel der Medizin*, pp. 42–3.

7 During this time, the afflicted person experiences discomfort while writing in a single pen stroke letters and signs that include twisted lines (such as the treble clef, the digit 8, the letter B, and so on). This is often caused by an imbalance between the flexors and extensors, caused by the weakening of the latter. When this is the case, the writer attempts writing such figures in several separate motions.

8 Gothic cursive, also known as *Kurrent*, *Kurrentschrift* or *Alte Deutsche Schrift*.

9 See, for example, the title page of BWV 772–801, *Auffrichtige Anleitung* (Mus. ms. Bach P 610, 1723); Johann Christoph Bach's letter, sent on April 4, 1686, from Eisenach to the municipality council of Schweinfurt [*BJ* 85 (1999): pp. 198–9] and Theodor Benedict Borman's log on J.S. Bach's arrest (*BD* II/84, p. 65, picture facing p. 81).

10 *BD* I, plate facing p. 192.

11 Reinhard Ludewig, *Johann Sebastian Bach im Spiegel der Medizin* (Grimma, 2000), p. 39. The original document is kept at the Stadtarchiv Eilenburg. A facsimile of this document also appears in Peter Wollny, 'Neue Bach-Funde', *BJ* 83 (1997): p. 39.

32   Part I: Toward the history of the conception

12 Letter to Johann Elias Bach, from October 6, 1748, and the above mentioned reference for Johann Nathanael Bammler, from April 12, 1749.
13 '… daß sich bei Bach in dieser Zeit ein gravierender Vitaleinbruch ereignet hat', (Ludewig, *Johann Sebastian Bach im Spiegel der Medizin*, p. 41).
14 '… im Gegenteil, wie wenn sich das vitale Leben zurück zöge' (ibid.).
15 Reinhard Ludewig interprets these signs as reflecting anxiety and irritation ('Störungen und Irritationen' ibid.). The contents and the tone of the letter, however, do not bear such signs.
16 [As time is short, I will say much in a few words] *BD* I/49, p. 117; translated in *NBR*, no. 257, p. 234.
17 [… das vitale Leben zurück zöge]. Alfred Dürr thinks that the periods of deteriorations and remissions may have alternated: 'Entweder hat Bach die Kunst der Fuge schon relativ früh vor seiner letzten Krankheit aus der Hand gelegt (…) oder aber er war in seinem Alter einmal vorübergehend krank – BWV 195, 245! – und hat danach in wieder gebesserter Gesundheit geschrieben hat.' [either Bach's *The Art of Fugue* was already set relatively early, before his last illness (…) or that he was, in his old age, temporarily ill – (creating) BWV 195, 245! – and had subsequently returned to better health, and then continued his work on *The Art of Fugue*.] Alfred Dürr, 'Neue Forschungen zu Bachs "Kunst der Fuge"', *Die Musikforschung*, 32/2 (1979): p. 158.
18 Georg von Dadelsen, *Beiträge zur Chronologie der Werke Johann Sebastian Bachs*, Tübinger Bach-Studien, vols. 4–5 (Trossingen, 1958): p. 116.
19 [Such late trembling-clumsy handwriting as in the Cantata BWV 195, in the latest insertions to the St John Passion and in the last sections of the Mass in B minor can be found nowhere else.] Alfred Dürr, 'Neue Forschungen …', p. 158.
20 'zittrig-klobige', ibid.
21 The insertion 'Finis', positioned in a comfortable writing spot in the Continuo instrumental part, on p. 108, was drawn in proportional font with a matching slant to the right. Near it is the insertion 'Wird mit gemacht'.
22 Shelfmark SA 5142–5144 in the archive of the Sing-Akademie zu Berlin.
23 Wolff, *Johann Sebastian Bach: The Learned Musician*, p. 451.
24 This assertion is based on similar traces in the handwriting, close style of inscriptions, same ink colour, and so on.
25 Ludewig, *Johann Sebastian Bach im Spiegel der Medizin*.
26 Ibid. p. 36. The original document is kept at the Stadtarchiv Naumburg. The same facsimile was also published in Werner Neumann, *Auf den Lebenswegen Johann Sebastian Bachs* (Berlin, 1953; 4th edition, 1962), p. 285.
27 Ibid. p. 38. The original document is kept at the Mary Flagler Cary Collection of music manuscripts, The Morgan Library and Museum, New York. Its facsimiles were also published in Robert Ammann, *Die Handschrift der Künstler* (Bern, 1953), p. 76, and in three publications by Paul Hindemith: (1) *Johann Sebastian Bach. Heritage and Obligation* (London, 1952), p. 6; (2) *Johann Sebastian Bach. Ein verpflichtendes Erbe* (Wiesbaden, 1954), plate facing p. 5, and (3) *Johann Sebastian Bach. Arv og forpliktelse* (Oslo, 1954), plate facing p. 7.
28 Ibid. p. 39; see also note 11.
29 Ibid. p. 40. The original document is kept at the Archiwum Głównym Akt dawnych, Warsaw. The facsimile also appears in two publications by Teresa Zielińska: (1) 'Osiemnastowieczna transakcja zakupu fortepianu', *Kwartalnik Historii Kultury Materialnej*, 3 (1967): p. 524, and (2) 'Nieznany autograf Jana Sebastiana Bacha', *Muzyka*, 4 (1967): p. 69.
30 Ibid. p. 40. The original document is kept at the Stadtarchiv Eilenburg. Discovered by Peter Wollny, the letter is discussed in his 'Neue Bach-Funde', *BJ* 83 (1997): pp. 7–50. The facsimile appears on p. 41.
31 For example, in the name 'Sebastian', the letter 'S' and the combination 'ſt' (it was customary, in this combination, to use the Latin lower case long 's').

32 This inscription (manuscript kept at the Berlin, Staatsbibliothek zu Berlin – Preußischer Kulturbesitz D-B Mus. ms. Bach P 180, and can be seen in www.bach-digital.de/receive/BachDigitalSource_source_00001048) provides evidence of the last alteration in the 'Et incarnatus est'. See Christoph Wolff, 'The Agnus Dei of the B Minor Mass: Parody and New Composition Reconciled', in *Bach: Essays*, p. 332: 'Along with the 'Et incarnatus est', the Agnus Dei represented not only the final steps in the completion of the entire work, but also Bach's last major efforts with respect to vocal composition in general'.
33 Anatoly Milka, 'Zur Datierung der H-Moll-Messe und der Kunst der Fuge', *BJ* 96 (2010): pp. 53–68.
34 Yoshitake Kobayashi, 'Bemerkungen zur Spätschrift Johann Sebastian Bachs …' *BJ* 74 (1988): p. 25. See Marshall (note 35) for details about the Nathan Bequest.
35 Robert Lewis Marshall, 'The Nathan Bequest: Payment Receipts in the Hand of Johann Sebastian Bach, 1746 to 1748 (With a Fragment for the Year 1749 in the Hand of His Son).' *The Moldenhauer Archives – The Rosaleen Moldenhauer Memorial, the Library of Congress*. http://memory.loc.gov/ammem/collections/moldenhauer/2428108.pdf.
36 Wollny, 'Neue Bach-Funde', p. 41.
37 Wollny, ibid. p. 42.
38 Wolff, *Johann Sebastian Bach: The Learned Musician*, p. 447.
39 Christoph Wolff, '"Et incarnatus" and "Crucifixus": The Earliest and the Latest Settings of Bach's B-Minor Mass', in Mary Ann Parker (ed.), *Eighteenth-Century Music in Theory and Practice: Essays in Honor of Alfred Mann* (New York, 1994), pp. 1–17.
40 *Berlinische Privilegierte Zeitung*, April 1, 1750. Quoted in *BD* II, no. 598, p. 468; translated in *NBR*, no. 269, p. 243.
41 Ibid.
42 '… theils auf Anrathen einiger seiner Freunde, welche auf einen damals in Leipzig angelangten Augen Arzt, viel Vertrauen setzten, durch eine Operation heben lassen.' The Obituary by Carl Philipp Emanuel Bach and Johann Friedrich Agricola (1750) published 1754 in *MMB* IV/1 (1754): p. 167, quoted in *BD* III, no. 666, p. 85. Translated in *NBR*, no. 306, p. 303.
43 See Part III for an extended discussion of this point.

Part II
The principal documents
The Autograph and the Original Edition

4   The Autograph

The Autograph of *The Art of Fugue* is kept in the Department of Music at the Berlin State Library (Musikabteilung mit Mendelssohn-Archiv von Staatsbibliothek zu Berlin, Preußischer Kulturbesitz) under the shelfmark Mus. ms. autogr. Bach P 200.[1] The Autograph includes four groups of manuscripts: the main body and three supplements (P 200/1–1, P 200/1–2 and P 200/1–3).

The main body contains 15 pieces: 12 fugues in score layout and three canons. Two of these canons are presented in both cryptic and decrypted forms. The third canon is composed on the same theme as the second one, but is presented only in its full, decrypted version. This collection opens with a title page that reads: *Die / Kunst der Fuga / d. Sig. Joh. Seb. Bach.* This title was inscribed by Bach's student, Johann Christoph Altnickol. Lower on the title page appears a postscript: 'in eigenhändiger Partitur' (in handwritten score), written by one of the Autograph's owners, Georg Johann Daniel Poelchau (Figure 4.1).[2]

P 200/1–1 contains the penultimate[3] version of the Canon in Augmentation and Inversion (*Canon p[er]. Augmentationem contrario motu*), BWV 1080/14, written on one side only of three sheets of paper, all oiled for engraving. On the first page, above the music notation and next to the title, there is an inscription made by Johann Christoph Friedrich Bach:

> NB: Der seel Papa hat auf die Platte diesen Titul stechen laßen *Canon / per Augment: in Contrapuncto all octava*, er hat es aber wieder / ausgestrichen auf der Probe Platte und gesetzet wie forn stehet[4]

> [N.B.: The late Papa had the following heading engraved on the plate, *Canon per Augment: in Contrapuncto all octava*, but he had crossed it out of the proof plate and put it in the above-noted form].

P 200/1–2 consists of two sheets of paper, showing the mirror fugue for two claviers (BWV 1080/18). One sheet presents the *rectus* of the fugue and the other—its *inversus*. P 200/1–3 consists of five sheets of paper with the 'unfinished' fugue BWV 1080/19, written on two staves, in keyboard layout. The music notation appears on one side only of each sheet. On the verso of the fourth sheet there is a list, inscribed in C.P.E. Bach's handwriting, of errata he had identified in the 1751 edition of *The Art of Fugue*, probably soon after its publication. The fifth (and last) sheet carries two inscriptions. One is by C.P.E. Bach:

38 *Part II: The principal documents*

NB Ueber dieser Fuge, wo der Nahme / BACH im Contrasubject / angebracht worden, ist / der Verfaßer gestorben[5]

[Over this fugue, where the name BACH is stated in the countersubject, the author died].

The other inscription, by an unknown scribe,[6] appears on the verso of the same sheet: 'und einen andern Grund Plan' [and another fundamental plan]. After C.P.E. Bach's death in 1788, the Autograph of *The Art of Fugue* was found among his possessions.[7] It was purchased in 1790 by C.F.G. Schwenke,[8] after whose death, in 1824, it passed to Poelchau. In 1841, Poelchau's

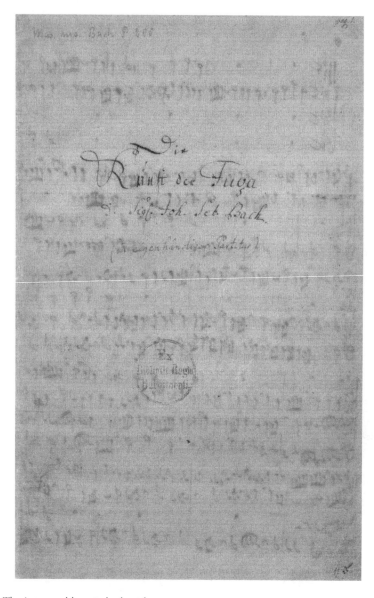

Figure 4.1 The Autograph's main body, title page.

son sold his father's music collection to the Royal Library in Berlin (today The Staatsbibliothek zu Berlin), where the manuscript is presently kept.

Diplomatics data

A thorough inspection of the paper on which manuscripts are written is particularly important for their study: definition of the paper's type, identification of its manufacturer and the time of its production, analysis of its watermarks, its material constitution and its binding—all these affect and contribute toward an accurate assessment of its content. The visual attributes of the text, too, have to be inspected, such as the handwriting and the physical condition of the document. Such a combination of multiple investigations is usually dubbed *diplomatics*.[9] A careful deliberation concerning the above elements is cardinal for an appropriate analysis of the Autograph P 200.

The paper constituting the main part of the Autograph in its present state[10] is a combination of five *binios*.[11] Its structure is shown in Scheme 4.1 (see p. 42). Bach used three types of paper in the main part of the Autograph, each type denoted by a different watermark. These are represented in the scheme by thin, thick and dashed lines and by conventional symbols (WZ 67, WZ 65 and WZ 21, respectively).[12] According to Kobayashi, the paper with the watermark WZ 67 (pp. 1–24, marked in Scheme 4.1 by a thin line) was used by Bach around 1742, 'but probably earlier (before August 1742)'.[13] The paper with the watermark WZ 65 (p. 25–34 and 39–40, marked in Scheme 4.1 by a bold line) was probably used in 1742 later than WZ 67 (starting in May).[14] The paper that has the watermark WZ 21 (pp. 35–8, dashed line in Scheme 4.1) was used during the period of 1743–46/47.[15]

P 200/1–1 (the Canon in Augmentation and Inversion, BWV 1080/14) is written on paper without any watermarks. Based on certain handwriting peculiarities, Kobayashi dated it as 'from 1747 till August 1748'.[16] P 200/1–2 (the fugue for two claviers, BWV 1080/18) uses paper watermarked WZ 21, implying that it was written around the same time as the music on pages 35–8 (the end of the four-part mirror fugue, the three-part mirror fugue in full and the beginning of the second Canon in Augmentation and Inversion), sometime between 1743 and 1746/47. The first two sheets of P 200/1–3 (the 'unfinished' fugue BWV 1080/19, written on five sheets) are watermarked WZ 19. Kobayashi dates these as 'after August 1748 to October 1749',[17] allocating the fifth and last sheet (watermarked WZ 24) to a similar date.

Numeration

Each page of the Autograph carries several numerations, a fact that deserves special attention. Sometimes there are three different numbers on a page and sometimes four. They were inscribed by a number of individuals, on various occasions. Certain scribes did not fully understand the meaning of their predecessors' numerations, subsequently introducing their own 'corrections'. This practice created a great deal of confusion, requiring careful and detailed consideration.

The Autograph carries four numeration systems. The first is a simple pagination, marking the pages from 1 to 40. The second appears only on the top left corner of the verso pages (1–4, in Bach's handwriting, and 5–19 and 22 by another hand). The third is the first numeration of the pieces in the cycle (1–9), and the fourth is the second numeration of the pieces in the cycle, written in Roman numerals i–xv. Table 4.1 shows these four numeration systems and their distribution in the Autograph.

Table 4.1 Numerations and content plan of the Autograph main body (P 200)

Pagination	Folio numeration	Primary composition numeration	Secondary composition numeration	Type of composition	Serial composition number
p. 1.	[1]			title: *Die Kunst der Fuge* ...	
p. 2.					
3		1	I	simple fugue	1
				(ending)	
4	[2]	2	II	simple fugue	2
5				(ending)	
6	[3]	3	III	fugue in rhythmic counterpoint	3
7				(ending)	
8	[4]	4	IV	fugue in rhythmic counterpoint	4
9				(continuation)	
10	5	5	V	(ending) + fugue with a consistent countersubject	5
11				(continuation)	
12	6			(continuation)	
13				(ending)	
14	7	6	VI	fugue with a consistent countersubject	6
15				(continuation)	
16	8	7	VII	(ending) + fugue with a stretto in diminution	7
17				(continuation)	
18	9			(continuation)	
19				(ending)	
20	10	8	VIII	fugue with a stretto in diminution	8
21				(continuation)	
22	11			(ending)	
23		9	IX (faded)	*Canon in Hypodiapason* + *Resolutio Canonis*	9, 10
24	12			(continuation)	
25			X	(ending) + double fugue	11
26	13			(continuation)	
27				(continuation)	

28	XI	(ending) + double fugue	12
29		(continuation)	
30		(continuation)	
31		(continuation)	
32	XII	(ending) + canon in augmentation (decrypted)	13
33	XIII	(ending) + *Canon in Hypodiatesseron, al roversio e per Augmentationem, perpetuus.* (cryptic) + mirror fugue	14, 15
34		(continuation)	
35		(ending)	
36	XIV	mirror fugue	16
37		(continuation)	
38	XV	(ending) + *Canon al roversio e per Augmentationem*	17
39		(ending)	
40		blank page	

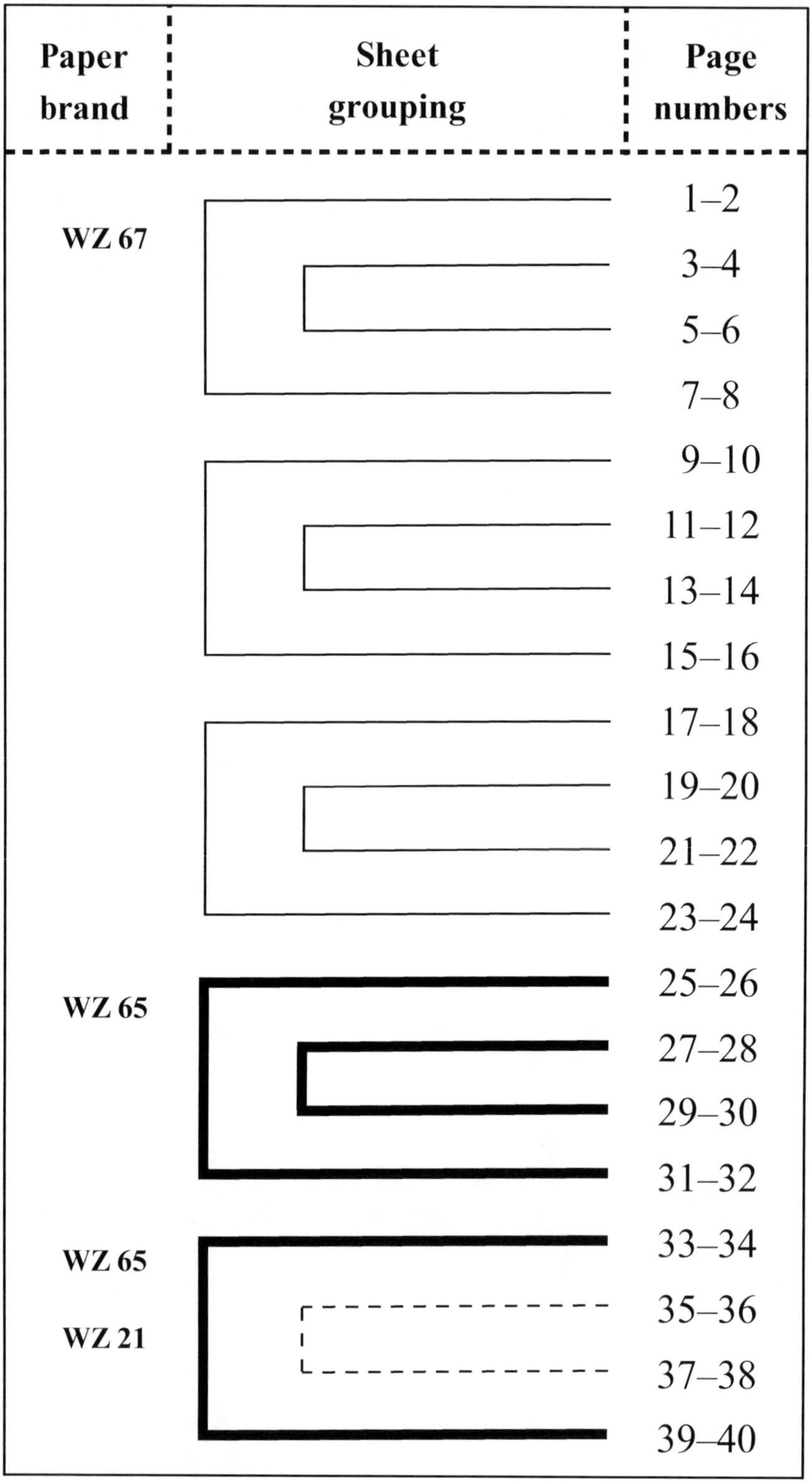

Scheme 4.1 The disposition of music sheets in the main body of P 200.

The pagination starts from the title page, that shows '*pag. 1.*' inscribed on the top right corner. The handwriting suggests Siegfried Wilhelm Dehn,[18] probably c.1842–43 (Figure 4.2a). On the verso the numeration looks like p. 2 (Figure 4.2b) and continues to the end, digits only (3–40; Figure 4.2c); starting on page 10, the page numbers are circled or (more rarely) half-circled (Figure 4.2d).

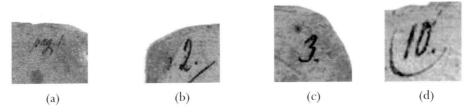

Figure 4.2 Examples of pagination numbers in the Autograph: (a) top right corner of the title page; (b) top left corner of the title page's verso (beginning of fugue 1); (c) top right corner of the same page spread (end of fugue 1); (d) top left corner of the fifth page spread (end of fugue 4).

Several digits are followed by a colon (1:, 4: and 5:); others—by a dot (2., 3., 6., 9., 10., 12., 15., 16., 18., 32., 36. and 39.). All other page numbers (7, 8, 11, 13, 14, 17, 19–31, 33–35, 37, 38 and 40) are not followed by any visible punctuation marks.

A librarian in the Royal Library, Emil Gottlieb Friedländer (1805–78), marked the numeration of page spreads, probably in 1841, before Dehn's pagination.[19] There is an inscription written by Friedländer on the additional cover of the main part of the Autograph: *Zwei u[nd]. Zwanzig Blätter / 18 Nov[ember] 41. / Fr[iedländer]*. The handwriting is identical to the numeration on the page spreads. The reason for following such a rare system is that the librarian might have interpreted Bach's numeration of pieces in the Autograph as page spreads' numeration, because the composer wrote digits at the top left corner of the left page of each spread for the first four fugues (Figure 4.3):[20]

Figure 4.3 Numeration of the first four fugues in the Autograph, misinterpreted by Friedländer as page spread numbers.

However, while the first four fugues begin at the top left of the page spread, the fifth begins at the middle of the page. Naturally, its serial number appears at that position, between the systems. This could be the reason that Friedländer, who followed the imaginary designations of page spreads on their top left corners, might not have noticed it, adding the digit '5' at the top left corner of the fifth spread (Figure 4.4).

The fifth fugue is longer than the former four, and its notation required one more page-spread, which Friedländer marked with the digit '6'. The next fugue, which is the sixth in the Autograph, starts on the seventh spread. Sticking to his way of thought, the librarian struck through the original digit '6' (which in fact marks the beginning of the sixth fugue), and wrote a '7' instead. The seventh *fugue*, on the other hand, starts at the middle of the left side of the eighth spread, and it is marked in a way similar to that of fugue 5 (Figure 4.5).

44   Part II: The principal documents

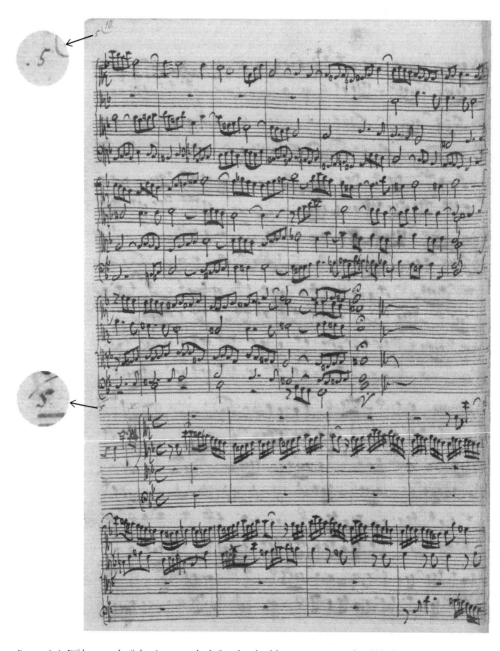

Figure 4.4 Fifth spread of the Autograph, left side: double numeration. The fifth fugue's original serial number appears where the fugue starts, at the middle of the page; Friedländer added a digit '5', at the top of the same page.

The eighth fugue, however, again begins from the left upper corner of a page spread, and its numeration, '8', is marked there. This time Friedländer did not strike it out, but just added his own page spread numeration, '10'. At this point, four numerations appear at the same place: the page number '20', the spread number '10', the serial number of the piece '8' and the secondary numeration of the same piece 'VIII' (Figure 4.6).

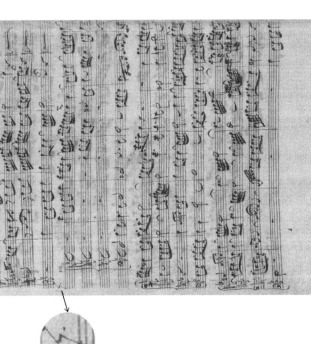

Figure 4.5b Page 16 of the Autograph: the original serial numbering of fugue 7.

Figure 4.5a Seventh spread of the Autograph (p. 14), top left: erroneous 'correction'; the fugue's serial number '6' is deleted, and the digit '7' is marked instead.

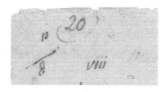

Figure 4.6 Tenth spread of the Autograph, top left: four different numerations. The eighth fugue is marked by both Arabic '8' and Roman 'viii' numerals; the page spread is marked as '10' and the page itself as '20'.

It appears that the next piece is the canon (*Canon in Hypodiapason*). It is written on page 23 of the Autograph, that is, on the right side of a page spread. The serial number of the composition is nine. This time, however, the digit '9' is not written on the left of the notation, near the beginning of the work, but on the top right corner of the page. It seems as if the composer hesitated concerning this particular ordering, his doubts revealed on paper in quite a unique way. The first sign of uncertainty is the position of the inscription, different from the numerations of previous fugues, which were always located on the verso.[21] The unusual location could be an attempt to indicate a new, different type of composition (canon), which up till then had not appeared in *The Art of Fugue*. Bach's deliberations seem to have remained unresolved, because he did not continue this numeration (hereafter marked as 'the first', since all the fugues were later renumbered by different hands).

A secondary numeration, marked by the Roman numerals I–XV, is probably the latest in the main body of the Autograph.[22] The handwriting indicates that the authors of this numeration were Franz Espagne[23] (I–VI) and, probably, Albert Kopfermann[24] (VII–XV).[25] Hans Hoke, though, suggests that it was Dehn.[26] Our discussion of the compositions in the Autograph will be based on this numeration. It is likely that the author of the secondary numeration chose Roman numerals to differentiate it from the other three numerations and avoid more confusion (such as Friedländer's, who misinterpreted the primary numeration of the pieces as page-spread designations).

In which order were these four numerations recorded on the Autograph's pages? A close inspection of the bottom right of the title page (p. 1) reveals the inscription *11 B.*, under which we can, albeit with difficulty, detect the number 22 (see Figure 4.7).

Figure 4.7 Bottom of the title page: inscription designating bifolios in the Autograph's main body.

This inscription states the number of bifolios (*11 B[ögen]*, or 22 single folios, that is, 44 pages), constituting the main body of the Autograph. It should be noted that the numeration sequence of page spreads made by Friedländer (in the main body of the Autograph) is 1–19, 22.

Two folios are missing: numbers 20 and 21. A quick check of the Autograph reveals that P 200/1–2 consists of two single folios, one with the *rectus* and the other with the *inversus* of the fugue for two claviers. As a reminder, this piece is written on paper bearing the same watermark as the end of fugue XIII, which is the first of another pair of mirror fugues: XIII and XIV (pp. 33–8 of the Autograph).[27] Bach wrote all of them in the same size, proportions and graphic style and using the same rastrum.[28] Each sheet of the fugue for two claviers carries, on its upper left corner, the Arabic numerals '20' and '21' respectively, identical in their handwriting and type to the numeration made by Friedländer: clearly the missing ones from the numeration series of the Autograph main body's page-spread (see Table 4.1).

The handwriting and its graphic style (the letter *B*, the digit *2* and their flawed condition) suggest that the inscription predates the 1841 receipt of the Autograph at the Royal Library. Hoke suggests that its author was Poelchau.[29] However, this could hardly be the case, since the manuscript reached the Royal Library directly from his own collection. Poelchau had no reason to write an inscription that did not correspond with the factual state of the manuscript in his possession. The inscription *11B.*, referring to the number of bifolios (Bögen) that constituted the Autograph, did not coincide with the form received by the librarian Friedländer, who catalogued and paginated the manuscript in 1841 or thereafter. He received 10 bifolios and two single folios (bifolio 11 cut in two). Therefore, the inscription *11B.* was probably written much earlier, before leaving C.P.E. Bach's own archive: not earlier than 1747 and not later than 1790, when it was purchased by Schwenke. We, however, propose that the date of the inscription belongs to an even narrower time frame, sometime between 1747 and 1751/52, that is, between the completion of the fugue for two claviers and the publication of *The Art of Fugue*.

Since the title page of the Autograph (p. 1) indicates the total number of bifolios (*11 B[ögen]*), and since the only supplemental material that could fit the missing number of folios and was attached to the manuscript, is the double fugue of P 200/1–2, then sometime during the period between the appearance of this inscription and Friedländer's pagination, the two separate sheets of P 200/1–2 existed as one double sheet (Bogen).

However, even if the assumption that P 200/1–2 must have formed a part of the main Autograph's body as a bifolio is correct, it could not have been inserted into the last binio as Friedländer's numeration suggests, since this would have split the second Canon in Augmentation and Inversion (pp. 38–9). Neither could it have been inserted between p. 36 and p. 37, to form a ternio, because it would have split the second mirror fugue on these pages.[30] The distribution of the compositions over the last binio admits only one combination in which the discussed double sheet could be incorporated into the last binio (see Scheme 4.2).

Yet, as the numeration of folios demonstrates, by the time the Autograph was deposited in the Royal Library, both sheets with the fugue for two claviers appeared as appendices (see Scheme 4.3).[31]

Judging by the remaining markings on the Autograph, it seems that three librarians—Dehn, Espagne and Kopfermann—believed that the fugue for two claviers should not be included in *The Art of Fugue* and left it out as a supplement. The analysis of the situation shows that this decision was made after—and in spite of—Friedländer's numeration, that is, after 1841. Dehn introduced most of the earliest inscriptions, notes and comments into the additional paper covers of the supplements ('*Beilage 1*', '*Beilage 2*' and '*Beilage 3*'). It is therefore feasible that he was the one who separated the fugue for two claviers from the main body of the Autograph, to form P 200/1–2 (around 1842/43). If this is the case, then most probably he was also responsible for the entire compilation of the three supplements. Being thus considered as a

48   Part II: The principal documents

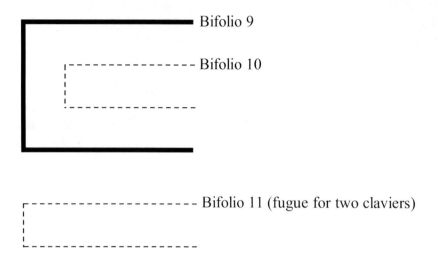

Scheme 4.2 P 200: last three bifolios (Bögen) prior to its acquisition by Poelchau.

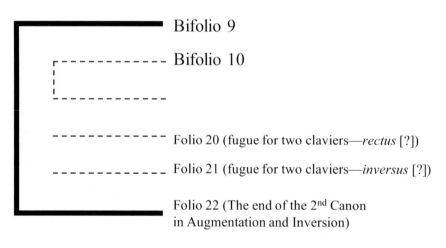

Scheme 4.3 P 200: Organisation of sheets at the time of their deposit in the Royal Library.

supplement, the fugue for two claviers is marked only by Friedländer's numeration and carries no pagination or composition-number by Dehn, Espagne or Kopfermann.[32]

At this point, a tentative chronology of the Autograph's various numeration systems may be offered:

- 1742/47: Johann Sebastian Bach numbered the first nine pieces in *The Art of Fugue* using the Arabic numerals 1–9.
- Second half of 1749: Johann Christoph Friedrich Bach, most probably, marked the page numbers '33' and '35' on two pages of P 200/1–1 (which were later, in 1750, marked by J.S. Bach as '26', '27' and '28').[33]

- 1785(?) or 1822(?): Either Carl Philipp Emanuel Bach or Christian Friedrich Gottlieb Schwenke inscribed, on the title page, the number of bifolios included in the Autograph as *11B*.
- 1841: Emil Gottlieb Friedländer marked Arabic numerals on the top left of each page spread. He also numbered the two folios with the mirror fugues (which later became P 200/1–2) as '21' and '22'.[34]
- 1842/43: Siegfried Wilhelm Dehn paginated the Autograph using the Arabic numerals 1–40, on the outer top corner of every page.
- Sometime between 1858 and 1878: Franz Espagne numbered the first six compositions with the Roman numerals I–VI.
- Sometime between 1878 and 1914: Albert Kopfermann, probably, completed Espagne's numeration, adding the Roman numerals VII–XV.

These conclusions will affect further discussions, especially those concerning the Third Version of *The Art of Fugue*.

Rastrum and page layout[35]

In Bach's Germany, manufactured manuscript paper was used only for exceptional occasions, and staves were usually drawn by hand. To do that, a special five-quill rastrum was used, either over a ruler, or just by hand.

Bach used a ruler mostly when preparing pages for musical texts that were planned as gifts or for engraving copies (*Abklatschvorlage*). For all other purposes he usually used the rastrum freely, by hand.

The staves layout in the Autograph of *The Art of Fugue* looks as following:

- The main body (P 200): the rastration in all the pages (1–40) was done by free hand.
- P 200/1–1 (Canon in Augmentation and Inversion): the rastration in all three pages was done using a ruler.
- P 200/1–2 (the mirror fugue for two claviers): the rastration in all four pages was done by free hand.
- P 200/1–3 (the manuscript with the 'unfinished' fugue): the rastrum was used on pages 1–4 with a ruler, but on page 5, by free hand.

In preparing a paper for score writing, Bach usually calculated the number of staves needed for each system and grouped the systems accordingly. The space left between the bottom staff of a system and the top staff of the following one was usually slightly larger than the distance between the staves within a system.

The paper on which the core of *The Art of Fugue* is written—the first eight fugues, consistently numbered by J.S. Bach (p. 1–22), was thus prepared for four-part scores. Each page has 20 staves grouped into five four-stave systems.[36] The same grouping (four staves per system, five systems on each page) is present in pages 23–4, although the canon written on them has only two parts. Moreover, this canon is first written (on the top two-thirds of p. 23) in a cryptic form, that is—on a single staff, and then decrypted—on two staves. Each presentation of this canon has its own title, as if there were two separate compositions: the cryptic

50   Part II: The principal documents

form is titled *Canon in Hypodiapason* [canon at the lower octave] and the decrypted—*Resolutio Canonis* [resolution of the canon]. The cryptic canon, on a single staff, occupies 15 staves. The inscription *Resolutio Canonis* occupies one staff, and the decrypted version that follows uses the remaining four staves as two two-part systems (see Figure 4.8).

Figure 4.8 Canon in Hypodiapason: the cryptic canon on single staves, the header of the decrypted canon on a blank staff, and the start of the decrypted canon on a two-stave system.

It is possible that Bach assessed the number of pages needing rastration only approximately, given that *The Art of Fugue* was planned as a large-scale work, knowing that the texture of most compositions in it would be in four-part and assuming that any spare pages would be used anyway.

As the manuscript and Table 4.2 show, the first 24 pages were prepared for eight four-part fugues. The paper size allowed a comfortable distribution of five four-stave systems.

Table 4.2 Rastration in the Autograph's main body (P 200)

Page	Type of composition	Rastration (systems x staves)	Use	Number of staves
1–22	I–VIII	5 x 4	5 x 4	20
23	Canon IX (cryptic);	5 x 4	15 x 1; 1 blank;	20
	Canon IX (decrypted, bars 1–13)		2 x 2	
24	Canon IX (decrypted, bars 13–74)	5 x 4	10 x 2	20
25	Canon IX (decrypted, bars 74–103); X (bars 1–35)	5 x 2; 4 x 3	5 x 2; 4 x 3	22
26–27	X (bars 36–155)	8 x 3	8 x 3	24
28	X (bars 156–188); X (bars 1–19)	5 x 3; 2 x 4	5 x 3; 2 x 4	23
29–31	X (bars 19–177)	6 x 4	6 x 4	24
32	XI (bars 178–184); Canon XII (decrypted, bars 1–35)	1 x 4; 9 x 2	1 x 4; 9 x 2	22
33	Canon XII (decrypted, bars 35–44); Canon XII (cryptic); XIII (bars 1–10)	3 x 2; 4 x 4	3 x 2; 6 x 1; 2 blank; 2 x 4	22
34–35	XIII (bars 11–56)	3 x 8	3 x 8	24
36–37	XIV (bars 1–60)	4 x 6	4 x 6	24
38	XIV (bars 61–71); Canon XV (decrypted, bars 1–29)	4 x 6	2 x 6; 6 x 2	24
39	Canon XV (decrypted, bars 29–55)	10 x 2	7 x 2; 3 x 2 blank	20

The first eight fugues fit on 22 pages prepared in this way (see Table 4.2, first line). The two remaining rasterised pages (23 and 24) were used for the *Canon in Hypodiapason*, which, although not needing four-stave systems, could be quite adequately written on these pages.

Here appears a certain peculiarity. Bach had never presented a canon in both cryptic and decrypted forms, let alone as two separate pieces, each with its own title. Given that this manuscript is a fair copy,[37] this unique double presentation of a canon can be considered intentional, deserving some discussion.

It is quite possible that Bach had initially intended to present the canon only once (most probably in cryptic form). In such a case, the first unit of eight fugues with their closing canon would fit in 24 pages and constitute, in a certain sense, a completed whole: four pairs of fugues on one subject sealed by a canon as a 'smart vignette'.[38] All these pieces are written on a model typical to Bach's 'cycles of six':[39] a six-sheet group of three binios (see Scheme 4.4).

The perception of this structure, combined with the inspection of the paper type, music content and handwriting, substantiates our view that after composing the first eight fugues and the subsequent canon Bach had paused his work on this composition, returning to it only several months later.[40] Was this the earliest variant of *The Art of Fugue*? It cannot be

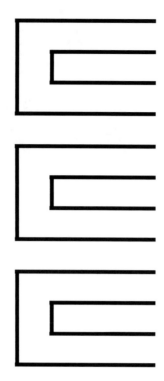

Scheme 4.4 Bach's 'six-sheet' group model.

ruled out that Bach might have changed his mind during those gap months and decided to continue this cycle of fugues. In such a case, though, the canon would be presented as a united pair.[41] It is suggested (particularly by Klaus Hofmann) that the canon was originally presented in both cryptic and decrypted forms, while its ending (five double staves) was completed on a separate sheet.[42] Hofmann suggests that this sheet was later either discarded or lost and the end of the canon was rewritten on a paper of another type.[43] Indeed, the new paper (p. 25) seems to have been prepared intentionally for that purpose: five two-stave systems for the canon and four three-stave systems for the three-part fugue x, adding up to a total of 22 staves on the page (instead of a total of 20 on each one of the former pages—see Table 4.2).

In order to continue fugue x, Bach drew on pages 26–7 eight three-stave systems, that is, 24 staves on each page. The following page (28) is reserved for the end of fugue x and the beginning of fugue xi. The former is a three-part fugue while the latter a four-part one. For this end a special rastration is applied: five three-stave systems for the end of fugue x and two four-stave systems for the beginning of fugue xi, making a total of 23 staves on page 28.

The continuation of fugue xi (pp. 29–31) is written on similarly stave ruled pages, each with six four-stave systems (24 staves in total). Page 32, however, was designed for the end of this fugue and the beginning of another two-part canon (*Canon in Hypodiateßeron, al roversio e per Augmentationem, perpetuus*).[44] Similarly to page 25, page 32 was thus laid out, too, for two different purposes: one four-stave system for the end of fugue XI and nine two-stave systems for the beginning of the canon.[45]

Page 33, too, carries two types of rastration: one for the end of the canon and the other for the beginning of fugue XIII. Three two-stave systems were used for the completion of the canon's decrypted variant, and four four-stave systems were probably intended for the next fugue. However, only the two bottom four-stave systems were used for fugue XIII, while the lion's share of the other two systems was used for the cryptic variant of the canon, to which the title '*Canon in Hypodiateßeron, al roversio e per Augmentationem, perpetuus*' had been added. Two staves before fugue XIII were left blank.

Fugue XIII continues on pages 34–5, prepared for a typical four-part mirror fugue, in three eight-stave systems, 24 staves on each page, while pages 36–7, on which the three-part mirror fugue XIV is written, are laid out, appropriately, as four six-stave systems—a total of 24 staves per page, too.

Page 38 presents the end of the three-part mirror fugue XIV and the beginning of the last canon of this Autograph (*Canon al roverscio et per augmentationem*). It seems that the page as a whole had been prepared just for the fugue's ending, because it is laid out exactly like the previous ones, with four six-stave systems (most probably, pages 36–8 had been primarily designed for this fugue and were lined with staves at the same time). The end of the fugue, however, occupies only the first two systems of the page, presumably a shorter span than anticipated. Thus, the two remaining systems served for the beginning of the canon and grouped as six two-stave systems.

The last page, 39, is laid out in a significantly more casual manner: 20 staves, grouped as 10 two-stave systems. The musical text on this page displays, too, a more relaxed writing, drastically contrasting the very dense and meticulous graphics of the preceding page. Lastly, only seven out of the 10 two-stave systems were utilised, leaving three systems blank.

As the analysis shows, Bach prepared the pages for the main body P 200 in different ways, distributing 20, 22, 23 or 24 staves per page, numbers always dictated by the particular requirements of the planned compositions. Since it mainly depended on the number of parts required for each individual piece, the rastration particularities reflect, to a considerable extent, the composer's plans for ways in which the material would be set on paper. A comparison between his plans (as apparent from the distribution of staves) and the actual musical text may be of importance, since the information derived from such a comparison could help understand significant details about certain compositional processes. These directions will be discussed further.

Notes

1 Many studies often mention this manuscript as P 200. We use both variants: the Autograph and P 200.
2 G.J.D. Poelchau (1773–1836) was a music collector, a member of the Berlin Sing-Akademie (from 1814) and the director of its library (from 1833).
3 This canon's last version appears in the Original Edition.
4 Emphasis in the original, translated in *NBR*, no. 280, p. 256. The 'above-noted form' is the *Canon p[er]. Augmentationem contrario motu*.
5 C.P.E. Bach's handwriting here dates from the late 1770s or the early 1780s.

6   'Der Schreiber ist unbekannt' [The scribe is unknown]. See: Klaus Hofmann, *NBA KB* VIII/2, *Die Kunst der Fuge: Kritischer Bericht* (Kassel, 1996), p. 60.
7   See the inventory of C.P.E. Bach's estate: *BD* III, no. 957, pp. 490–504. See also: Elias N. Kulukundis, 'Die Versteigerung von C.P.E. Bachs musikalischem Nachlaß im Jahre 1805', *BJ* 81 (1995): pp. 145–76. It is not quite clear from the inventory whether P 200 (the main manuscript and the three supplements) belonged to C.P.E. Bach's estate in whole or in part.
8   Christian Friedrich Gottlieb Schwenke (1767–1822), a composer and music publisher, served after C.P.E. Bach's death as cantor and music director in Hamburg.
9   Diplomatics exists as a complementary discipline of history, establishing documents' reliability through the study of the paper properties (including watermarks) and the means of inscription. The term originates in the Greek word *diplöma* – a sheet of paper folded in half. The word was further carried to the Latin *diploma* – an official letter.
10 The main part of the Autograph was bound sometime between 1751 and 1789, that is, after J.S. Bach's death or even after C.P.E. Bach's death. It was rebound in the process of restoration (in 1940 and in 1976) and regained its original, unbound form, only in the late 1990s.
11 The following terms are used here for the study of manuscripts: a *sheet* [*Blatt*] is one piece of paper; when a sheet is folded in half it is called a *bifolio* [*Bogen*], which is now divided (by a fold) into two *folios*, forming four *pages*. A folio, thus, is a two-sided folded half of a bifolio, and each side of a folio is a *page* [*Seite*]. The folios are numbered, while the pages are marked by the folio number with the modifiers 'recto' or 'verso' specified (usually just 'r' or 'v', respectively). The 'recto' is the page that has the fold on its left side, and a 'verso' is the page that has the fold on its right side. A *binio* is a combination of two bifolios folded one into the other (thus forming four folios and eight pages). Following that, a *ternio* is a combination of three bifolios folded into each other (thus forming six folios and 12 pages), and so on. When a bifolio, binio, ternio and the like are opened, showing the verso of a certain folio and the recto of the next folio, it is called a *page spread*.
12 In Bach's time, the manufacturing paper mills watermarked the different types of paper. Since manufacturers changed their trademarks periodically, watermarks can indicate the origin, time and place of specific documents. Here we use data from Wisso Weiss and Yoshitake Kobayashi, *Katalog der Wasserzeichen in Bachs Originalhandschriften*, Neue Bach-Ausgabe, Serie IX: Addenda. vol. 1–2 (Kassel, 1985). The digit next to the abbreviation WZ (*Wasserzeichen*) designates the watermark's serial number in this catalogue.
13 '… Um 1742, vermutlich aber früher (vor August 1742).' Kobayashi, 'Zur Chronologie', p. 11.
14 Ibid. p. 3.
15 Ibid. p. 16.
16 '… Um 1747 bis August 1748', Ibid. p. 59–60.
17 '… Nach August 1748 bis Oktober 1749', Ibid.
18 Siegfried Wilhelm Dehn (1799–1858) was a German bibliographer, publisher and music theorist. In 1842, on Giacomo Meyerbeer's recommendation, he was appointed as the head of the Berlin Royal Library's Music Department.
19 Friedländer seems to have a system of numeration practiced among certain music copyists, who numbered page spreads rather than folios. These numbers were written on the top left corner of a verso, and included the verso of a folio (marked with an 'L' for 'left') and the recto of the next folio (marked with an 'R' for 'right'). See the description of manuscripts 90–91 and 942–43 in the online introduction to the *Music Catalogue of the Christ Church Library at Oxford*.
20 Another reason for this choice of numeration system could be a comparison that Friedländer might have done with the 1751 edition of *The Art of Fugue*, where the music notation starts on the verso side of the leaf, numbered as 1. Thus, uncharacteristically to printed editions, all the recto pages of the edition have even numbers, while the verso pages have the odd numbers.
21 This substantiates the view that these digits designate the serial number of the compositions and not of the folios.
22 Hofmann, too, estimates it as a later numeration: 'eine offenbar jüngere Satzzählung'. *NBA KB* VIII/2, p. 23.

23 Franz Espagne (1828–78) was a German music librarian and editor. A student of Dehn, he was appointed in 1858 as assistant curator at the Berlin Royal Library. Five years later he succeeded Dehn in the task of completing the music catalogue.

24 Albert Kopfermann (1846–1914) was a German librarian and curator. He joined the Berlin Royal Library in 1878, and was appointed professor and director of its music division in 1908, a post that he held until his death.

25 The marking 'ix' is seen only in the original; in the facsimile it is practically indistinguishable.

26 See Hans Gunter Hoke, 'Zur Handschrift Mus. ms. autogr. Bach P 200 der Deutschen Staatsbibliothek Berlin,' in H.G. Hoke (ed.) *BACH, Die Kunst der Fuge BWV 1080: Autograph, Originaldruck* (Leipzig, 1979), p. 3. Dehn could not be its author because the Roman numerals do not appear in his handwriting.

27 The two first pages of fugue XIII are written on paper with the watermark WZ 65.

28 Judging by the dimensions of the rastrum and by its 24 staves-per-page pattern.

29 Hoke, 'Zur Handschrift …', p. 3.

30 Of course, a similar problem, this time splitting the first mirror fugue, would arise if such bifolio would be inserted between p. 34 and p. 35.

31 The most feasible explanation for Friedländer's peculiar insertion is that at this stage he was just occupied with organising a general inventory of the materials he received from Poelchau's library, dealing first with compiling various papers into general groups, without going into the details of inspecting the music itself; this would be done later by other librarians.

32 As a reminder, the earliest, *first* numeration stops abruptly after the ninth composition.

33 The page that should be marked '34' does exist, but it is a new one, replacing the first page that was marked with the digit, and which was probably lost or spoiled. The newly copied page replaced the original one at a later stage and therefore was not marked (maybe because by that point the new pagination, 26–8, was being inscribed).

34 Obviously Friedländer could not mark here page spreads since he had only two loose folios. Nevertheless, he kept writing the numbers on the top left corner of the verso.

35 On the rastration in Bach's manuscripts see: Christoph Wolff, 'Die Rastrierungen in den Originalhandschriften Joh. Seb. Bachs und ihre Bedeutung für die diplomatische Quellenkritik', in *Festschrift für Friedrich Smend zum 70. Geburtstag: dargebracht von Freunden und Schülern.* (Berlin, 1963), pp. 80–92.

36 See Figure 16.1 in Chapter 16.

37 There is no consensus among scholars on this matter; copying and copyists are discussed later in this book.

38 For more on this device as one of Bach's stylistic features see: Anatoly Milka, *Muzykal'noye prinoshenie I.S. Bakha: K rekonstruktsii i interpretatsii* [The *Musical Offering* by J. S. Bach: Reconstruction and Interpretation] (Moscow, 1999), pp. 101–12.

39 See Anatoly Milka's 'Bakhovskie "shestërki": Printsip organizatsii bakhovskikh sbornikov v kontekste osobennostei barokko' [Bach's "cycles of six": the organisation principle of Bach's collections in the context of baroque characteristics], *Muzykal'naya kommunikatsia* [Musical Communication], series Problemy muzykoznaniia, vol. 8 (St Petersburg, 1996), pp. 220–38.

40 Other scholars share this opinion too, given certain changes in Bach's handwriting on page 25 as well as changes in paper type. The estimated time gap between page 24 and 25 is several months. See Hofmann, *NBA KB* VIII/2, pp. 20–1 and 81; Kobayashi, 'Zur Chronologie …', pp. 51–2, 60, 62 and 70.

41 This point is discussed in detail in Chapter 7 ('The First Version of *The Art of Fugue*').

42 Hofmann, *NBA KB* VIII/2, p. 81.

43 Ibid.

44 [a perpetual (loop) canon at a fourth below, inverted and augmented].

45 Like the previous one, this canon is inscribed in two forms, albeit in opposite order: first appears the decrypted canon and only then the cryptic version. It is also significant that here only the cryptic variant of the canon carries a title.

5   The Original Edition

The term *Original Edition* [*Originalausgabe*], when associated with *The Art of Fugue*, refers to the two publications of this work that were issued one after the other: the first published edition was offered for sale on September 29, 1751;[1] the second on April 2, 1752.[2] Despite the different dates, both printings are called The Original Edition, because their notation was printed from the same engraving plates. Additionally, the second print features all the errata found in the first one.[3]

The edition was engraved on copper plates [*Kupferstich*], a method extensively used in music printing during the eighteenth century. Johann Heinrich Schübler from the Thuringian town of Zella performed the engraving in its entirety.[4] He was familiar with Bach's work since back in 1747, when he took part in the engraving of the *Musical Offering*.[5]

The following materials must be produced during the copper plates publishing process, starting from the composer's creative idea to the final print:

- drafts[6]
- handwritten fair copies[7]
- engraving copies[8]
- copper plates with the engraved music text[9]
- proofreading prints of all the pieces[10]

After proofreading, the plates were delivered to the print shop, where the final copies were produced.

Engraving and printing of *The Art of Fugue*

Since the engraving process of copper plates requires handwritten engraver copies, the identity of their transcribers can be determined with considerable accuracy. Studies ascertain the active involvement of Johann Sebastian Bach in the preparation of the engraver copies, himself writing those for 11 items in *The Art of Fugue*:[11] Contrapuncti 1, 2(?), 3, 4, 11, 12_2, $[13]_2$,[12] as well as all four canons. His son, Johann Christoph Friedrich, wrote the engraver copies of the eight Contrapuncti 5(?), 6, 7, 8, 9, 10, 12_1, and $[13]_1$. The person(s) who prepared the engraver copies of the four Contrapuncti [10a],[13] $[18_1]$ (*Fuga a 2. Clav:*), $[18_2]$ (*Alio modo. Fuga a 2. Clav.*) and [19] (*Fuga a 3 Soggetti*) as well as of the choral setting *Wenn wir in hoechsten Noethen sein* still has not been established.[14] It is only known that they were written after Bach's death, in the period of preparation of *The Art of Fugue*'s edition, probably in the winter of 1750–51.

Unfortunately, there is no direct information that Carl Philipp Emanuel proofread the sample printouts. While his list of errata in the 1751 edition is written on the blank verso of the fourth sheet in P 200/1–3,[15] the 'unfinished' fugue, it is impossible to establish a link between this list and either the sample proofreading sheets or the published edition.

It is known, however, that Johann Sebastian took particular care of the sample proof sheets when preparing *The Art of Fugue* edition for print. Johann Christoph Friedrich Bach's inscription on the engraving copy of the Canon in Augmentation (P 200/1–1) tells about his late father's proofreading of the sample printouts of *The Art of Fugue* and making the necessary amendments himself.[16]

Where was the printing performed?

The place where *The Art of Fugue* was printed has not yet been established. Klaus Hofmann, summarising years of multiple efforts in Bach studies, had to conclude: 'Die näheren Umstände der Drucklegung der Kunst der Fuge sind unbekannt' [The details of the circumstances surrounding the print of *The Art of Fugue* are unknown.][17] However, at least three places can certainly be identified as having some relation to this process: Zella, Berlin and Leipzig.

Schübler's engravings, made out of engraving copies prepared by Johann Sebastian and Johann Christoph Friedrich Bach, took place in Zella. However, while it is possible that the sample prints were issued there, it seems that the run printing was not performed in that town. It is hard to believe that Zella had sufficient printing capacities: else, the whole run printing would be done there, too. As a reminder, four years earlier the *Musical Offering* was engraved in Zella, too, but its run printing was performed in Leipzig. *The Art of Fugue* required even more printing resources than the *Musical Offering*.

Another possible printing place for *The Art of Fugue* is Berlin, the residing place of Carl Philipp Emanuel Bach and Johann Friedrich Agricola, who managed the whole publication process. The fact that Emanuel was deeply involved in this process is beyond doubt, since he was the one who initiated and drafted all the newspaper announcements about the Original Edition. It is known that he did not leave Berlin during the period of publication, that is, from the end of November 1750 to the beginning of 1751. He owned and kept the Autograph and all the supplements,[18] and it was in his house that almost all the engraved copper plates were later offered for sale to interested music publishers.[19] However, circumstantial evidence indicates that Berlin was not the place of printing and publication of *The Art of Fugue*.

First, as Georg Kinsky shows,[20] the important introductions to two publications—the *Musical Offering* (the title page and the dedication to the King) and the 1752 edition of *The Art of Fugue* (the title page and the Preface)—were not engraved, but typeset with the cast sorts of the Breitkopf Publishing Company in Leipzig. Furthermore, the music pages were printed on the same kind of paper as the title page of the 1752 *The Art of Fugue*, which would be too much of a fortuitous coincidence, were they printed in two different cities. Second, it is documented that on May 19, 1752, Anna Magdalena Bach brought to the Magistrate of Leipzig several copies of *The Art of Fugue*.[21] This was most probably the fresh edition of 1752. Finally, as already mentioned, both editions were prepared to coincide with the Leipzig Fairs.[22] It is likely, therefore, that at least the second edition was printed in Leipzig. As for the first (1751) edition, there are still many unclear points. On one hand, the above considerations point to Leipzig; on the other hand, the letterset of the title page and the Preface of the 1751 edition is not identical, and it is yet not established whether Breitkopf used it or not.

Since the editions of 1751 and 1752 are printed on different types of paper,[23] one could argue that one of the editions might have been printed in Berlin and the other in Leipzig. However, were the first edition printed in Berlin and not in Leipzig, it would entail a rather unwieldy transfer of the engraved copper plates: more than 60 plates, about a hundredweight[24] of copper, about 175 miles northeast from Zella to Berlin, then about 90 miles southwest from Berlin to Leipzig, and then back northeast to Berlin, a cumbersome total distance of 355 miles. It would thus seem more feasible to travel the approximate distance of 85 miles northeast from Zella to Leipzig and then continue in the same direction, another 90 miles, to Berlin, less than half the distance of the latter route, which even without taking into account the awkward and partly fragile load would logically be a preferred one. Such a choice, however, would locate the 1751, first edition, in Leipzig, and the 1752 second one in Berlin. Yet, it was the Leipzig edition that appeared in 1752.

Thus, there is not enough direct proof for affirming that it is Leipzig where both editions of *The Art of Fugue* were printed. Nevertheless, such a conclusion could be quite reasonable within the wider context of direct and indirect information. Klaus Hofmann, for example, writes: 'Als Druckort kommt in erster Linie Leipzig'.[25] Christoph Wolff shares this opinion and even more decisively names Leipzig as the location where both editions of *The Art of Fugue* were printed.[26]

Thus, the following unfolding of events concerning the publication of *The Art of Fugue* can be tentatively drafted. Based on the known facts and whereabouts of the individuals that had a role in the publication process, it becomes apparent that Johann Heinrich Schübler from Zella dealt just with the engraving, that is, with the preparation of the 67 copper plates. Thereafter, they were all transported to Leipzig for the printing of (probably) both editions, and eventually sent to Berlin, to Emanuel.

Carl Philipp Emanuel, in all likelihood, was the one responsible for writing the engraving copies of the pieces located on the edition's pages 45–7 and 57–67 (*Contrap: a 4*; *Fuga a 2 Clav.*; *Alio modo, Fuga a 2 Clav.*; *Fuga a 3 Soggetti*; *Choral. Wenn wir in hoechsten Noethen sein*), which he sent to Zella. He provided the general design of the whole collection and further took upon himself the advertising of the edition, taking advantage of his connections among both enlightened and merchant circles and drafting practically all the related announcements and notices. Finally, he wrote the preface to the first edition, although it is possible that Johann Friedrich Agricola helped him in that.

As for Anna Magdalena Bach, her participation in preparing the fair and/or the engraver copies for *The Art of Fugue*—either when Bach was still alive or in a later stage of the publishing process—has left no trace. Most probably, her mission was limited to maintaining contacts with the Breitkopf publishing house and printing press.

Wilhelm Friedemann Bach left no evidence of immediate involvement in writing any kind of copies. Also, there is no indication of Altnickol being connected with this project. On the other hand, Agricola probably assisted C.P.E. Bach in preparing *The Art of Fugue* for print.

Two editions

As already mentioned, the publications of 1751 and 1752 differ only in their title pages and prefaces. The title pages of the two editions carry identical texts, in slightly different designs. The letters are larger in the 1752 edition, and the text is spread over seven lines rather than five. The two prefaces, however, differ significantly. The preface to the 1751 edition is titled *Nachricht*, and is printed on the verso of the title page:

Nachricht.

Der selige Herr Verfasser dieses Werkes wurde durch seine Augenkrankheit und den kurz darauf erfolgten Tod ausser Stande gesetzet, die letzte Fuge, wo er sich bey Anbringung des dritten Satzes namentlich zu erkennen giebet, zu Ende zu bringen; man hat dahero die Freunde seiner Muse durch Mittheilung des am Ende beygefügten vierstimmig ausgearbeiteten Kirchenchorals, den der selige Mann in seiner Blindheit einem seiner Freunde aus dem Stegereif in die Feder dictirert hat, schadlos halten wollen.[27]

[Notice.

The late Author of this work was prevented by his disease of the eyes, and by his death, which followed shortly upon it, from bringing the last fugue, in which at the entrance of the third subject he mentions himself by name (in the notes B A C H, i.e., B♭ A C B♮), to conclusion; accordingly it was wished to compensate the friends of his muse by including the four-part church chorale added at the end, which the deceased man in his blindness dictated on the spur of the moment to the pen of a friend.][28]

The preface to the 1752 printing (here titled *Vorbericht*) is signed by Friedrich Wilhelm Marpurg. It has been expanded into two full pages and carries an additional remark: 'in der Leipziger Ostermeße / 1752' [during the Leipzig Easter Fair / 1752.][29]

The music in the Original Edition

As indicated above, the musical text in the Original Edition is identical in both 1751 and 1752 prints. However, when the edition is compared with the Autograph, significant differences emerge:

- Six compositions that appear in the Original Edition are absent from the Autograph:

  - *Contrapunctus 4*
  - *Contrapunctus 10. a. 4. Alla Decima*
  - *Canon alla Decima Contrapunto alla Terza*
  - *Canon alla Duodecima in Contrapunto alla Quinta*
  - *Fuga a 3 Soggetti*
  - *Choral. Wenn wir in hoechsten Noethen ... Canto Fermo in Canto*

- The compositions in the Original Edition have different titles than those appearing in the Autograph. The first 14 compositions in the edition are fugues. While the fugues in the Autograph are just numbered (as a reminder, J.S. Bach numbered only the first eight), those in the edition are all titled Contrapunctus (*Contrapunctur*[30] for the fifth fugue) except for the 14th, which is titled *Contrap: a 4*. Additionally, fugues 1–12 are also numbered.[31]

- The remaining three fugues appear in the edition after the presentation of the canons. They are not numbered and use *Fuga* in their titles:

  - *Fuga a 2 Clav:*
  - *Alio modo. Fuga a 2. Clav.*
  - *Fuga a 3 Soggetti*

Part II: The principal documents

- The first four fugues and the last one (*Fuga a 3 Soggetti*) have no indication of the number of voices.
- The canons are not numbered. To indicate the interval in which the second part enters, Italian designations were used (Ottava, Decima, Duodecima), while in the Autograph the designations are Greek (Hypodiapason, Hypodiateßeron).
- The order of compositions in the Original Edition differs from their order in the Autograph (see Scheme 5.1). The order of compositions and their titles in the entire cycle is shown in Table 5.1.

Autograph	Original Edition	BWV
I	*Contrapunctus 1.*	1
II	*Contrapunctus 2.*	2
III	*Contrapunctus 3*	3
—	*Contrapunctus. 4*	4
IV	*Contrapunctur 5.*	5
V	*Contrapunctus 6. a 4 in Stylo Francese.*	6
VI	*Contrapunctus 7. a 4. per Augment et Diminut:*	7
VII	*Contrapunctus 8. a 3.*	8
VIII	*Contrapunctus 9. a 4. alla Duodecima*	9
IX *Canon in Hypodiapason (cryptic)*		
[IXa] *Resolutio Canonis*	*Contrapunctus 10. a 4. alla Decima.*	10
X		
XI	*Contrapunctus. 11. a 4.*	11
XII [Canon]	—	
[XIIa] *Canon in Hypodiateßeron. al roversio e per augmentationem, Perpetuus (cryptic)*	—	1080
XIII$_{1,2}$	*Contrapunctus inversus. 12 á 4.*	12$_2$
	Contrapunctus inversus a 4	12$_1$
XIV$_{1,2}$	*Contrapunctus a 3*	13$_2$
	Contrapunctus inversus a 3	13$_1$
	Contrap: a 4.	10a
XV *Canon al roverscio et per augmentationem* (+ Supplement 1)	*Canon per Augmentationem in Contrario Motu.*	14
—	*Canon alla Ottava.*	15
—	*Canon alla Decima Contrapunto alla Terza.*	16
—	*Canon alla Duodecima in Contrapunto alla Quinta.*	17
Supplement 2$_{1,2}$	*Fuga a 2 Clav:*	18i
	Alio modo. Fuga a 2. Clav.	18$_2$
Supplement 3	*Fuga a 3 Soggetti*	19
—	*Choral. Wenn wir in hoechsten Noethen sein. Canto Fermo in Canto.*	**668a**

Scheme 5.1 Ordering changes between the Autograph and the Original Edition.

- In the Autograph, only the canons are supplied with textual comments:

  - *Canon in Hypodiapason*
  - *Resolutio Canonis*
  - *Canon in Hypodiateβeron. al roversio e per augmentationem,* Perpetuus
  - *Canon al roverscio et per augmentationem*

- Several fugues, however, have additional textual comments (see below).

Other differences relate to the general layout.

- The Original Edition has an unusual pagination system, which starts not from the title page, as does the Autograph, but from the left page of the first spread. Consequently, the odd numbers appear on the verso pages while the even numbers on the recto ones.
- The fragment of the 'unfinished' triple fugue's presentation in the Original Edition differs from that of the Autograph (P 200/1–3) in three elements. First, it is titled *Fuga a 3 Soggetti* in the edition, while in the Autograph it has no title; second, in the Autograph the fugue is written in a two-stave clavier layout while in the edition it is presented in a four-stave score; finally, in the Original Edition, the seven last bars of this fugue, as it appears in the Autograph, are missing. Most probably, Emanuel made all these changes.

Table 5.1 Order of pieces in the Original Edition (in bold: not in the Autograph)

Position in the cycle	Title of composition
1	*Contrapunctus 1.*
2	*Contrapunctus 2.*
3	*Contrapunctus 3*
4	**Contrapunctus. 4**
5	*Contrapunctur 5.*
6	*Contrapunctus 6. a 4 in Stylo Francese.*
7	*Contrapunctus 7. a 4. per Augment et Diminut:*
8	*Contrapunctus 8. a 3.*
9	*Contrapunctus 9. a 4. alla Duodecima*
10	**Contrapunctus 10. a. 4. alla Decima.**
11	*Contrapuntus. 11. a 4.*
12_1	*Contrapunctus inversus. 12 á 4.*
12_2	*Contrapunctus inversus a 4*
13_1	*Contrapunctus a 3*
13_2	*Contrapunctus inversus a 3*
14	*Contrap: a 4.*
15	*Canon per Augmentationem in Contrario Motu.*
16	*Canon alla Ottava.*
17	**Canon alla Decima Contrapunto alla Terza.**
18	**Canon alla Duodecima in Contrapunto alla Quinta.**
19_1	*Fuga a 2 Clav:*
19_2	*Alio modo. Fuga a 2. Clav.*
20	*Fuga a 3 Soggetti*
21	**Choral. Wenn wir in hoechsten Noethen sein. Canto Fermo in Canto).**

Changes in rhythm and metre

The changes between the Autograph and the Original Edition involve not only the number of works in the set, their ordering and layout, but also modifications of the music itself: change of metre, double rhythmic values, double number of bars, addition of bars and the reworking of a one-theme simple contrapunctus into a double fugue.

- The metre of most fugues (Contrapuncti 1, 2, 3, 8, 9, 11, 12, [13] and [14]) and of the *Canon per Augmentationem in Contrario Motu* was changed in the Original Edition in comparison with the Autograph.[32] Consequently, these pieces (except the first three) have doubled rhythmic values in the edition.
- Contrapuncti 1, 2, 3 and 10 underwent further changes on their way to the Original Edition, including additional musical fragments. In the first three fugues these modifications were limited to several extra bars in the cadenza. In Contrapunctus 10, however, the simple (monothematic) fugue with the regular countersubject was re-worked into a double one. The Original Edition includes both Contrapuncti 10 (the re-worked variant) and [14] (the Autograph version with the augmented rhythmical values that doubled the number of bars).
- While the two mirror fugues (Contrapuncti $12_{1,2}$ and $[13]_{1,2}$) have their metre changed in relation to the Autograph ($\frac{3}{2}$ instead of $\frac{3}{4}$ and $\mathbf{C}$—instead of $\frac{2}{4}$), the third mirror fugue (*Fuga a 2. Clav* in both *rectus* and *inversus*), that had been derived from the second one, did not undergo such a transformation.[33] This particular case requires special explanations and leads to a discussion relevant not only to the mirror fugues but to the entire cycle.

Table 5.2 shows that transformations of metre and rhythm from the Autograph to the Original Edition are the rule rather than an exception.[34] The following types of changes in metre and rhythm are found in the Original Edition:

- Doubled metre with no rhythmic or bar number modifications. Such is Contrapunctur 5 (in the Autograph it is fugue IV), where the metre $\mathbf{\phi}$ in the Autograph is replaced by $\mathbf{C}$, though neither rhythmic values nor number of bars changed in the fugue.
- Changed metre and doubled rhythmic values, leaving the bar numbers intact, happen in Contrapuncti 8, 11, 12_1, 12_2, $[13]_1$ and $[13]_2$.
- The rhythmic values and bar number were doubled in Contrapuncti 9 and 10 while their metre was left intact.
- In the first three contrapuncti, the number of bars was doubled but the metre and rhythmic values remained unchanged.

As follows from the Original Edition and Table 5.2, all metre and rhythm changes were performed when Bach was still alive and—evidently—on his initiative, while Emanuel did not intervene at all in Bach's text.

Table 5.2 Rhythm and metre from the Autograph to the Original Edition

Position in the cycle	Title of composition	Change in time signature	Doubled duration	Doubled number of bars	P 200 (see note 35)
1	Contrapunctus 1.	—	—	+	
2	Contrapunctus 2.	—	—	+	
3	Contrapunctus. 3	—	—	+	
4	Contrapunctus. 4				
5	Contrapunctus 5.	¢ → c	—	—	
6	Contrapunctus 6. a 4 in Stylo Francese.	—	—	—	
7	Contrapunctus 7. a 4. per Augment et Diminut:	—	—	—	
8	Contrapunctus 8. a 3.	$\frac{2}{4}$ → ¢	+	—	P 200
9	Contrapunctus 9. a 4. alla Duodecima	—	+	—	P 200
10	Contrapunctus 10. a 4. alla Decima.	—	+	+	
11	Contrapunctus. 11. a 4.	$\frac{2}{4}$ → ¢	+	—	
12₁	Contrapunctus inversus. 12 á 4.	$\frac{3}{4}$ → $\frac{3}{2}$	+	—	
12₂	Contrapunctus inversus a 4	$\frac{3}{4}$ → $\frac{3}{2}$	+	—	
13₁	Contrapunctus a 3	$\frac{2}{4}$ → c	+	—	
13₂	Contrapunctus inversus a 3	$\frac{2}{4}$ → c	+	—	
14	**Contrap: a 4.**	—	+	+	
15	Canon per Augmentationem in Contrario Motu (see note 35)	c → ¢	+	+	P 200
16	Canon alla Ottava.	—	—	—	
17	Canon alla Decima Contrapunto alla Terza.				
18	Canon alla Duodecima in Contrapunto alla Quinta.				
19₁	Fuga a 2 Clav:	—	—	—	
19₂	Alio modo. Fuga a 2. Clav.	—	—	—	
20	Fuga a 3 Soggetti				
21	Choral.Wenn wir in hoechsten Noethen [...]	—	—	—	

Notes

1. September 29 is St Michael day, on which the yearly Leipzig Fall Fair takes place. See: Christoph Wolff, 'Die Originaldrucke Johann Sebastian Bachs: Einführung und Verzeichnis,' in Willi Wörthmüller (ed.), *Die Nürnberger Drucke von J.S. und C.P.E. Bach: Katalog der Ausstellung* (Nürnberg, 1973), p. 20; Hofmann, *NBA KB* VIII/2, pp. 13 and 16.
2. The date of the Leipzig Easter Fair. There are 18 surviving copies of this edition. See Hofmann, ibid. pp. 13 and 17–20.
3. There is a controversy concerning the number of editions. Johann Nikolaus Forkel, for example, claimed that *The Art of Fugue* was published only in a 1752 edition. See Johann Nikolaus Forkel, *Ueber J.S. Bachs Leben, Kunst und Kunstwerke: für patriotische Verehrer echter musikalischer Kunst ... Mit Bachs Bildniß und Kupfertafeln* (Leipzig, 1802), p. 52; translated to English by Charles Sanford Terry as *Johann Sebastian Bach: His Life, Art and Work* (New York, 1920), p. 212. Walter Kolneder, on the

64 Part II: The principal documents

other hand, suggested that there were three editions: a first in 1751; a second in 1752, with the errata already detected but not yet revised; and a third, which is identical to the 1752 edition, except for the errata that are here corrected. See Walter Kolneder, 'Die Datierung des Erstdruckes der Kunst der Fuge,' *Musikforschung*, 30/3 (1977): pp. 329–32. Wolfgang Wiemer severely criticised Kolneder's proposal, calling it 'ein fataler Irrtum' [a fatal mistake]. See Wolfgang Wiemer, 'Zur Datierung des Erstdrucks der Kunst der Fuge,' *Musikforschung*, 31/2 (1978): p. 182.

4 Currently called Zella-Mehlis. Bach required the services of the Schübler family of engravers several times, the older brother of Johann Heinrich being his former student. See: Wolfgang Wiemer, 'Johann Heinrich Schübler, der Stecher der Kunst der Fuge', in *BJ* 65 (1979): pp. 75–95.

5 Other projects of Johann Heinrich Schübler during this period included an engraving of the sonata for clavier in E-flat major by Wilhelm Friedemann Bach (1748) and the engraving of *The Art of Fugue*, which took place sometime between 1749 and 1751. Finally, there is a note in his handwriting attached to an engraved supplement including 18 samples from six sonatas, proposing expected completion dates for the engraving of Carl Philipp Emanuel Bach's first part of his *Versuch über die wahre Art das Clavier zu spielen* (Berlin, 1753).

6 The draft of *The Art of Fugue*, very probably, did not survive.

7 The fair copies of *The Art of Fugue* are the main body of the P 200, P 200/1–2 and P 200/1–3.

8 The only surviving engraver copy from *The Art of Fugue* is P 200/1–1.

9 The copper plates of *The Art of Fugue* are lost.

10 The proofreading prints of *The Art of Fugue* were never found, but Johann Christoph Friedrich Bach reported that his father proofread them (see section 'The proofs' in Chapter 10).

11 Richard Koprowski, 'Bach "Fingerprints" in the Engraving of the Original Edition,' in the seminar report 'Bach's "Art of Fugue": An Examination of the Sources,' *Current Musicology*, 19 (1975): pp. 61–7; Wolfgang Wiemer, *Die wiederhergestellte Ordnung in Johann Sebastian Bachs Kunst der Fuge: Untersuchungen am Originaldruck* (Wiesbaden, 1977). Gregory Butler, 'Scribes, Engravers and Notation Styles: The Final Disposition of Bach's Art of Fugue,' in Gregory Butler, George B. Stauffer and Mary Dalton Greer, *About Bach* (Urbana and Chicago, 2008), pp. 11–124; Hofmann, *NBA KB* VIII/2, p. 90.

12 When attached to the number of a mirror fugue, the subscript numbers 1 and 2 indicate its rectus and inversus versions, respectively.

13 10a is the conventional indication of Bach's older version for the autograph's fugue VI, before it was reworked as Contrapunctus 10.

14 All the spelling peculiarities of the composition titles are presented here as they appear in the original.

15 The errata list relates only to pp. 21–35. There are no data concerning the rest of the pages.

16 See more details about this inscription in note 3 of Chapter 4.

17 Hofmann, *NBA KB* VIII/2, p. 90.

18 See the inventory of his estate: *Verzeichniß des musikalischen Nachlasses des H. Capellmeisters Carl Philipp Emanuel Bach*. (Hamburg, 1790), p. 69.

19 *BD* III, no. 683, pp. 113–14.

20 Georg Kinsky, *Die Originalausgaben der Werke Johann Sebastian Bachs* (Wien, 1937), pp. 79 and 118.

21 For these she was paid 40 talers (*BD* III, no. 650, p. 17). If the Magistrate paid her the price of four talers per copy, as announced by Emanuel (*BD* III, no. 683, p. 113) it means that she brought 10 copies there.

22 See notes 1 and 2 above.

23 The first edition was printed on paper of medium quality, watermarked with the inscription WOLFEG and a coat of arms with a crown. Christoph Wolff states that similar paper was used for one of the sheets of the *Musical Offering*. (Christoph Wolff, *Neue Bach Ausgabe, Musikalisches Opfer, NBA KB* VIII/1, p. 50). The second edition is printed on paper of better quality and a larger size, its watermark WZ ICV and a fleur-de-lis emblem.

24 '… einen Centner': approximately 112 pounds or 51 kg. This weight estimation appears in C.P.E Bach's sale announcement in Marpurg's Berlin journal *Historisch-Kritische Beyträge zur Aufnahme der Musik*, on September 14, 1756, pp. 575–6 of vol. 2. (See *BD* III, no. 683, p. 113.)
25 [as for printing place, Leipzig stands first.] Hofmann, *NBA KB* VIII/2, p. 91.
26 Wolff, 'Die Originaldrucke …', p. 20.
27 *BD* III, no. 645, pp. 12–13.
28 *NBR*, no. 284, p. 258; the additional comment in brackets was added by the *NBR* editors.
29 This Fair took place on April 2, 1752.
30 All existing subsequent editions consider this spelling 'Contrapunctur' a misprint and correct it without any comments.
31 The 14th fugue in the Original Edition is not numbered here, but is positioned as number 6 in the Autograph (see Scheme 5.1). In the Original Edition this fugue is written in doubled values but the metre is unchanged. It is most probable that Bach himself wrote it this way, also naming it with its new title.
32 The numeration of contrapuncti given in italics is positional, because in the Original Edition only the first 12 contrapuncti are numbered.
33 See discussion in the section 'The oddities of *Contrap: a 4.*' in Chapter 13.
34 As Table 5.2 shows, three of the pieces—Contrapuncti 8 and 9 and the Canon in Augmentation and Inversion—carry Johann Sebastian's indications concerning such changes in the Autograph (fugues x and v respectively). The P 200 column in Table 5.2 marks the works for which Johann Sebastian Bach indicated with pencil marks the required changes of metre. These marks can be easily seen in P 200 near the beginning of fugues x and v. Christoph Wolff, using infrared light, found the pencil marks for the '*Canon per Augmentationem in Contrario Motu*'. See his 'The Last Fugue: Unfinished?' *Current Musicology*, 19 (1975): p. 77. As for the canon, the relation recorded in Table 5.2 is between the earlier version of the canon in P 200 (composition No. 15) and the Original Edition. However, there is no change of metre, rhythmic values or number of bars in the Original Edition version of this canon from P 200/1–3 (see description above in Chapter 4).

Part III
J.S. Bach's work on *The Art of Fugue*

6   The versions in Bach's music

One of the characteristics of Bach's musical output is the existence of several versions of a single composition. Such versions appear in a variety of genres, ranging from small two-part clavier pieces, such as the Invention in C major, to grandiose instrumental and choral works and cycle organisation, such as the Inventions and Sinfonias, a number of cantatas, St John Passion and the Mass in B minor, to mention just a few. This procedure is so common that it may be regarded as typical to Bach's creative process. These versions are not parodies, where the same musical material of one composition is used for another (as happened in the case of the second part of the cantata BWV 12, *Weinen, Klagen, Sorgen, Zagen*, that was reused in the Crucifixus of the Mass in B minor), but a creation of different versions of one and the same work. Moreover, a version usually emerged once the composition of the previous one had been completed.

Various circumstances led Bach into such operations.[1] In certain cases he continued to modify and correct a work while preparing its fair copy, to a point in which the changes were so substantial that a new version of a composition emerged. This happened, for example, with the Invention in C major and with Contrapunctus 10 in *The Art of Fugue*.[2]

In other cases, new versions stemmed from the need to repeat a performance (usually of a cantata) with a different ensemble of musicians, or when a new performance context required changes; several cantatas went through such modifications, as well as the two Passions.

A new conception of the general structure of a cycle could create a new version of the work. New versions that did not occur as a result of practical or other circumstantial reasons, but rather as a change of structural conception, are particularly important in the present book. Ending a composition seems, therefore, to have been just one stage in Bach's creative process, since even after its completion a work continued to live and transform in the composer's mind. That is why there usually is a certain period of time between versions. For example, 16 years passed between the first and the second versions of the Mass in B minor; approximately nine years between the two versions of the Magnificat (BWV 243 and BWV 243a), and it took three years for the Præambula and Fantasias of the *Clavier-Büchlein vor Wilhelm Friedemann Bach* to become the Inventions and Sinfonias BWV 772–801.

In most cases each new version became an independent work, with its own conception and structure. However, sometimes Bach switched away from a first variant of a composition while still in the process of writing and, without completing the version in work, moved into the new idea that had captivated his mind.

Such was the case of that grand fresco, the *Symbolum Nicenum* from the Mass in B minor, which has at least two versions. The last one is present in the 1749 autograph. An analysis of the corrections in that autograph, however, reveals the initial idea and enables backtracking Bach's steps in the process of recomposing the piece.

A comparison: the *Clavierübung III*[3]

An account of Bach's *Clavierübung III* may prove useful for a comparison in the context of the present study, since its composition process was quite similar—mainly in regard to their versions—to that of *The Art of Fugue*. As studies show, a number of facts point to the existence of at least three versions of the *Clavierübung III*, all initiated during its composition.[4] Based on these studies, the earliest of the versions was recorded in a lost autograph, and the third is the one printed in the original edition of 1739.

The first version was completed as a cycle of choral settings organised in two parts: the first part (nine pieces) corresponds in its structure to the Lutheran 'short Mass', and the second (six pieces) to the *Symbolum Nicenum* in the Mass in B minor (see Scheme 6.1).[5]

	Kyrie, Gott Vater in Ewigkeit, BWV 669 Christe, aller Welt Trost, BWV 670 Kyrie, Gott heiliger Geist, BWV 671
MISSA	Kyrie, Gott Vater in Ewigkeit, BWV 672 Christe, aller Welt Trost, BWV 673 Kyrie, Gott heiliger Geist, BWV 674
	Allein Gott in der Hoch sei Ehr, BWV 675 Allein Gott in der Hoch sei Ehr, BWV 676 Allein Gott in der Hoch sei Ehr, BWV 677 (Fughetta)
	Wir glauben all an einen Gott, BWV 680 Vater unser im Himmelreich, BWV 682
SYMBOLUM NICENUM	Christ, unser Herr, zum Jordan kam, BWV 684 Jesus Christus, unser Heiland, BWV 688
	Dies sind die heiligen zehen Gebot, BWV 678 Aus tiefer Not schrei ich zu dir, BWV 686

Scheme 6.1 The first version of *Clavierübung III*.

However, after the composition had already entered the engraving process, Bach had a new idea that led to a second version, in which the structural reference to the *Symbolum Nicenum* of the Mass was replaced by that of the Catechism. The new approach required the addition of six chorale preludes for the Catechism (BWV 679, 681, 683, 685, 687 and 689) and some reordering of the existing ones (see Scheme 6.2).

\multicolumn{2}{c}{Praeludium pro Organo pleno BWV 552₁}
Mass	Kyrie, Gott Vater in Ewigkeit, BWV 669 Christe, aller Welt Trost, BWV 670 Kyrie, Gott heiliger Geist, BWV 671
	Kyrie, Gott Vater in Ewigkeit, BWV 672 Christe, aller Welt Trost, BWV 673 Kyrie, Gott heiligerGeist, BWV 674
	Allein Gott in der Hoch sei Ehr, BWV 675 Allein Gott in der Hoch sei Ehr, BWV 676 Allein Gott in der Hoch sei Ehr, BWV 677 (Fughetta)
Catechism	Dies sind die heiligen zehen Gebot BWV 678 Dies sind die heiligen zehen Gebot BWV 679 (Fughetta)
	Wir glauben all an einen Gott BWV 680 Wir glauben all an einen Gott BWV 681 (Fughetta)
	Vater unser im Himmelreich BWV 682 Vater unser im Himmelreich BWV 683
	Christ, unser Herr, zum Jordan kam BWV 684 Christ, unser Herr, zum Jordan kam BWV 685
	Aus tiefer Not schrei ich zu dir BWV 686 Aus tiefer Not schrei ich zu dir BWV 687
	Jesus Christus, unser Heiland BWV 688 Jesus Christus, unser Heiland BWV 689 (Fuga)
\multicolumn{2}{c}{Fuga a 5 con pedale pro Organo pleno [not BWV 552₂]}

Scheme 6.2 The second version of *Clavierübung III*.

The first part (the 'Mass' structure) remained unchanged, but a newly composed prelude (BWV 552₁) now precedes it. Also, a new fugue in E-flat major was added to conclude the cycle. This fugue is referred to as BWV 552₂, since it is written, like the prelude, in E-flat major and for a full organ.[6]

The internal structure of the Catechism part follows a principle akin to the Credo section of the first version. In both versions adjacent movements are organised in pairs. Here, however, each pair of movements is based on one and the same chorale: the first prelude in each pair is larger and written for both manual and pedal keyboards (*pedaliter*), while the second is composed on a smaller scale, for manual keyboard only (*manualiter*).

This second version (Scheme 6.2) originated as an extension of the finished first version (Scheme 6.1). The process was performed under great pressure and took only a short time (one to two months), because the first version was already at the engraver's workshop. The new pieces were inserted at the beginning, the middle and the end of the cycle, leading to two subsequent versions.[7]

There are grounds to suggest that Bach composed the last fugue in *Clavierübung III* as a response to Johann Mattheson's challenge in *Der vollkommene Capellmeister*:[8]

> Von Doppelfugen, mit dreien Subjecten ist, so viel man weiß, nichts anders im Kupffer-Druck herausgekommen, als mein eignes Werck, unter dem Nahmen: Der wolklingenden Fingersprache. Erster und zweiter Theil, 1735, 1737, welches ich, aus Bescheidenheit niemand anpreisen mag: sondern vielmehr wünschen mögte, etwas dergleichen von dem berühmten Herrn Bach in Leipzig, der ein grosser Fugenmeister ist, ans Licht gestellet zu sehen.[9]

> [Of double fugues with three subjects, there is, as far as I know, nothing else in print but my own work under the name, *Die wolklingende Fingersprache*, parts one and two (1735, 1737), which I, out of modesty, would comment to no one. I would much rather see something of the same sort published by the famed Herr Bach in Leipzig, who is a great master of the fugue.[10]]

In this context, the continuation of this passage is interesting, too:

> Indessen legt dieser Mangel einer Seits die Nachläßigkeit und den Abgang gründlicher Contrapunctisten, andern Theils aber auch die geringe Nachfrage heutiger unwissenden Organisten und Setzer nach solchen lehrreichen Sachen…[11]

> [In the meantime, this lack exposes abundantly, not only the weakened state and the decline of well-grounded contrapuntists on the one hand, but on the other hand, the lack of concern of today's ignorant organists and composers about such instructive matters.[12]]

Besides being direct, this caustic sentence, mentioning 'the weakened state and the decline of well-grounded contrapuntists' and 'ignorant organists and composers' right after Bach's name, makes it even more overtly invective. Bach could not have missed it.

The *Musikalische Bibliothek*, the Society's official publication, announced the upcoming publication of Mattheson's work as early as winter 1738:

> Herrn Matthesons vollkommener Capellmeister, eine Schrift, auf welche sehr viele Musikverständige schon lange begierig gewartet, ist nun in Leipzig würklich unter der Presse, und wird ohnfehlbar kommende Oster Messe zum Vergnügen und Nutzen der Musikliebenden zum Vorschein kommen.[13]

> [Herr Mattheson's *Vollkommener Capellmeister*, a writing which a great many people discerning in music have been awaiting eagerly for quite some time, is now actually 'under the press' in Leipzig, and will make its appearance for the coming Easter fair without fail for the delight and profit of music lovers.[14]]

The following Easter Fair took place in Leipzig on Sunday, March 29, 1739, but the full treatise was published in Hamburg only after May 1739. Nevertheless, materials from *Der vollkommene Capellemeister* were published in Leipzig even before the aforementioned Easter Fair, but not in the publishing house of Adam Heinrich Holle, in an edition that nobody has ever seen as Butler suggests, but in Mizler's *Musikalische Bibliothek*. In fact, a review of its first chapter appeared in the very same issue in which the above announcement was printed.[15] More reviews and parts of the treatise were published in various issues of the *Musikalische Bibliothek* between 1739 and 1747.[16] Even in the extremely unlikely case that Bach might have missed these publications, his friends from Mizler's Society of Musical Sciences (or perhaps even Mizler himself), who closely watched for new treatises, would surely have informed him of this passage.

Mattheson's challenge presented a peculiar kind of fugue (most probably of his own imagination). Other contemporary theoretical treatises do not consider double fugues on three themes at all, just as Mattheson stated: 'of double fugues with three subjects, there is, as far as I know, nothing else in print but my own work …' there were no compositions of this sort in contemporary music literature.

Bach could not ignore the challenge, and indeed, there are several indications that he took up the gauntlet. BWV 552_2, which closes the *Clavierübung III*, is the one and only double fugue with three subjects that Bach had ever written, either before or after Mattheson's invective. The chronology of events confirms this suggestion, too: *Der vollkommene Capellmeister* was published around May 1739; the final version of *Clavierübung III was* offered for sale on the 29th of September, about five months later.

If Fugue BWV 552_2 was Bach's response to Mattheson's challenge, it could not have been composed before the publication of *Der vollkommene Capellmeister*. The dedication page of the treatise, to Ernest Ludwig, the Landgrave of Hessen, is marked 'Hamburg, im May 1739.' Dedications (and other kinds of introductory notes) were usually written last, thus reflecting in some measure the date of publication (for example, the preface to the 1752 edition of *The Art of Fugue* carries the date of its sale in the Leipzig Easter Fair of 1752: 'in der Leipziger Ostermeße 1752'). Thus, it is reasonable to establish May 1739 as the approximate date of *Der vollkommene Capellmeister*'s publication. If this is the case, then Bach had no more than two to three months (from May/June to July/August) to introduce any changes in the earlier version of the *Clavierübung III*. Moreover, the design of its last version may indicate that the final fugue, BWV 552_2, was written at the very end of this period, when the entire collection, which included four duets, was being printed (or at least engraved).

Thus, the reason for the *Clavierübung III*'s final version (as shown in Scheme 6.3) might have been the composition of that last fugue. The process leading to this result could develop along three possible scenarios.

First scenario: it is possible that before the publication of Mattheson's treatise, the second version of *Clavierübung III* closed with the four duets, and that the E-flat major fugue did not exist at all at that point in time. In such case, the fugue could have been composed later, probably only at the end of summer 1739.

Second scenario: another fugue in E-flat major, unknown today, was composed for the position later occupied by BWV 552_2. The replacement occurred in the last revision as a response to Mattheson. If this is the case, it is highly likely that Bach would not destroy the earlier fugue but rather keep it for another composition. However, among his organ fugues there is not a single one that would fit both typology and approximate composition date.

Third scenario: the hypothetical earlier Fugue in E-flat major could have been written on the very same three themes, but instead of a double fugue, as Mattheson suggested, it might have been a triple one. In such a case, to remodel it into one that would respond to the challenge would not be a difficult task. One should only replace the statements where all three themes are combined with paired ones: first and second, second and third, and first and third themes.[17]

74   Part III: J.S. Bach's work on The Art of Fugue

Praeludium pro Organo pleno, BWV 552₁	
Mass	Kyrie, Gott Vater in Ewigkeit, BWV 669 Christe, aller Welt Trost, BWV 670 Kyrie, Gott heiliger Geist, BWV 671 Kyrie, Gott Vater in Ewigkeit, BWV 672 Christe, aller Welt Trost, BWV 673 Kyrie, Gott heiligerGeist, BWV 674 Allein Gott in der Hoch sei Ehr, BWV 675 Allein Gott in der Hoch sei Ehr, BWV 676 Allein Gott in der Hoch sei Ehr, BWV 677 (Fughetta)
Catechism	Dies sind die heiligen zehen Gebot, BWV 678 Dies sind die heiligen zehen Gebot, BWV 679 (Fughetta) Wir glauben all an einen Gott, BWV 680 Wir glauben all an einen Gott, BWV 681 (Fughetta) Vater unser im Himmelreich, BWV 682 Vater unser im Himmelreich, BWV 683 Christ, unser Herr, zum Jordan kam, BWV 684 Christ, unser Herr, zum Jordan kam, BWV 685 Aus tiefer Not schrei ich zu dir, BWV 686 Aus tiefer Not schrei ich zu dir, BWV 687 Jesus Christus, unser Heiland, BWV 688 Jesus Christus, unser Heiland, BWV 689 (Fuga)
	Duetto I, BWV 802 Duetto II, BWV 803 Duetto III, BWV 804 Duetto IV, BWV 805
Fuga a 5 con pedale pro Organo pleno, [not BWV 552₂]	

Scheme 6.3 The third and fourth versions of *Clavierübung III*.

The most likely is the last scenario. An analysis of the melodic features and thematic structure of BWV 552₂ reveals various options that Bach could have used of triple counterpoint simultaneities among the three themes. Moreover, these themes seem to call for such contrapuntal combinations, as shown, for instance, in Examples 6.1 and 6.2.

Example 6.1 juxtaposes a fragment of our hypothetical fugue with bars 100–103 of BWV 552₂. The top system in the example (variant *a*) represents the hypothetical variant of a triple E-flat major fugue, which, after being completed, could have been readapted to a final form in the Fugue BWV 552₂ (variant *b*, bottom system). In variant *a*, the first theme is stated in the pedal, the inverted second theme[18] in the soprano and the third theme in the tenor. To

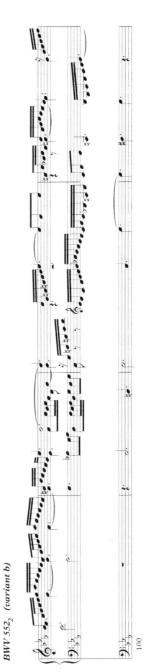

Example 6.1 Possible variants for bars 100–103 of fugue BWV 552_2.

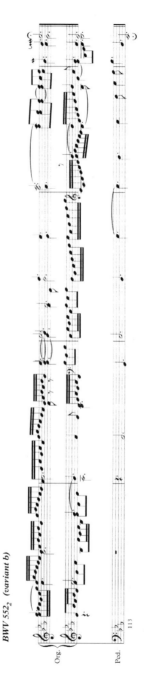

Example 6.2 Possible variants for bars 113–17 of fugue BWV 552$_2$.

turn this three-part combination into a two-part one, a little change of the soprano line in the last quarters of bars 100 and 101 should suffice. This manipulation results in variant *b*. The counterpoint is thus significantly simplified, albeit responding to Mattheson's idea.

Even more interesting in this respect is Example 6.2, which compares the closing statements of the hypothetical triple fugue (variant *a*) with bars 113–117 of BWV 552$_2$ (variant *b*).

An analysis of the combined statements and variants of the fugue's three themes (including the inverted second theme) inspires their combination into a quite complex contrapuntal construction. The second and third themes of variant *a* in Example 6.2 appear twice against the cantus firmus style backdrop of the first theme, written as a canon in the lower octave. Each of the themes is presented in statement–answer tonal relations. Additionally, the second theme appears in both original and inverted forms. In such a closing section, therefore, each of the three themes would be stated twice simultaneously, realising a triple thematic counterpoint, a worthy closure for a triple fugue.

Surely Bach would not miss the latent potentials of such a variant. After all, he used the *canto fermo in canone* principle at least twice in other pieces of the *Clavierübung III*,[19] and the inversion of the second theme, as has already been said, already appears in this very fugue.

In order to turn variant *a* of the closing section into a double fugue on three themes, one should just simplify it. For this, it would suffice to remove the canonic statement of the first theme, leave only the answer in the pedal part, and abandon the idea of the second theme's double appearance (in both its direct and inverted forms).[20] This would result in variant *b*, shown in the lower system of Example 6.2.

The first two scenarios accept the possibility that the Prelude and Fugue in E-flat major could have been composed at the same time. However, obviously, these scenarios would prevent the particular Fugue in E-flat major, BWV 552$_2$ of being itself.

The composer's four versions of the *Clavierübung III* were described here in detail not only to show that creating several versions of a given composition is typical to Bach's working methods, but also because the publication histories of this composition and *The Art of Fugue* have much in common, and not just in regard to the composition of several versions.

The above examples confirm that the emergence of several versions of one work during its composition is not an isolated case but a characteristic of Bach's creative process. Therefore, the existence of several versions in the composition process of *The Art of Fugue* can be looked upon as a natural phenomenon.

There are four versions of *The Art of Fugue* that can be detected in its two earliest sources: the Autograph and the Original Edition.

Notes

1 David Schulenberg discusses essential performance factors causing the creation of versions in Bach's music. See: David Schulenberg, 'Versions of Bach: Performing Practice in the Keyboard Works,' *Bach Perspectives*, 4 (1999): pp. 111–35.

2 'Contrapunctus 10 a 4 alla Decima' (BWV 1080/10) is a reworked fugue that appears in the Autograph as vi. The older version is titled in the Original Edition as '*Contrap. a 4*' (BWV 1080/10a).

3 Also known as The German Organ Mass, the *Clavierübung III* is Bach's most extensive collection of compositions for organ.

78   Part III: J.S. Bach's work on The Art of Fugue

4 There are reasons to believe that there were four versions. The data collected from the study of sources, in particular those related to the circumstances surrounding the lost manuscript Sp 1438, allows one to consider that this autograph reflected a version of the *Clavierübung III*, which chronologically preceded the final one as it appears in the original edition (see: Friedrich Smend, 'Bachs Kanonwerk über Vom Himmel hoch da komm ich her,' *BJ* 30 (1933): pp. 1–29; Hans Klotz, *Die Orgelchoräle aus der Leipziger Originalhandschrift*, NBA KB IV/2, p. 50; Christoph Wolff, *Johann Sebastian Bachs Klavierübung: Kommentar zur Faksimile-Ausgabe* (Leipzig/Dresden, 1984), p. 31; Gregory Butler, *Bach's Clavier-Übung III: The Making of a Print, with a Companion Study of the Canonic Variations on Von Himmel hoch BWV 769* (Durham, N.C., 1990), p. 50. The loss of the manuscript in 1945, however, leaves the hypothesis unconfirmed. Our discussion considers the three known versions of the *Clavierübung III* and proposes several suggestions regarding a fourth one.

5 The Latin text of the *Symbolum Nicenum* (Credo) has three paragraphs dedicated to the Trinity. The first refers to God the Father, the second to God the Son (Jesus Christ) and the last to God the Holy Spirit. There is a clear similarity between the early version of the *Symbolum Nicenum* in the Mass in B minor, where each textual paragraph is set into a pair of movements, and the 'six' of the second half in the *Clavierübung III* (see the Cathechism in Scheme 6.2).

6 I will challenge this view below.

7 This hypothesis is reflected in Butler's *Bach's Clavierübung III*, pp. 83–5, where he points at three versions of the *Clavierübung III* that resulted from the composition process.

8 Gregory G. Butler, '*Der vollkommene Capellmeister* as a stimulus to J.S. Bach's late fugal writing,' in George J. Buelow and Hans Joachim Marx (eds.), *New Mattheson Studies* (Cambridge, 1983), pp. 293–5. Gregory Butler was the first to suggest *Der vollkommene Capellmeister* as a stimulus to J.S. Bach's late fugal writing.

9 Johann Mattheson, *Der vollkommene Capellmeister* (Hamburg, 1739) Part 3, Chapter 23, paragraph 66, p. 441.

10 Gregory G. Butler, '*Der vollkommene Capellmeister* …' p. 295.

11 Johann Mattheson, *Der vollkommene Capellmeister*, paragraph 66, p. 441.

12 Butler, 'Der *vollkommene Capellmeister*'… p. 295.

13 *MMB* I/6 (1738): pp. 97–8.

14 Butler, 'Der *vollkommene Capellmeister*'… p. 293.

15 'Der vollkommene Capellmeister, Erster Stück' *MMB* I/6 (1738): pp. 76–85.

16 The preface to the treatise was published in *MMB* II/1 (1740): pp. 38–71; 'vollkommene Capellmeister …' A sequel—'Fortsetzung von Matthesons vollkommenen Capellmeister'—appeared in the next issue of *MMB* II/2 (1742): pp. 204–47. Five more sequels followed in the same series: 'Zweite Fortsetzung von Matthesons vollkommenen Capellmeister', II/3 (1742): pp. 72–119; 'Dritte Fortsetzung von Matthesons vollkommenen Capellmeister', II/4 (1743): pp. 96–118; 'Vierte Fortsetzung von Matthesons vollkommenen Capellmeister', III/1 (1746): pp. 46–61; 'Fünfte Fortsetzung von Matthesons vollkommenen Capellmeister', III/2 (1746): pp. 276–304, and 'Sechste und letzte Fortsetzung von Johann Matthesons vollkommenen Capellmeister', III/3 (1747): pp. 477–539.

17 The possible variant combining the second and third themes was not used by Bach in BWV 552_2.

18 In the fugue BWV 552_2 only the second theme undergoes inversion, which appears several times (for example, in bars 47–53).

19 In 'Dies sind die heiligen zehen Gebot', BWV 678 and in 'Vater unser im Himmelreich', BWV 682.

20 The second theme is absent from bars 114–15 of BWV 552_2. Its inversion in bars 113–14 is essentially a transformation, but the uninterrupted motion of the sixteenth notes is preserved.

7 The First Version of *The Art of Fugue*

The Autograph P 200 consists of materials that can be separated into two groups, each characterised by the use of a certain type of paper, different rastration and specific particularities of writing, all pointing at two different periods of composition. The first group, called here the First Version, reveals three principles of organisation characteristic to Bach: contrasting pairing (*Paarungsprinzip*), ascending (*Steigerungsprinzip*) and numerical signification. They can be characterised as following:

- The contrasting pairing principle: the fugues are organised in pairs; the members of each pair share visible features and also contrast each other in certain properties or parameters.[1]
- The ascending principle: each fugue (or pair of fugues) is, in some respect, more complex than the previous one. Another application of this principle is the organisation of consecutive pieces in ascending keys, either in whole or half steps.[2]
- Numerical meaning: certain numbers related to the fugues (for example, a fugue's serial number within a sequence of compositions) acquire special meaning, usually—but not exclusively—expressed in numerical symbolism.[3]

Each one of the fugue pairs that comprise the first version of *The Art of Fugue* will be now described and discussed in detail, looking at the various ways in which Bach applied these three principles in every case.

The first two fugues are simple, and their themes clearly contrast each other; the first fugue presents the main theme of the collection, while the second presents the theme's tonal answer in inversion (Example 7.1).

Example 7.1 The themes of fugues I and II.

Fugues III and IV are simple, too. Like the first pair, they are related through the contrast between the main theme (in fugue III) and its inversion (in fugue IV) (Example 7.2):

80   Part III: J.S. Bach's work on The Art of Fugue

Example 7.2 The themes of fugues III and IV.

In addition, in both fugues Bach applies one of the classified types of rhythmic counterpoint: the 'dotted note'. In seventeenth-century treatises it appears under various names, most often as *contrapunto della minima col punto* (or *di minima puntate*), or *contrapunto di semiminime puntate* (also named *della semiminima col punto*).[4] The first case refers to a pattern of a dotted half note and a quarter note (which, for the sake of convenience, will be nicknamed here 'large dotting'); Berardi's second description refers to a pattern of a dotted quarter note and an eighth note (correspondingly nicknamed 'small dotting').

The themes of fugues III and IV (in the above examples) consist of two segments each, connected by a tie. In fugue III, the first part of theme features equal rhythmic values, while the second part consists of dotted eighth notes complemented by sixteenth notes (one might call it 'micro dotting'). In fugue IV, on the other hand, the theme's first part contains three patterns of 'small dotting'[5] while the second part features equal rhythmic values. This structure affects the developmental processes in both fugues: in fugue III the dotted pattern is related to non-thematic fillers, while in fugue IV it is ingrained within the theme statements. Still, it cannot be ignored that the unifying contrast between the first two fugues is far more effective and convincing than the 'dotted opposition' between fugues III and IV. The themes of these fugues appeared too different because of the rhythmic cross-manipulation. This weakness was no doubt apparent to Bach himself, since he chose to end the fugue with a half cadence, on the dominant, uniting the two fugues in the vein of toccatas that lead to a subsequent fugue by pausing on the dominant. This is the only time in the first two versions of *The Art of Fugue* that such procedure was applied. Furthermore, in the process of further remodelling the work, this particular pair will be disbanded and the half-cadence removed, allowing the fugue to end on the tonic.[6]

Fugues V and VI are simple, with regular countersubjects. Alongside the contrast created by the presentation of the main theme in straight and inverted forms, other contrasts are at work, too, adding some complexity. There is an exchange of roles: in fugue V the main theme of the collection acts as countersubject to a completely new theme. Fugue VI inverts this picture: here the theme of the fugue is the main theme of the collection, and the consistent countersubject presents new material (Example 7.3).

Fugues VII and VIII form a contrasting pair, too. However, in addition to manoeuvring the main theme in both its straight and inverted forms, now becoming themes in these two fugues, a new type of contrast appears in the rhythmic characteristic of the themes: fugue VII is based on a rhythmic variant of the inverted theme of fugue IV, while fugue VIII presents its diminution, which, on its turn, is the inverted theme of fugue VI (compare Example 7.4 with Example 7.3).

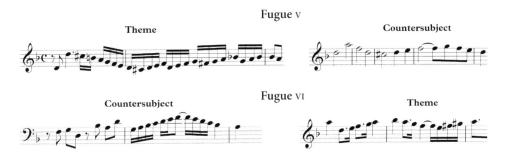

Example 7.3 Themes and countersubjects of fugues v and vi.

Example 7.4 Stretto theme entries in fugues vii and viii.

Adding complexity, this pair incorporates three more fugue types. First, these are *stretto fugues*, as can be seen from the ways that themes and answers are juxtaposed in both of them.[7] Second, these are *fugues in inversion*: each answer presents an inversion of the theme.[8] The third typological contrast between these fugues is rhythmic: fugue vii uses diminution and fugue viii augmentation.[9]

Next in the First Version of *The Art of Fugue*, numbered ix and ix$_a$, is the Canon in Octave. It is presented twice (hence the double numbering), first in an cryptic form, and then as a *resolutio canonis*, decrypted. This unusual pair could allude to the pedagogical leaning of *The Art of Fugue*, as an attempt to demonstrate that every canon may be presented in these two different ways. However, if the work is viewed as an artistic composition rather than as a textbook, this canonic pair looks rather peculiar. It is not by coincidence, therefore, that practically all studies of the Autograph's structure had never considered the two presentations of this canon (nor of the other canon in this cycle) as a pair. Yet, the assumption that Bach counted the canon as one of the pairs in the collection is supported by a contextual analysis, based on several indicators:

- Each presentation of the canon—cryptic and decrypted—is written separately, as a stand-alone, independent piece.
- Each one of this canon's presentations has its own title.

82   Part III: J.S. Bach's work on The Art of Fugue

- Except for *The Art of Fugue*, Bach had never presented both cryptic and decrypted forms of one canon. He acted this way only when the canon was incorporated into a sequence of paired pieces.
- The First Version of *The Art of Fugue* includes yet another perpetual canon—in augmentation and inversion—which will be discussed below. It is written in the same two presentation forms, but this time in the opposite order: first the decrypted variant and then the cryptic one.

This substantiates the interpretation of the two presentations of the Canon in Octave as the fifth pair of pieces in the First Version of *The Art of Fugue*:

IX: *Canon in Hypodiapason*
IX$_a$: *Resolutio Canonis*

The 11th and 12th pieces (marked in the Autograph as X and XI) are both double fugues with consistent countersubjects; both are based on the same motivic material (see Example 7.5). The example shows that the themes and consistent countersubject of the second fugue are the same as in the first one, albeit inverted. Besides, as expected after the third and fourth pairs of fugues, the order in which the themes appear in each of these pieces has been reversed, too. These fugues, therefore, comprise a contrasting pair, like all the preceding ones.

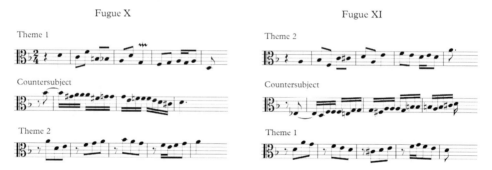

Example 7.5 Thematic materials of fugues X and XI.

The Canon in Augmentation and Inversion occupies positions 13 and 14 in the First Version, and its first presentation is marked in the Autograph with the single Roman numeral XII. Like the Canon in Octave (marked here as IX and IX$_a$), this pair consists of two presentations of the canon, decrypted and cryptic:

XII (decrypted): carries no title
XII$_a$ (cryptic): *Canon in Hypodiateßeron, al roversio e per augmentationem, Perpetuus*[10]

This appearance raises at least two questions:

   a)   Why is it that the first member of the pair, marked XII, has no title?
   b)   Why is it that the decrypted and cryptic presentations of this canon follow an order opposite to those of the Canon in Octave (IX and IX$_a$)?

To answer the first question, one must remember that the usual practice for a canon's double presentation positions the cryptic form first. The reverse order, in which the solution to a puzzle is given before its presentation, would be odd. Here, however, the *resolutio canonis* appears first.

The possibility that Bach noticed this oddity—maybe right after the canon was written—cannot be excluded. This could be a reason for his temporarily leaving the full presentation of the canon without a title, with the intent of somehow sorting this out at a later stage. If this were the case, however, the order could have been easily corrected in the fair copy, exchanging the positions of XII and XII$_a$ to present the puzzle before its solution. The fact that Bach had not done so means that the interchange of the presentation order was intended. This would coincide with a general characteristic of Bach's approach, creating contrasts in every aspect of possible pairings.[11]

The analysis of the fugues' sequencing and their individual peculiarities, as well as of their interrelationship and combination capacities, allows the entire collection to be seen as one whole and complete polyphonic cycle. These properties are not limited to the unifying key of D minor, nor to the single common theme with its variants, but are ingrained in its internal logic, responding to Bach's three principles of cyclisation: all the pieces are grouped in pairs based on common elements while still opposing each other; each pair of fugues or canons is more complex than its predecessor not only in its compositional devices but also in the types of contrasts that are invariably enriched and complicated. The importance that Bach related to numbers is apparent in the total number of 14 compositions (fugues and canons) organised in seven pairs, reflecting the numerical value of the letters that form the name Bach.[12]

Scheme 7.1 shows a structural summary of the First Version of *The Art of Fugue*. It demonstrates yet another element of numeric symbolism that defines the cycle's internal logic. An analysis of Bach's works written in the last decade shows that the composer consistently associated the concept of canon with the numbers 10 and 4.[13]

The scheme shows that the two canons are located on positions 9–10 and 13–14.[14] It is also clear from the scheme that these canons could appear on the even positions of 10 and 14 only if each one of them were written twice, on both odd- and even-numbered positions. In other words, in order to epitomise the symbolism of the numbers 10 and 4, a canon must be the *second in a pair*. It is possible that by including in the cycle two presentations of one and the same canon Bach tried to create such a constellation, affecting the general structure of the First Version.

Thus, beyond its already listed particularities, *The Art of Fugue* is also a bipartite composition. Its two parts, of unequal length, reflect the proportion between the symbolic numbers 10 and 4, each part crowned by a canon. Its first part features eight fugues and a canon, and the remaining part—two fugues and a canon. The fugues in the first part are all based on one single theme; the second part features double fugues.

The First Version of *The Art of Fugue*, therefore, reveals itself, rather than a mere collection of short pieces, as one integral composition, the wholeness of which is warranted by several factors and characterised by a certain type of logic and numerological symbolism. Nevertheless, there remained several weak points. Bach's next steps could be interpreted as attempts to overcome these weaknesses, which, in all probability, led to the emergence of the Second Version of *The Art of Fugue*.

It looks as if some time had passed between the completion of the First Version and the creation of the second one, which forms an integral part of the Autograph P 200 but

84   Part III: J.S. Bach's work on The Art of Fugue

includes additional materials. There are several circumstantial indications that lead to this conclusion:

- Different types of paper: Scheme 4.1 shows that the two types of paper that Bach used in 1742, watermarked WZ 67 (until August 1742) and WZ 65 (after May 1742), were not used anymore after the ninth bifolio. Thereafter he wrote on a new paper, which he used from 1743 until 1746/1747.[15]

General Structure	Serial Number	Autograph Numeration	Pairs	Type or Title
	1	I		Simple fugues
	2	II		
	3	III		Fugues with dotted counterpoint
	4	IV		
	5	V		Fugues with consistent countersubjects
	6	VI		
	7	VII		Stretto fugues in inversions
	8	VIII		
	9	IX		Canon in Octave: cryptic and decrypted
	10	IX$_a$		
	11	X		Double fugues with consistent countersubjects
	12	XI		
	13	XII		Canon in Augmentation and Inversion: decrypted and cryptic
	14	XII$_a$		

Scheme 7.1 Structure of the First Version of The Art of Fugue.

- Different rastration: there are 22 staves on each of pages 32–3 of the Autograph, where the Canon in Augmentation and Inversion is written; the following pages (34–8) encompass 24 staves each, and
- Different note-head size: starting on p. 34, note-heads are smaller than on the previous pages.

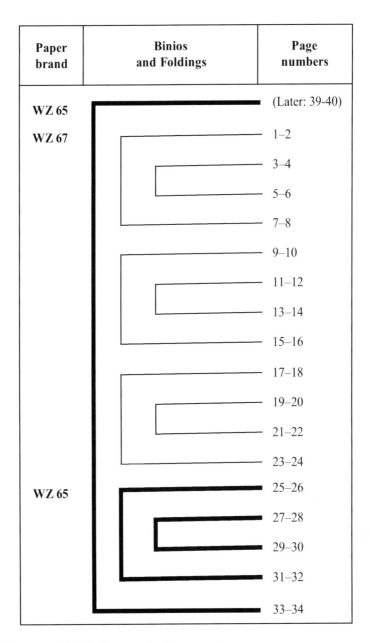

Scheme 7.2 Structure of the First Version, showing paper types.

Still, it cannot be ignored that an earlier paper (WZ 65) was used when writing new pieces too, for example, most of the first mirror fugue (the bottom part of page 33 and the whole of page 34), and the end of the second presentation of the Canon in Augmentation and Inversion (p. 39), followed by a blank page (p. 40). This can mean that the First Version left pages 34, 39 and 40 blank and that the last bifolio was meant to serve in part as a cover folder (see Scheme 7.2). Later, in the Second Version, rastration was added to pages 34 and 39, to be used for new musical text. This means that at some point in time, between 1743 and 1746/47, Bach revised the First Version, writing the additions partly on the available old blank sheets, and partly on new paper (WZ 21).

Notes

1 Contrasts of major versus minor keys, straight versus inverted subject statements, high versus low registers, equally divided versus dotted rhythm, and so on.
2 For example, such is the organisation of *The Well-Tempered Clavier* and in the collections of Inventions and Sinfonias.
3 For example, the total number of canons on the Christmas choral in the Canonic Variations BWV 769 is eight (as a symbol of the Nativity); in the *Musical Offering* BWV 1079 there are 10 canons, as the number of commandments, and the total number of movements is 13 (the numerological equivalent of the abbreviation FG: Friedrich der Grosser). Similarly, there are 14 canons (BWV 1087) on the bass theme of the *Air and 30 Variations* (the Goldberg Variations, BWV 988): 14 is the numerological equivalent of Bach's name. As a reminder, this aspect of the eighteenth-century German culture engaged not only the curiosity of the general public, but — particularly in the 1740s — was also one of Bach's fields of interest. The composer's perceptions of numerology and its symbolism were epitomised especially in the second section of the Mass in B minor, the *Symbolum Nicenum*, which was composed during the second half of the 1740s.
4 Alongside widespread types of complex counterpoint that relate mainly to the shifting of pitch relations, seventeenth- and eighteenth-century treatises also considered various types of rhythmic counterpoint as a coherent part of the *obbligato* counterpoint series. Thus, a metric/rhythmic pattern applied to the initial melodic structure (or to a combination of melodies) generates the corresponding derivatives of the structure. For example, Angelo Berardi, to whose *Documenti Armonici* Mattheson refers several times in his book, specifies such types of rhythmic counterpoint as *contrapunto alla zoppa, contrapunto alla diritta, contrapunto della minima col punto, contrapunto di semi-minime puntate*, and so on (Angelo Berardi, *Documenti Armonici* [Bologna, 1687], pp. 12–21). Berardi's work is discussed in Mattheson's *Der vollkommene Capellmeister*, particularly in part 3, Chapter 21 (about canons), paragraph 13, p. 395; pp. 740–1 in Mizler's translation. Mizler quotes Mattheson's two references to Berardi's works, once in relation to the above mentioned Chapter 21, in the last issue of *MMB* (1747) and much earlier, in *MMB* II/4 (1743): p. 106.
5 The dotting here is not universally applied, since several half notes remained intact. Else, the main tones of the theme would be moved into the metrically weak positions, which would cause the theme to be hardly recognisable. Moreover, such transformation would relate to other kinds of rhythmic counterpoint (*per arsin et thesin*, as well as *alla zoppa*). It is apparent that Bach preferred to keep the musical coherence of his theme rather than follow theoretical techniques, an approach that also characterises his handling of rhythmic textures. The axis of the theme's inversion is F, the mediant. This same note (in the second bar, tied) also acts as an axis for the dotted counterpoint's symmetry: 'small dotting' in the bottom line before the F and equal rhythmic values in the top line; after the F the rhythmic texture is reversed: the dotted rhythm moves to the top line (in 'microdotting'), and the equal rhythmic values move to the bottom.
6 This structural readjustment is discussed in Chapter 8.

7 In a *stretto fugue* the exposition is structured as a stretto, a chain of stretti or several stretti.
8 In an *inverted fugue* the answer is the inverted theme.
9 In a *diminution fugue* the answer consists of the theme in rhythmic diminution; respectively, in an *augmentation fugue* the answer consists of the theme in rhythmic augmentation.
10 Henceforth, the original spelling in the titles of the pieces of *The Art of Fugue* is kept.
11 This principle is apparent in the sequence of similarly paired fugues (for example, fugues XI and XII). It will become even more obvious during the analysis of the mirror fugues (Chapter 8).
12 B = 2; A = 1; C = 3; H = 8. 2 + 1 + 3 + 8 = 14.
13 In this context it is worth mentioning the 10 canons of the *Musical Offering*, structured as a combination of 6 and 4; the Canonic Variations BWV 769 (4 + 4) and the four duet canons from the *Clavierübung III*. Most relevant to our discussion here are the 14 canons, of BWV 1087 (10 + 4) as well as the 10 Canonic Variations (nine + the Quodlibet) in BWV 988 (Goldberg Variations).
14 Bach considered the position occupied by a movement in a cyclic composition as highly significant. The composition history of the *Symbolum Nicenum* in the Mass in B minor provides a good example, in which, while still in the process of composition, he undertook a major reworking of already composed music in order to place the 'Crucifixus' in the fifth position, a number to which he attached relevant symbolic meaning.
15 See Chapter 4.

8 The Second Version

Perceiving the double presentation of a canon as two separate pieces was a structural weakness of the First Version. Indeed, in the Second Version of *The Art of Fugue* Bach removed this awkwardness, counting each canon as one piece rather than two. This resulted in a total number of 12 pieces rather than 14. Since the general guiding rule, requiring 14 pieces in total for the whole set, stayed intact, two more pieces were needed. These Bach provided in the last six pages (33–8) of the Autograph: two mirror fugues, the first, marked in the Autograph as XIII, in four parts, and the second, marked as XIV, in three.[1]

The two mirror fugues

Each mirror fugue consists of two fugues that 'mirror' each other, providing the inversion of its companion. Each of these two mirror fugues presents its two component fugues on the page, one on top of the other, tied by a brace, and thus clearly demonstrating the 'mirroring' effect (Figures 8.1 and 8.2).[2]

The first (top) fugue of each pair of mirror fugues is usually called the *rectus* (or *fuga recta*), and the second—the *inversus* (or *fuga inversa*). Usually this terminology is quite straightforward,

Figure 8.1 P 200, pp. 33–5: the first mirror fugue (marked XIII).

Figure 8.2 P 200, pp. 36–8: the second mirror fugue (marked XIV).

but in monothematic cycles, such as *The Art of Fugue*, some complexities may emerge, since the theme undergoes various transformations, most importantly inversion. Consequently, the theme itself exists in two forms: straight (*rectus*) and inverted (*inversus*). Therefore, special attention is paid here to clarify whether the subject of discussion is a fugue or its theme.

The mirror fugues in the Second Version of *The Art of Fugue*, like the former pairs, are similar and yet contrast each other. The themes of the two *fugae ractae* oppose each other; the theme of fugue XIII recta is the rectus of the cycle's main theme, while the theme of fugue XIV recta is the inversus of that same theme's ornamented variant (Example 8.1). The two fugae inversae present the same type of contrast, albeit inverted. The theme of fugue XIII inversa is the inversus of the cycle's main theme, while the theme of fugue XIV inversa is the ornamented variant of the main theme rectus (Example 8.2).

Example 8.1 The themes of the two *ractae* mirror fugues XIII and XIV.

Example 8.2 The themes of the two *inversae* mirror fugues XIII and XIV.

90   Part III: J.S. Bach's work on The Art of Fugue

A new canon

Bach's Second Version concludes with a new canon—*Canon al roverscio et per augmentationem* (Canon in Inversion and Augmentation). Such a canon is already included in the First Version of *The Art of Fugue*: it capped that version after the second double fugue with consistent countersubject, on pages 32–33. Why did Bach decide to write yet another canon on the same theme? Did he want a pair of similar canons, or was the new one aimed to replace the previous? If the latter is the case, what was wrong with the first one?

A comparison between these two canons may lead to an answer and to a better understanding of Bach's way of thinking. In the following discussion, the canon that concludes the First Version, marked in P 200 as XII (decrypted and then cryptic) is called 'the first canon', while the later one, marked as XV, 'the second canon'.

The main reason for writing the second canon seems straightforward; it was meant to provide a closure to the new, Second Version of *The Art of Fugue*, an approach concurrent with each one of the First Version's two parts ending with a canon. This closure function of canons was probably highly significant for Bach and is characteristic of his style.[3] Thus, the first canon, which, with the addition of the two mirror fugues lost its capping function, should be moved to a new position after these fugues. Indeed, the striking similarities between the two canons' openings point at exactly such an idea (Figures 8.3a and 8.3b).

Figure 8.3 (a) P 200, p. 32: the opening of the first canon (marked XII); (b) P 200, p. 38: the opening of the second canon (marked XV).

However, Bach had never just reproduced any musical text—whether his own or other composers'—*ad literam*. Rather, without exception, he introduced corrections that, depending on context, could result in radical changes.

The first canon and its corrections

Bach's intention to revise the first canon and copy it with the new amendments to its new position is apparent from the correction marks in the manuscript (Figure 8.3a). The corrections in the second and third beats of bars 3 and 4 of the proposta (the top part) can be clearly seen: thirty-second notes replaced the two groups of sixteenth notes, corrections that were clearly made after this canon had been completed; its cryptic presentation reveals the initial version without the corrections (Figure 8.4).

Figure 8.4 P 200, p. 33: beginning of the cryptic canon (xii, unmarked).

The corrections, however, could not be fully implemented. Correcting a completed canon—even a simple one, let alone one with sophistications such as inversion and augmentation—is virtually a hopeless enterprise.[4] Generally, then, rather than fixing problems in a given canon, it is simpler to compose a new one.

Bach, no doubt, was aware of these facts, and quickly relinquished the corrections: the risposta in bars 7 and 8, where he should repeat—in augmentation and inversion—the correction was made in bars 3 and 4 of the proposta. The risposta, however, does not follow the correction, preserving the initial variant of the counterpoint (Figure 8.5).

Figure 8.5 P 200, p. 32: beginning of the decrypted canon (marked xii), corrected proposta (bars 3–4) and the uncorrected risposta (bars 7–8) encircled.

Most probably, thus, Bach did plan to rewrite the canon with the necessary corrections, sealing the cycle. However, if the augmentation and inversion rules were to be followed, the correction, when applied to the risposta, would result in parallel fifths and octaves as well as other non-stylistic slips, demanding either correction or removal.[5] The corrections he made on bars 3–4 of the first canon, therefore, were intended to serve him just as initial clues for a further rework of this canon, a kind of a memo draft. Eventually, realising the unavoidable contrapuntal problems, he kept just the theme of the first canon and some melodic gestures from its counterpoint, literally composing a new canon, now marked in P 200 as xv.

The second canon and its corrections

Creating counterpoint to a given melody, be it a theme, a cantus firmus or a new melodic statement, is a cornerstone of polyphonic imitation composition techniques. Whereas the main melodic line, in principle, should not be subjected to changes, its counterpoint may be corrected, in the process of composition, as many times as needed. In other words, in the composition of canons, the counterpoint is the part that adjusts itself to the theme that remains intact.[6] This particular trait requires the composition of a canon on paper, usually calling for preliminary drafts, especially when various material transformations need to be applied.[7]

92 Part III: J.S. Bach's work on The Art of Fugue

Despite its corrections, verbal annotations and the title that was later added to its cryptic presentation in the manuscript, the first Canon in Augmentation, marked as XII in P 200, is a fair copy. While minor corrections are quite common even in fair manuscript copies, the kind of corrections that appear are introduced in one part only and are not further implemented. Moreover, if realised, they would destroy the canon. These corrections, therefore, do not belong here, but refer to a new variant of the canon, which at that point in time was yet to be composed.

Thus, when the corrections, annotations and inscription were added on the clean copy of the canon, it was not regarded anymore as such, and became instead raw material for a new piece: a draft. The inscription, defining the canon's nature, changed, indicating that Bach's approach to it had changed, too.

As later transformations of *The Art of Fugue* show, from that point the first canon was no longer considered as part of the cycle, and its role as closure was transferred to the new canon, in a new location, after the two new mirror fugues. Bach changed its title. It was now called *Canon al roverscio et per augmentationem* (instead of the former *Canon in Hypodiateßeron. al roversio e per augmentationem, perpetuus*). Unlike the first canon, which was marked as infinite (*perpetuus*), or a round, the new canon appears to be a finite one, and that despite the fact that it could easily be made a round, too.[8] The composer, however, did not do so, maybe to avoid repeating the same trait as the Canon in Octave (IX and IX$_a$). Furthermore, Bach removed from the title the interval designation of the risposta's entry (*in Hypodiateßeron*—the lower fourth), probably because the canon is in inversion.

It is generally believed that the second canon is a draft (*Konzeptschrift, erste Niederschrift*), made at the moment of composition. This view is based on the fact that, starting on the second half of bar 14, Bach had to write the thirty-second notes so small that the text became almost unintelligible. The assumption is that this happened because Bach, while transferring the material from the proposta to the risposta, (quarter, eighth and sixteenth notes), spaced them erroneously, without taking into account that thirty-second notes should appear in the top part counterpoint.[9]

However, if this were a draft, then the composition procedure of the canon would undoubtedly be following. First, at the entrance point of the risposta (the bottom part for a canon's first half and the top part of its second half), the previous segment of the proposta—in augmentation and inversion—needs to be written. Then, a counterpoint to this risposta is to be composed. In a canon's composition draft, this process must be kept all the way along the first half of the canon.

An analysis of this Autograph score, however, shows that this is not always the case. For example, in the first canon, as early as the entrance of the risposta, when the material is allegedly transferred from the proposta (bars 3–6), it is apparent that it was not the lower part that determined the inscription, but the top one (see Figures 8.3a and 8.5, bars 3–6).

A careful examination shows that bar 4 occupies more space (48.5 mm) than bar 3 (40.5 mm). This difference is a result of the top part. A closer look at the bottom part reveals that the distance between the opening barline of each one of these two bars and the half notes that fall on the second beat of each is equal in both cases (15 mm); however, the distance between these half notes and the quarter notes that follow each of them is different (16 and 20 mm, respectively); further, the distance from the quarter note to the following barline is different, too (10 and 14 mm, respectively). It is apparent that these differences relate to the top part. Here, in bar 4, appear a series of alteration signs, which are missing from bar 3.[10] It leads to the conclusion that the top part (at least in these particular bars) was written first, and only afterwards the bottom part was copied in.

A similar case is presented in bar 5, which is protracted even further (54.5 mm), although the number of notes in bars 4 and 5 of the bottom part is equal. The number of notes in the top part, on the other hand, has significantly increased: while bar 4 has 16 notes, bar 5 includes 22. Therefore, the physical length of bar 5 is defined, too, by the top part, which in bars 3–5 was written first. All this indicates that the second segment of the Canon in Augmentation (bars 3–6) was not composed 'on the spot.' This conclusion, by itself, should suffice to claim that this manuscript is not entirely a composition draft. At least the two first segments of the canon were copied from an earlier draft that must have preceded the Autograph.

However, the third segment, bars 7–14, presents a different picture.[11] Here the bottom part was written first, following the usual process of *canon composition rather than copying*. A similar order of writing can be seen in the shortened fourth segment (bars 15–26). The first half of this canon, then, *combines copying and composition*: the first and the second segments are copied, while the third and the shortened fourth segments are composed 'on the spot,' in the Autograph itself.

It is apparent, thus, that this is a particular kind of manuscript, which could cautiously be qualified as the result of *composing* (or correcting) *while copying*.[12] Such a copying procedure is typically intertwined with a subsequent correction, which sets off a complete revision process. This classification is based on evidence indicating, first, the coexistence of copying and composing, and second, the position of copying traces in the document's beginning, and of composition traces toward its later parts. The second canon reflects both.

The start of the canon's second half (bars 27–52) is identical to the start of the first canon's second half in both subject and counterpoint (see Figure 8.6, comparing bar 21 in the first canon with bar 27 in the second canon), implying that both parts of the first half (bars 1–26) were, at least in part, copied from the first canon.

Figure 8.6 (a) P 200: canon xii, bar 21; (b) canon xv, bar 26.

The composition process of a canon in augmentation and inversion ends at the middle of the piece (here, at bar 26). The manuscript shows a significant difference in density of the music inscription between the first and second halves, the latter being sparsely inscribed. This is not coincidental. Scholars often focus on the high density of the canon's first half (until bar 26) but do not bestow enough meaning to its quite sparsely written second half (after bar 26). It is possible that Bach strove to fit the piece within page 39 in order to avoid a possible turn of the page. The new canon seemed to be 11 bars longer than its predecessor (the middle point of the

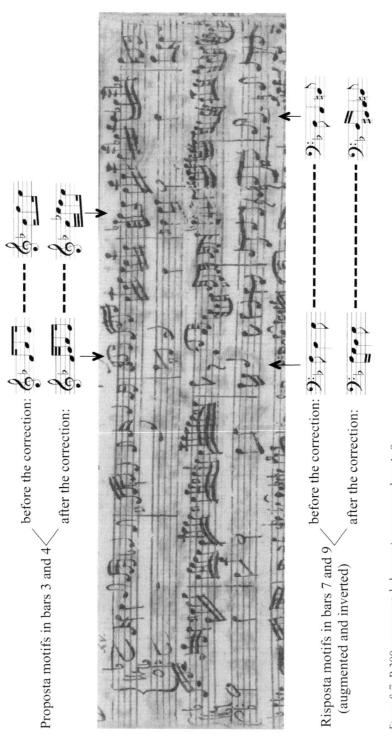

Figure 8.7 P 200: ornamental changes in canon xv, bars 1–9.

first canon is on bar 21). During the process of correction-composition Bach may have been unsure of its final length. Once he reached bar 26, however, the picture cleared up, offering more than enough writing space to complete the work.

Bach continued to correct the canon even while composing its new version. The later correction of canon xv is of a special interest for two reasons. First, it substantiates the hypothesis that the canon was corrected after its inscription. Second, it holds indirect data concerning Bach's ideas after the *Canon al roverscio et per augmentationem* had been written down.

For example, a close examination of bars 3 and 4 shows that the second note in each of these bars is an insertion: both notes were added after the canon had been inscribed. The corrected version was more ornamented (Figure 8.7).

In the risposta, where these figures are augmented and inverted, corresponding modifications appear in bars 7 and 9. However, judging by the specifics of the musical text, another reason for the changes in the latter could point at a wish to avoid a rhythmic slowdown toward the cadenza, on the strong beat of bar 7, which might have inspired Bach to introduce the sixteenth-note motion. Only later the parallel correction was copied into the proposta (the second note of bar 3, top part); the sequential motion required a similar modification of bar 4.

Similar corrections, determined by those in the first half, appear in the second half of the canon, (bars 29, 30, 33, 35), all introduced into the text after the inscription of the whole canon. These corrections were possible precisely because of their triviality (in the first case an added melodic passing note; in the second, a note related to the harmonic figuration): none required any further changes in the counterpoint.

There is another correction, however, which, although performed after the canon's completion, promises to be much more significant. It appears in bar 11 of the proposta (top) part, and includes both colouration and additional notes (Figure 8.8). The correction was copied to bar 37 (the proposta in the bottom part), with no further changes, in double counterpoint at an octave (Figure 8.9).

However, the same correction was not followed through in the risposta of the canon's first half (bars 23–24), nor in its second half (bars 49–50), though this would not have involved any changes in the counterpoint and therefore could easily have been done (Figure 8.10).

It seems that Bach abandoned the idea after making the correction, leaving it only in the proposta without transferring it into the risposta. This, however, would betray the essence of a canon, which is defined by an exact repetition, in the risposta, of a previous proposta segment. The fact that the canon rules were not followed here up to the letter may mean that Bach inserted the corrections just as a hinting reminder for a future revision. Like in the case of the first canon (marked xii), it is possible that Bach, at a certain point, started to regard the manuscript as a draft into which he jotted some suggested ideas for later amendments, maybe preparing a new variant of the canon. Indeed, as his later actions show, he did prepare a new, Third Version of *The Art of Fugue*.

The structure of the Second Version

The coherent structure of the Second Version can be seen in the Scheme 8.1, which shows the distribution of the pieces in the cycle, and in Scheme 8.2, which displays the grouping of the score sheets in the manuscript.

Figure 8.8 P 200: canon xv, corrections in bars 10–14; enlarged: bar 11, correction visible in the proposta; bottom: (a) transcription of the original inscription; (b) transcription of the correction, made after the canon was finalised.

Figure 8.9 P 200: canon xv, correction in bars 34–38. Bar 37 is enlarged at bottom left, correction copied ad literatim; transcribed in bottom right.

Figure 8.10 P 200: canon xv, corrections discontinued. Top: bar 11, followed by its original inscription and the correction; bottom: bars 23–24 and 49–50 showing no corresponding corrections in the augmented and inverted rispostas.

As in the First Version, the principal factor that determined the number of pieces in the cycle is the numerological symbol of Bach's name: 14. The cycle's central structuring principles, such as contrasting pairing and ascending complexity, remain valid, with the addition of the pair of mirror fugues, introducing yet one more degree of complexity in composition technique.

The Second Version of *The Art of Fugue*, thus, displays a deliberate thinking of a complete cycle that is a corrected, enriched and perfected extension of the First Version.

Yet, there is ground to believe that in the process of finalising this plan, Bach altered it yet further. The decision to do so was probably made at the time of completion of the two mirror fugues and before composing the last canon's new version, which could explain its dense note writing. Such interpretation requires some explanation.

A hypothesis, often mentioned in scholarly literature but most clearly articulated by Klaus Hofmann, suggests that the autograph of this canon's present version is a composition manuscript, that is, an initial inscription of the piece at the moment of its composition;[13] our hypothesis, on the other hand, regards this canon's autograph as a special kind of manuscript that we defined as *a secondary inscription (or revision) in the process of copying*.[14]

According to Hofmann's hypothesis, the canon's dense script is the result of Bach's oversight, which caused him to copy the augmented and inverted proposta to the risposta in a standardised proportion rather than taking into account the numerous notes that would be written above it, leading to jammed thirty-second notes in the counterpoint. This hypothesis could be accepted were it not for two deterrents.

First, as the analysis showed, this manuscript reveals the traces of *secondary* inscription, that is, of copying. If this is the case, then the model draft would undoubtedly include thirty-second notes, which would prevent Bach from writing down a risposta in standard proportion when actually requiring wider spaces. Second, he used several gestures in this version that were

General Structure	Serial Number	Autograph Numeration	Pairs	Type or Title
14 — 4 pairs of fugues	1	I	⎫⎬⎭	Simple fugues
	2	II		
	3	III	⎫⎬⎭	Fugues with dotted counterpoint
	4	IV		
	5	V	⎫⎬⎭	Fugues with consistent countersubjects
	6	VI		
	7	VII	⎫⎬⎭	Stretta fugues in inversions
	8	VIII		
	9	IX		Canon in Octave: (decrypted)
4 fugues	10	X	⎫⎬⎭	Double fugues with consistent countersubjects
	11	XI		
	12	XII	⎫⎬⎭	Mirror fugues
	13	XIII		
	14	XIV		Canon in Augmentation and Inversion (decrypted)

Scheme 8.1 Structure of the Second Version of *The Art of Fugue*.

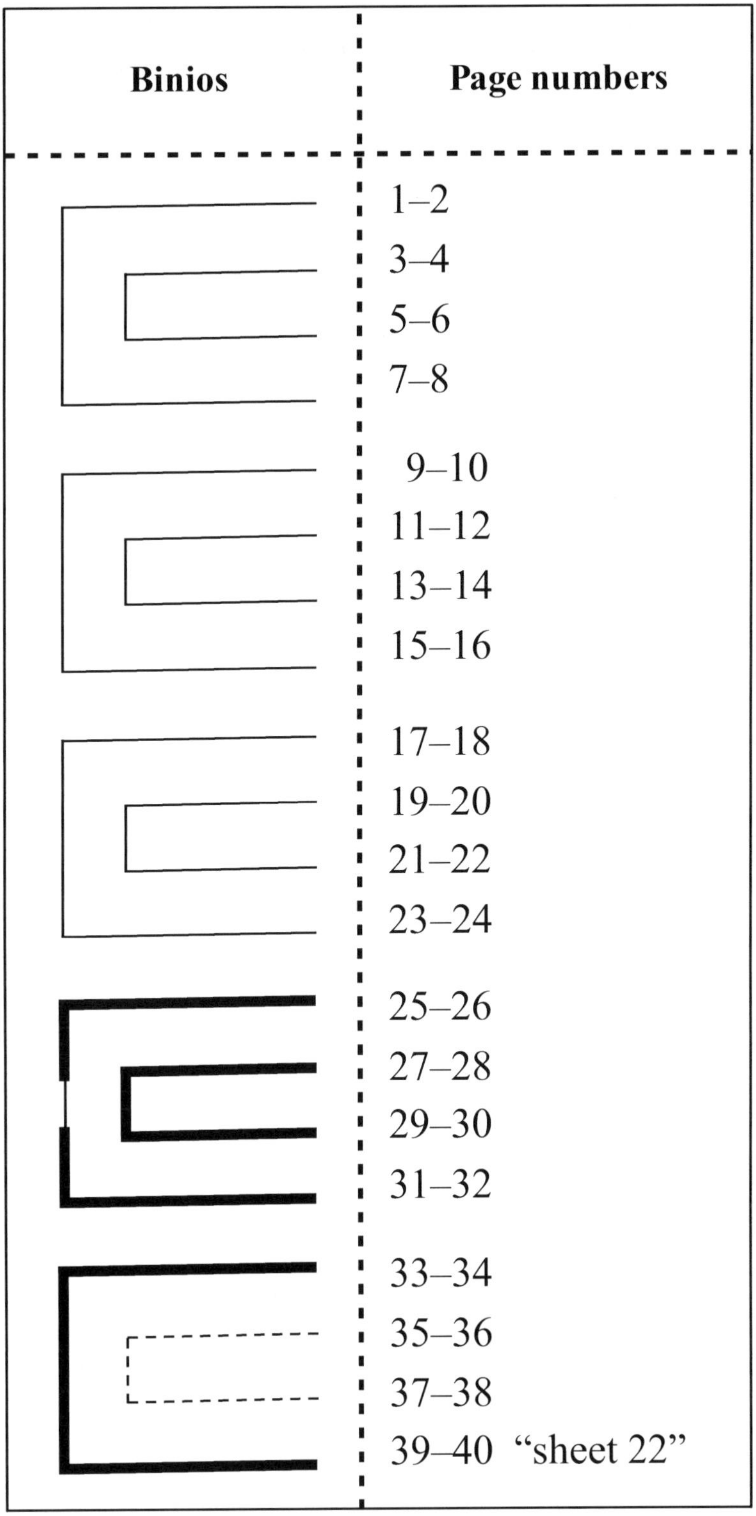

Binios	Page numbers
	1–2
	3–4
	5–6
	7–8
	9–10
	11–12
	13–14
	15–16
	17–18
	19–20
	21–22
	23–24
	25–26
	27–28
	29–30
	31–32
	33–34
	35–36
	37–38
	39–40 "sheet 22"

Scheme 8.2 Sheet structure of the Second Version of *The Art of Fugue*.

taken from its previous version. There, the thirty-second notes are quite prominent. Moreover, Bach drafted similar gestures in the unrealised correction of the first Canon in Augmentation (see Figure 8.5), as reminders to realise them in the Second Version. However, it is hardly possible that bearing these in mind from a previous version of the canon, as well as from the model from which he copied, he would write the augmented risposta in standard proportion. Besides, Hofmann does not take into account the fact that the left side of the manuscript's spread (p. 38) dramatically differs in its scale of writing from the right side (p. 39): the latter is written in an absolute flow and in larger notes.

Another hypothesis explaining the crammed handwriting and the difference in scale between the left and right sides of the spread could be offered. This is a bipartite canon, its second part deriving from the first. Having composed the first part, Bach knew exactly the scale of the second, and the space it would need. The remaining blank page allowed for more than enough room, creating a palpable difference of inscription size between the canon's two last pages.

Still, certain facts contradict this conclusion, too. First, two and a half blank pages were available for the inscription of this canon, a space of which Bach was well aware. If Bach had chosen to raster these two blank pages (39 and 40) in the same way as the preceding ones, 24 staves per page, he would have had available, together with the 12 staves on page 38, 60 blank staves for the canon. Finally, the inscription of the previous version of the canon in its decrypted and spaciously written form occupied 24 staves. The new version was 11 bars longer, which would demand no more than six additional staves. In other words, the whole canon, written in the standard proportion, would comfortably fit into no more than 30 staves and arrive at its conclusion before filling up page 39, leaving page 40 blank. Bach could not have missed that. There was absolutely no need for that narrow, congested script.

Nevertheless, the inscription of the canon's first half is quite jammed. The two hypotheses are thus unconvincing and were presented and discussed only to highlight what lies out in the open, which is that *Bach needed to fit the whole canon into a formerly defined space*. The density of writing indicates that this space seemed insufficient for the fulfilment of the composer's intentions. While such an interpretation might put everything into place, it still requires knowing what Bach had planned for this space. Certain traits of the Autograph could provide clues for Bach's actions in organising this part of the manuscript.

Notes

1 The first fugue is written on pp. 33–5 of the Autograph; the second on pp. 36–8. Both fugues are followed by a canon. For a discussion of the paradoxes of mirror fugues see Chapter 10.
2 As is always the case with complex counterpoint, the composer must consider the particularities of each line, its combinations and restrictive limitations.
3 For example, in the Goldberg Variations each group of three variations is capped by a canon, while the Quodlibet, a kind of 'generalised canon,' seals the whole cycle. See Boris Katz, 'O kul'turo-logicheskikh aspektakh analiza' [Analysis through the lens of cultural studies] in *Sovetskaya muzyka*, 1 (1978): pp. 37–40. In a way, the thematic canon from the *Musical Offering* and the canonic duets in the *Clavierübung III* serve a similar purpose.
4 In the process of composing a canon, the material of the *proposta* is being transferred to the *risposta* at a certain pitch interval and after a certain time interval. These components affect the subsequent progress of the proposta and limit its counterpoint, one correction inevitably leading to the next,

requiring further corrections in both parts. The challenge is dramatically increased if specific transformations of the material (such as augmentation and/or inversion) are involved, particularly when these are called for beyond and above the shifts in pitch and in time.

5   The first description and analysis of the possible results of such a correction were made by Thomas Baker, 'Bach's Revisions in the Augmentation Canon,' *Current Musicology*, 19 (1975), pp. 67–71.
6   This fact enables the unveiling of the order of composition elements in a canon, and thus distinguishes the compositional manuscript from a copy.
7   In this respect, the preserved fragments of drafts written by J.S. Bach and his son Wilhelm Friedemann are interesting. Several drafts relate to the technique of canon composition. See Peter Wollny, 'Ein Quellenfund in Kiew: Unbekannte Kontrapunktstudien von Johann Sebastian und Wilhelm Friedemann Bach,' in Ulrich Leisinger (ed.) *Bach in Leipzig – Bach und Leipzig*: Konferenzbericht Leipzig, Leipziger Beiträge zur Bach-Forschung, vol. 5 (Hildesheim, 2002), pp. 275–87.
8   It would suffice to transpose the last proposta of the canon theme an octave lower (bars 53–55) and to put the repeat signs in the proper places.
9   See, for example, Hofmann, *NBA KB* VIII/2, p. 44.
10 The reason for the protraction of bar 4 is the last three flats (out of four; the first flat was added later).
11 Since this is a canon in augmentation, each segment in the risposta is double the length of its presentation in the proposta.
12 A manuscript with corrections introduced in the process of copying is usually called a *revision copy* (*Umarbeitungsschrift*).
13 Hofmann, *NBA KB* VIII/2, p. 44 (compare note 9).
14 See note 12. In this particular case the term *revision copy* would not define the size of the correction introduced while copying, which could be anything from two notes to several bars.

9 Toward the Third Version

There are reasons to suggest that the jammed writing in the first half of canon xv was intended to fit it into a given page space (Figure 9.1). Since this is a bipartite canon, its second half should be equal to the first in length, and since the first half occupied less than 12 staves, the whole canon could fit into 24 staves. That succeeding, and assuming that page 39 and page 40 would each be rastered with 24 staves, Bach might still have had at his disposal 36 blank staves. What would these staves be intended for?

The most likely candidate among the pieces composed around this same time is the mirror fugue for two claviers. Indeed, each of its two components, written on P 200/1–2—the *fuga recta* and the *fuga inversa*—occupies exactly 36 staves. It very well may be that Bach planned to write on the available staves so that the *fuga recta* would end at the bottom of page 40. Its mirror, the *fuga inversa*, should begin on page 41, for which manuscript paper would be added.

To consider how many additional manuscript papers were needed, certain information has to be taken into account. A substantial part of Bach studies devoted to his creative process emphasises the careful attention that the composer paid to the organisation of pieces in his composition collections. He regarded as important not only the musical and rational aspects of these works, but also the physical organisation of its material embodiment.

Pairing was an important structural principle in Bach's collections and cycles, and no less so in *The Art of Fugue*, where it is expressed by a sequence of fugue pairs. Schemes 7.1 and 7.2 show how the same principle was applied to the binio-structure of the Autograph's main body. Since it was Bach who chose this particular combination of bifolios,[1] it would be reasonable to assume that he would proceed with the same structural principle and add one more binio, that would result in pages 41–8.

It is also likely that Bach would retain his approach concerning the fugues, and since the pairing principle lies at the core of *The Art of Fugue*, he would probably add a pair of fugues rather than just one. In this case the first fugue was written for two claviers. Therefore, another fugue of the same type was to be expected. According to this way of thinking, Scheme 9.1 would describe the assumed last two binios with their additional pieces and Scheme 9.2—the whole Autograph's hypothetical new plan.

This plan is, of course, just a hypothesis of a possible structure. Its only trace in the Autograph is the exceptionally crammed writing of the first half of canon xv and the assumption that it was written like that in order to fit it all into 24 staves, so that the remaining 36 staves would be available for the next planned piece.

Figure 9.1 P 200: canon xv, written over the spread of pages 38–9; crammed writing on the left page, clear and flowing on the right one.

Page	Type of Piece
33	Canon in Augmentation (end); 1st mirror fugue (beginning)
34	1st mirror fugue (continuation)
35	1st mirror fugue (end)
36	2nd mirror fugue (beginning)
37	2nd mirror fugue (continutation)
38	2nd mirror fugue (end); Canon (beginning)
39	Canon (ending); 1st fugue for two claviers, *rectus*, (beginning)
40	1st fugue for two claviers, *rectus*, (ending)
41	1st fugue for two claviers, *inversus*, (beginning)
42	1st fugue for two claviers, *inversus*, (ending)
43	2nd fugue for two claviers, *rectus*, (beginning)
44	2nd fugue for two claviers, *rectus*, (ending)
45	2nd fugue for two claviers, *inversus*, (beginning)
46	2nd fugue for two claviers, *inversus*, (ending)
47	Canon
48	Blank page

Scheme 9.1 A hypothetical additional binio allows the inclusion of a new pair of mirror fugues for two claviers.

This plan did not materialise; the second half of canon xv is so clearly written in a flowing, relaxed notation, occupying 14 rather than 12 staves, that clearly the intention to leave space for another fugue was abandoned.[2] This probably happened sometime in mid-realisation, and likely for a new compositional idea, so clear and evident in the structural plan, that Bach surely had noticed it.

Schemes 9.3 and 9.4 show how the cycle might have looked after adding the pair of mirror fugues for two claviers. The pieces of the cycle are numbered in the schemes in Roman numerals from I to xv, just like in the Autograph. Three additional numbers—those related to hypothetical insertions—are printed in italics: *xvi, xvii* and *xviii*.

Number *xvi* was assigned to the extant fugue for two claviers, (P 200/1–2). It is marked in italics because in the manuscript it does not carry a serial number. This fugue would follow the canon xv, and it is possible that Bach had planned for it the space of 36 staves in the manuscript.

The second number in italics, *xvii*, indicates a hypothetical second mirror fugue for two claviers that, presumably, would have paired with the extant fugue *xvi*.

Number *xviii* indicates a canon that, following the logic of *The Art of Fugue* and of several other Bach's cycles, would seal the whole work. The numbers that are boxed in Scheme 9.3 indicate canons (marked C_1, C_2, C_3 and C_4, referring respectively to canons IX, XII, XV and *xviii*). The first three canons exist in the Autograph under the very same numeration that appears in the scheme. The fourth is assumed, based on Bach's habit to cap a cycle with a canon.

Does this hypothetical canon actually exist?

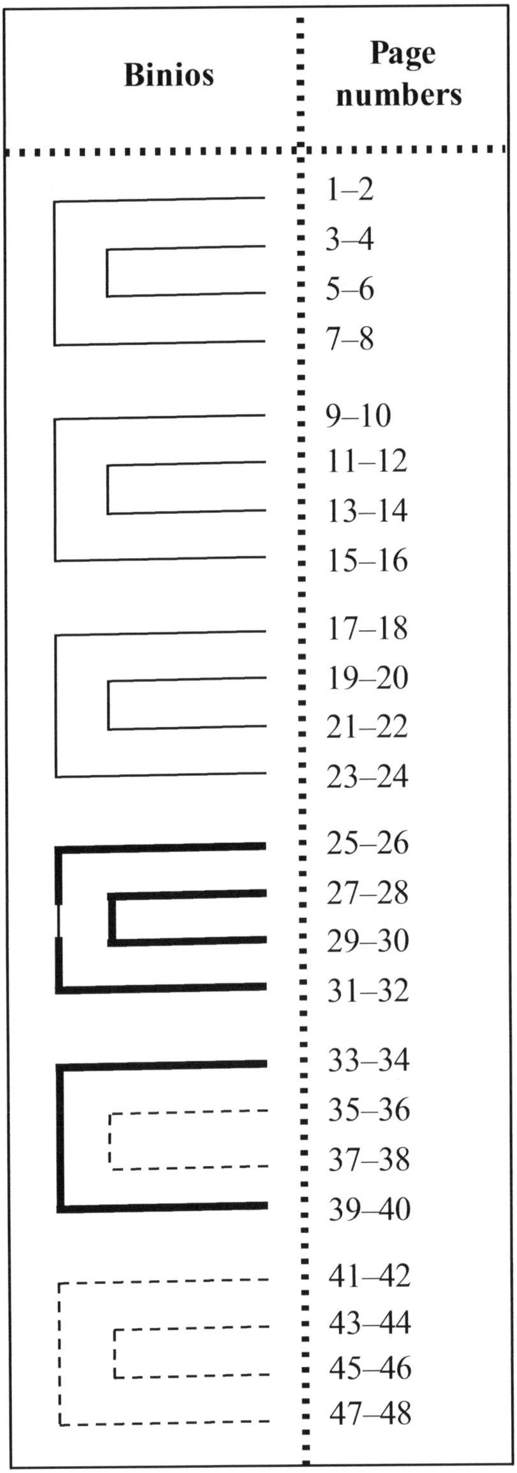

Binios	Page numbers
	1–2
	3–4
	5–6
	7–8
	9–10
	11–12
	13–14
	15–16
	17–18
	19–20
	21–22
	23–24
	25–26
	27–28
	29–30
	31–32
	33–34
	35–36
	37–38
	39–40
	41–42
	43–44
	45–46
	47–48

Scheme 9.2 Hypothetical unrealised plan of the entire Second Version.

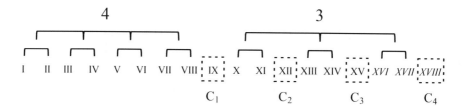

Scheme 9.3 Hypothetical structure of the Autograph, before the creation of the Third Version.

Yes, most probably so. The compositional approach detected in canons XII and XV is consistent: Bach starts to correct the *proposta* of a completed piece but does not transfer the corrections into the *risposta*. Once the melodies of the *proposta* and *risposta* are not identical, the work becomes a draft for a new composition. Thus, the corrections made in canon XII are realised in canon XV, and those marked in the *proposta* of canon XV would be realised in both *proposta* and *risposta* of canon *XVIII*.

Such a correction does exist. It appears in P 200/1–1 and is titled *Canon p[er]. Augmentationem contrario motu*.[3] The fact that this supplement is a canon reinforces the assumption that it was planned as the closing piece of the cycle.

In this new version of the canon Bach continued to develop the corrections even further. What started as a 'memo annotation' in bar 11 of canon XV developed into its realisation in the canon P 200/1–1, proposed here as the planned canon *XVIII*.[4]

In canon XV this correction was marked only in the *proposta*. In P 200/1–1, on the other hand, the correction appears in both the *proposta* and the *risposta*, albeit in a more elaborated variant. Example 9.1 shows the development of this elaboration. For the sake of clarity, the example shows the motif in P 200/1–1 twice: once preserving the rhythmic values of canon XV and once as it appears in the supplement.

Example 9.1 P 200: canons XV and *XVIII*, motivic comparison.

It therefore looks most probable that the canon tentatively marked in Scheme 9.3 as number *XVIII* is actually the one written on P 200/1–1, where it appears as an engraver copy. If, indeed, once becoming 'drafts' the canons marked as XII and XV should not be present in the final work, then the structure of the cycle might be as the one shown in Scheme 9.4. The scheme looks like a simple development of the Second Version. However, the composition described in it does not exist in actuality. In the Autograph, canons XII and XV are present, making *The Art of Fugue* a composition that is both finalised and in the process of becoming.

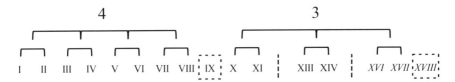

Scheme 9.4 Proposed hypothetical structure of *The Art of Fugue* (without the 'draft' canons).

This scheme presents an image that could not have escaped Bach's attention and which, by providing him with a vision of the final version of *The Art of Fugue*, did motivate him to realise it. Entering the mind of a composer without a factual verification is indeed adventurous, but in order to better understand this masterpiece, it is imperative to conceive what could be the general scheme that the composer had in mind while planning the next stage of the cycle's composition.

The vision: Structure, form and numbers

One significant trait of Bach's multi-partite cycles, especially those consisting of pieces of one type, is their clear tendency to subdivide into two groups, which in a certain sense can be interpreted as pairing on a higher level.[5] This type of subdivision exists in the Inventions and Sinfonias, the Goldberg Variations, the *Clavierübung III* and the Canonic Variations, to name just a few.

Such a division is apparent even in the sheer physical appearance of the planned Autograph; as Scheme 9.2 shows, the expanded manuscript would consist of 12 bifolios, which symmetrically divided the content into two equal parts of six bifolios each. The first part, ending with canon IX, would reflect the earlier First Version; while the second group of bifolios, all on newer paper, would be the result of later thought. The division of six plus six, whether coincidental or planned, had special significance for Bach.[6]

Further, like in others of his bi-partite works, here, too, the second half seems also to reflect a possible realisation of the ascending principle (*Steigerungsprinzip*). Presenting two double fugues and the two mirror fugues for two claviers, it would include compositions that are more complicated than the fugues in the first half, which are relatively simpler.

The number of fugues in each part is significant. Here, however, the division would not be symmetrical, showing eight fugues in the first part and only six in the second. On top of that, Scheme 9.3 shows a first part capped with one canon, while the second seems to include three other canons spread throughout it. However, one should bear in mind that two of the dash-framed canons shown in Scheme 9.3 cannot really partake in the same structure. The last three canons (XII, XV and possibly *XVIII*, which could be the canon of P 200/1–1) are based on one and the same theme: there should be, in fact, just one canon. Following Bach's use of canons to mark the completion of a group of fugues, one would tend to opt for Scheme 9.4 as a more likely structure, featuring only canons IX and *XVIII*.

Alternatively, another possible plan could, in fact, include the four canons. The work now consisted of 14 compositions, the numerical symbol of Bach's name, a number to which he persistently adhered throughout his work on the various versions of *The Art of Fugue*. These 14 compositions, reflecting both the pairing principle and the symbolically significant numeral 7, might allow a double organisation: seven pairs on one hand, and one meta-pair of two groups of seven fugues on the other (both 7 × 2 and 2 × 7). Moreover, the number 7 itself, following Bach's system of numerical signification, should be divided into 4 + 3,[7] which is exactly the division of pairs shown in Scheme 9.4: four pairs of fugues, capped by canon ıx, and three pairs of fugues, capped by a final canon xvııı.

A division of the 14 fugues into two groups of seven each, however, presents a completely new structure (Scheme 9.5).

$$14$$

$$7 + 7$$

$$4+3 \;+\; 4+3$$

$$(+ \text{ conclusion: 4 canons})$$

Scheme 9.5 A hypothetical interpretation of the phrase 'einen andern Grund Plan', scribbled on the verso of the last page of P 200/1 3.

The special symbolic significance that is imbued in seeing the number 14 as a combination of (4 + 3) + (4 + 3) may have been the reason for which Bach considered this particular structure.[8]

The thought of a meta-structure might have led Bach to yet another idea, that of a 'meta-fugue', in which the individual fugues may be seen as statements and the canons as episodes.[9] To actualise such an interpretation, Bach would need to compose one more fugue that would provide an appropriate closure to the whole structure. Eventually, he would do so.

The particulars mentioned here support the view that at the moment in which Bach settled in to write a Third Version, he also decided to abandon the plan to seal the work with the two mirror fugues for two claviers. Therefore, there was no more need of condensed writing in order to save space for another fugue (xvı) that would follow the canon, nor to compose yet one more (xvıı) as its pair.[10] Bach completed the canon with no further plans to add a fugue on that page, eventually recording the fugue on a separate bifolio, which is now known as P 200/1–2.[11]

The new composition required both new structure and new pieces, which would form the Third Version of *The Art of Fugue*.

Notes

1 For example, in the Mass in B minor Bach uses the sequence of 12 binios (12 × 2) for the Kyrie, while in the *Symbolum Nicenum* he combines three quarternio (3 × 4), although he could continue with the same structure as before. These preferences reflect numerical symbolism to which Bach attached particular importance.

2 The music is inscribed on this page with less attention to graphic density, and written more quickly than on page 38. The rastration on this page was done more hastily, too: the staves were drawn in a less accurate way, and their number — 20 instead of 24 in the former page, drawn with no particular calculation — implies, too, that Bach abandoned his previous plan.

3 See note 4 in Chapter 4.

4 This 'memo annotation' is discussed in Chapter 8.

5 See Kira Yuzhak, 'O prodvigayushchey i svertyvayushchey tendentsiakh v Iskusstve fugi: "Alio Modo" i parnost' vysshego poryadka' [Expanding and contracting tendencies in *The Art of Fuge*: "Alio Modo" and the pairing of the highest order], in K. Yuzhak, *Polifoniya i kontrapunkt*. vol. 1, (St Petersburg, 2006), pp. 165–94.

6 Quite often Bach organises compositions within his collections or cycles in groups of six. This is not coincidental or whimsical. One of the many reasons that this number was chosen is that it was the first of the so-called perfect numbers (*perfectus primus*). Another reason is that it rounds the first number series in the senary numerical system; besides, it also has a special symbolic significance in the Pythagorean system of thought, admired by the Society of Music Sciences members. Finally, its combinatorial properties and convenience in modeling a composition (3×2 or 2×3, that is, the organisation of three two-piece pairs or one 'meta-pair' with three pieces in each) provided flexible opportunities of compositional organisation. For a more detailed account see Anatoly Milka, 'Bakhovskie "shestërki": Printsip organizatsii bakhovskikh sbornikov v kontekste osobennostei barokko' [Bach's 'cycles of six': the organisation principle of Bach's collections in the context of baroque characteristics], in *Muzykal'naya kommunikatsia*, Seria Problemy muzykoznaniia, vol. 8, (St Petersburg, 1999), pp. 220–38.

7 The first to present such structure was Olga Kurtch, 'Ot pomet kopiistov — k strukture tsikla Iskusstvo fugi' [From scribes' annotations — to the structure of *The Art of Fugue*] in Anatoly Milka (ed.) *Vtorye Bakhovskie chtenia: 'Iskusstvo fugi'* (St Petersburg, 1993), pp. 83–4. Fifteen years later Gregory Butler confirmed this hypothesis: Gregory Butler, 'Scribes, Engravers and Notation Styles: The Final Disposition of Bach's Art of Fugue,' in Gregory Butler, George B. Stauffer and Mary Dalton Greer (eds.), *About Bach* (Urbana and Chicago, 2008), p. 120.

8 The significance of the particular division of the number 7 into 4 + 3 is explained and discussed in Chapter 20.

9 The analogy between *The Art of Fugue*'s structure and the idea of a 'meta-fugue' had been first promulgated by Philipp Spitta, *Johann Sebastian Bach*, vol. 2 (Leipzig, 1880), pp. 682–3.

10 The assumption that Bach dropped his initial decision to connect the fugue for two claviers (XVI) with the canon XVIII is supported by his writing it on a separate bifolio. It is important to bear in mind that making a decision and later abandoning it represent two separate stages. If Bach had not initially intended to place the fugue for two claviers on pages 39–40, there would be no need for the congested writing on page 38. Equally, had he not made up his mind to abandon that idea, the inscription's characteristics on page 39 would not be so different from those of page 38.

11 The bifolio was cut into two halves and brought in that form to the Berlin Royal Library later on, in 1841. Until then the fugue for two claviers was an inseparable part of *The Art of Fugue*, as confirmed by the inscription in the left bottom corner, written, as Klaus Hofmann suggests, by J.S. Bach himself: 'eigentlichen Originalhandschrift vermerkt (*11 B.*)'. Hofmann, *NBA KB* VIII/2, p. 22. If indeed this is the case, the composer himself established the pertinence of the fugue for two claviers (at least of this particular manuscript) to *The Art of Fugue*.

10 The Third Version

Indications of a Third Version in P 200[1]

The new version offered a completely new outlook on the cycle, requiring the realisation of a fugue sequence structured as (4 + 3) + (4 + 3) and supplemented by four additional canons.[2] This structure differs significantly from the one shown on Schemes 9.3 and 9.4. Most importantly, it breaks, at least in part, the pairing principle developed in the First and Second Versions. Thus, while the numerical expression of Bach's name, the number 14, does play a decisive role in the cycle's structure, the Third Version includes a total of 14 individual fugues *without* counting in the four canons. Allegedly, an alternative positioning of the canons could be considered, in a way more similar to the former model, distributing them among the fugue groups (Scheme 10.1, top). This structure would agree with Spitta's idea of a meta-fugue.[3] However, it did not happen. The final version of the composition, presented in the first printed edition, suggests that Bach decided to group the four canons at the end of the cycle (Scheme 10.1, middle). A group of 14 fugues, then, constitutes the main body of the cycle.[4]

$$4 + C + 3 + C + 4 + C + 3 + C$$

$$\underset{\text{FUGUES}}{(4+3+4+3)} + \underset{\text{CANONS}}{4}$$

$$\underbrace{1\ 2\ 3\ 4}_{4}\ \underbrace{5\ 6\ 7}_{3}\ \underbrace{8\ 9\ 10\ 11}_{4}\ \underbrace{12\ 13\ 14}_{3}$$

Scheme 10.1 The Third Version of *The Art of Fugue*: structural options and solutions. Top: optional model — fugue groups alternating with individual canons; middle: structure of the Third Version — 14 fugues and four canons; bottom: the Third Version — fugue groups organisation.

The fugues of the cycle are organised in two structurally identical halves, a pair of 7 + 7 fugues. To make this new division more persuasive, the resemblance between the new pair of components needed to be highlighted, so that the correspondence is expressed not just in their sheer numerical subdivision into 4 + 3 but in other properties, too. Bach's next steps served this purpose.

Based on the composer's vein of thought and the two former versions of *The Art of Fugue*, present in the Autograph, each group of four and of three fugues will be examined separately.

Fugues 1–4

Promoting in part Spitta's perception of the cycle's structure as a meta-fugue, the first four fugues could be looked upon as a meta-exposition, in which each one of the fugues is regarded as an entry stating the theme. Obviously, each should present the theme in its basic form (the first four notes as half notes).

However, only the three first fugues of the Autograph comply with this description: they are simple and present the main subject of the collection in its original form, while all the subsequent fugues present thematic variants that include passing notes and other figurations. Further, in each of these first three fugues the theme is first stated by another part: the alto presents the theme in fugue I; the tenor opens fugue II with the inverted theme; the bass opens fugue III, again with the main theme. An expected fourth fugue would thus open with the treble, stating the inverted theme. It should also be a simple fugue, presenting the theme with no ornamentation or additional figurations.

There is no such fugue in the Autograph. It does appear, however, as Contrapunctus 4 in the Original Edition of *The Art of Fugue*.[5] Bach composed it especially for the Third Version, moreover, with precisely all the expected parameters. It is a simple fugue; its theme, introduced in the treble voice, is presented in inversion but without any ornamentation (Example 10.1).

Example 10.1 Beginning of Contrapunctus 4 in the Original Edition.

The new structure, presented in the Third Version, shows both its affinity to the first two versions (which are realised in the Autograph) and the features in which it differs from them.[6] The top of the scheme shows the first pair of the two simple fugues, composed on the original and the inverted themes. The third and fourth fugues present a similar structural unit. Bach's subsequent actions would aim to move away from a 'two pairs' structure, integrating instead the four fugues so that they form a cohesive group.

The musical theme of the collection creates a basic, general similarity among all its fugues. To mark a group of fugues within this collection as an interconnected unit, Bach resorted to parameters of contrast. The most obvious contrasts among the first four fugues are the theme inversions. To highlight these, the composer exchanged the position of fugues II and III, weakening the link of the initial pair I–II and creating instead a strongly interrelated set of four, shown at the centre of Scheme 10.2.[7] The cohesion of this new set is now based, on one hand, on the contrast between the two fugues that present the theme in its original form and the two that present its inversion, and on the other hand on the simulacrum to an exposition of a meta-fugue, where each fugue introduces the theme in a different part: alto, bass, tenor and treble. This first quartette, created by the addition of a new fugue and the repositioning of pre-existing ones, can be seen at the bottom of Scheme 10.2.

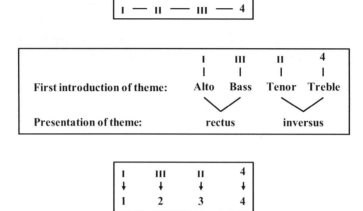

Scheme 10.2 The first set of four fugues. Top: adding a new fugue (number 4); centre: repositioning fugues II and III to create an interlocked set of four; bottom: the resulting set renumbered 1–4.

Bach addressed a specific trait in the resulting set of four fugues. Fugue III (number 2 in the Third Version) is the only one in the first two versions that ends on a half-cadence, a very unusual ending for any independent piece. Bach's decision to use such a cadence in the first two versions was intended to connect fugue III to fugue IV, since these two fugues did not gravitate toward each other as the other pairs did (see Example 7.2).[8] The half-cadence at the end of fugue III would compensate for this shortcoming, creating an expectation for continuity, thus leading toward fugue IV. In the Third Version, however, there was no more need for this half-cadence, since the pair III–IV disappeared. The new fugue, number 4, replaced fugue IV, and fugues II and III interchanged positions. Consequently, fugue III (now numbered 2) rather than calling for continuation, closed a pair, and the half-cadence was replaced by an authentic one.

The scheme of the first set of fugues in the Third Version, thus, presents four simple fugues, in which the pair 1–2, where the theme is presented in its original form, contrasts the pair 3–4, where the theme is inverted. Each of the four fugues starts on a different voice (Table 10.1).

Table 10.1 The first set of four fugues in the Third Version

Fugue's serial number in the Third Version	Presentation of theme	Part first presenting the theme	Type of fugue
1	rectus	alto	simple
2	rectus	bass	simple
3	inversus	tenor	simple
4	inversus	treble	simple

Fugues 5–7

The second group in the Third Version of *The Art of Fugue* is a set of three fugues. To form it, Bach combined the stretto fugue IV, which in the first two versions belonged to the second pair, with the pair of stretto fugues VII and VIII, creating a group of the three stretto fugues on positions 5, 6 and 7 respectively, ordered in increasing complexity. Fugue IV is a stretto fugue in inversion with no diminution or augmentation. Next comes fugue VII, which is inverted with diminution, and last is fugue VIII, based on double augmentation[9] (Table 10.2).

Table 10.2 The first set of three fugues in the Third Version

Serial number in the Third Version	Serial number in the Autograph	Presentation of the theme	Ornamentation of the theme	Type of fugue
5	IV	inversus	ornamented	Stretto in inversion
6	VII	rectus	ornamented	Stretto in inversion and diminution
7	VIII	rectus	ornamented	Stretto in inversion and augmentation

Table 10.2 shows one more detail: fugues VII and VIII are based on the *original* theme, giving the impression that in this particular pair Bach transgressed the principle, otherwise strictly observed by him, that requires a pair of fugues to be joined by contrasting forms of the theme. Example 10.2, which presents the initial bars of both fugues, shows, however, that this principle is, in fact, closely followed.

Example 10.2 The first bars of fugues VII and VIII.

While the first appearance of the theme is indeed related to its original presentation (that is, opening with an ascending fifth), the immediate answer, in both cases, is its inversion. Further, the theme in the lower part of fugue VIII is, in fact, the inversion of its dotted, inverted form in the top part of fugue VII. Indeed, the most visible contrast here is the diminution—the theme's rhythmic appearance and its position within the texture of the fugues.[10] A comparison between the positions in which the theme in diminution appears in the initial strettos of both fugues and the positions of the augmented theme shows an opposite result (Tables 10.3 and 10.4). Thus, the principle of opposition is realised in the stretto fugues not only in their theme presentations and in their types but in their initial stretto constructions, too.

Table 10.3 The first appearance of the theme in diminution in fugues VII and VIII

Fugue	Function of the first appearance of the diminution	The part in which the first diminution appears	Presentation of the theme
VII	risposta	top	inversus
VIII	proposta	bottom	rectus

Table 10.4 The first appearance of the theme in augmentation in fugues VII and VIII

Fugue	Function of the first appearance of the augmentation	The part in which the first augmentation appears	Presentation of the theme
VII	proposta	bottom	rectus
VIII	risposta	top	inversus

Fugues 8–11

The second set of four fugues in the Third Version was meant to consist of double fugues. The most suitable double fugues in the Autograph are X and XI. Fugue V, on a cantus firmus, which has two themes, would fit here, too.[11] The set of four fugues is thus short of one double fugue. No other fugues of this type were available in the Autograph. One possible solution would be to compose a new fugue, as Bach did for the first set of four. Instead, he remodelled fugue VI—a simple fugue with a consistent countersubject—into a double one. Upgrading the status of the consistent countersubject into a main subject, he composed a new exposition and inserted it at the very beginning of the fugue. In this way the consistent countersubject becomes its first subject, its exposition preceding the original beginning of fugue VI. There are no further changes in this fugue. The second set of four fugues is presented in Table 10.5.

Table 10.5 The second set of four, based on double fugues

Serial number of the fugue in the Third Version	Serial number of the fugue in the Autograph	Presentation of the theme	Style of the theme	Type of fugue
8	X	inversus	Hocketus	double
9	V	rectus	Cantus firmus	'double'
10	VI (modified)	inversus	ornamented	double
11	XI	rectus	Hocketus	double

The process of formation of the second set of four fugues was similar to that of the first one: Bach revised and remodelled one of the fugues and changed the order of the other three. Following the logic that lies at the foundation of this cycle, the permutation of these fugues served two purposes: to deconstruct the solid fugue pair x–xi and to ensure the alternation of original and inverted theme presentations. As in the first set, these steps were taken in order to weaken the perception of these fugues as a pair and to highlight instead the cohesion of the four as an integrated group.

Fugues 12–14

The last triad of fugues was present in the Autogaph and did not require any additional actions for its organisation. These are the three mirror fugues. The first two were fugues xiii and xiv in P 200. The fugue for two claviers to which the serial number *xvi* was assigned, when discussing the Second Version, was put into this group but deserves a special discussion.[12]

In Bach studies, starting from Philipp Spitta's description, fugue *xvi* always appears as a 'setting' or an 'arrangement'[13] of fugue xiv and is therefore usually removed from *The Art of Fugue*. There are many reasons to support such an opinion. The chief one was the fact that the material of fugue *xiv* (Contrapunctus a 3 rectus and inversus, pp. 41–4 in the Original Edition) was fully used for fugue *xvi*. The first to draw attention to this fact were Robert Schumann and the librarians of the Berlin Royal Library.[14] Since then, the perception of the fugue for two claviers as an arrangement, disconnected from *The Art of Fugue*, reappeares regularly to this day, and there is hardly any study expressing doubt on this account.

Such an attitude would be justified if *The Art of Fugue*, as a cycle, were intended for performance on the concert stage. In such a case, the repetition of musical material, even as a different type of fugue, might create certain monotony and be ineffective. However, just like *The Well-Tempered Clavier*, the Clavierübungen, Inventions and Sinfonias and some other collections and cycles, *The Art of Fugue* was not composed for concert performance. All Bach's contemporaries, and especially Philipp Emanuel, described it as a kind of manual for composition, a practical guide for writing fugues.

The fugue for two claviers (*xvi*) demonstrates a new composition technique and an additional type of fugue, which had not yet been featured in the cycle: a fugue with an accompaniment. Fitting it into the cycle, Bach proved that practically any imitational form—a fugue or a canon—could be composed with or without an accompaniment. There are other such examples in Bach's own output, several in the *Musical Offering* (the Fuga canonica, two fugues in the sonata, and the Canon perpetuus) or the fugue *Allein Gott in der Höh sei Ehr* (BWV 676) from the *Clavierübung III*.

An accompaniment could be of various types: one melodic line, as in the Fuga canonica or in BWV 676; several voices; a chordal harmonic support or a figured bass that a cembalo player would extemporise (for example, in the fugues of the *Musical Offering*). In doing this, Bach demonstrates a certain kind of counterpoint originating in cantus firmus technique: composition of new counterpoint to an already existing melody (or melodies), applied here into the major-minor system. The fugue is first presented as a contrapuntal structure in its purest form, without any accompaning voices; then the text moves to a derivative combination: the same fugue with new contrapuntal voices, some of which act as accompaniment. This is the reason for which the second clavier was introduced.[15]

The opinion that this fugue belongs to The Art of Fugue is indirectly supported by the fact that, being technically more complex than the preceding one, it complies with the 'ascending complexity' principle, which is one of the cycle's main characteristics.

Earlier we considered Bach's intention to fit this fugue in a given space, next to canon xv (see Scheme 9.3). Later, so it seems—probably as a result of a new idea—he wrote the fugue on a separate bifolio. It is unlikely that Bach would write into the Autograph of The Art of Fugue an arrangement that he did not intend to include in the cycle. On top of that, the paper type, on which the fugue was written, is the same one used for the previous mirror fugues (XIII and XIV). The size and dynamics of the handwritten notes, the ink and the rastration are absolutely identical to the two previous fugues. All this indicates that they were written during the same period of time and with the same purpose.[16]

This can be confirmed by other factors, too. Initially, the fugue was written on a separate bifolio. Eventually, the double sheet was cut in two and in this form deposited in the Berlin Royal Library. Until then, the fugue for two claviers was an integral part of the Autograph as evidenced by the manuscript's features. The inscription '*eigentlichen Originalhandschrift vermerkt (11 B.)*' on the right bottom corner of the title page (see Figure 4.7), made by J.S. Bach, as Klaus Hofmann thinks, also supports this notion.[17] This inscription indicates that the whole set of music sheets that formed part of the Autograph's main corpus consisted of 11 bifolios. Consequently, the double sheet with the fugue for two claviers (*XVI*), which coincides precisely with all the material characteristics of the 11th bifolio, should be considered part of the collection. Moreover, if Hofmann's notion is correct, and the discussed inscription was indeed the composer's own, then the pertinence of the fugue for two claviers to this cycle was designated by J.S. Bach himself, and its exclusion from the whole happened only as late as 1841, in the Royal Berlin Library.[18]

Permutations, permutations, permutations…

The exclusion of this bifolio from the manuscript, though seemingly solving the repetition of materials in fugues XIV and *XVI*, created new questions. For example, the function of this mirror fugue, separate from The Art of Fugue, becomes unclear and quite problematic: why would Bach use the modified theme from this cycle for an instrumental ensemble (two claviers without accompaniment), which he had never used for any independent pieces? Besides, it is hard to believe that while working on such a grandiose project as The Art of Fugue, Bach would engage in arranging and clean copying a fugue that he did not intend to include in the cycle. It does make sense that this fugue is not leftover 'refuse' but an actual, integral part of the great work.

A short discussion of mirror fugues may be in order here. Deciding whether the first presentation of a theme in a mirror fugue is in prime or inverted position is impossible, unless some artificial labelling is imposed, simply to facilitate discussion of these pieces and a better understanding of their organisation in the cycle.

Two mirror fugues appear in the Autograph, numbered there as XIII and XIV; the third is the mirror fugue for two claviers, written on P 200/1–2. The two mirror fugues in the

Table 10.6 The mirror fugues defined by theme presentation

Autograph mark	Autograph pages	Autograph system	Recta or inversa	Opening theme	Theme presentation
XIII	33–5	top	XIII$_1$		**rectus**
XIII	33–5	bottom	XIII$_2$		inversus
XIV	36–8	top	XIV$_1$		**inversus**
XIV	36–8	bottom	XIV$_2$		rectus
Two claviers	Supplement 2	Folio 20	*XVI*$_1$		**rectus**
Two claviers	Supplement 2	Folio 21	*XVI*$_2$		inversus

Autograph's main body, numbered XIII and XIV, are written in double systems, one above the other, each member visually mirroring its companion fugue. Since each one of these fugues is, actually, two fugues, they will be individually labelled XIII$_1$, XIII$_2$, XIV$_1$ and XIV$_2$. The fugues written on the top systems are thus marked XIII$_1$ and XIV$_1$ and are regarded as the two recta fugues. The two fugues on the bottom systems are marked, accordingly, XIII$_2$ and XIV$_2$ and regarded as the inversae fugues. The importance of this differentiation will become apparent in the Original Edition, where rather than one above the other, as in the Autograph, the fugues are printed one after the other. Here, the presentation of the theme in the fugue positioned first in a pair will define the subject as rectus or inversus *for the pair*.

The third mirror fugue, written for two claviers and marked in this discussion as XVI, poses a difficulty. Here the two mirror fugues were not written one above the other, but on a bifolio, which was torn in the middle into two folios (P 200/1–2), one fugue on each folio. Here there is not even an implied hierarchy of a 'top system' versus a 'bottom system'. However, the two folios were marked as '20' and '21', which will be respectively substituted, when this fugue is under discussion, with the markings 'XVI$_1$' and 'XVI$_2$', regarding XVI$_1$ as the recta of this pair.

Thus, the mirror fugues, as presented in the Autograph and their internal hierarchy defined, can be described as in Table 10.6.

This set of three mirror fugues, after having been adopted into the Third Version in chronological order, introduces yet another unifying element: all three fugues allude to dance topics, a first such reference in the cycle (Table 10.7).

It is unlikely, however, that Bach would leave the group as in Table 10.7. The fugues in positions 13 and 14 share the same theme and, in fact, are constructed identically. The main difference is that the second among them has an additional accompaniment (the contrapuntal part). Thus, the fugue in position 13 presents an initial composition, and the one in position 14 its derivative. In this aspect, these two fugues are correctly positioned, since they demonstrate a gradual increase of contrapuntal complexity, which is a main didactic principle in *The Art of Fugue*. Nevertheless, Bach could not ignore the motivic repetition in adjacent parts of

Table 10.7 The second set of three: mirror fugues (initial variant)

Serial number in the Third Version	Serial number in the Autograph	Presentation of theme	Genre	Type of fugue
12	XIII	rectus	Sarabande	mirror
13	XIV	inversus	Gigue	mirror
14	XVI	rectus (?)	Gigue	mirror

Table 10.8 The second variant of the set of three mirror fugues

Serial number in the Third Version	Serial number in the Autograph	Presentation of theme	Genre	Type of fugue
12	XIV	inversus	Gigue	mirror
13	XIII	rectus	Sarabande	mirror
14	XVI	rectus (?)	Gigue	mirror

the cycle. However, there was no way to get around this problem, since the repeated musical material is here ingrained in the composition itself.

While Bach could renounce this fugue and thus avoid repetition, such a step would prevent him from presenting a more complex type of counterpoint, which was one of his two most important principles of composition. Another option would be to somehow diminish the perception of repetition by reordering the fugues' dance topics, creating a slightly more diversified scheme (see Table 10.8).

The canons in the Third Version

The Art of Fugue should be concluded, according to its Third Version, with a group of four canons. Two of them—the Canon in Octave (*Canon in Hypodiapason*) and the Canon in Augmentation (*Canon in Hypodiateßeron. al roversio e per augmentationem, Perpetuus*), already exist: they occupy positions ix and xv in the Autograph. Bach composes two additional canons, built on the intervals of 10th and 12th, respectively. The order of their presentation requires inspection.

There are several organising criteria according to which a series of canons could be ordered. One criterion would be their sequencing by the interval in which the voices are introduced, starting from the smallest interval. Another criterion would adhere to degrees of sophistication, starting from simple counterpoint and proceeding to more complex forms. The four canons that Bach wanted to introduce into *The Art of Fugue* show that these two criteria were inconsistently applied.

Presenting the canons in the order in which they might have been composed is tentative at best. There is no doubt regarding the chronology, reflected in the Autograph, of the first two canons. However, the Autograph of the remaining two canons is lost, and therefore they are recorded here in the order they appear in the Original Edition. In fact, this order seems to follow the ascending complexity principle, having the simple counterpoint canon being followed by three canons in double counterpoint. These last three are sequenced according to an ascending interval size: octave, 10th and 12th (Table 10.9).

This order is consistent with tradition and coincides with the ways in which most common types of counterpoint are described in treatises known to Bach.[19]

The logic in this order is highlighted by the title of the Canon in Augmentation, explicitly stating that it is written in counterpoint of an octave. Bach's special indication of this fact is confirmed by Johann Christoph Friedrich Bach's note at the top of the first page of P 200/1–1, where the canon was inscribed: 'Der seel. Papa hat auf die Platte diesen Titul stechen laßen *Canon / per Augment: in Contrapuncto all octava*, er hat es aber wieder / ausgestrichen auf der Probe Platte und gesetzet wie forn stehet'.[20] The 'as follows' states: *Canon p[er] Augmentationem contrario motu* [Canon in Augmentation and Inversion]. Bach's original title, therefore, did specify the counterpoint at an octave in the canon's title. This may explain why one variant of the canons' organisation was the one presented in Table 10.9.

Still, there was one more detail that Bach might have found unsatisfactory: following intervallic order, the Canon in Augmentation and Inversion is positioned here second, while usually the composer would have preferred to position such a complex canon at the very end.[21]

The difference in the author's view of these two canons becomes clear when noticing that, while the first canon in Table 10.9 is titled after its entry interval (the octave), the title of the second describes its type of counterpoint (in augmentation and inversion).

Table 10.9 Ordering of canons in the Third Version (first variant)

Title of canon in the Third Version	Title of canon in the Second Version	Interval of the second part entry	Type of counterpoint	Theme transformations in the risposta
Canon alla Ottava	Canon in Hypodiapason	lower octave	simple	without change
Canon al roverscio et per augmentationem	Canon in Hypodiateßeron al roversio e per augmentationem, perpetuus	lower fourth	double counterpoint at the octave	augmented and inverted
Canon alla Decima. Contrapunto alla Terza		upper tenth	double counterpoint at the tenth	without change
Canon alla Duodecima in Contrapunto alla Quinta		upper twelfth	double counterpoint at the twelfth	without change

The titles of the two remaining canons in this group indicate both the entry interval and the type of counterpoint: *Canon alla Decima Contrapunto alla Terza*, and *Canon alla Duodecima in Contrapunto alla Quinta*. Moreover, the name of the entry interval coincides with the type of counterpoint. This double criteria (by type and by interval) of classification allowed ordering manipulations. Johann Christoph Friedrich's inscription reflects Bach's indecisiveness concerning the classification principle and the canons' sequence. A hypothetical order that follows exclusively the ascending entry interval principle (fourth–octave–tenth–twelfth) is shown in Table 10.10.

Table 10.10 Organisation of the canons by an increasing entry interval

Title of canon in the Third Version	Title of canon in the Second Version	Interval of the second part entry	Type of counterpoint	Theme transformations in the risposta
Canon al roverscio et per augmentationem	Canon in Hypodiateßeron al roversio e per augmentationem, perpetuus	lower fourth	double counterpoint at the octave	augmented and inverted
Canon alla Ottava	Canon in Hypodiapason	lower octave	simple	without change
Canon alla Decima. Contrapunto alla Terza		upper tenth	double counterpoint at the tenth	without change
Canon alla Duodecima in Contrapunto alla Quinta		upper twelfth	double counterpoint at the twelfth	without change

However, this organisation does not allow for the ascending complexity principle to be followed, given that the most complicated canon is now located at the beginning of the group sequence (instead of at its end), while the simple canon is occupying the second place (instead of being at the beginning, as in Table 10.10). Table 10.11 shows that Bach then moved the Canon in Augmentation and Inversion to the last position, to better comply with his ascending complexity criterion.

In fact, this step may have accommodated the entry interval principle, too, given that the entry interval of a fourth is now below the main line, rather than above it. Most Bach studies agree that this is, most likely, the final order intended by the composer.[22]

Nevertheless, the order in which these canons actually appear in the Original Edition follows, unexpectedly, the one presented in Table 10.10.[23]

The inscription that Johann Christoph Friedrich Bach wrote on P 200/1–1 leads to several key inferences:

- It ascertains that the Third Version of *The Art of Fugue* was the one that had been sent by Johann Sebastian to the engraver.
- It confirms that Bach received the proofs and was able to insert his corrections in them.
- If the engraving followed the order of the print, from the beginning of the cycle to its end,[24] the inscription could serve as proof that with the revision of the Canon in Augmentation and Inversion, as written on P 200/1–1, J.S. Bach had finished the engraving proofreading of the whole *Art of Fugue* in its Third Version.
- In such a case there would be grounds to suggest that this version was not only wholly prepared—with a full set of clean engraver copies—but even existed as proof copies, which Bach revised.

Table 10.11 Final organisation of the canons in the Third Version

Title of canon in the Third Version	Title of canon in the Second Version	Interval of the second part entry	Type of counterpoint	Theme transformations in the risposta
Canon alla Ottava	Canon in Hypodiapason	lower octave	Simple	without change
Canon alla Decima. Contrapunto alla Terza		upper tenth	double counterpoint at the tenth	without change
Canon alla Duodecima in Contrapunto alla Quinta		upper twelfth	double counterpoint at the twelfth	without change
Canon al roverscio et per augmentationem	Canon in Hypodiateßeron al roversio e per augmentationem, perpetuus	lower fourth	double counterpoint at the octave	augmented and inverted

The Third Version in print?

The Third Version was not published, although Bach did prepare it for publication and visualised its printed edition.

How was the Third Version supposed to look in print? As the analysis of the Autograph shows, Bach did not finalise it, although he did make several attempts to that end, as betrayed by the Canon in Augmentation on pages 38–9 of the Autograph.[25]

All the facts point to this canon's second part (on p. 39) concluding the composer's work on the five binios folder that constituted the main body of P 200 and left it at that. As it stands, the Autograph holds the First and Second Versions, and it also served as a draft for the Third Version.[26]

The accomplishment of the Third Version required the reworking of several pieces,[27] permutation of others[28] and composition of new ones.[29] Bach could not use P 200 for the new composition, into which the Third Version eventually turned. It is only natural that the folder's structure of the Third Version would turn out to be completely different from the first two.

It seems reasonable to regard the fugue for two claviers (P 200/1–2) as the only evidence left of a once existent Third Version's folder. The fact that this fugue is written on a separate bifolio (despite the apparent initial intention to start it on the middle of page 39 in the Autograph), shows that at that point, with the new idea of the cycle, Bach dropped the principle of continuous inscription, where each piece may begin at any position on a page. From the Third Version onwards he maintains another principle, according to which every piece is written separately, starting at the top of the page. Such an approach to the performance of permutations—and there were quite a few of them—became easily operable.

Indeed, starting from Contrapunctus 12, as the first mirror fugue is called in the Original Edition, every piece (the three mirror fugues and the four canons) is written on two pages, or more precisely—and eventually—on one page spread.[30]

The sequence of pieces in the Third Version and their provisional order on the printed pages is presented in Scheme 10.3.

It is interesting to note that the two mirror fugues in the positions 12 and 13 (XIII and XIV in the Autograph) are not organised in consecutive order. The order in the Original Edition is inverted: 12_2, 12_1, 13_2 and 13_1. It is unclear why would Bach choose to do it this way, but it is possible that he decided to start with an inverted theme as a contrast to Contrapunctus 11, which was based on the theme's rectus presentation, or to create contrast with the new fugue that will replace XVI in the Fourth Version. However, it is clear that this reordering required a considerable process of repagination.[31] The pagination, as it appears in Scheme 10.3, can only be assumed, since in reality it could have been just a collection of pieces in engraver copies (*Abklatschvorlagen*) and in proofs (*Probe Platten*); it is reasonable to assume that they were printed. After all, both the engraver copies and the proofs did exist in reality. The printouts, made from the engraver copies of the Third Version, are present in the Original Edition of 1751 and 1752. As for the proofs, the *Nota Bene* by J.C.F. Bach on the first page of the Canon in Augmentation does imply that J.S. Bach revised them.

The proofs

The first to call attention to the proofs created in the process of Bach's publications was probably John Alexander Fuller-Maitland, in his study of the *Clavierübung II*, which is

BWV 1080	Work group	Work titles	Pagination
1	⎫	*Contrapunctus 1.*	1–2
2	⎬	*Contrapunctus 2.*	3–5
3	⎬	*Contrapunctus 3*	6–8 (sys. 1)
4	⎭	*Contrapunctus 4*	8–12 (sys. 2–3)
5	⎫	*Contrapunctur 5.*	13–15
6	⎬	*Contrapunctus 6. a 4 in Stylo Francese*	16–18
7	⎭	*Contrapunctus 7. a 4. per Augment et Diminut:*	19–21 (sys.1)
8	⎫	*Contrapunctus 8. a 3*	21–25 (sys. 2–3)
9	⎬	*Contrapunctus 9. a 4. alla Duodecima*	26–28
10	⎬	*Contrapunctus 10. a. 4. alla Decima*	29–31
11	⎭	*Contrapunctus. 11. a 4.*	32–36
12$_2$	⎫	*Contrapunctus inversus. 12 á 4.*	37–38
12$_1$	⎬	*Contrapunctus inversus a 4*	39–40
13$_2$	⎬	*Contrapunctus a 3*	41–42
13$_1$	⎬	*Contrapunctus inversus a 3.*	43–44
18$_1$	⎬	*Fuga a 2. Clav:*	45–46
18$_2$	⎭	*Alio modo. Fuga a 2. Clav.*	47–48
15	⎫	*Canon alla Ottava.*	49–50
16	⎬	*Canon alla Decima Contrapunto alla Terza*	51–52
17	⎬	*Canon alla Duodecima in Contrapunto alla Quinta*	53–54
14	⎭	*Canon per Augmentationem in Contrario Motu*	55–57

Scheme 10.3 The order of pieces in the Third Version.

kept at the British Library in London. Fuller-Maitland identified one of them (shelfmark K.8.g.7) as a set of proofs: 'a close comparison of this with the second state of the publication makes it clear that this copy of the first state was used by the composer as a set of proof sheets.'[32] Fuller-Maitland, however, did not ask whether the set he was studying was a preliminarily printout, before the main run, or if Bach simply used one of the final copies from the run.

Decades later, in 1990, Gregory Butler discussed a similar problem while studying materials from the original edition of *Clavierübung III*.[33] He drew attention to two printed copies of this work, which are referred to as A7 and A15 in Manfred Tessmer's study.[34] Tessmer, however, did not identify these documents as proofs. The first to do that was Butler, after a meticulous analysis of both sources and their comparison with other preserved copies. The edition proofs of the part of A7 that was printed in Leipzig (marked by Butler as 'L') were poorly printed on a paper of low quality and of three different types, and this in contrast to the main run, the print quality of which was much higher, the paper of good quality and of one type. Butler describes this set:

> Physically, L in A7 presents a striking contrast to its counterpart in all of the other nineteen exemplars of the print. The pages are covered with creases, blots, and streaks of printer's ink, and overall present a very messy appearance. Also, in some cases, there are multiple impressions, which create a blurred effect.[35]

Butler also draws conclusions from these documents: 'Its unsightly appearance and the poor quality of the paper would further suggest that L in A7 was a proof copy of the section printed in Leipzig'.[36]

However, the proof pages in A7, printed in Nuremberg, were of the same kind of paper as the main run. Nevertheless, they belong to A7, which, in Butler's view, 'remained in Bach's possession until his death'.[37] If this is the case, it means that any sort of paper could be used for proofs prior to printing the main run.

Another source considered by Butler to be a set of proofs is encoded as A15. It carries no corrections and is printed on a high quality paper: 19 sheets on the same paper that was used for the main run of the *Musical Offering* (BWV 1079), eight sheets on the paper of the Leipzig portion of the *Clavierübung III*'s main run and the remaining 13 on the paper of the Nuremberg portion of the same run.

The situation with *The Art of Fugue* seems more complicated, because the only documented evidence for the existence of proofs for this work is Johann Christoph Friedrich's *Nota Bene* on the first page of the engraver copy of the Canon in Augmentation (P 200/1–1). Strictly saying, it is only this particular canon that is mentioned in the *Nota Bene*. This might be the reason nobody ever discussed proof sheets (in plural) in regard to *The Art of Fugue*. In this case, it is assumed by default that one can safely talk only about a single proof sheet.

There is more indirect evidence, besides J.C.F. Bach's note, of the existence of proofs. It does not coincide with the notion of one single proof sheet. The distance between Leipzig, where Bach lived, and Zella, where the engraver resided, is more than 200 km, with part of the way, after Arnstadt, through the difficult path of Thuringia's forested mountains.

The communication in Bach's times—either by post or by personal travel—was possible but still far from easy. In such conditions, organising the delivery of the single Canon in Augmentation's proof copy or, even worse, sending the proofs one by one, would hardly be cost effective.

It is unlikely that the Canon in Augmentation was the sole piece to be printed for proof reading. What would be the special need for a proof copy of this piece, specifically, to be checked by Bach? Taking into account the manuscript, the engraver copy, the genre of the piece, the construction of the whole cycle, the particularities of the Original Edition and any accompanying documentation, there is nothing that casts any light on such a special need.

According to the preserved inventory of Bach's property after his death, the engraver Johann Heinrich Schübler received an honorarium of 2 Reichsthalers and 16 Groschen for the engraving of *The Art of Fugue*.[38] This is 25 percent more expensive than the cost of a golden ring (as marked in the same inventory) and almost equal to the cost of the spinet.[39] It is highly questionable that the price for engraving one canon, or even half of *The Art of Fugue*, could be the same. More likely, a much larger body of texts stands behind this commission to the engraver: the whole Third Version. If the composition were to be engraved as a whole, however, it is doubtful that the proofs would be printed just of one canon and not of the whole cycle, as was the usual practice.

The fact that a set of proofs was made during the publication process of the *Clavierübung III* is essential.[40] It supports the view that a similar set was prepared for *The Art of Fugue* and that Bach revised it before sending the engraved material to print.

Christoph Wolff suggests that the gray-blue folder P 200/1 contained, at a certain point in time (seemingly earlier than their deposit at the Royal Berlin Library) the missing part of the whole set of engraver copies: '... the wrapper inscribed by Johann Christoph Friedrich Bach, which possibly contained the engraver's copy'.[41] Indeed, a careful examination of the blue cover reveals traces of vertical folding marks, probably produced by its wrapping a significant amount of papers, larger than just the supplements it contained.

Wolff deems that those were engraver copies.[42] However, engraver copies, usually, would not be returned to the composer. Therefore, if Wolff's hypothesis concerning *The Art of Fugue*'s printing materials being included in that folder is correct, then these could be the set of proofs rather than the engraver copies.[43] This means that the proof sheet (*Probe Platte*) referred to by J.C.F. Bach could, most probably, be a part of that whole set.

It is quite plausible, thus, that J.S. Bach himself prepared the Third Version for print: it was fully engraved, its proofs revised and corrections introduced. The whole cycle would have been issued in this form, unless one point was judged by Bach as a gaucherie: the repetition of musical material in the fugue for two claviers and, more generally, the very introduction of two claviers into the cycle.

Two points must be considered when discussing the fugue for two claviers. First, it should not be excluded that the appearance of such an instrumental ensemble could be one of Bach's ideas for reinforcing the concluding role of a last piece in a multi-movement cycle. Second, Bach's steps might indicate that he thought some trait of the fugue for two claviers unsatisfactory and therefore decided to remove it. In doing so he revised the Third Version and created

126   Part III: J.S. Bach's work on The Art of Fugue

a fourth one, the main point of which would be the replacement of the fugue for two claviers with a new fugue, more suitable to its function as closure of the whole cycle.[44]

The Third Version of The Art of Fugue was thus fully engraved with the exception of the fugue for two claviers, which occupied the 14th position in the collection. This means that the idea of yet another new plan occurred to Bach no later than the time in which the first 13 counterpoints had been engraved. It is even possible that Bach managed to warn the master engraver not to engrave this fugue, which would be replaced by a new one. If this is the case, then this fugue was missing not only from the engraving plates, but also from the set of proofs.

Notes

1 The Third Version is evident in the Original Edition. However, the first part of this chapter deals with the plan that predates the printing of the edition.
2 The symbolic aspect of this structure is discussed in Chapter 20.
3 'Dieses letzte Werk Bachs ist im Grunde nur eine einzige Riesenfuge in fünfzehn Abschnitten' [In reality this last work of Bach's is a single gigantic fugue in fifteen sections.] Philipp Spitta, *Johann Sebastian Bach*, vol. 2 (Leipzig, 1880), p. 682. English translation in Philipp Spitta, *Johann Sebastian Bach: His Work and Influence on the Music of Germany, 1685–1750*. Translated by Clara Bell and J.A. Fuller-Maitland, (London, 1899), vol. 3, p. 203.
4 Unlike the two previous versions, the serial number of each fugue in the following discussion, except for the first few annotations that describe the transition (see note 6), is marked by Arabic numerals as they appear in the Original Edition.
5 It is marked in Schemes 10.2 and 10.3 as number 4.
6 The Roman numerals (I–III) denote the fugues from the Autograph, and the Arabic numeral 4 — the new fugue composed for the Third Version of *The Art of Fugue*.
7 Beyond the creation of a set of four fugues, there may have been another reason, perhaps even more essential, for this exchange. This will be discussed in Chapter 15.
8 The pairing of fugues III and IV was based, mainly, on the juxtaposition of the original and inverted theme and on its transformation to a dotted rhythm. The latter was expressed not quite convincingly because the similarity between 'small dotted rhythm' and 'large dotted rhythm' is not easily identified by ear.
9 These terms usually relate to canons, where the first risposta states the theme in augmentation (a quarter note becomes a half note), and the second — in double augmentation (the quarter note becomes a whole note). In the exposition of fugue VIII the bass part states the theme in double augmentation.
10 The order in which the contrasting types of dotted rhythm appear echoes the affinity between the themes of fugues III and IV of the Autograph: the 'microdotting' in fugue VII stands for 'small dotting', while in fugue VIII — in contrast, the 'small dotting' is responsible for the 'microdotting'.
11 A fugue on a cantus firmus presents a certain paradox: strictly speaking, it is a simple fugue with an additional accompaniment (if the cantus firmus is stated only once) or with consistent countersubject (if the cantus firmus appears several times). In both cases, two themes participate in the fugue, making it possible to regard it as a 'double' fugue, that is, a fugue with two themes.
12 This fugue is usually referred to in Bach literature as BWV 1080/13$_{1,2}$.
13 'Die letzteren sind Arrangements jener beiden dreistimmigen Fugen' [Both these last (Spitta means the two versions of the fugue for two claviers — A.M.) are arrangements of those two three-part fugues …]. Spitta, *Johann Sebastian Bach*, vol. 2, p. 677. English translation in Bell and Fuller-Maitland, vol. 3, p. 198.

14 In 1841, when the Autograph was deposited in the Berlin Royal Library.
15 The view that the second clavier in this fugue (XVI) was needed to support an earlier variant (the second mirror fugue, 13$_2$, which was too difficult for performance) was voiced as early as in Philipp Spitta's book: '...Welche (zwei Fugen für zwei Claviere) zum Theil sehr schwer, je nach Bachscher Art gar nicht zu spielen sind' [portions of this are very difficult, nay, impossible, to play] and then also 'auch schon durch die Einführung eines zweiten Claviers aus dem Stil des Ganzen herausfallt' [... while the introduction of a second clavier radically alters its style and character ...], Spitta, *Johann Sebastian Bach*, vol. 2, pp. 677–8. English translations in Bell and Fuller-Maitland, vol. 3, p. 198.
16 Several scholars think that Bach planned the fugue for two claviers as a separate arrangement for music-making sessions with his sons and students. For example: 'Bach hat sie vielleicht für das Zusammenspiel mit einem Schüler geschaffen — etwa für seinen 1732 geborenen Sohn Johann Christoph Friedrich oder für Johann Christoph Altnickol, der in der Zeit zwischen 1745–1748, also genau in der mutmaßlichen Entstehungszeit von sowohl Contrapunctus 13 als auch der 'Fuga a 2. Clav:' von Bach unterweisen wurde.' [Bach perhaps created it for the interaction with a student — maybe for teaching his son Johann Christoph Friedrich, born in 1732, or for Johann Christoph Altnickol, between 1745 and 1748, exactly the composition time of both Contrapunctus 13 and the fugue for two claviers.] Pieter Dirksen, *Studien zur Kunst der Fuge von Joh. Seb. Bach: Untersuchungen zur Entstehungsgeschichte, Struktur und Aufführungspraxis* (Wilhelmshaven, 1994), p. 55.
17 Hofmann, *NBA KB* VIII/2, p. 22, note 12.
18 'der fragliche Bogen dem Hauptmanuskript nicht ursprünglich angehört hat und nachmals von der Berliner Bibliothek zu Recht separiert worden ist.' [...the sheets in question initially did not belong to the main manuscript (of *The Art of Fugue* — A.M.) and were rightfully separated from it.] Ibid.
19 Johann Mattheson writes in a chapter dedicated to double counterpoint: 'Nunmehr aber kommt die Reihe an solche Contrapuncte, die nach einem gewissen Intervall benennet werden, und deren drey sind: Nehmlich 1) der doppelte Contrapunct *all'Ottava*, 2) der *alla Decima*, und 3) der *alla Dodecima*' [Now, however, we turn to a series of such counterpoints, which are named for one certain interval, and of which there are three: namely 1) double counterpoint *all'Ottava*, 2) *alla Decima*, and 3) *alla* Dodecima] Johann Mattheson, *Der vollkommene Capellmeister* (Hamburg, 1739), p. 422. Translation based on Ernest C. Harriss *Johann Mattheson's* Der volkommene Capellmeister: A Revised Translation with Critical Commentary (Ann Arbor, 1981), p. 777. The same kinds of counterpoint are described in Johann Joseph Fux's *Gradus ad Parnassum* and Angelo Berardi's *Documenti armonici*. All three texts existed in Bach's personal library.
20 [The dec[eased] Papa ordered to engrave on this page [:]*Canon per Augment. in Contrapuncto all octava*, but on the proof printout he erased it and wished to leave it as follows]
21 This preference is applied in most cases. For example, in the Canonic Variations BWV 769 (the variant of the autograph), where the cycle is concluded by a canon in augmentation and inversion; the 14 canons on the bass of the Air from the Goldberg Variations, BWV 1087, end with a canon in augmentation and inversion; the beginning of the Quodlibet in BWV 988 looks as such a canon in which both proposta and risposta are introduced simultaneously; finally, the penultimate of the six thematic canons from the *Musical Offering* BWV 1079 is, too, a canon in augmentation and inversion.
22 See for example: Wolff, *Johann Sebastian Bach: The Learned Musician*, p. 434; Schulenberg, *The Keyboard Music*, pp. 348–9; Schwebsch, *J.S. Bach und Die Kunst der Fuge*, pp. 310–23; Dirksen, *Studien zur Kunst der Fuge*, p. 20.
23 This is one of the mysteries of *The Art of the Fugue*. It will be discussed in Chapter 11.
24 To the best of our knowledge, all recent studies concerning the history of *The Art of Fugue*'s printing essentially state that the fugues and canons were intentionally engraved in an order different from

the one present in the printed edition. 'Three phases' of the engraving process are usually discussed. The first phase (1748/1749): fugues 1, 3, 4, 11, 12$_1$,13$_1$ and the four canons; the second phase (1749): Fugues 2, 5, 6, 7, 8, 9, 10, 12$_2$ and 13$_2$, and the third phase (1751) 10a, the fugue for two claviers, the unfinished concluding fugue and the 'posthumous choral'. See, for example, Wiemer, *Die wiederhergestellte Ordnung in Johann Sebastian Bachs Kunst der Fuge: Untersuchungen am Originaldruck* (Wiesbaden, 1977), p. 50; Butler, 'Ordering Problems', p. 58; Schleuning, *Johann Sebastian Bachs 'Kunst der Fuge'* (München, 1993), p. 169.

25 See Chapter 9.
26 The Autograph is considered here as a clean manuscript containing materials of both the First and the Second Versions of *The Art of Fugue*.
27 As a result, the following pieces were modified: fugues I, II, III and VI (and to a lesser degree IV, V, VIII, X, XI and XVIII) and the Canon in Augmentation (XV). Reworking fugue VI (in the Third Version of *The Art of Fugue* it is number 10) required *copying it from scratch*. Therefore, its inscription in P 200 could not be used for the Third Version.
28 Fugues II, III, IV, V, VI, X and XI changed positions in the Third Version.
29 Fugue 4, the canon at a 10th and the canon at a 12th were composed specifically for the Third Version.
30 The only exception is the last canon (in augmentation and inversion), which is written on three pages. This was not as essential for the order, because it occupied the last position in the cycle's Third Version.
31 The process that will bring these fugues change in internal ordering is discussed and analysed in Chapter 11.
32 J.A. Fuller-Maitland, 'A Set of Bach's Proof-Sheets,' *Sammelbände der Internationalen Musikgesellschaft*, II/4 (August 1900): p. 643.
33 Gregory Butler dedicated a special section to the problem of proof copies. Butler, *Bach's Clavier-Übung III*, pp. 65–71.
34 Manfred Tessmer (ed.), *NBA KB IV/4, Dritter Teil der Klavierübung* (Kassel, 1974), pp. 17 and 19. A7 is kept in the British Library in London (shelfmark Hirsch III.39) and A15 in the Oesterreichische Nationalbibliothek in Vienna (shelfmark *Hoboken 1.5.Bach.33*).
35 Butler, *Bach's Clavier-Übung III*, p. 66.
36 Ibid.
37 Ibid. p. 69.
38 The exact nature of Bach's commission to Schübler, for which this sum was paid, is not indicated. However, according to preserved documents, at that time Schübler's only commision from Bach was *The Art of Fugue*. See Wolfgang Wiemer, 'Johann Heinrich Schübler, der Stecher der *Kunst der Fuge*,' *BJ* 65 (1979): pp. 75–95.
39 *BD* II/627, p. 490.
40 Butler, *Bach's Clavier-Übung III*, pp. 65–72.
41 Wolff, *Bach: Essays*, p. 270. Wolff writes about *the set* of engraver copies, using the word *copy* in singular: 'engraver's copy (principal portion)'. (p. 269).
42 Ibid. p. 270.
43 This folder also contained the score of the church cantata by Johann Friedrich Fasch. This may refute Wolff's thesis because the traces of vertical folding marks could be made by Fasch's cantata. The cantata, however, became part of the folder many years after *The Art of Fugue* had been published, probably after 1765. In addition, the note, written by Emanuel's hand 'Herr Hartmann hat das eigentliche' [the original is at Mr Hartmann's] was attached to this file during the period when materials from *The Art of Fugue* were already included in it. Emanuel's note will be discussed below more in detail.
44 The note 'und einen andern Grund Plan,' written on the verso of page 5 of P 200/1–3 may provide an additional clue, which is discussed in Chapter 18.

11 The Fourth Version

Bach had one more adjustment impending: to replace the fugue for two claviers (marked here as Cp[14]) with a new concluding one (marked here as Cp[14F]).[1] Given the logic that lies at the basis of the cycle's structure, some traits of this new fugue could be foreseen:

- It should differ from Cp[14] in its thematic material, since the latter was discarded, among other reasons, because it was based on the same theme as Cp[13].
- It had to be a mirror fugue, just like Cp[14], because it would belong to the mirror fugues group.
- It should be written for one clavier, like all the preceding fugues.
- It had to possess characteristics and qualities fitting to its role as the concluding fugue in the collection.[2]

It might seem that Bach could decide to go ahead with this amendment although the Third Version already was in the process of being engraved because the sequence of the engraving procedures would be practically unaffected. Engraving the new fugue (Cp[14F]) in place of Cp[14] should be simple, because in the second half of the cycle (starting from Cp12) all the pieces were placed on page spreads.[3] Only the Canon in Augmentation occupied three pages, but since it was planned to be the last piece in the cycle, it would not affect the ensuing pagination.

Nevertheless, the task was not so simple. Cp[14F] turned out to be much longer than Cp[14], which would change the pagination of the subsequent canons. Bach needed to figure out how much space should be reserved for Cp[14F] and calculate how to distribute the following canons, so that they could appear, as planned, on page spreads.

Another issue, which extended to the two mirror fugues Cp12 and Cp[13], would affect the pagination of the Fourth Version. These two fugues appeared for the first time in the Second Version (that is, as early as the Autograph P 200). Presenting two musical topics—Sarabande in Cp12 and Gigue in Cp[13]—they contrasted in their presentation of the theme, which was rectus in Cp12 and inversus in Cp[13] (see Table 11.1).[4]

Table 11.1 Cp12 and Cp[13] in the Third Version, before the introduction of Cp[14]

Order of appearance	Fugue	Genre	Presentation of theme
1	Cp12$_{1,2}$	Sarabande	rectus
2	Cp[13]$_{1,2}$	Gigue	inversus

Table 11.2 The mirror fugues after the introduction of Cp[14]

Order of appearance	Fugue	Genre	Opening theme	Theme presentation
1	Cp12₁	Sarabande		**rectus**
2	Cp12₂	Sarabande		inversus
3	Cp[13]₁	Gigue		**inversus**
4	Cp[13]₂	Gigue		rectus
5	Cp[14]₁	Gigue		**rectus**
6	Cp[14]₂	Gigue		inversus

Table 11.3 The mirror fugues after the first reordering

Order of appearance	Fugue	Genre	Opening theme	Theme presentation
1	Cp[13]₂	Gigue		**rectus**
2	Cp[13]₁	Gigue		inversus
3	Cp12₂	Sarabande		**inversus**
4	Cp12₁	Sarabande		rectus
5	Cp[14]₁	Gigue		**rectus**
6	Cp[14]₂	Gigue		inversus

However, the addition of the third mirror fugue (Cp[14], for two claviers) in the Third Version of *The Art of Fugue* changed the situation, positioning a set of two (in fact four) consecutive fugues that present the same musical topic, tempo and—what might have probably be the last straw—fugue Cp[14]$_1$ would start on a theme absolutely identical to Cp[13]$_2$, albeit with the additional contrapuntal line and a second clavier (Table 11.2).

To follow his creative principles and the structural logic of *The Art of Fugue*, Bach would most probably remove the impending monotony by establishing a new order. Thus, beyond reordering the mirror pairs to avoid four consecutive fugues on the same dance topic, this may be the point where Bach also decided to reorder the component fugues of Cp12 and Cp[13]. The result of this double interchange would create not just the required contrasts of Gigue–Sarabande–Gigue dance topics and rectus-inversus-rectus presentation of theme, but also a kind of an A–B–A form, so characteristic of dance topics (Table 11.3).

It seems that this order was kept until the moment when Bach decided to replace the fugue for two claviers with a new one. However, the removal of Cp[14] and its replacement with Cp[14F], which in the Original Edition appears as the incomplete *Fuga a 3 Soggetti*, created a new situation and posed a new problem. The initial section of Cp[14F] (exposition and first episode) is slow and reserved (it could be described as *Grave*). Thus, it resulted in two consecutive slow pieces, both presenting the theme in rectus form (Table 11.4).

It is quite probable that Bach would reorder the pieces yet again and return the Sarabande fugue to its original position, at the head of the three mirror fugues group (Table 11.5).

This variant would perfectly comply with all the structural principles that Bach cared about: organising a group into a cohesive unit by contrasting slow–fast–slow tempi; gradually increasing contrapuntal and compositional complexity, from the simply stated theme, to an ornamented derivative and ending with a multi-subject fugue and no less important, concurrence with a significant number: 'three' after 'four' in the second half of the work.[5]

Table 11.4 The mirror fugues after the replacement of Cp[14] with Cp[14F]

Order of appearance	Fugue	Genre	Presentation of theme
1	Cp[13]$_{1,2}$	Gigue	inversus
2	Cp12$_{1,2}$	Sarabande	rectus
3	Cp[14F]	Grave	rectus

Table 11.5 Probable repositioning of the mirror fugues, avoiding juxtaposition of similar tempi, topics and presentation of themes

Order of appearance	Fugue	Genre	Presentation of theme
1	Cp12$_{2,1}$	Sarabande	inversus
2	Cp[13]$_{2,1}$	Gigue	rectus
3	Cp[14F]	Grave	rectus

Repagination

Sticking to the last variant would require a change in the pagination of the first two mirror fugues. Since these fugues occupied separate page spreads, this change would have a purely formal character. However, the canons positioned after Cp[14F] would pose a more complex challenge.

The insertion of the new mirror fugue (Cp[14F]) would create repagination problems of the three ensuing canons, because Cp[14F] was significantly longer than Cp[14]. This called for considerable additional work by both composer and engraver, because after composing the *fuga recta*, the *inversa* had to be inscribed and then a clean copy prepared, followed by the engraver copy. The problem lay not only in the increased amount of work, but also in predicting the pagination: knowing exactly how many pages would be needed for this fugue would be possible only after the engraver copy was ready.

At this point, the strenuous procedure of changing page numbers had to be done. It was hard because the changes had to be introduced in all nine pages on which the canons were already engraved. The entailed repagination of engraved plates was expensive and demanded the engraver attention and absolute accuracy.[6] Sometimes musicians preferred to make such corrections by hand on the printed run, in black or red ink, rather than engrave corrections into the plates. Master engravers preferred to etch the page numbers as the last step in the engraving process.[7]

For the repagination of the two mirror fugues Cp12 and Cp[13], the engraver had only to confirm (or reorder) their sequence and the sequence of their parts, while for the repagination of the canons he had to know the exact number of pages required for the new fugue that would follow Cp[13] and appear before the four canons. Bach, however, would be able to supply these particulars only once the fugue had been completed. It is unclear, however, if Bach had, at this point, the necessary information.

Alfred Dürr took a step toward a possible answer. Analysing vulnerable points in Wolfgang Wiemer's hypothesis concerning the three engraving phases of *The Art of Fugue*,[8] Dürr notes: 'Da nun aber die Kanons zur ersten Stichphase gehören, ist es schwer zu sagen, ob Bach zur Zeit ihrer Niederschrift schon sicher wußte, daß die letzte Fuge vor den Kanons auch wirklich mit einer Recto Seite enden würde.'[9]

Indeed, if Bach indicated that the first canon should start from an uneven page, it means he knew that the engraver copy of the fugue preceding this canon would end on an even page. Bach's calculation, however, was not precise, which indicates that the engraver copy was not ready as yet, and all that he had at hand was a compositional manuscript, or at the very best a clean copy.

On the other hand, the numbers written by J.S. Bach on the engraver copy of the Canon in Augmentation (P 200/1–1) suggest that Bach did know the positioning of the canon's pages. This means that he must have been aware of the ending point of Cp[14F], the piece immediately preceding the group of canons.

The final permutation of the mirror fugues and the canons Bach planned would have required a repagination of the already engraved 17 plates; this means that literally all the pages of the cycle's second part, the two mirror fugues and the four canons, had to be repositioned.

The Autograph bears marks suggesting that Bach, in order to solve this problem, resorted to a subsidiary pagination for this group of pieces.

The subsidiary pagination in the second part of *The Art of Fugue*

Wolfgang Wiemer and Gregory Butler drew attention to the subsidiary pagination in the Autograph of *The Art of Fugue*, pointing at the numbers 26, 27 and 28 that are inscribed on the top left corner of each of the three pages of P 200/1–1—the Canon in Augmentation and Inversion (see Figure 11.1, left):[10]

Wiemer and Butler, however, differ in their interpretation. Wiemer states that 'die Funktion dieser Zahlen erklärt sich mühelos, wenn wir sie mit dem Bestand der von Bach vorbereiteten Stichvorlagen in Verbindung bringen'.[11] He assumes that the subsidiary pagination started from Cp1. Moreover, he includes a copy of Cp2 in the count of Bach's engraver copies, although he himself affirmed that it was not the composer who inscribed it.[12] Thus, in Wiemer's view, page 1 of the subsidiary pagination corresponds to page 1 of the Original Edition, while its last page (which Wiemer deems to be number 30) falls on the second page of the Canon in Octave (!), which he trusts to close the set of four canons.

Butler, too, holds that Bach used a subsidiary pagination while composing *The Art of Fugue*. However, he suggests that it had another role. In his opinion, it should not be juxtaposed with Bach's engraver copies but with the second part of the cycle, following the consecutive order and not reordered as in Wiemer's hypothesis. Butler proposes therefore that the subsidiary pagination starts with Cp11 and continues to the end of the cycle—the last page of the Canon in Augmentation.[13] These two hypotheses are schematically presented in Table 11.6:

Table 11.6 Comparison of Wiemer's and Butler's subsidiary paginations

The subsidiary pagination	First page in relation to the Original Edition	Last page in relation to the Original Edition	First piece	Last piece	Total numbers of pages
Wiemer	1/1	30/52	Cp1	Canon in Octave	30
Butler	1/32	28/59	Cp11	Canon in Augmentation	28

Either way, both authors agree that the music materials of *The Art of Fugue* include a secondary pagination that is related to a group of pieces and formed over a marker that could not adhere to the main pagination. Without accepting this premise, the very existence of the page numeration 26, 27 and 28 (Figure 11.1, left) would be senseless. Unfortunately, while Wiemer's hypothesis was criticised for clarifying very little,[14] Butler's analysis does not cast much more light on the identity of the pieces and pages that underwent repagination.

Butler's main argument is based on his detection of what are, in his view, preserved traces of former numbers that had been erased, and publishes their picture, enlarged. Unfortunately, the photographs of these alleged marks are unclear, leaving room for interpretations of quite an array of numerals beyond the one he claims to have identified. Further, the boundaries of the subsidiary pagination are not substantiated by a motivation, which makes his choice of the starting point rather fortuitous. Moreover, remembering that in this cycle all the left-side pages of the spreads carry odd numbers and the pages on the right side even numbers may help the composer to form the general layout, indicating the left-and-right positions of the pages

134   Part III: J.S. Bach's work on The Art of Fugue

on the spreads. Therefore, if Bach would begin a new pagination from an *even* (right) page, giving it an *odd* number (32 = 1), he would significantly complicate his own imminent work.

While generally agreeing with the existence of a subsidiary pagination in the Autograph, I feel that its boundaries seem to require careful inspection and redefinition.

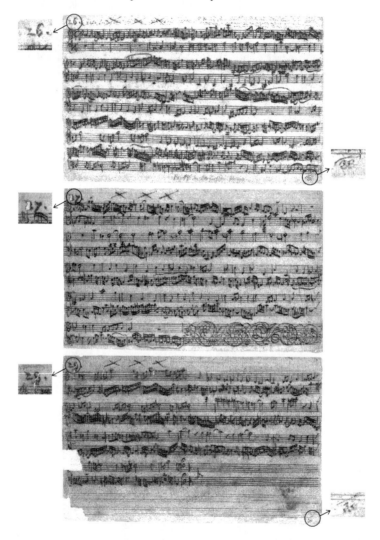

Figure 11.1   P 200/1–1: subsidiary pagination of the Canon in Augmentation. Centre: the three pages of the Canon in Augmentation; left: top subsidiary pagination 26, 27 and 28; right: bottom subsidiary pagination 33 and 35

The beginning of the second half of *The Art of Fugue* seems to offer such a boundary. This part, which went through a series of changes, is marked by a structural border: Cp12, which opens the group of mirror fugues.

Various signs in both the Autograph and the Original Edition reinforce the assessment that the cycle's second half starts precisely on Cp12.

The main numeration of contrapuncti in the Original Edition ends with Cp12. This is not coincidental, because the cycle's final structure, on which Bach had been working through various permutations, would be finalised only during the first three months of 1750, shortly before the ophthalmological surgery. Contrapunctus 12, written in the title of this fugue on page 37 of the Original Edition, serves here as a kind of 'custus', marking the position of both inversa and recta fugues of the first piece in the cycle's second half, after which the order of contrapuncti was yet to be determined.[15]

There are several additional indications that Cp12 marks the beginning of the subsidiary pagination. Until the mirror fugues, the creation process of the layout for the set of engraver copies was straightforward, and all the contrapuncti fit in order into the layout as expected. Here, however, due to the numerous permutations, the order became unclear. Its dependency on the interrelations between the pieces according to their tempo, topic, form, presentation of theme and so on, while also following the vein of thought that dictated the construction and development of the whole cycle according to groups with a specific number of pieces in each one, required several permutations and repaginations of practically every piece in the cycle's second half. This could not but be confusing, creating the need for subsidiary paginations.

Given all the permutations, it is very likely that the process of repagination went through several stages. Indeed, the Autograph does provide evidence for that. It is strange that neither Wiemer nor Butler considered the marks of yet another secondary pagination, located at the bottom right corner of two pages of P 200/1–1, the very same that carry the marks 26, 27 and 28 on the top left corners of the pages. The numbers marked are 33 and 35 (Figure 11.1, right).

An analysis and comparative assessment of these two subsidiary paginations are of great interest. While the digit 5 in the latter numeral bears marks of Christoph Friedrich Bach's hand, too, the general opinion is that these numbers were written by J.S. Bach.[16] If so, the handwriting suggests that the pagination shown on the right-hand side of Figure 11.1 is the earlier one, while the numbers shown on the left side (26, 27 and 28) were added at a later stage. This means that at an earlier stage of the permutations, the Canon in Augmentation was meant to be located on pages 33, 34 and 35, thus reserving pages 27–35 of the Original Edition for the set of four canons, making sure that each of them starts at the left-hand side of the spread, on an odd-numbered page, to avoid a turn of page during its reading (Scheme 11.1).

With that in mind, the starting point of this subsidiary pagination can be calculated. Given that all odd page numbers in the Original Edition are positioned on the left-hand side of the spreads, page 1 of this new pagination had to fall on a spread's left page where a new piece begins. The Original Edition has only four such places: Cp5, starting on page 13; Cp7, on page 19; Cp10 on page 29 and Cp12$_2$ on page 37.

The three first options—starting on Cp5, Cp7 or Cp10—must be discarded. Starting the count on Cp5 would locate the end of Cp[13]$_1$ on page 33, leaving pages 34–5 for the beginning of Cp[14F], far from the originally planned position for the Canon in Augmentation. Starting on Cp7 would not only superimpose the end of Cp[13]$_1$ with the first page of the Canon in Octave, but also leave no space at all for Cp[14F]; finally, starting on Cp10 would leave only nine pages for Cp[14F], about half the amount that Bach would need for it. The only logical place to start the new subsidiary pagination was, therefore, on Cp12.

Early subsidiary pagination	Titles of Canons
25–26	(reserved for the two last pages of Cp[14F])
27–28	*Canon alla Ottava*
29–30	*Canon alla Decima…*
31–32	*Canon alla Duodecima…*
33–34	*Canon per Augmentationem in Contrario Motu*
35	

Scheme 11.1 The early subsidiary pagination of the group of canons

The later subsidiary pagination, however, reserves pages 26, 27 and 28 for the Canon in Augmentation, thus moving its starting point from the verso, odd-numbered page to a recto page, carrying an even number. In this particular case, however, it did not matter much, since the canon was written on three pages, and a turn of page was thus unavoidable. Knowing the reason for this change, however, may lead to a better understanding of the Fourth Version's whole structure.

Given that page 26, which according to the earlier subsidiary pagination would be reserved for the end of Cp[14F], was not so anymore suggests that this page was no longer needed for this fugue and that some permutation must have taken place.

Moving the whole group of canons seven pages up (starting on page 20 instead of on page 27 of the subsidiary pagination) would leave just 11 pages for Cp[14F], an unlikely short span for a mirror fugue for which Bach had originally planned 18 pages (see Scheme 11.3). Moreover, it would create a situation in which all the canons start on an even numbered page, requiring a turn of page in the reading of each one. It is therefore more likely that the new subsidiary pagination indicates that Bach decided to compromise the ascending complexity principle and located the Canon in Augmentation before the other three. This also means that page 26, which was reserved for Cp[14F]'s ending, was actually blank and thus available (Scheme 11.2).

A comparison between Schemes 11.1 and 11.2 shows that the new subsidiary pagination presents the fugue Cp[14F] as one page shorter than originally planned. Given that Bach, in moving the Canon in Augmentation ahead of the other canons, clearly compromised the ascending complexity principle, it seems likely that this permutation was caused by some change in length of Cp[14F].

Information about Bach's situation at that time may shed light on the reason for this change. The numbers 26, 27 and 28 marking the later subsidiary pagination are awkwardly written. They were inscribed by Bach during the time that his handwriting deteriorated to the point

Early subsidiary pagination	Titles of Canons
25–26	(reserved for the last page of Cp[14F]) / ***Canon per***
27–28	***Augmentationem in Contrario Motu***
29–30	***Canon alla Ottava***
31–32	***Canon alla Decima…***
33–34	***Canon alla Duodecima…***
35	Blank page

Scheme 11.2 The second subsidiary pagination of the group of canons

that he was unable to write any more clean copies, let alone prepare engraver copies. At that time he had to entrust such tasks into the hands of a copyist.[17] This—in all probability—happened upon his completion of Cp[14F]. A comparison between the musical notation in engraver copies made by Bach himself and that by his copyists shows that Bach's notation, with its larger musical characters, allows a considerably smaller number of bars per page than his copyists' work, because their handwriting was notably smaller and more parsimonious than his. There is no need for analysis to clearly see this on the pages of the Original Edition. It is likely that Bach calculated the space needed for writing the fugue in his own hand. His copyist, meaning probably to save his master on the high expenses for engraver plates and paper, unintentionally did him a disservice by saving one page, creating the need to somehow fill up the gap. That is why the next (and final) permutation of the pieces was applied, and the Canon in Augmentation moved backward, now leading the group of canons.

The engraver, nevertheless, had to continue his work on the permutations and repaginations in the second part of the cycle. If Bach, as Alfred Dürr correctly noted, knew that the set of four canons was to begin on a *recto* page, because the preceding fugue had to end on a *verso*,[18] he must have calculated that on the basis of the number of bars in Cp[14F].

How many bars does the last fugue have?

Many scholars, composers and performers tried to establish this number. These attempts applied diverse methods, such as mathematical calculations, musicological approaches, performance practices and other combinations of various research procedures. Mathematical calculations have usually rendered a lower number than reconstructions based on performance practices. Thus, Vincent Dequevauviller and Herbert Kellner consider the question of the last fugue as an algebraic problem,[19] suggesting that the new fugue should comprise 276 bars. Gregory Butler relies on the evaluation (which is generally correct) that each section in Bach's

Subsidiary Pagination	Title of Pieces
1 – 2	Contrapunctus 12$_2$
3 – 4	Contrapunctus 12$_1$
5 – 6	Contrapunctus [13]$_2$
7 – 8	Contrapunctus [13]$_1$
9 – 10	
11 – 12	
13 – 14	
15 – 16	
17 – 18	
19 – 20	
21 – 22	
23 – 24	
25 – 26	
27 – 28	*Canon alla Ottava*
29 – 30	*Canon alla Decima...*
31 – 32	*Canon alla Duodecima...*
33 – 34	*Canon per Augmentationem*
35	*in Contrario Motu*

Scheme 11.3 The plan of the second half of *The Art of Fugue*, before the insertion of Cp[14F].

multi-subject fugues tends to be shorter by 30 percent than the previous one, suggesting a total number of 279 bars.[20] Helmut Walcha considers, based on his rich experience as an organist, that the fugue is 310 bars long.[21] Michael Ferguson agrees with the '30 percent shorter' hypothesis for each section, but his reconstruction of the fugue is based on his performance practice and organist's intuition; according to his calculation, the last fugue should be 324 bars long.[22] Zoltán Göncz, relying on his performance experience, considers the themes' individual profiles, their development in Bach's style, the particularities of a multi-subject fugue and the ratio between the sections; the result of his analysis is 350 bars.[23] Erich Bergel attempts to reconstruct the missing part of the fugue, departing from the peculiarities of its themes; he opts for 381 bars.[24] Wolfgang Graeser relies on aesthetic proportions, too, and thinks that the number of bars should reach 400.[25] Ferruccio Busoni, in his quite interesting reconstruction, lets his romantic fantasy free, creating a fugue that recalls not just the great works by Bach himself, but also the many other arrangements created and performed by this outstanding pianist and composer. According to Busoni, the fugue reaches the remarkable length of 414 bars.[26] One could state, then, that the range between 276 and 414 bars represents the range of the fugue's possible length. Still, this range, spanning over 138 bars, is too large. Its middle point, marking the length of the fugue at around 350 bars, is in fact quite possible.[27]

The hypothesis suggested here concerning the number of bars in Cp[14F] is exclusively based on traces left by J.S. Bach in the Autograph: the two subsidiary paginations and their correlation, and his own handwriting.

The correlation between Schemes 11.2 and 11.3 is shown in the next two schemes, in context. Scheme 11.4 represents a tentative layout of *The Art of Fugue*'s second half, starting the subsidiary pagination from Cp12, before the engraver copy of Cp[14F] was inserted. It shows that Bach allowed 18 pages (numbers 9–26 in the subsidiary pagination) for the last fugue. Since this was intended to be a mirror fugue, each of its parts—*recta* and *inversa*—should be allocated nine pages, or four and a half spreads.

The density of Bach's typical music handwriting for a four-part composition with a $\frac{4}{4}$ metre, taking Cp11 as a model, is 36.1 bars per page.[28] The fugue, engraved on nine pages, should therefore be 325 bars long. Compared with the mathematical, musicological and performance practice reconstructions discussed above, which range between 276 and 414 bars, this result lies around the middle, closer to the lower boundary (49 bars away from its lowest points and 89 bars from the highest one).

Scheme 11.5 shows that the copyist needed less space for the fugue: eight and a half pages for each of its presentations instead of the planned nine, leaving page 26 of the subsidiary pagination blank. Bach decided to fill the gap by relocating the Canon in Augmentation from the last position in the cycle, to the first position in the set of four canons.

Knowing the exact date in which the layout of *The Art of Fugue* was completed is of major importance. Unfortunately, due to a lack of documented data, it cannot be established; tentatively, however, it is possible to give an approximate estimate within the general outline of Bach's life at that time.

In the last days of December 1749, just a few days before the beginning of the new year 1750, Johann Christoph Friedrich left for Bückeburg. Before his departure he saw only a part of this fugue and was not aware of the last canons' permutation in the layout.[29]

Subsidiary Pagination	Title of Pieces
1 – 2	Contrapunctus 12_2
3 – 4	Contrapunctus 12_1
5 – 6	Contrapunctus $[13]_2$
7 – 8	Contrapunctus $[13]_1$
9 – 10	nine pages reserved for the quadruple mirror fugue (Cp [14F]) (rectus)
11 – 12	
13 – 14	
15 – 16	
17 – 18	
19 – 20	nine pages reserved for the quadruple mirror fugue (Cp [14F]) (inversus)
21 – 22	
23 – 24	
25 – 26	
27 – 28	*Canon alla Ottava*
29 – 30	*Canon alla Decima...*
31 – 32	*Canon alla Duodecima...*
33 – 34	*Canon per Augmentationem in Contrario Motu*
35	

Scheme 11.4 The plan to insert Cp[14F] to the second half.

Subsidiary Pagination	Title of Pieces	Main Pagination
1 – 2	Contrapunctus 12$_2$	37 – 38
3 – 4	Contrapunctus 12$_1$	39 – 40
5 – 6	Contrapunctus [13]$_2$	41 – 42
7 – 8	Contrapunctus [13]$_1$	43 – 44
9 – 10	eight and a half pages of the quadruple mirror fugue (Cp [14F]) (rectus)	45 – 46
11 – 12		47 – 48
13 – 14		49 – 50
15 – 16		51 – 52
17 – 18		53 – 54
19 – 20	eight and a half pages of the quadruple mirror fugue (Cp [14F]) (inversus)	55 – 56
21 – 22		57 – 58
23 – 24		59 – 60
25 – 26	*Canon per Augmentationem in Contrario Motu*	61 – 62
27 – 28		63 – 64
29 – 30	*Canon alla Ottava*	65 – 66
31 – 32	*Canon alla Decima...*	67 – 68
33 – 34	*Canon alla Duodecima...*	69 – 70
(35)	Blank (back cover)	(71)

Scheme 11.5 The layout of the cycle's second half after the insertion of the engraver copy of Cp[14F].

142   *Part III: J.S. Bach's work on* The Art of Fugue

At that moment, the upcoming publication of *The Art of Fugue* looked reassuringly bright, and the whole project was near completion. Only a few minor tasks remained to be done: concluding the fugue, preparing its engraver copy and sending it to Schübler. After the departure of his son, the most competent of his assistants, Johann Sebastian finished the composition of the quadruple fugue (Cp[14F]) and handed it to the copyist, who would write the engraver copy.

If everything went according to plan, *The Art of Fugue* would probably be published while Bach was still alive. Unfortunately, two unrelated circumstances, which accidentally coincided in time, caused delays and loss of precious time: the work of the copyist and the arrival of the oculist John Taylor. The engraver copy, which turned out to be one page shorter than planned, added extra work for the canon's permutation and, yet one more time, its repagination. All this had to happen in exactly three months—from the very end of December 1749 to the very end of March 1750. These actions, however, completed the layout.

It was exactly at the end of March 1750 that the oculist John Taylor arrived in Leipzig, stirring much public excitement. Documents and biographical reports show that Bach had never thought or prepared himself for this surgery, but his friends and relatives believed that this was a lucky moment, an opportunity to improve his drastically deteriorated eyesight, and convinced him to go into surgery. The idea caught him by surprise; this is probably why, hoping for a fast and successful recovery, he agreed, leaving all his current business as it were. The following events, however, took a disastrous turn.

Bach, probably, did not manage to send the engraver copy to Schübler before the surgery, and the assistant who prepared it—if indeed it was Bammler—left Leipzig soon after its completion. In the general disarray that followed, both the clean and the engraver copies disappeared without a trace. Bach's relatives took over the publication of this immortal masterpiece, chief among them Carl Philipp Emanuel. In his edition, however, the structure of *The Art of Fugue* significantly differs from the one that had originally been planned by his father.

Notes

1 Contrapuncti [fugues as designated in the Original Edition] are marked by the abbreviation Cp and followed by their serial number. As the Original Edition does not give serial numbers after 12, numbers 13 and 14 are in square brackets. The fugue for two claviers and the final piece (*Fuga a 3 Soggetti*) are distinguished as Cp[14] and Cp[14F], respectively.
2 That is, the last *fugue*. It would still be followed by four canons.
3 The ratio in the numbers of pages between the first and the second halves of the cycle differed in the Fourth Version from the third one. In the Third Version, the ratio is 36 and 26 pages; in the fourth, it respectively became 36 and 33.
4 Since mirror fugues initially had been positioned by Bach under the same accolade, in each case the theme of the fugue written on the top system is considered as the rectus.
5 On the symbolic meaning of the sequence 4 + 3 see Chapter 20.
6 Describing the process of repagination, Gregory Butler uses the words 'erasing and re-engraving of page numbers'. Butler, *Bach's Clavier-Übung III*, p. 39.
7 The pagination in the process of engraving on copper (*Abklatschvorlage*) could be made in various ways, but usually it was done last, by directly etching the page numbers onto the copper plates. The traces of this praxis can be seen on page 25 of the Original Edition, where the page number

is printed in a mirrored reflection, most likely a trace of an absentminded etching of the straight (rather than mirror) number into the copper plate.
8   See note 24, Chapter 10.
9   [However, since the canons belonged to the first phase, it is difficult to say whether Bach, at the time of their being copied, knew for certain that the last canon would really end on the recto side of the sheet.] Alfred Dürr, 'Neue Forschungen', p. 157.
10 Wiemer, *Die wiederhergestellte Ordnung*, pp. 13–14; Butler, 'Ordering Problems', pp. 50–3.
11 [The function of these numbers can easily be explained if we juxtapose them with Bach's prepared folder of the engraver's copies.] Wiemer, *Die wiederhergestellte Ordnung*, p. 13.
12 Ibid. pp. 13–14 and 50.
13 Gregory Butler, 'Ordering problems', pp. 51–2.
14 For example, see Dürr, 'Neue Forschungen', p. 158; Wolff, 'Zur Kunst der Fuge', *Musica*, 33 (1979): pp. 288–9; Butler, 'Ordering problems', p. 52.
15 The inversus of Cp12 appears in the Original Edition before the rectus. As a reminder, this happened in an earlier permutation, when Bach exchanged the order of $Cp12_1$ and $Cp12_2$, as well as that of $Cp[13]_1$ and $Cp[13]_2$ (see Table 11.3).
16 See, for example, Hofmann, *NBA KB* VIII/2, p. 49. The page where number 34 should be is unnumbered. An examination of the original, indistinguishable in the facsimile, shows that the initial copy of this page was replaced by a newer engraver copy. There are several signs of this replacement, besides the lack of the numeral 34: different ink, a new rastration and other formatting details that differ from the two other sheets. This new copy of the page was also written by J.S. Bach, who had probably left it unnumbered because all three sheets would receive new page numbers: 26, 27 and 28. The page order in the first subsidiary pagination should thus be read as 33, [34] and 35.
17 As Peter Wollny established, Bach's main copyist at that time was his student Johann Nathanael Bammler. Wollny, 'Neue Bach-Funde', p. 44.
18 Alfred Dürr, 'Neue Forschungen', p. 158.
19 It is not coincidental that Dequevauviller highlights this approach in the title of his article. Vincent Dequevauviller, '*L'art de la fugue*', un problème algébrique: étude sur les caractéristiques numériques et les raisons de l'inachèvement de la dernière œuvre de Jean-Sébastien Bach (Paris, 1998); Herbert Kellner, *Die Kunst der Fuga [i.e. Fuge]: how incomplete is the fuga a 3 sogetti [sic]? (BWV 1080/19, Contrapunctus 14)* (Darmstadt, 2002).
20 Butler, 'Ordering problems', pp. 51–7.
21 Helmut Walcha, 'Weiterführung und Beendigung der Schlüßfuge' in *Johann Sebastian Bach: Die Kunst der Fuge — Übertragung für Orgel von Helmut Walcha* (Frankfurt am Main, 1967), pp. 129–32.
22 Michael Ferguson, *Bach-Ferguson. Contrapunctus XIV: a Completion of J.S. Bach's Unfinished Quadruple Fugue from The Art of Fugue* (St Paul, MN, 2nd ed., 1990).
23 This reconstruction offers a substantial and one of the best discussions of the subject: Zoltán Göncz, 'Reconstruction of the Final Contrapunctus of The Art of Fugue,' *International Journal of Musicology*, vol. 5 (1995): pp. 25–93 and vol. 6 (1996): pp. 103–19.
24 Erich Bergel, *Bachs letzte Fuge* (Bonn, 1985), pp. 196–259.
25 Wolfgang Graeser, 'Bachs Kunst der Fuge', *BJ* 21 (1924): pp. 57–8.
26 Ferruccio Busoni, *Choral-Vorspiel und Fuge über ein Bachsches Fragment: der Fantasia contrappuntistica* (Leipzig, 1912), pp. 8–21.
27 For example, Bach's fugue from the Sonata for violino solo in C-dur (BWV 1005/2) is 354 bars long. Thus, assuming a number around 350 bars for the last fugue in *The Art of Fugue* is quite reasonable.
28 The engraver copy of Cp11, prepared by J.S. Bach, occupies five pages and is 184 bars long, thus above average.
29 The fast deterioration in Bach's handwriting allows the dating of his manuscripts from the end of 1749 with relatively high accuracy. In this case it relies on date-range and handwriting particularities in the unfinished fragment of the quadruple fugue on one hand and in the Canon in Augmentation (pp. 26, 27 and 28) on the other.

Part IV

Carl Philipp Emanuel Bach's work toward the publication of *The Art of Fugue*

12 Settings, attitudes and circumstances

Who was responsible for the Original Edition? Who planned it, outlined its final form and brought it to print? Clearly, the first planning was Johann Sebastian's. Bach scholars are practically unanimous in agreeing that the sequence of pieces until Cp12 is the composer's own and that Philipp Emanuel followed his father's wishes at least to that point of the work. The rest of the cycle, however, does not provide a clear picture of its internal ordering, and there are still no absolute conclusions of this matter in the existing literature.

Several people partook in the process of publication besides Carl Philipp Emanuel. It is agreed that, to a larger or lesser extent, these were Johann Friedrich Agricola, and perhaps also Johann Christoph Altnickol, Wilhelm Friedemann Bach and even Johann Christoph Friedrich Bach, bearing in mind that he could consult Emanuel, in one way or another, concerning the composition of the cycle. However, although scholars mention these names in this context, there is no factual trace of their working with the musical texts of *The Art of Fugue* or participating in the publishing process during 1750–1751.[1] Moreover, even if their influence affected the process to some extent, it was Emanuel who had to make the final decisions.

Knowing the degree to which the Original Edition reflects the composer's design is cardinal, but also very difficult to assert. While Bach scholars disagree concerning the design itself, it is also unclear how Emanuel saw that his father's intentions were met, how their realisation matched with his own purposes and which operative steps he considered legitimate (or less so) in achieving his goals.

Former chapters described a hypothetical process in which *The Art of Fugue* was created, comprising four versions of the cycle. According to this hypothesis, there were four versions of this work, the first three prepared for publication and revised by Johann Sebastian. The only change required for the Fourth Version was the replacement of the mirror fugue for two claviers with the new quadruple mirror fugue.

Finding out whether, and to what extent, Philipp Emanuel understood his father's plan (and diverted from it) requires a clarifying appraisal of his views, motivations and attitudes, since these undoubtedly affected his decisions and actions.

'Emanuel did not understand'

Contemporary Bach scholars quite unanimously agree that the reason the Original Edition does not correspond with what most assume was the composer's plan for *The Art of Fugue*, is quite simple: Emanuel did not understand. This means that he published Johann Sebastian's great opus with obvious errors that are clear to anyone acquainted with the work. It is almost two centuries since serious shortcomings of this edition were first criticised, starting a debate that continues to this day.

Among the first critics was Robert Schumann who published in 1841 an eloquently titled article, where he pointed at the exact spots in *The Art of Fugue* that he deemed 'corrupted'.[2] He noticed that *Contrap: a 4.* and the *Fuga a 2. Clav:* (with the *Alio modo, Fuga a 2. Clav.*) which are incorporated in the cycle, repeat, to a certain degree, other fugues in the collection (for example, *Contrapunctus 10. a. 4. alla Decima* and *Contrapunctus* [13] *a. 3*). In the same year and following Schumann, Maurice Hauptmann stated that the Canon in Augmentation is misplaced in the edition and that the group of canons should start at the Canon in Octave.[3]

The number of scholars criticising the Original Edition grew with each new work dedicated to *The Art of Fugue*. Among them can be counted Siegfrid Dehn (1845), Wilhelm Rust (1878), Philipp Spitta (1880), Gustav Nottebohm (1880–1881), Wolfgang Graeser (1924), Hans Theodor David (1927) and others.[4] Later works render similar conclusions.[5] The reasons indicated for the errors are various, but the one that appears in most cases is Bach's conception being misunderstood by his son. Another assumption is that a misunderstanding emerged in the process of printing between Emanuel and the engraver.[6] Bottom line, the responsibility for the Original Edition's structure is down to Emanuel, and any mistake in it happened under his aegis.

The hierarchy of composers, copyists and engravers in the mid-eighteenth century was strictly kept, engravers and copyists being subservient to the composer. The engraver's initiative and independence were limited, and some kind of control system, such as preparation of proofs and their revision by the author, was always applied. Nothing would be done without the explicit approval of the author or commissioner.

However, it is rather bizarre that all the critics, from Robert Schumann up to the most recent authors, understood Johann Sebastian's ideas about *The Art of Fugue*'s composition, while the one and only person who did not understand his father's intentions was Philipp Emanuel. Seemingly, he did not understand the simplest things; for example, he missed the fact that *Contrap: a 4.* uses entire sections from Cp10; he did not notice that the *Fuga a 2. Clav:* (together with *Alio modo, Fuga a 2. Clav.*) is just an 'arrangement', as scholars brand it, of the second mirror fugue Cp[13]. Further, he did not even understand why the fugues in this composition are called 'contrapuncti' rather than 'fugues', since in his own *avertissement* and even in his preface to the work he relates to 'fugues and contrapuncti' without paying attention to his father's specific nomenclature.

How could that be possible? Who could declare, like Philipp Emanuel, that 'he had no other teacher' than J.S. Bach—when speaking about his keyboard studies and composition? Who would better understand the variants of *The Art of Fugue*, which he knew first hand? Did any of the critics who studied *The Art of Fugue* and fugue composition watch Johann Sebastian in the process of composition? And who among present-day Bach scholars—more than a quarter of a millennium after his death—dare claim knowledge of the peculiarities of Bach's musical style and subtleties more accurately than Philipp Emanuel, who was at Bach's side all his formative years? How could it be that all these musicians and scholars understood Bach's intentions, while only Philipp Emanuel remained so incredibly oblivious?

To answer this question, one needs to contextualise the state of affairs at the time of the publication of *The Art of Fugue,* to look at facts concerning not only the specifics of Bach's compositional process, but also details about his other publications, the relations within the Bach family, particularities of his lifestyle, the Potsdam court and the circle of Emanuel's friends and acquaintances. All these need to be carefully considered, weighed and analysed.

Father and son

Wilhelm Friedemann, the oldest son of the great composer, was his favourite. As far as Johann Sebastian was concerned, Friedemann was the most gifted among his sons. The composer invested time and effort developing the child's talent, creating for him a special collection of pieces, which he named the *Clavier-Büchlein vor Wilhelm Friedemann Bach*,[7] where he included not only pieces of his own and of other composers, but also of Friedemann himself, who was only nine years old at the time.[8] The father's approach was more balanced toward Philipp Emanuel, who was more than three years younger than Friedemann[9] and was not spoiled by similar attention.

Bach's sons differed in their attitude toward their father, too. It is known, for example, that neither of the two older sons, nor Christoph Friedrich, his fifth son, was present at Bach's deathbed or even attended the funeral. As for Emanuel, it is absolutely clear that his court service as the king's personal accompanist did not enable him to get away even for a short period. Christoph Friedrich was in Bückeburg, which is quite far from Leipzig, and although he was almost a week late to the funeral, he nevertheless did arrive in Leipzig. On the other hand, Halle, where Friedemann resided, is situated just 40 km from Leipzig, and the regime of his service did allow him to get a short vacation in case of bereavement. Nevertheless, Friedemann would arrive only six weeks later, for the inventory and division of property.[10]

The brothers' stance toward their father's legacy was different, too. Emanuel literally cherished every piece of Bach's writing, recording his works in a special catalogue. Having concerns about Johann Sebastian's works, he decided to give or sell his compositions only to those he trusted to safe keep them. Further, he did his best to distribute only printed copies or manuscript copies. He allowed copies to be made of original manuscripts but made sure that the originals would be treated carefully and returned to him.[11]

Friedemann, on the other hand, cannot be suspected of a similar reverence for his father's legacy. Not only did he not record the precious manuscripts: he simply squandered them. It is due to his negligence that a vast number of J.S. Bach's autographs disappeared without a trace. He even claimed authorship of several of his father's compositions while in other instances offered his own manuscripts to interested parties claiming they were his father's.[12]

Emanuel venerated his father. For him, Johann Sebastian was the greatest authority in many respects, but his utmost admiration was reserved for his professional knowledge and mastery. In his autobiography, Emanuel wrote: 'In der Komposition und im Clavierspielen habe ich nie einen andern Lehrmeister gehabt, als meinen Vater'.[13] One might think, however, that there was more to it than Emanuel's own personal relation or opinion. He did realise the greatness of his father's public reputation. This can be confirmed by his additional comments in the autobiography:

> Die Grösse dieses meines Vaters in der Komposition, im Orgel und Clavierspielen, welche ihm eigen war, war viel zu bekannt, als daß ein Musikus vom Ansehen, die Gelegenheit, wenn es nur möglich war, hätte vorbey lasse sollen, diesen grossen Mann näher kenne zu lernen.[14]

> [The greatness that was my father's in composition, in organ and clavier playing, was so far too well known for a musician of reputation to let the opportunity slip of making the closer acquaintance of this great man if it was at all possible].

Emanuel indeed understood that his father was the great master and valued him more highly than all the contemporary composers of which he knew. The evidence of this can be found in Emanuel's letter to the writer and philologist Johann Joachim Eschenburg, who translated Charles Burney's essay about the performance of Handel's music in Westminster Abbey.[15] Despite being in quite friendly relations with Burney, who visited him and was an active subscriber to his compositions, Emanuel did not let this essay go unchallenged. Reacting to the Englishman's comparison between the organ playing of Handel and that of Bach, Emanuel criticises Burney's writing, English organs and Handel himself:

> But to write with regard to organ-playing: that he had surpassed my father; this should not be said by a man who lives in England, where organs are of slight value, N.B. all without pedals, and who, consequently, has no insight into what constitutes the excellence of organ-playing; who perhaps never saw nor heard any things [works] for the organ; and who, finally, does certainly not know my [father's] works for the keyboard and especially for the organ, and in these the obbligato use of the pedal to which now the chief melody, now the Alto or the Tenor is given, always in fugues where a voice is never abandoned and the most difficult passages occur while the feet are occupied with the greatest fire and brilliance, *en fin*, innumerable things about which Burney knows nothing.[16]

As if this rebuke was not sufficient, Emanuel published his own essay in the *Allgemeine deutsche Bibliothek*, where he wrote about his father in a similar superlative tone, making it publicly available.[17]

Clearly, unlike Friedemann's position, anything written in his father's hand was perceived by Emanuel as coming from the unquestionable high authority and status of its author's will. Changing anything in his father's text would have been unthinkable for Emanuel, let alone appropriating anything that came from his pen. In some cases, when it was unavoidable (for example on occasions of new performances of Bach's works), Emanuel took care to clearly mark his father's text and differentiate it from his own. In this respect, his approach, which followed working principles of a professional restorer, was rooted in the environment in which he lived and worked: the Prussian court of King Frederick II ('Frederick the Great'), where he served as the King's harpsichordist.[18]

The interest in ancient culture and art restoration

Between 1740, the year in which Frederick became King of Prussia, and 1750, when Carl Philipp Emanuel Bach began the publication process of *The Art of Fugue*, Frederick also constructed his court as a main European cultural centre. The *petites soupers*—dinners in which the king engaged in scholarly conversations with eighteenth-century intellectual luminaries who were invited to and often even resided in his palace[19]—were a hub of new ideas about philosophy, government, history, literature and the arts: painting, architecture and music. Frederick, who was an avid art collector, personally planned and supervised the building of his favourite residence, the Sanssouci Palace, discussing (and arguing for) its details with the chief architect of the project, Georg Wenzeslaus von Knobelsdorff, and with the court painter Antoine Pesne, as well as with other builders, designers and constructors that were involved in this project.

Knobelsdorff was a loyal follower of the fashionable Palladian style in architecture, which copied Renaissance interpretations of Classical structures and buildings. Indeed, Sanssouci is imbued with characteristics of this style, such as the Marble Hall and the vestibule of the palace with its Corinthian pillars. This approach, however, was markedly revitalised by the 1738 discovery and excavations of Herculaneum. The uncovering of this whole city, which for many centuries was buried under the Vesuvius' ashes, constituted a major event in Europe's intellectual life. Throughout the following decades, the site became a main attraction for an international host of visitors and scholars.

An important figure among these was the French writer, traveller and scholar Charles de Brosses (1709–1777), who spent several months in Italy during the fall of 1739, devoting a considerable part of his sojourn to visiting the Vesuvius and the excavations at Herculaneum. While his *Lettres sur l'état actuel de la ville souterraine d'Herculée et sur les causes de son ensevelissement sous les ruines du Vésuve* were published only in 1750, he presented his findings a year earlier to the *Académie des inscriptions et belles lettres*, of which he became a member in 1746. Several of the Académie's members were in contact with the intellectual circle of Frederick the Great. Moreover, the large collections of letters that De Brosses wrote to friends and family during his 1739 travels must have become a subject of further social elitist discussions.[20] These letters, describing the Herculaneum findings and conditions in detail, were addressed, among others, to nobility, intellectuals and scholars, such as Jean Bouhier (1673–1746), the French jurist, historian, translator, bibliophile and scholar, as well as the Count De Buffon (1707–1808), the naturalist and scholar who was in friendly contact with several members of Frederick's circle. For example, the letter of De Brosses to Bouhier, from November 28, 1739, expresses his admiration for the beauty of the findings, his sorrow for their dilapidated state and sensitivity not only to their historical signification but also to possible interpretations of their style:

> Quant aux peintures à fresque trouvées à Ercolano, elles sont d'autant plus précieuses qu'il ne nous restoit presque rien d'antique en ce genre. (…) Ceux d'Ercolano sont en grand nombre; mais la plupart en pièces, ou du moins fort gâtés. (…) J'ai ouï parler de plusieurs autres (…) d'autres, enfin, où l'on remarque des choses si semblables à nos modes actuelles les plus bizarres, qu'on est prêt à les soupçonner d'y avoir été ajoutées après coup.[21]

[As for the fresco paintings found at Herculaneum, they are all even more precious because almost nothing [else] remained for us from the ancient type. ... Those from Herculaneum are many, but most of them are in pieces, or at least very decayed. ... I have heard of several others ... as of the others, effectively, in which we see things so similar to our present bizarre manners, that one is willing to suspect them of having been added at a later stage.]

Interest in Classical art—architecture, sculptures and even painting—was the cultural norm since the Renaissance. Now, however, it was rekindled, gaining a new point of view: that of *authenticity*. While Frederick was far from being unique in this interest, he manifested it in avid purchase of ancient artefacts and sculptures, although most were still heavily restored by contemporary artists.[22]

Indeed, since the Herculanean—and excavated sculptures from other places—artefacts were often found damaged, art restoration became popular: assumed attires, additional objects held in marble broken hands, limbs—and sometimes even heads—that were deemed as missing were added to excavated sculptures that were found in derelict conditions. Such interpretations, in their turn, gradually became a subject of lively discussion in European academies. Aesthetic criteria, historical authenticity and art interpretation, which were only implied in the 1739 letter of De Brosses became, during the 1740s, a fashionable subject of both professional and social conversations, and the vocation of *art criticism* began to form. In this context, the person of Count Francesco Algarotti, a close friend of Frederick and a constant and influential presence at the court's social dinners, is of major importance.

Algarotti (1712–1764) was a philosopher, poet, essayist, art critic and art collector. A member of Frederick's intellectual circle since 1736, that is, from before the crown prince became King, he acted during the 1740s as the King's Chamberlain and emissary to many tasks. Algarotti was also friend of most of the leading authors of his times: Voltaire, Marquis d'Argens, Pierre-Louis de Maupertuis and the Comte de Buffon. After Knobelsdorff fell from his King's grace, in 1746, Algarotti took over some of the architectural responsibilities of Sanssouci and other buildings. While there is no record of the discussions he might have had with Knobelsdorff or Frederick on the subject of art restoration, his *Saggio sopra l'Architettura* (Essay on Architecture), published in 1756, gives an impression of his opinions about art conservation. It is very likely that these were different from those of other artists in Frederick's court, where heavily restored sculptures were the norm rather than the exception. It is to these courtly ideas, so it seems, that the writer is elliptically referring in the opening lines of his Essay, written after he had left Frederick's court:

Molti, e vari sono gli abusi, che per una o per altra via entrarono d'ogni tempo in qualunque sia generazione di arti, e di scienze. E benchè per essi ne venga oltremodo disformata la faccia di quelle; pur nondimeno ad avvertir gli non bastano le viste volgari, ma necessario è l'acume di coloro, che penetrano più addentro nella sostanza delle cose. Conviene perciò risalire quasi in spirito sino a principi primi, vedere quello che legittimamente da essi deriva, non riputare virtù ciò che ha in se del maraviglioso, ciò che è protetto da un qualche nome che abbia il grido, e dall'autorità sopra tutto, che danno alle cose l'abitudine e il tempo, la quale ha forza appresso gran parte degli uomini di sovrana ragione.[23]

[Many and various are the mishandlings, which in one way or another, throughout time, penetrated into several genres of art and sciences. And although, because of them, their appearance is rendered deformed, while not yet sufficiently to recognise them in a vulgar view, still visible enough for the insight of those who penetrate deeper into the essence of things. It is worthy, therefore, to turn one's thoughts toward the first principles, to see what can legitimately be derived from them, and not count upon a virtue of being stunning in itself, or upon whatever is protected by a 'sweetly sounding' name, and above all, upon an authority relying on habit and time, and which exerts power over most people, even those blessed by supreme reason.]

Thus, during the 1740s, basic principles of restoration were discussed and developed. Archaeology and restoration had to join forces to admire, interpret and analyse artistic findings. This approach had further repercussions, affecting historicism: the very sight of a broken, effaced sculpture rescued from the soil acquired its own value, as an irreplaceable constituent of reality, witness to the passing of time. Of no less significance was the emerging concept of authenticity. Authorial materials needed to be clearly marked as different from a restorer's work, while, at the same time, the most important criterion of a restorer's work was now his success to come as close as possible to the authorial intention and work.

The extent to which Carl Philipp Emanuel Bach was aware of these discussions can be deduced not only from his commitment to conserve his father's work, but moreover from his connections in Frederick's court and, more generally, in Berlin's mid-eighteenth-century cultural milieu. Philipp Emanuel was hired as keyboard player in 1738, while Frederick was still the crown prince. In spite of his experience at the court, he did not enjoy any special position in the palace, and was not particularly favoured by the King, who preferred the music of Johann Joachim Quantz (1697–1773), his flute teacher and composer of hundreds of flute concertos written especially for the King, and Carl Heinrich Graun (1704–1759), who composed operas that were mainly performed in the newly built Berlin Opera House.[24] As performers, the King admired the Benda brothers as well as several of his opera singers. In fact, Frederick thought that Carl Philipp Emanuel Bach was 'irksome'.[25] The composer is mentioned in the literature about (and by) Frederick II only in lists of court musicians, while his father's 1747 famous visit to Sanssouci, which instigated the composition of the *Musical Offering*, is described to a far larger extent.

Regardless of courtly rank, however, Carl Philipp Emanuel was a man of letters, whose interest in art and literature combined well with his congeniality, leading to a network of connections among the main court's artists and entourage. It is not hard to imagine him conversing with Knobelsdorff, Pesne and even with Algarotti, none of whom belonged to the nobility by birth. Some of Knobelsdorff's bitterness and frustration of 1746, the year he was released from his Sanssouci duties by the King, were possibly shared with Emanuel. Thus, although the composer might not have directly read it, Algarotti's words were probably based on discussion subjects of which he was informed, becoming well aware of the authenticity question and the importance of the research of original facts.

Sometime after 1748, Philipp Emanuel became active in Berlin's musical life, too, making acquaintance with the city's wider intellectual circles. Gotthold Ephraim Lessing (1729–1781), for example, to whom the composer was introduced in 1748, became a life-long influence.

Indeed, during the late 1740s Lessing wrote only dramas (his famous *Laocoon* essay is of a much later date),[26] but since early in his life he was avidly interested in art, art criticism and art history, an interest that surely would be expressed during educated discussions. The Berlin *Musikalische Assemblés* that started in 1749, and in which Bach had an active role, were another venue in which to air ideas and thoughts about literature, art, and ongoing cultural issues.[27] This background may corroborate the assumption that the inclusion of a composition's several versions in *The Art of Fugue* is rooted in Carl Philipp Emanuel's increased sensitivity to the importance of authenticity and, probably, also in his wish to avoid controversies and misinterpretations of the work by supplying in the Original Edition at least several of his father's available drafts and versions.

Emanuel's knowledge of sources concerning the internal order of *The Art of Fugue*

To understand Philipp Emanuel's contribution to the ordering of pieces in *The Art of Fugue*, the sources of his knowledge about this cycle need to be revealed and clarified: how did he learn about the cycle's composition process, and how did he use and apply this information in the publication of the work. Both direct and indirect data about materials concerning *The Art of Fugue*, which he saw and/or possessed, may serve as clues leading to a sharper image of his decisions and actions toward the final product: the Original Edition.

An analysis of the Edition's oddities, then, should shed some light on their operative source. A first cardinal step in such analysis would be the separation between Johann Sebastian's requirements and the results as they are presented in Philipp Emanuel's work. This means that a careful comparison between the two is called for, focusing on their differences, which could appear in any of the following four elements:

- In the pieces' order of appearance
- In the pieces' titles
- In metre and rhythm
- In the music texts themselves

During the months in which Philipp Emanuel prepared *The Art of Fugue* for publication—from autumn 1750 to spring 1751—he could gather information about the cycle's structure from several sources. First, his father. In May 1747, when the composition of this large-scale and fascinating work was in full swing, Johann Sebastian visited Sanssouci and demonstrated his artistry to Frederick II. During this visit, Bach stayed at his son's home. It is highly unlikely that he would neglect telling his son about the new work, perhaps even playing for him what probably was, at that time, the Second Version of *The Art of Fugue*. At this early date, neither the Third nor, surely, the Fourth Version would have been part of such session.

Another possible source could be Johann Christoph Friedrich, who assisted his father as copyist and proofreader until the very last days of December 1749, when the 17 years old left the family home to serve as harpsichordist at the court of Wilhelm, Count of Schaumburg-Lippe in Bückeburg. Besides the composer himself, Johann Christoph was probably the only person who had an accurate image of *The Art of Fugue* final version: it was he who wrote on the autograph of the quadruple fugue the comment related to the cycle's last version: *einen andern Grund Plan*.

However, as the study of Bach's interfamilial contacts shows, the brothers did not meet until June–July of 1751, when Emanuel, as part of the king's entourage, visited Bückeburg. By that time, however, the preparation of the Original Edition was completed, and the score had been sent to the print shop. It means, therefore, that the brothers did not see each other during Emanuel's editorial work or prior to the moment of its being sent to print, so Christoph Friedrich could not inform Emanuel concerning the composition of *The Art of Fugue*.

The third source of information regarding the structure of the cycle must have been the music materials that were available to Emanuel. Which materials could these be? In his article on the history of the creation and publication of *The Art of Fugue*, Christoph Wolff describes the presumed set of materials that should have come out from J.S. Bach's pen before he would send his work to print.[28] In Wolff's opinion, the following documents must have been included:

- Materials preceding P 200: compositional manuscripts of pieces I–XIV: lost
- Fair copies. P 200, pieces I–XIV
- Arrangements: P 200/1–2, *Fuga a 2 Clav:* (fair copy)
- Compositional manuscript of the Canon in Augmentation: P 200, XV
- Compositional manuscripts of Contrapuncti 4 and 10, as well as the Canons in Decima and Duodecima: lost
- The engraver copy of the Canon in Augmentation (P 200/1–1)
- The engraver copies of Contrapuncti (according to Wolff's numeration) I–XIV, as well as copies of the Canons in Octave, Decima and Duodecima: lost

It should be noted that Wolff did not count the Canon in Augmentation and Inversion among the lost engraver copies, presuming that it had been preserved in P 200/1–1. In reality, however, this canon, as it appears in the Original Edition, was printed from *another engraver copy* (which, also, was originally prepared by Johann Sebastian).[29] It could be, therefore, that Wolff's list is missing some materials, first and foremost the pieces that Bach revised in relation to the Autograph, P 200.

Further, and even more essential: after the music materials listed by Wolff were completed, Bach received proof sheets (that is, of the Third Version), which he carefully revised, most likely just shortly before Christoph Friedrich left for Bückeburg.[30]

It is quite difficult to establish which part of the listed set of music materials could have reached Emanuel. It is true that compositional manuscripts carry priceless information not only concerning traits of the compositional process in the creation of the specific work but also about composition processes of an entire period. However, in the mid-eighteenth century there was no norm of keeping what might have been perceived as dispensable materials, which offered little interest, even to people in Bach's circle.[31] Such documentation acquired value only in later centuries. In any case, even if the compositional manuscripts had been preserved, and were in Emanuel's possession, they would hardly have served as a source of information about the general structure of the cycle and the order of pieces, since in most cases they would have been written on loose manuscript paper.

Several of the fair and revision copies did arrive in Emanuel's hands.[32] A closer examination of the type of information concerning the composition of the cycle, which may have been found on the pages of P 200 and P 200/1, is nevertheless due. By consensus, these are considered fair copies or at least revision ones. It should be noted that Bach's pagination is absent from the main corpus, P 200.[33] The only extant numeration is that of the pieces and only the first nine pieces (including the Canon in Octave).

The supplements of P 200 render a similar picture. The Canon in Augmentation (P 200/1–1) has two secondary paginations (26–27–28, and also 33–[34]–35) related to the cycle's second part and carries no indication of the piece's serial position. The autograph of the fugue for two claviers (P 200/1–2) and the unfinished copy of the quadruple fugue (P 200/1–3) have neither page numbers marked by the composer nor any other indication of their serial position in the work; in fact, they don't even have a title. Judging by the described manuscript design of *The Art of Fugue*, the copies that Emanuel saw, (most probably proof copies), did not carry full information about the cycle's structure and its ordering of pieces.

The absence of such information is of no real surprise. Bach changed the order of pieces in his work several times throughout the composition process. This led to several changes in pagination, in serial numeration of the pieces and even in their titles.[34] It is possible that he did not consider any of these versions as final, anticipating further changes, some of which indeed took place.

The final pagination, piece numeration and titles appear only in the final stage of the engraving process, sometimes even on the already engraved copper plates.[35]

What could, then, provide any indication, for both Emanuel and the engraver, to a correct order of pieces? After all, the correct reproduction of a composition in print depended on the accuracy of the engraver's actions. Butler suggests that there were 'clear instructions concerning the pagination scheme' that accompanied this process.[36] Bach research studies provide no instances of such instructions. However, several engraver plates of works by Bach carry certain minuscule marks made with some very fine instrument. Those are reminders concerning the order of pages and pieces, transferred by the engraver from the stacks of music sheets to the copper plates. Butler mentions one such case.[37]

One phenomenon deserves special attention: the order, in which the sheets of a manuscript (of any composition) are stacked. In the eighteenth century the sheets-stacking order was important no less than the pagination or the serial numeration of pieces, although the only thing that held them together was a bifolio—a double sheet that served as a filing folder.[38] Sometimes, however, they were not bound at all and just left as a stack of folded sheets of paper.

In this respect, some information concerning *The Art of Fugue*'s structure could be derived from the fair and revision copies of the work. Still, and regardless of whether these copies were or were not marked with page or title numbers, they most probably were stacked in a certain order. Unfortunately, the fate of these copies is unknown.

A study of the Original Edition shows that Schübler engraved copper plates of almost all *The Art of Fugue* from engraver copies prepared while J.S. Bach was still alive, and that the composer did review the proof copies. While it is possible that the engraver copies remained with Schübler, it is unlikely. Usually, engravers discarded these copies, since the engraving needle damaged them and they could not be reused. Moreover, they were covered with a layer of varnish, resulting in a product that would hardly be enjoyable.[39]

The proof copies, on the other hand, were used in practice, at least by J.S. Bach. As Butler established, in his meticulous study of the engraving process of the *Clavierübung III*, the first stage of the work, preceding the print of the run, was the creation of two sets of proof sheets that Bach received for revision. Bach kept them. One set was used for the preparation of a preliminary model of the final product.[40] For this purpose the proof sheets were folded and stacked in the proper order, and then secured with special glue.[41] This set was intensively used. It contains numerous handwritten corrections, and its general appearance is telling: the printouts are made on a paper of low quality, porous and thin; the folding marks show that several sheets were folded in two, others in four, and so on. A second set of the *Clavierübung III* proof copies is tidier.[42] Its function in the process of publication remains unclear; Butler suggests that it might have been intended for sale.

The publication process of *Clavierübung III* may shed some light on the printing history of *The Art of Fugue*, since it is possible that in similar situations Bach took similar steps. And if Johann Christoph Friedrich stated, before leaving for Bückeburg, that Bach tackled the proof sheet of the Canon in Augmentation (apparently the last piece of the cycle), one can safely assume that by that moment, not only the printouts of this canon, but the whole *Art of Fugue* cycle had already existed in print sheets.[43]

It is probable that the set of proofs of *The Art of Fugue* engraved materials received by Bach was similar to the proofs of the *Clavierübung III*. If he had them, it is unlikely that they were stacked in random order. Rather, it is most likely probable that the proper order of the sheets was observed and perhaps they were even fastened together by glue. Indeed, such a final touch could be applied only to the first half of the cycle (until Cp12), where, by that time, the sequence of pieces was not subject to any further changes. The remaining pieces underwent several permutations: in all likelihood Bach did not finalise their order.

Emanuel could be guided by the numeration of contrapuncti, reflected in the original edition, which was kept intact until Cp12. The sequencing of the remaining pieces, however, depended on the conception of the whole cycle and on Emanuel's thoughts. It is clear that he had a view of the order of the pieces after Cp12, too (regardless of its coincidence with the composer's intention). Thus, when advertising subscriptions for *The Art of Fugue* he wrote:

> Die Letzten Stück sind zwey Fugen für zwey unterschiedene Claviere oder Flügel, und eine Fuge mit drey Sätzen, wo der Verfasser bey Unbringung des dritten Satzes seinen Namen *Bach* ausgeführt hat.
>
> [The last pieces are two fugues for two keyboard instruments and a fugue with three themes, in which the author, writing the third theme, has displayed his name *Bach*.][44]

Note that Emanuel lists the two last pieces in the order in which they are placed in the Original Edition. He refers to this sequence as the *author's*, without any caveat: 'The last pieces *are* ...'. On the other hand, he deliberately informs the reader that the chorale, although composed by Johann Sebastian, is included in the cycle by the editor, and then explains the reason for his intervention:

> Den Beschluß macht ein Anhang von einem vierstimmig ausgearbeiteten Kirchen-Choral, den der selige Verfasser in seinen letzten Tagen, da er schon des Gesichtes beraubet war, einem seiner Freunde in die Feder dictiret hat.

[The conclusion is provided by an appendix of a church-chorale, elaborated in four parts, which the late composer, during his last days and already deprived of eyesight, had dictated to one of his friends.][45]

Emanuel refers to the mentioned 'last pieces' (which are not numbered in the manuscript) in the announcement of the subscription without expressing any doubt concerning their being part of *The Art of Fugue* or their position in the cycle. How could he be so sure, given the lack of numeration on these pieces in the Autograph? Our assumption is that Emanuel relied on the order in which the pieces had been stacked, relating to this order as a fact that informed him of the composer's will.

There are grounds to believe, therefore, that *The Art of Fugue* reached Emanuel as a set of proofs corrected and properly stacked by his father in an order on which the son relied in his decisions. This stack was probably the Third Version of *The Art of Fugue*. That set of proofs was supplemented by three pieces: the fugue for two claviers, the quadruple fugue and the engraver copy of the Canon in Augmentation.

Several peculiarities should be noted regarding these music materials as they reached Emanuel. First, as already noted, the set of proofs was the Third Version of *The Art of Fugue*, and therefore the presence of the *Contrap: a 4.* in place of the fugue for two claviers is inconceivable.[46] It is unlikely that Emanuel, who was so careful to follow his father's intention, would have distorted the composer's idea with a personal whim. Only Johann Sebastian himself could take such an extreme step. But why would he place this piece here, against the internal logic of *The Art of Fugue*?

A second peculiarity is that the fugue for two claviers is placed not within the set of proofs, but as a supplement. This means that Johann Sebastian himself had placed it together with the supplements; in other words, it was *extracted* from the cycle. It is important to note that this fugue exists not as a proof copy but as an autograph, which had been engraved for the Original Edition only after Bach's death. It had never appeared as a proof copy during Bach's lifetime. It is not by coincidence that Emanuel had to commission for the Original Edition both the engraver copy and the engraving itself. This confirms the proposition that Bach himself extracted this piece from the cycle's Third Version. This happened, most probably, during the engraving process of the Third Version, when Bach decided to replace the fugue for two claviers with the new quadruple fugue, thus creating the Fourth Version of *The Art of Fugue*.[47] Had the fugue been engraved earlier, Emanuel would have used its plates for printing in the Original Edition. He would then have placed it on the 14th position, where *Contrap: a 4.* had been—*before* the four canons and before the *Fuga a 3 Soggetti*.

The set of music materials that Emanuel received had been closed, thus, with the autograph of the mirror fugue for two claviers (to which Emanuel refers, in his announcement, as two fugues) and with the unfinished copy of the quadruple fugue, stacked—according to the same announcement—precisely in this order. The set also contained a copy of *Contrap: a 4.*, which seems quite strange. This peculiarity, however, will serve as an index for Johann Sebastian's actions in the composition process and for those of his son in the publication process: Emanuel, as it was noted before, interpreted the sequence of pieces in the set of proofs as his father's direct instruction.

Notes

1. There are two documents containing information on this subject. The first is Carl Philipp Emanuel's advertisement, offering subscriptions to *The Art of Fugue* in the *Critische Nachrichten aus dem Reiche der Gelehrsamkeit* (Berlin, May 7, 1751; *NBR*, no. 281, pp. 256–8). Here 'the heirs of the great composer' [*Die Erben des großen Componisten*], as well as other 'gentlemen entrepreneurs' [*Herren Unternehmer*], are mentioned as those who decided to publish the composition that Johann Sebastian left in manuscript. The second source is Emanuel's other announcement offering the same kind of subscriptions in the Leipzig newspaper (Leipzig, June 1, 1751; *BD* III/639, pp. 8–9). Here are mentioned the 'Widow of Bach in Leipzig' [*in Leipzig bey der Frau Witthe Bachin*], the 'Music director Bach in Halle' [*in Halle bey dem Hrn. Music-Director Bach*], the 'Royal chamber-musician Bach in Berlin' [*in Berlin bey dem Königl. Cammer-Musicus Bach*] and the 'organist Altnickol in Naumburg' [*in Naumburg bey dem Organist Altnicol*]. These four individuals – Anna Magdalena, Wilhelm Friedemann, Carl Philipp Emanuel Bach and Johann Christoph Altnickol – are here referred not as publishers or contributors to the editorial process, but as individuals whom one can address for a subscription rather than subscribing in one of 'the distinguished bookstores' (*in den vornehmsten Buchhandlungen*). Agricola's name does not appear in any of these documents.
2. Robert Schumann, 'Ueber einige muthmaßlich corrumpirte Stellen in Bach'schen, Mozart'schen und Beethoven'schen Werken', *Neue Zeitschrift für Musik*, 38 (1841): pp. 149–51.
3. Maurice Hauptmann, *Erläuterungen zu Joh. Sebastian Bach's Kunst der Fuge* (Leipzig, 1841).
4. Hofmann, *NBA KB* VIII/2, p. 94.
5. Christoph Wolff, for example, notes that *Contrap: a 4.* 'is erroneously included,' and that 'the Augmentation Canon is erroneously placed at the beginning of the canon group.' Wolff, *Johann Sebastian Bach: The Learned Musician*, p. 434. However, he does not consider the fugue for two claviers as mistakenly incorporated into the cycle. In this case the culprit for the alleged mistakes (whether the engraver or Emanuel) is not named. By default, however, it is understood that it was not Johann Sebastian.
6. David Schulenberg, *The Keyboard Music of J.S. Bach* (New York, 2nd edition, 2006), p. 399.
7. [J.S. Bach] *Clavier-Büchlein / vor / Wilhelm Friedemann Bach. / angefangen in / Cöthen den / 22. Januarij / A[nn]o 1720.*
8. Friedemann was born on November 22, 1710.
9. Emanuel was born on March 8, 1714.
10. He returned to Halle almost half a year later, receiving a penalty for such a long absence. This fact shows that in any case he had the possibility to be present at the father's funeral, even more so than his brothers.
11. Thus, sending to Forkel the manuscript of the organ sonatas, Emanuel requests: 'Da sie sehr zerlästert sind, so belieben Sie solche gut in acht zu nehmen'. [Since they are very worn out, please be careful in handling them] (letter from October 7, 1774; *BD* III/795, p. 279). However, presenting Forkel with a copy of the *Clavierübung III*, he explains that he can give it for copying or even offer it for sale, because the Autograph stays in his possession (*BD* III/792, p. 277).
12. While serving in Halle, in the Marienkirche, he was required to write music for a university ceremony. For that he took one of his father's cantatas, set to it a new text and presented it as his own composition. A scandal ensued, and Friedemann was deprived of the 100 thalers honorarium. In another opportunity he used Bach's autograph of the organ arrangement of Vivaldi's concerto in D minor (BWV 596) and marked it 'my composition, copied by my father's hand'. The deceit was revealed: Max Schneider, 'Das sogenannte *Orgelkonzert d-moll von Wilhelm Friedemann Bach*' *BJ* 8 (1911): p. 23.
13. *BD* III/779, p 255. [In composition and keyboard playing I never had any other teacher than my father]. Translated in William S. Newman, 'Emanuel Bach's Autobiography' *The Musical Quarterly*, vol. 51/2 (1965): p. 366.
14. Ibid. Translated in *NBR*, no. 359, p. 366.

15 Burney, K. (sic) *Nachricht von Georg Friedrich Handel's Lebensumstanden und der ihm zu London im Mai und Juni 1784 angestellten Gedächtnißfeyer* (Berlin, 1785).
16 Dragan Plamenac, 'New Light on the Last Years of Carl Philipp Emanuel Bach', *The Musical Quarterly*, 35/4, (1949): pp. 583–4.
17 *BD* III/927, pp. 437–45.
18 Emanuel was hired as harpsichordist in Frederick's court two years earlier, in 1738, when Frederick still was the crown prince.
19 Voltaire, Euler and Maupertuis are the most renowned persons in this group, which included philosophers, historians, mathematicians and other men of letters.
20 *Le Président De Brosses en Italie: Lettres Familières écrites d'Italie en 1739 et 1740 par Charles de Brosses*. Quatrième édition authentique d'après les manuscrits annotée et précédée d'une étude biographique par R. Colomb (Paris, 1885).
21 Ibid. Letter to Jean Bouhier, pp. 373–84; quotation from p. 379.
22 Most famous among these were the *Lykomedes Family* group of statues, purchased in 1742, and the *Praying Boy* statue, purchased in 1747.
23 *Saggio sopra l'Architettura* del Co. Algarotti, Cavaliere dell'Ordine del Merito e Ciambellano di S. M. Il Re di Prussia (Venice, 1784), p. 7 (originally published in Bologna, 1756).
24 The famous painting by Adolph von Menzel, which shows Frederick playing the flute at Sanssouci Palace, while C.P.E. is sitting by the keyboard and accompanying him, is from 1852, and relies rather on a later mythology of the Bach family than on eye witnessing. In fact, it was mostly Quantz who accompanied the King's flute playing.
25 Giles MacDonogh, *Frederick the Great: a Life in Deed and Letters* (New York, 2000), p. 187.
26 *Laokoon oder Über die Grenzen der Malerei und Poesie* (1766).
27 Hans-Günter Ottenberg, *C.P.E. Bach* (Leipzig, 1982), translated by Philip J. Whitmore (Oxford, 1987), pp. 62–5.
28 Wolff, 'The Compositional History of the Art of Fugue' in *Bach: Essays on his Life and Music*, pp. 268–9.
29 Issues concerning the engraver copies of this canon are discussed in Chapter 17.
30 As a reminder, the evidence of this is Christoph Friederich's inscription on the engraver copy of the Canon in Augmentation (P 200/1–1).
31 Autographs of this kind were usually kept only under exceptional cases, for example, if they were written by royalty or their family members. In this regard, the archive of the Prussian Princess Amalia, Frederick II's younger sister, at the Staatsbibliothek zu Berlin (Musikabteilung), is of interest. Thanks to her preserved composition drafts scholars attained priceless information concerning the pedagogical principles of Bach's school. Amalia studied with Johann Philipp Kirnberger who was one of J.S. Bach's students and who often stated that he was following the methodical principles of his teacher. (See Alla Irmenovna Yankus, 'Predvaritel'naya rabota nad fugoy v rukopisyakh Anny Amalii Prusskoy: sistema I.F. Kirnbergera' [Preliminary work over fugues in manuscripts by the Princess Anna Amalia of Prussia: the method of J.P. Kirnberger], in Anatoly P. Milka and Kira I. Yuzhak (eds), *Rabota nad fugoy: metod i shkola I.S. Bakha: Materialy Vos'mykh Bakhovskikh chteniy 20–27 aprelya 2006 goda* [Working on fugues: the Method and School of J.S. Bach: Materials from the Eighth Bach Reading, April 20–27, 2006] (St Petersburg, 2008). English Abstract on p. 286.
32 See Chapter 5.
33 See Chapter 4.
34 A piece of evidence of Bach's careful attention to the titles of the pieces is the inscription of Johann Christoph Friedrich on the first page of the Canon in Augmentation (P 200/1–1). According to this inscription, Bach changed this canon's title for the third time, each time with a new variant and did that at the latest stage of the work's engraving.
35 Several scholars raised this possibility. A detailed discussion on this subject is found in Gregory Butler's publications. While studying the process of the engraving and printing of *Clavierübung III*

Butler established that Bach could change both pagination and even the structure of the cycle when it had already been at the engraver's desk. Butler, *Bach's Clavier-Übung III*, pp. 39–71.
36 Butler, 'Ordering Problems', p. 58.
37 Butler, ibid. pp. 51–2.
38 The handwritten legacy of Johann Sebastian and his sons includes numerous bifolios that function as folders.
39 As an exception, the engraver copy of the Canon in Augmentation was returned to Bach, although not for practical use but for revision, since its size appeared larger that the copper plate allowed (see Table 17.1 and the following discussion of this copy in Chapter 17). The traces of varnish show that Schübler handled it and that he even attempted to transfer it to a copper plate. However, the engraver had to cut short the process because of the discrepancy in size between the manuscript copy and the copper plate. This is probably why it reached J.S. Bach undamaged and was preserved.
40 This copy is kept in the British Library in London (shelfmark Hirsch III. 39). In Manfred Tessmer's study the part of edition that was engraved in Leipzig, is marked by an 'L', while the set of the proofs under discussion is marked by an 'A7' (Tessmer, *NBA KB* IV/4 (Kassel, 1974), p. 26).
41 Butler, *Bach's Clavier-Übung III*, pp. 65–71.
42 This copy is deposited in the Austrian National Library in Vienna, shelfmark *Hoboken. 1.5.Bach.33*. In Tessmer's study it is branded 'A15'.
43 Christoph Wolff, too, thinks that Bach did receive the full cycle from the engraver, but deems that it was not in proof copies but engraver copies. Wolff, *Bach: Essays*, pp. 269–70 and 212.
44 *Critische Nachrichten aus dem Reiche der Gelehrsamkeit* (May 7, 1751): p. 146. Translated in *NBR*, no. 281, p. 256.
45 Friedrich Wilhelm Marpurg, 'Carl Philipp Emanuel Bach', in *Historisch-Kritische Beyträge zur Aufnahme der Musik*, vol. 2, (Berlin, 1756), p. 576. In all the documents Philipp Emanuel—and thereafter Marpurg—highlight this circumstance, using the words *supplement* (Anhang), *appended* (beygefügten) [sic, in his preface to the Original Edition of 1751] and *added* (zugefügte; in Marpurg's introduction to the 1752 edition of *The Art of Fugue*).
46 The *Contrap: a 4.* is discussed in Chapter 13.
47 As already mentioned, this process is akin to Bach's composition of *Clavierübung III*, when, after the composition had already been completed and sent to the engraving, he decided to change its structure, adding new pieces to the existing version. There, too, the addition is not reflected in the title page.

13 Sequencing and titles in the Original Edition

Several features of the Original Edition seem odd and demand interpretation. All of these peculiar traits carry important information about the construction of the edition by Philipp Emanuel as well as about the shape that his father gave to *The Art of Fugue* prior to his death.

Philipp Emanuel paid careful attention to every piece of information left in the materials related to the composition, such as the work's title, its musical text and even the order in which the music sheets had been stacked. Striving to follow Johann Sebastian's idea as closely and precisely as possible, he made independent decisions only where it was absolutely necessary.

The sequence of pieces in the Original Edition (shown in Table 13.1) presents a practically indisputable first half, with pieces numbered consecutively up to Cp12. The presence of this numbering led to a consensual impression that in the process of preparing *The Art of Fugue* for publication J.S. Bach controlled the engraving and the order of pieces until this point.

Bearing in mind the hypothesis that there were four versions of *The Art of Fugue*, as well as the view that Bach proofread the Third Version that he was preparing for publication, it is easy to realise that this version is visible in the Original Edition as the first 18 pieces. The completion of the Third Version in the Original Edition is represented in Table 13.1 by a solid line, while the serial numbers marking the order of pieces, absent in the Original Edition, are written within square brackets.

In the 14th position appears, however, what became 'redundant material': the *Contrap: a 4.*, which Bach remodelled for the Third Version as Cp10, only to completely remove it from the cycle at a later stage. According to his assumed plan for the Third Version, the 14th piece should have been the fugue for two claviers. However, for the Fourth Version Bach intended to replace it with the new quadruple fugue. It was Emanuel who decided to include *Contrap: a 4.* in the Original Edition. Thus, in Table 13.1, under the column 'who determined the serial position', this piece is marked as positioned by both Carl Philipp Emanuel and Johann Sebastian.

The scholarly conviction that Bach controlled the order of the pieces up to Cp12 is based on the fact that these pieces carry serial numbers. This implies that Emanuel could have based

Table 13.1 Plan of the Original Edition

Serial number	Title	Who gave the title	Who determined the serial position
1	*Contrapunctus 1.*	J.S.	J.S.
2	*Contrapunctus 2.*	J.S.	J.S.
3	*Contrapunctus 3.*	J.S.	J.S.
4	*Contrapunctus 4.*	J.S.	J.S.
5	*Contrapunctus 5.*	J.S.	J.S.
6	*Contrapunctus 6. a 4 in Stylo Francese.*	J.S.	J.S.
7	*Contrapunctus 7. a 4. per Augment et Diminut:*	J.S.	J.S.
8	*Contrapunctus 8. a 3.*	J.S.	J.S.
9	*Contrapunctus 9. a 4. alla Duodecima*	J.S.	J.S.
10	*Contrapunctus 10. a 4. alla Decima.*	J.S.	J.S.
11	*Contrapunctus. 11. a 4.*	J.S.	J.S.
12_1	*Contrapunctus inversus. 12 á 4.*	J.S.	J.S.
[12_2]	*Contrapunctus inversus a 4*	J.S.	J.S.
[13_1]	*Contrapunctus a 3*	J.S.	J.S.
[13_2]	*Contrapunctus inversus a 3.*	J.S.	J.S.
[14]	**Contrap: a 4.**	**J.S.**	**C.P.E. (J.S.)**
[15]	*Canon per Augmentationem in Contrario Motu.*	J.S.	J.S.
[16]	*Canon alla Ottava.*	J.S.	J.S.
[17]	*Canon alla Decima Contrapunto alla Terza.*	J.S.	J.S.
[18]	*Canon alla Duodecima in Contrapunto alla Quinta.*	J.S.	J.S.
[19_1]	*Fuga a 2 Clav:*	C.P.E.	C.P.E.
[19_2]	*Alio modo. Fuga a 2. Clav.*	C.P.E.	C.P.E.
[20]	*Fuga a 3 Soggetti*	C.P.E.	C.P.E.
[21]	*Choral.Wenn wir in hoechsten Noethen sein Canto Fermo in Canto.*	C.P.E.	C.P.E.

his sequencing decisions on only these first 12 numbers, and that since there is no numeration after Cp12, all the remaining pieces could follow in a random order.

However, if the Third Version was completed, then all its engraved plates, the titles of the pieces and their serial numbers (except for the fugue for two claviers) were settled, too. Remembering that the canons, unlike the contrapuncti, were not numbered (because they were not included in the first 14 pieces, the number symbolising Bach's name), only two pieces were left unnumbered in the Original Edition, Cp[13] and Cp[14], the latter supposedly the quadruple fugue that reached Emanuel not only unnumbered and untitled, but also unfinished; that is, not Cp[14] but Cp[14F]. As for Cp[13], the lack of numeration here can be explained by a closer examination of the titles Cp12 and Cp[13]. It is not by chance that the number 12 was inscribed just on the title of the first half of the mirror fugue (the rectus) and is absent from its second half (the inversus). Figure 13.1 shows the titles of these contrapuncti as they appear in the Original Edition:

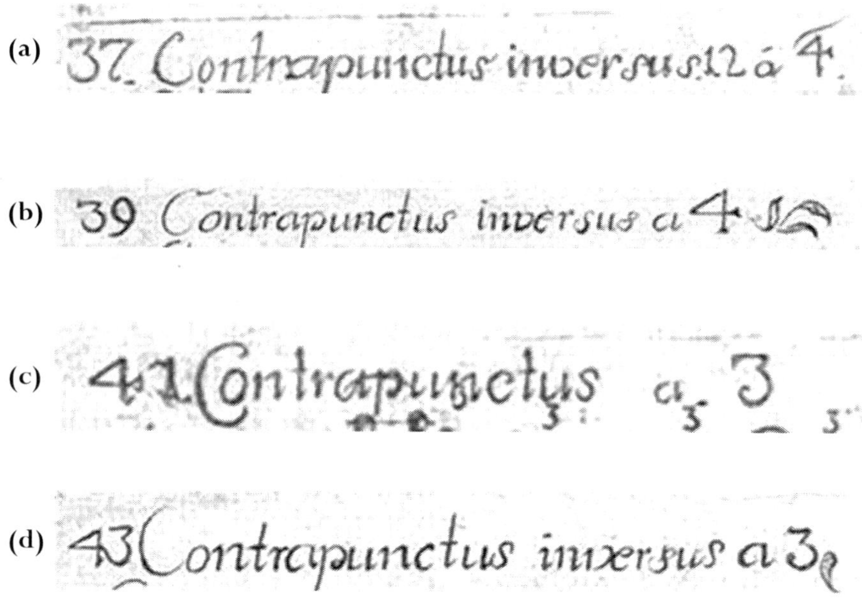

164 Part IV: Carl Philipp Emanuel Bach's work toward the publication of The Art of Fugue

(a) 37. Contrapunctus inversus 12 á 4.

(b) 39 Contrapunctus inversus a 4

(c) 41 Contrapunctus a 3

(d) 43 Contrapunctus inversus a 3

Figure 13.1 The titles of the two mirror fugues in the Original Edition.

An analysis of these inscriptions reveals several points:

- In the first inscription, the number 12 was inserted with some difficulty into a relatively small space (6 mm) between the words *inversus* and *á 4*, an insertion made, in all likelihood, after the inscription of the title.
- The same space in the three remaining titles is even smaller: 2.5, 5 and 2 mm respectively.
- The lack of numeration of these mirror fugues may not have been due to the lack of space as much as for their frequent permutation by Bach during the last stage of composition.
- By implication, it is therefore likely that the number 12 here functioned rather as a 'custus', connecting the group of mirror fugues with the numeration sequence of the first group of contrapuncti.

In other words, it seems that the contrapuncti listed in Table 13.1 above the solid line represent the Third Version of *The Art of Fugue*, and those listed below the line are those added by Philipp Emanuel. The difference is clear. In the first part, J.S. Bach's original titles are preserved; the titles in the second part, on the other hand, were prescribed by Emanuel, who also intervened in the general title of the work. Fugues number 19 and 20 (the two fugues for two claviers and the *Fuga a 3 Soggetti*) carry no titles in the Autograph, yet Emanuel could not send them to print untitled. Nevertheless, when the titles above the solid line in the table are compared with those below it, Emanuel's efforts to show the change of hands in the Original Edition are apparent.

Another indicator of this division can be seen in the metric and rhythmic differences between the last four pieces and those preceding them.

The oddities of *Contrap: a 4.*

The peculiar title

A first oddity is seen in the uniquely abbreviated title. This abbreviation could not be Emanuel's because he was so careful to preserve intact anything that was made by his father. He would not, by his own initiative, add the title *Contrapunctus* to any piece or transform it even by way of abbreviation. The fact that he had never done so in similar cases only substantiates this assertion.[1] Therefore, he would name *Contrap: a 4.* neither a 'contrapunctus' nor a 'fugue'. If this particular title, in its abbreviated form, is present in the Original Edition, it means that Emanuel had seen the words *Contrap: a 4.* written in exactly such a manner: the inscribed title must have been done by Johann Sebastian.

Rhythmic peculiarity

Contrap: a 4., which is based on the sixth fugue in the Autograph, presents the original rhythmic values doubled, (just as Cp10, which was derived for the Third Version from the same fugue's countersubject, has its original rhythmic values doubled). This trait, which strengthens the similarity of *Contrap: a 4.* to Cp10, is an exception. Since it is quite clear that Emanuel would not bother to transform rhythmic values and/or metre, preferring to leave a variant in its original form, the fact that *Contrap: a 4.* is written in rhythmic augmentation suggests that it reached Emanuel precisely in this form.

The position in the Original Edition

Another peculiarity is apparent in the position of *Contrap: a 4.*: right after the second mirror fugue and before the Canon in Augmentation and Inversion.[2] Beyond its awkward position in the sequence, this piece is mostly a repetition of Cp10 and therefore should not have been included in the final version at all. Regardless of the fact that the scholarly literature about *The Art of Fugue* has noticed this, Emanuel could not help but see how illogical such an insertion would be and subsequently remove it from the series or admit that he did not understand this point in his father's compositional conception by simply accepting the order of pieces as they were found in the stack of proofs. However, that was the position reserved, in the Third Version, for Cp[14] (the fugue for two claviers). How, then, did a copy of *Contrap: a 4.* arrive in that position in the stack?

An external insert

Studies of the Original Edition and the engraving style show that the engraver copy of *Contrap: a 4.* was produced after Bach's death, during Emanuel's preparation of *The Art of Fugue* for print. It looks odd, because all of the contrapuncti, from 1 to [13] and also the four canons were engraved while Johann Sebastian was still alive, forming the Third Version: a full set of proof copies for the future printing of *The Art of Fugue*. However, in the whole set there was no proof copy of *Contrap: a 4.* Had such a copy existed, this fugue would be printed in the Original

166 Part IV: Carl Philipp Emanuel Bach's work toward the publication of The Art of Fugue

Edition from a copper plate, engraved while Bach was still alive and not after his death. This means that the musical text of *Contrap: a 4.* existed within the set of the musical materials, but as a *manuscript* (a handwritten copy) and not as a proof copy. This is why, following Emanuel's instructions, *Contrap: a 4.* had to be especially engraved for the Original Edition.

At this point, however, it is still unclear why the fugue for two claviers (Cp[14]) was missing from the proof copies set of the Third Version, and how the manuscript of the formerly discarded *Contrap: a 4.* appeared among the proof copies in its stead. Further, while in the Third Version the fugue for two claviers occupied this place, in the Fourth Version it was removed from this position by Johann Sebastian in order to be replaced by the new, quadruple fugue (which does appear in the Original Edition in its unfinished form and under the title *Fuga a 3 Soggetti*).[3]

It seems that the strange insertion of *Contrap: a 4.* reflects a particular moment in the materialisation of the Fourth Version. The fugue for two claviers was removed; in its stead should appear the new fugue, which was still incomplete. *Contrap: a 4.* was thus inserted as a temporary bookmark, indicating the *position of a still missing proof copy*. This fugue is basically a recycled piece of used paper that temporarily marked the place where the closing fugue should have been inserted. The fact that *Contrap: a 4.* did not look like a proof copy, but rather like a fair copy, different from the other proof copies in the stack, supports this interpretation. In this particular context it clearly 'does not belong here': something else should be positioned at this particular location.

Contrap: a 4. occupies a special place in *The Art of Fugue*'s printing history. It was not strictly *added* by Emanuel to the printed version of the composition, because it was already present in the set, as a handwritten copy, among the proof copies left by his father. While Sebastian did not intend to include this contrapunctus in the final version, it was nevertheless physically present there, placed by J.S. Bach's very hand. This was probably the reason that Emanuel did not move it to another position nor remove it from the cycle, but left it exactly in the position where it was found.

Emanuel's initiative

The fugue for two claviers was removed from the Autograph. The bifolio was torn, separating the pair of mirror fugues, and recorded as P 200/1–2.[4] This fugue was formerly a part of the cycle's Third Version but was extracted from it and replaced by the new, quadruple fugue. If indeed this is the copy that was excluded by the composer from the cycle's Fourth Version, it was not engraved. Emanuel had to prepare it from scratch. An analysis of the Original Edition's engraving shows that this is exactly what happened. While doing this, Emanuel did not dare to write it in double rhythmic values, although he surely could not help seeing the similar case, Cp[13], where Johann Sebastian reworked the fugue from the Autograph precisely in this way.

The quadruple fugue reached Emanuel unfinished, without closure, in a two-stave clavier setting (P 200/1–3). Naturally, he could not know what position within the cycle it was supposed to occupy, but its unfinished state might have suggested that it should be the last piece. Indeed, this is where he positioned it in the Original Edition and how he described it in the announcement of the subscription from May 7, 1751. In all likelihood he had to commission a special engraver copy of this fragment, interpreted from the clavier layout in the Autograph into an open score layout. This arrangement was mandatory, because Emanuel could not include in the Original Edition just one piece that was not yet ready in an open score layout.[5]

However, Emanuel made his mark on the titles of the three pieces that were added to the Third Version and positioned at the end of the Original Edition. The title *Contrapunctus* and numbering were missing from the following three fugues (the two mirror fugues for two claviers and the *Fuga a 3 Soggetti*).

Emanuel was not aware that the fugue for two claviers should not be part of *The Art of Fugue*'s final version. To add it to the Original Edition he would have needed a title and a number. However, since it was not part of the Third Version stack, he would not have used the term *Contrapunctus*. He thus compromised on the most general and obvious feature of the piece: it was a fugue, and it was written for two claviers, and consequently titled *Fuga a 2. Clav*. Moreover, in its inversus, Emanuel went as far as to avoid pointing at the inversion, although he surely understood that this fugue continues the compositional logic of the previous mirror fugues. He circumscribed himself into an even more general term: *alio modo*, which can be understood as *the same, but in another way*.

As for the 'unfinished' fugue, Emanuel did not envision its position, although he (mistakenly) assumed, judging by the documents he had available at the time, that it should be the last in the cycle. As P 200/1–3 it does not carry a serial number, pagination or title. As with the fugue for two claviers, Emanuel neither called it *Contrapunctus* nor gave it a number, although the general logic of the cycle would have allowed it.[6] Here, too, he indicated only the features of which, at the beginning of 1751, he was completely certain and which he published in press: he saw a fugue with three subjects and cautiously titled it *Fuga a 3 Soggetti*.[7]

An analysis of Philipp Emanuel's steps throughout the publication process of *The Art of Fugue* shows that he acted with great sensitivity to questions of restoration and authenticity. Like a skilled curator he avoided, as much as he could, any intervention in the composer's conception of his work. He broke this rule only when conditions compelled him to introduce his own marks, and even then he did it in such a way that his contribution was clearly distinguishable from the composer's. Although his professional competence and knowledge of Bach's style surely enabled him to realise that these additional pieces were indeed contrapuncti, and he could easily organise them in a numerical order, he chose to take no responsibility over either nomination or numeration.[8]

Emanuel's attitude toward the restoration of *The Art of Fugue* in the Original Edition allows a hypothetical reconstruction of the material that was available to him before the publication of the work, as well as a delineation of what he did for the publication. These facts suggest that he received the materials of *The Art of Fugue* as a set of proof copies (or, although much less likely, engraver copies), after they had been reviewed by his father and stacked in a certain order.

This given set of pieces, in that particular order, constituted the final version of *The Art of Fugue*,[9] as determined by Johann Sebastian, with one exception: the place where Bach *temporarily* inserted a simple fair copy of *Contrap: a 4.*, which was planned for the closing quadruple fugue. Emanuel, however, left the ill-fated *Contrap: a 4.* in the cycle, obediently following the received order of pieces and preserving it in the Original Edition.

The main protagonist in this story was the quadruple fugue that should replace the fugue for two claviers which occupied that position in the Third Version. Indeed—the three pieces that in a way did not belong to the Third Version of *The Art of Fugue* (*Contrap: a 4.*; the fugue for two claviers and the quadruple fugue) were still connected by the same thread: they were steps toward the cycle's unfinished Fourth Version. However, on the way toward the Fourth Version, the fugue for two claviers was removed, while the quadruple fugue, which should be positioned in that spot, was not yet completed, and the placement was thus temporarily marked by the 'bookmark' of *Contrap: a 4*.

It is possible that two manuscripts were later added to this set: the fugue for two claviers and the quadruple fugue, most probably in the same order in which they were to be included in the Original Edition.[10] To these—now by his own initiative—Philipp Emanuel added the choral *Wenn wir in hoechsten Noethen sein*, always—in the announcement of the subscription and in other documents—pointing out that it was an arrangement composed by Johann Sebastian but external to *The Art of Fugue*. Moreover, Philipp Emanuel and, following him, Marpurg highlighted this point in all the documents, using such words as 'addition' (*Anhang*), 'supplemented' (*beigefügten*), 'added' (*zugefügte*). This is yet another proof of the careful attention with which the son respected the will of his father.

Notes

1 The fugue for two claviers and the 'unfinished' fugue have no titles in the Autograph. Emanuel thus used in the titles the obvious term, the fact that they were *fugues*.
2 The position of *Contrap: a 4.* does not follow the logic of the cycle either in relation to the preceding pieces or to the following ones.
3 This is actually the quadruple fugue. The autograph that Emanuel received (P 200/1 3) did not have a fourth theme. It was only later that Gustav Nottebohm showed that there were four themes (see Nottebohm, 'J.S. Bach's letzte Fuge'). Indeed, the definition of this fugue is complicated: there is no fourth theme in the exposition: it appears as a *cantus firmus* in the closing section of the fugue. Hence, the correct classification of this fugue would be *a triple fugue on a cantus firmus*. The 'fourth theme' functions, in fact, as a countersubject. In this sense this fugue is similar to Contrapunctus 9, which is a simple fugue over cantus firmus (although there the cantus firmus is the main theme).
4 For a detailed discussion of the Autograph's materials see Chapter 4.
5 In this announcement Emanuel explains in detail the usefulness of presenting the fugues in a score format and specifies that *The Art of Fugue* is printed in this layout.
6 The following generation of Bach scholars marked both these fugues with serial numbers.
7 It was precisely this peculiarity (a triple fugue) that he indicated in all the advertisements, but even this careful definition, which initially appeared to him as irrefutable, proved eventually to be wrong.
8 In his announcement, Emanuel offered an expanded description of *The Art of Fugue*'s characteristics. Its content proves that he was aware and had an excellent understanding of the details and technical peculiarities of the cycle's collection of compositions. His only mistake concerning the structure of the cycle could owe itself to two issues. First, when preparing the first publication of *The Art of Fugue*, he surely did not know that Bach had 'einen andern Grund Plan', while he might have been impressed by information concerning the work's Second Version that Johann Sebastian might have shared with him during his visit to Potsdam, in May 1747. Second, the musical materials of *The Art of Fugue*, as received by Emanuel, did not easily render the final version of the composition; in fact, it was rather indistinguishable. He must have realised that the previous version had been changed, but he was also aware of his lack of knowledge about it. In such a situation, the optimal decision was to follow the order in which the music was folded and stacked, interpreting it as a direction indicated by his father.
9 It can, in fact, be presented as the Third Version of *The Art of Fugue*, with one exception: the fugue for two claviers should replace the *Contrap: a 4*.
10 Their order is kept in Emanuel's announcement of the subscription.

14   The history of the 1752 edition

The 1752 edition is puzzling. Regardless of how one might look at it, its reason and purpose seem senseless. The first edition was offered for sale on September 29, 1751. Six months later, on April 2, 1752, followed the second edition. This means that the second edition of *The Art of Fugue* was commissioned almost immediately after the publication of the first one. Six months may suffice for printing a given edition and having it ready for sale, but it is too short to prepare a whole new edition.[1]

What could be the purpose of such a hurried operation?

The financial argument has to be discarded. If a bigger run was required, it could have been done at the first printing. Were the first edition a bestseller, a desire to repeat it straightaway could be understandable. But it was not; the sales were slow, despite constant price reductions: from 10 Reichsthalers, announced by Emanuel at the beginning,[2] it went down to five,[3] and finally, to four.[4] In one of the publications, a few years after issuing both editions of *The Art of Fugue*, Emanuel wrote with regret that only about 30 copies had been sold in total.[5]

Perhaps the 'entrepreneurs' intended to make some changes in the new edition in order to improve revenue? The comparison shows that the 1752 edition differs from the previous one only in its cover, preface and the paper type. Everything else, including misprints, remain absolutely identical. Was it for such a result that Emanuel initiated a new, expensive and, yet again, commercially unsuccessful undertaking? It would be naïve to presume that a change of cover or paper quality might improve the sale results, and Emanuel could not but realise that. If he had had such hopes, he would have taken the necessary steps to advertise these particular changes. However, Emanuel does not mention any of these in any of the publications concerning the subscription or sale of the second edition.[6] Nevertheless, the second edition was issued, implying that there must have been another reason for its publication.

The motive for embarking on such an allegedly futile new edition may be connected to a meeting between Philipp Emanuel and Christoph Friedrich in Bückeburg (during the last days of June and the beginning of July 1751). This encounter took place when the first edition of *The Art of Fugue* was already in print. Given that the upcoming publication was a main family event, it is nearly impossible that Emanuel would not have told his brother about it, as well as how would it look once printed.[7] During this probable conversation, Christoph Friedrich would surely have corrected his brother and updated him about the latest structure of the cycle.[8] However, Emanuel's reaction to this news could not have been the publication of a new edition in which the only changes were the cover, preface and quality of paper; he would have made changes more in accordance with the composer's authentic plan. The new edition, however, carries no content changes. Why would that be?

The new information required substantial updating, a task that had to be done before sending the work to print. Such updating would consist of several steps:

- Finding the end of the last, 'unfinished' fugue, the overall size (rectus and inversus) of which had to cover about nine page spreads
- Removing *Contrap: a 4.* and the fugue for two claviers from the cycle
- If just a clavier-score of the last fugue is found, writing it in open score
- Preparing its engraver copy

While the two latter tasks were quite achievable, the first presented serious challenges. Emanuel, so it seems, did not realise, when ordering the second edition of *The Art of Fugue* practically right after issuing the first one, how difficult finding the fugue's closure might prove to be. At least part of his efforts may be traced through a short note written on a small piece of paper. According to Siegfried Dehn, the Berlin Staatsbibliothek's librarian who received the Autograph, this note was attached to the folder in which all three supplements to the Autograph of *The Art of Fugue* were kept. The writing on the paper stated that 'Herr Hartmann hat das eigentliche' [Mr. Hartmann has the real thing].[9] It is unclear who this Hartmann was, and trying to find out will probably prove to be quite futile. The piece of paper was lost, but Dehn, writing in the journal Cäcilia, ascribes the inscription to C.P.E. Bach.[10]

This information may suggest that Philipp Emanuel undertook a search for the completed quadruple fugue. Clearly, he failed, or else he would have published it in its finalised form. Unfortunately, when he had to accept that his efforts were in vain, it was too late to cancel the commission, and the content of the second edition remained identical to the first. Nevertheless, based on the information he received from Johann Christoph Friedrich, Emanuel did succeed in informing his readers what kind of fugue should appear at the end of his father's cycle. For this purpose he used Mizler's *Musikalische Bibliothek*. There, in the obituary for Johann Sebastian, he described the main features of this fugue. He did not mention either the fugue for two claviers or the triple fugue, not even the 'deathbed' choral. Only the two last fugues, which are connected to each other in a special way, and the information about the quadruple fugue are mentioned.

Notes

1 This period is characteristic. For example, in November 1751, when Johann Matthesohn's *Philologisches Tresespiel* was in print, he wrote that it would be issued only by the Easter Fair, in April of 1752. This in fact coincides with the issuing period of the second edition of *The Art of Fugue*. A similar time span was planned by J.S. Bach for the edition of the *Clavierübung III* (Butler, *Bach's Clavier-Übung III*, p. 125, note 4). True, Bach's constant revisions during the engraving process changed the deadline, but the very fact of its happening tells what was considered a reasonable period.

2 Thomas Wilhelmi, 'Carl Philipp Emanuel Bachs 'Avertissement' über den Druck der Kunst der Fuge,' *BJ* 78 (1992): p. 102: 'wird das Werck nicht unter 10 Reichstalern verkauft werden.' [After that time the work will not be sold under 10 Reichsthaler.] C.P.E. Bach's announcement is translated in *NBR* no. 281, p. 257.

3 See Johann Matthesohn, *Philologisches Tresespiel*: 'Wie wäre es denn, wenn ein jeder Aus- und Einlander an diese Seltenheit seinen *Louis d'or* wagte?' [How would it be, then, if every foreigner and every compatriot risked his louis d'or on this rarity?] (*BD* III/647, p. 12. Translated in *NBR*, no. 375, p. 377). In 1751, one *Louis d'or* was equal to five Reichsthalern.
4 See Emanuel's announcement for the sale of the engraved copper plates of *The Art of Fugue*: 'Dieses Werk wurde bisher 4 Rthlr. das Exemplar verkauft.' (*BD* III/683, p. 113). [This work has been sold hitherto at 4 Reichsthaler the copy.] (*NBR*, no. 376, p. 378).
5 Ibid.
6 The only advertising claim of the publication's high quality is in the announcement of the copper plates sale, which states that the engraving is 'neat and accurate' ['saubre und accurat' – ibid.]. However, since both editions had to be printed from the same plates, this comment gave no advantage to the new edition over the first one.
7 As a reminder, Philipp Emanuel had an idea about compositional steps that his father took concerning *The Art of Fugue* for its Second Version, of which he became aware during Johann Sebastian's visit to Sanssouci in May 1747. Christoph Friedrich, on the other hand, knew about later developments, possibly even about the Fourth Version (as it was by the end of December 1749).
8 The fact that such a conversation took place is substantiated in the obituary, written by the end of 1750 (*NBR*, no. 306, p. 297, note 28.) In paragraph 8 of the obituary Emanuel reports about *The Art of Fugue*, mentioning the plan for the quadruple fugue. His only possible resource for this information would be Christoph Friedrich (ibid. p. 304).
9 *NBR*, no. 377, p. 378.
10 Siegfried Wilhelm Dehn, 'Ueber einige Theils noch ungedruckte, Theils durch den Druck bereits veröffentliche musikalische Manuskripte von Johann Sebastian Bach, welche sich in der musikalischen Abteilung der König. Bibliothek zu Berlin befinden', *Cäcilia*, 24 (1845): p. 22. Wilhelm Rust, while preparing the first edition of Bach's works, stated that Philipp Emanuel failed to find this sheet. See: Wilhelm Rust, *Bach-Gesellschaft Ausgabe*, Band 25/1 *Die Kunst der Fuge* (Leipzig, 1878), pp. xix–xx.

Part V

Toward a new interpretation of *The Art of Fugue*

15 The title page as a 'letters and numbers game' and the question of authorship[1]

No Bach scholar has ever seen the title page of *The Art of Fugue* or, for that matter, even the name of the work written in Bach's own hand. This is why it is still uncertain who, in fact, conceived of the title. The problem first emerged when Philipp Spitta raised doubts, which later spread to other Bach studies,[2] as to whether the title *Kunst der Fuge* came from Bach himself.[3] We do know that the name *Kunst der Fuge* was altered throughout the formation process of the work as a whole. The reasons for these alterations, once revealed, might cast a light on the puzzle of the title's authorship.

Four variants of the title are known today: two handwritten and two in print. The earliest of those preserved was written by J.C. Altnickol (Figure 15.1).[4]

Figure 15.1 P 200: The title page of *The Art of Fugue*.

The inscription reads: *Die / Kunst der Fuga / d. Sig[?] Joh. Seb. Bach*.[5]

The next, chronologically, is probably the other handwritten variant, inscribed by Johann Christoph Friedrich Bach (?)[6] and Carl Philipp Emanuel Bach on the grey-blue cover of the folder that contained all three supplements to P 200 (Figure 15.2).

The inscription can be dated sometime between 1748 and 1752. It reads: *[Die] Kunst / der Fuge / Von J[.]S.B.*[7] The first printed variant of the title appears on the cover page of the 1751 edition (Figure 15.3).

176   *Part V: Toward a new interpretation of* The Art of Fugue

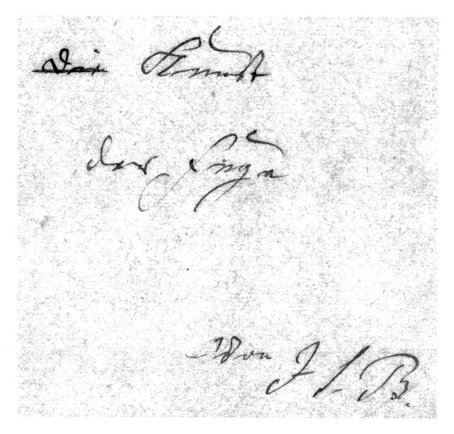

Figure 15.2 P 200/1: The title page of *The Art of Fugue* on the supplements folder.

Figure 15.3 The title page of the 1751 Original Edition.

It reads: *Die / Kunst der Fuge / durch / Herrn Johann Sebastian Bach / ehemahligen Capellmeister und Musikdirector zu Leipzig.* The title page of the 1752 edition has exactly the same wording, with only layout differences: here the word 'Herrn' is positioned in a separate line and is written all in capital letters; the words 'zu Leipzig' are separated in a last line: *Die / Kunst der Fuge / durch / HERRN / Johann Sebastian Bach / ehemahligen Capellmeister und Musikdirector / zu Leipzig.*

Each of these four title page variants has unique traits that deserve discussion. First, however, the possibility that the title itself, *Die Kunst der Fuge*, may have been invented not by Bach but by someone else, should be contemplated. The feasibility that by 1744, after several years of composing this new work, encircled by family members, pupils and friends who knew his work, and often copied parts of it, he had not given it even a temporary name, is very low to nil. The starting premise, therefore, is that J.S. Bach did have some kind of a working title, with which those in his close circle were probably familiar. Assuming that, giving a different title to this work without the author's consent, is hard to imagine. Therefore, the working assumption of this study is that Bach himself gave *The Art of Fugue* its title.

Still, the title of a work is not synonymous with the *title page*. The latter has its own structure, on which Bach bestowed a special significance that often transcended the literal meaning of the title itself. Nevertheless, the fact is that the title page of the fair copy of *The Art of Fugue* (P 200) remained blank for a long time (the exact period has not been established yet).

It has been established, though, that Bach began his work on *The Art of Fugue* in 'about 1740 at the latest, more likely the end of the 1730s.'[8] The beginning of Bach's cooperation with Altnickol is documented in the composer's letter of recommendation on the latter's behalf, written in September 1745.[9] It appears, therefore, that the recto of the Autograph's first page remained blank for several years (from about 1740)—an interval of time that seems rather strange. What might have been the reason for this delay? A comparison of Altnickol's inscription with the other three might provide an answer.

The title page of the autograph (P 200)

This title is organised in three lines:

Die

Kunst der Fuga

d. Sig[?] Joh. Seb. Bach.

The unnecessary juxtaposition of German and Italian, quite uncommon for a title page, immediately attracts attention. Its contrast with the three other variants of the title page, which are written exclusively in German, underscores the peculiarity of this combination. In fact, it had led several scholars to doubt the authenticity of the title.[10] What might have prompted this mixing of languages?

A look at paragrammatic compositions that were widespread in German culture throughout the seventeenth century and the first half of the eighteenth century may provide an explanation.[11] Figure 15.4 shows a fragment from the *Poetischer Trichter* [Poetic Bullhorn] by Georg Philipp Harsdörfer.[12] It features a paragrammatic composition where the words 'Jesus ist Christus' equal in their numerical value (218) to 'unser Helfter und Heile,' thus creating a pair of symbolic synonyms.

VII.

sich das vorhergehende geendet / den Mißlaut zuverhüten / als : er ist schreiend entsprungen/ den Reuter ergreiffen ꝛc.

70. Von den zweydeutigen Wörtern / von den Erfindungen so von der Zeit / den Namen/ den Zahlen ꝛc. hergenommen werden / ist hier nicht zu reden / weil solches alles in dem ersten Theil deß Poëtischen Trichters nach allen Umbständen erkläret worden / und müssen wir nur diese fast neue Erfindungsquelle anführen belangend die Zahl Buchstaben auf nachgehende Weise gesetzet:

a. b. c. d. e. f. g. h. i. k. l. m. n. o. p. q.
1. 2. 3. 4. 5. 6. 7. 8. 9. 10. 11. 12. 13. 14. 15. 16.

r. s. t. u. w. x. y. z.
17. 18. 19. 20. 21. 22. 23. 24.

Wann ich nun einen Namen habe / so finde ich einen Spruch/ der mit denselben/ gleiche Zahlen führet.

Jesus ist Christus   } bringet } 218
unser Helffer und Heile. }   } 218

Solche gleichzahlige Namen und Sprüche verursachen zu eigentlichen Erfindungen / und sind in den Philosophischen und Mathematischen Erquickstunden zu sehen.

Die

Figure 15.4 Numerical alphabet and paragram in Harsdörfer's *Poetischer Trichter*.

There are instances of Bach's use of similar techniques. It has been confirmed that Bach paid serious attention to paragrammatic constructions as early as the mid-1730s. In his later works, he applied this technique extensively, especially in the Mass in B minor (and most clearly in the *Symbolum Nicenum*).

The First Version of *The Art of Fugue*, finalised in the manuscript P 200, was created between 1740–42 and 1746.[13] The fact that paragrammatic compositions from that period have been frequently spotted in his cantatas and oratorios does not exclude their presence in instrumental music, too, where the compositional evolvement is not necessarily related to a text. In such cases, paragrams would feature in the title and the title page.

The length of the title supports attempts at its interpretation as a paragram. In comparison with other works by Bach, such as the Inventions, Sinfonias or *The Well-Tempered Clavier*, which feature longer titles, a longer title would be expected here, too, particularly since *The Art of Fugue* is such a fundamental work.[14] Yet, the first two variants of the title are brief.

It is most likely that Bach, always very particular with regard to signs and symbols of his own name in different variants (Bach = 14; J.S. Bach = 41; Johann Sebastian Bach = 158) would not have resisted the temptation to exploit the numerical proximity of the following:

$$\text{Die Kunst der Fuge} = 162$$
$$\text{Johann Sebastian Bach} = 158$$

Only four digits separate the title and the composer's name, and Bach did not miss this opportunity to create here, too, a pair of symbolic synonyms. The process of matching is not simple: one has not only to match digits, but also to retain the meaning of the text. Bach found a brilliant solution: in the word 'Fuge', he changed just the last letter, resulting in 'Fuga,' the Latin (and Italian) form of the same term. This resulted in a rather odd linguistic combination, particularly when compared with the more familiar later versions of the title where the spelling is entirely German. However, although not common, such spelling is acceptable as an 'admissible atypicality', widely spread among encrypted Baroque inscriptions. The composer, therefore, arrived at the unique title on the cover of P 200: 'Die Kunst der Fuga', generating the required match:

$$\text{Die Kunst der Fuga} = 158$$
$$\text{Johann Sebastian Bach} = 158$$

The result is a typical paragrammatic composition. Interestingly, 158 is not just the numerical expression of Johann Sebastian Bach; the sum of digits in this number equals the numerical value of Bach (2–1–3–8), a fact of great importance for the composer:

$$(1 + 5 + 8) = (2 + 1 + 3 + 8) = 14$$

It is hard to imagine that such a paragram is a mere coincidence and that Bach did not notice it. On the contrary, there is reason to believe that he invested intellectual effort in matching numbers and letters. We should remember, however, that the phrase 'Johann Sebastian Bach' is only a suggested abstraction, a possible reference whose numerical value the composer could have had in mind for the paragram of the first two lines in this title page.

180   Part V: Toward a new interpretation of The Art of Fugue

The above considerations encourage a similar approach to analysis of the third line of the title page. The numerical sum of its letters is 108. This number is so far away from 158 that in order to find its paragrammatic meaning one needs to look for some other principle of codification. The only datum we have, thus, at this stage, is the first expression of a possible paragram.

d. Sig[?] Joh. Seb. Bach = 108

It was Friedrich Smend who first mentioned the number '84' that Bach wrote at the end of the Patrem omnipotentem in the Mass in B minor, sealing the 84 bars of the section. Taking this as a starting point, Robin Leaver proposed an analytic method, looking at the symbolic meanings encapsulated in the number of bars of each section in the Credo. Later, Anthony Newman mentions the match between the number of letters in the poetic text (84) and the number of bars in the musical text (84).[15] Combining this method with our analysis of the titles of *The Art of Fugue*, we matched the third line on P 200's title page with the number of bars in the first three fugues of *The Art of Fugue*. The reason for choosing the first three fugues is that they share an important feature: they, and only they, leave the theme rhythmically intact (starting in half notes). Their total number of bars is 111. Although the numbers do not match, and therefore there is still no finalised paragram, the difference is small:

d. Sig[?] Joh. Seb. Bach   = 108
Number of bars in fugues I, II and III = 111

This small mismatch may be related to the fact that the numerical value of the title's third line is, actually, still unclear: one sign, here replaced by a question mark, is rather indistinct and although quite visible is not easily read. Unsurprisingly, various scholars have interpreted this mark in different ways. For instance, Christoph Wolff reads it as the abbreviation as 'di Sig.';[16] Peter Schleuning—as 'di Sign°',[17] and Klaus Hofmann as 'd. Sig*l*.', writing the last letter in cursive script.[18]

Yet, another reading could be offered. In eighteenth-century German manuscript practice, this figure used to serve as a conventional abbreviation. It had the character of a capital 'C' in cursive Latin. The sign is derived from the initial letter of the French word *coupure* (a cut), marking a truncated word.[19] Johann Christoph Friedrich Bach, for example, used it quite often to abbreviate certain words. For example, the word 'Graflicher' in his letter to the State Graf Wilhelm Schaumburg-Lippe, on May 24, 1759, written 'grafC' (Figure 15.5);[20] the word 'Bückeburg', from which he wrote a letter to Breitkopf, the publisher, on November 20, 1785, is written 'BückebC'; so is the word 'exempel' in another letter to Breitkopf from November 23, 1784, written 'exemC' and the word 'Herrn' in a letter, also to Breitkopf, from December 17, 1786, written 'HC'.[21] The sign 'SigC', therefore, probably means 'Signor', and the 'd.' marks the Italian word 'di' (or, to accept a further linguistic mixture—'der'), abbreviated here for the sake of the paragram.

 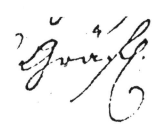

Figure 15.5 P 200: the inscription 'SigC' on the title page, probably meaning 'Signor' (left); the inscription 'GrafC' from J.C.F. Bach's letter to Graf Wilhelm Schaumburg-Lippe, meaning 'Graflicher' (right).

Interpreted as a 'C', the letter carries the numerical value 3, allowing the following calculation:

d. Sig[C] Joh. Seb. Bach = 111
Number of bars in fugues I, II and III = 111

The above findings indicate that what may seem at first a strange linguistic concoction of French, Italian and German abbreviations, truncations and so on is probably a result of paragrammatic games, introduced to suggest and supplement meanings to written excerpts.

Another puzzle relates to the choice of the inscription's writer. Why was the title page not written by J.S. Bach but by another person? What prevented Bach himself from inscribing it, especially since the title page had been left blank for such a long time? The presence of Altnickol's hand in the inscription is not coincidental: Bach needed his name to be written in the third person. Bach never referred to himself in the third person, nor did he ever write in his own hand the words Signor, Herr, or their variants in score inscriptions. The letters 'SigC', marking the word 'Signor', were needed for their numerical value. The solution might have been to ask someone else—Altnickol, in this case—to write the title in his own hand.

An understanding of the importance that Bach attached to paragrammatic constructs in his works might help in solving a question posed earlier: why was the cover of P 200 left without a title for such a long time? The many years that had passed between the completion of the work and the (paragrammatic) writing of the title might imply, at least to a certain extent, that the title somehow depended on the content of the composition itself. For example, the numbers of bars in each fugue—at least in the first three fugues—was correlated with the title inscription. It is clear, therefore, that the title could not have been finalised before at least several of the compositions in this cycle had been completed. Furthermore, it is probable that Bach's composition of the work as a sequence of fugues and his planning of the title page as a paragrammatic construction progressed in parallel. Finally, and most importantly, if the paragram contained in the title is the result of Bach's own work, then the title, too, should be considered as solely his.

The title on the cover of the supplements folder (P 200/1)

The title page that appears on the gray-blue folder cover (Figure 15.2) was probably written by Johann Christoph Friedrich Bach between August 1748 and the end of 1749, when he left Leipzig for Bückeburg. During this period the Third Version of *The Art of Fugue* was created. However, the possibility that this title (albeit not necessarily its composition) might have been written later, sometime between 1750 and 1752, cannot be excluded. The title reads:

>
> *[Die] Kunst*
> *der Fuge*
> *Von J[.]S.B.*

Any idea of linguistic mixtures is here abandoned: the whole title is in German.[22] The article *Die* was added later, by Philipp Emanuel, probably after his father's death, and could not reflect Johann Sebastian's intentions. Moreover, it is unclear if the word is crossed out or underlined. The numerical value of the whole text (233, without the article 'Die') does not tell much. The last line is odd, too; *von* is written in the middle of the line, suggesting that initially it might have been intended to stand alone in the line, just like the word 'Kunst'. The initials 'J[.]S.B.' look rather indecisive, more like a later addition to the line, instead of being symmetrically situated on the next line.

Like the title of the earlier version, this one is puzzling, too. Why was the title originally written here without the article 'Die'? Was it due to some kind of structural idea or manipulation of letters and numbers? And why would Emanuel add the article 'Die' to the title? Was it deleted or emphasised by an underline?

The title's brevity suggests that Bach had originally intended to present the title as a paragrammatic composition. As we see in the case with the title of the Autograph, it can be correlated with the musical text. However, the history of this whole cycle is rich with various versions of the music itself, and it is unknown to which one of them this particular title, written on the folder that contained later supplements, could relate. Given that, at this point it seems unproductive to look for the numerical sense of this title. Therefore, these and other questions related to this presentation of the title remain, for the time being, unanswered.

The titles in the two printed Original Editions (1751 and 1752)

Most studies share the opinion that the final wording on the title pages of the 1751 and 1752 printed editions (Figures 15.3 and 15.4) belongs to Carl Philipp Emanuel. J.S. Bach usually (and especially in printed editions) wrote his title as 'Directore Chori Musici Lipsiensis', and never as Musikdirector, particularly not with a 'k'. In fact, he always spelled words derived from 'music' with a 'c'. Comparing the two texts, we see that they differ only in their typographic design; their wording is identical. Judging by its laconic form and its meaning, the 1751 title page recalls the two earlier handwritten titles, both lacking a detailed description of the work's content and its purpose, stating only the title (*The Art of Fugue*) and the composer's name. This peculiarity supports the assumption that J.S. Bach was fashioning paragrams.

The last line on this page introduces an additional remark mentioning the former Capellmeister and Musikdirector. This addition could not have been inscribed by Johann Sebastian: it was Philipp Emanuel who published the printed edition. The incongruities within this variant of the title result from modifications originally initiated by J.S. Bach, which Emanuel edited while preparing the work for posthumous publication, without suspecting that he might be hindering the composer's intention. This interpretation is supported by the presence of words in the title that are uncharacteristic to both J.S. Bach and Philipp Emanuel. Any attempt to separate elements that, in all likelihood, were generated by paragrammatic intentions from those dictated by the new circumstances of a posthumous edition, should begin with a close examination of the first printed edition's title page (Figure 15.3):

Die
Kunst der Fuge
durch
Herrn Johann Sebastian Bach
ehemahligen Capellmeister und Musikdirector zu Leipzig

Judging by the design, Emanuel added only the last line and the word 'Herrn' before the name of the composer, as required by the new situation.

There are several reasons to suggest that Emanuel merely edited a title that he had seen in writing at an earlier time. The first indication is the presence of the word 'durch'. The point is that Emanuel's title pages, regardless of the ways in which the composer is presented, or whether they are in German, French or Italian, never present the word 'durch' despite its being very common in titles of other contemporary composers. Moreover, the handwritten title pages by Johann Sebastian, as well as those by Philipp Emanuel, never use the word 'durch' in a phrase presenting the author.[23] It is not likely that Emanuel would have decided to change his approach just in this case, and it would also be uncharacteristic that in the process of publishing *The Art of Fugue* he would concern himself with questions of paragrammatic composition. Therefore, it is improbable that the 'durch' came from Emanuel. If this is indeed the case, it is reasonable to deduce that the word was introduced here according to the expressed wish of J.S. Bach.[24]

What would the original title page have looked like? Removing from the printed title Emanuel's probable editing, that is, anything that J.S. Bach would not write, would result as follows:

Die
Kunst der Fuge
durch
Johann Sebastian Bach

Apart from the word 'durch' there is nothing special in this title, which is in complete accord with the two handwritten titles. This suggests that all of the variants of the title page could have originated from only one source: the creative mind of Johann Sebastian Bach.

We turn now to other 'admissible atypicalities', having already determined that they are, in the title page of P 200, results of paragrammatic manipulation of letters and numbers. The insertion of the word 'durch', in the title page of the printed edition, might have served a similar purpose. In such a case, the presence of this word in the title acts—if not as a proof—at least as an indication to the probability of such a process.

To conclude, the proposed reconstruction of the composer's original title page, intended for the first printed edition, is based here on three arguments:

- The four-line construct and its laconic presentation may suggest the possible presence of a paragrammatic component.
- The printed title no longer uses a German-Italian combination (the word Fuge is written in its German variant).
- This impression is reinforced by the uncharacteristic word 'durch' that is interpreted here as indicating paragrammatic manipulation.

What do the fugues tell us?

A comparison between the fugues in the Autograph and the contrapuncti in the printed editions shows that, while preparing *The Art of Fugue* for print, Bach refashioned the fugues in certain ways. Each change is puzzling for its seeming purposelessness, and there are no signs of any connection between them.

First, Bach changed the principle of organisation of the fugues at the beginning of the cycle. Instead of the existing sequence of pairs of fugues in the original Autograph, he grouped the first four fugues and renamed them as contrapuncti. To that end, he added to the printed edition a new fugue (*Contrapunctus 4*) on the basic theme, without any rhythmic changes—a fugue that does not exist in the Autograph at all. Moreover, comprising 138 bars, this new fugue is disproportionally long in comparison with the first three, which appear in the Autograph as, respectively, 37, 35 and 39 bars long. Why did he need this new giant fugue, and why was it located precisely at the fourth position in the printed edition?

The transformation did not leave the first three fugues untouched: while their rhythmic values remained intact, the metre was changed from $\frac{4}{2}$ to $\frac{2}{2}$, a procedure that doubled the number of bars, turning out to be 74, 70 and 78, respectively. Why?

In addition to doubling the number of bars, Bach added several bars to each of the first three fugues: four bars were added to the first fugue, two to the second one and six to the third (see Table 15.1). While we could regard these as simple corrections, a musical analysis shows that the new bars make no real difference. Each of these fugues could exist (and indeed still exists in concert practice) as it appears in the Autograph. It seems that the manuscript and the printed variants of these fugues have equal artistic value. What then could have been the reason for these inessential extensions?

Formerly, among the changes made from the Second to the Third Version, Bach had changed the ordering of the first three fugues. Fugues II and III in the manuscript changed places, respectively becoming *Contrapunctus 3* and *Contrapunctus 2* in the printed edition. The reasons for that were discussed in Chapter 9. However, it seems that there were some additional calculations that contributed to these modifications, summarised in Table 15.1.

Table 15.1 Reorganisation and resizing of the first set of four pieces

Autograph		Printed edition		
Name	Number of bars	Name	Number of bars before addition	Number of bars after addition
Fugue I	37	Contrapunctus 1	74	78
Fugue II	35	Contrapunctus 2	78	84
Fugue III	39	Contrapunctus 3	70	72
		Contrapunctus 4		138

While one might assume that these changes reflected Bach's artistic concept, it is nonetheless impossible to ignore the fact that they were all, in one way or another, related to one element: the number of bars. It is quite possible that a 'letters and numbers' manipulation has a role here, too. The hypothetical four-line design of the title could allude to the first four fugues of the cycle (just as the three-line design of the Autograph's title alludes to the first three fugues). The possible correspondence between the numerical value of the title's letters (a tentative paragram) in the first printed edition and the number of bars of the first four contrapuncti in that edition[25] is shown in Scheme 15.1.

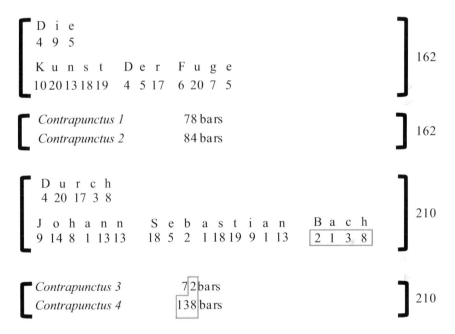

Scheme 15.1 Paragrammatic correspondence between number of bars and the hypothetical title page wording in the first Original Edition (1751).

This unbelievably precise correspondence could, of course, be a mere coincidence, but that would be very unlikely. Such significant changes in this part of the cycle would hardly have occurred except as a result of an intentional and sophisticated operation.

186 *Part V: Toward a new interpretation of* The Art of Fugue

The sequence of letters in the name Bach, 2–1–3–8, as reflected in the numeric alphabet, are framed at the end of the last line: 'Durch Johann Sebastian Bach'. They also appear, in this order, in the framed number of bars of Contrapuncti 3 and 4: [7]2, 138. The two sets (of words and numbers) end in the same way, both related to Bach's name.

The edge of the thread is the last fugue, known as *Contrapunctus 4*, which did not exist prior to the first printed edition. The number of its bars, 138, disproportionately differs in scale from fugues I–III of the manuscript, which were, initially, 37, 35 and 39 bars long, respectively. Its digits, 1–3–8, strangely coincide with the three last letters of Bach's name: A-C-H. The missing B, numerically equivalent to 2, was required just before this figure. The composer, thus, had to somehow envisage a way to manipulate the number of bars of *Contrapunctus 3* to end with the digit 2. If we assume that Bach wanted to construct a paragram that matched the total number of bars of Contrapuncti 3 and 4 to 210, which is the numeric expression of 'Durch Johann Sebastian Bach', we would be looking for a 72 bar long contrapunctus (210 − 138 = 72), thus requiring an addition of two bars to the existing 70 of *Contrapunctus 3*, which is exactly what happened.

None of the original three fugues in the manuscript, with their 37, 35 and 39 bars could approach—even remotely, either by itself or in any combination—this desired number of 72. Bach's 'Columbus's egg' solution was to double the number of bars in the three first fugues by changing the metre from $\frac{4}{2}$ to $\frac{2}{2}$ without altering even one note. The operation rendered three contrapuncti of 74, 70 and 78 bars respectively. Since cutting any finished fugue is infinitely more time consuming than extending it, and since the digit 2 was needed at the end of the third contrapunctus, Bach picked up the only candidate for this purpose—fugue II, added two bars to it and positioned it as third in the set of four first contrapuncti. In this way he both strengthened the four-set character of this group (rather than the former pairs) and also created a numerical paragrammatic equation between text and number of bars—the total paragrammatic value of the third and fourth line in the title with the total number of bars in the third and fourth contrapuncti, with the additional meaning of his name's letters reflected in the last group's bar numbers.

If the above reasoning is correct, a similar match should exist between the number of bars in the first two contrapuncti and the first two lines of the text: 'Die Kunst der Fuge'. The total of its numerical equivalent is 162. Indeed, this is exactly the sum of bars of Contrapuncti 1 and 2 in the printed edition. In order to reach the number 162 in the remaining fugue I and fugue III, which had 74 and 78, 10 more bars were required (74 + 78 = 152). Bach extended these fugues, adding four and six bars to them, respectively: the new *Contrapunctus 1* has now 78 bars, and *Contrapunctus 2*—84 bars, a total of 162 bars.

This analysis shows that there are absolutely no changes in this part of *The Art of Fugue* that cannot be explained as paragrammatic constructs entailing modifications based on numerical calculations made to match the text of the title page with new bar numbers of the first four contrapuncti.

The interpretation of the title pages of *The Art of Fugue* (Autograph and printed editions) as paragrammatic constructs offers answers to some of the questions presented above. It also relates to the changes made while preparing the handwritten variants of *The Art of Fugue* toward the printed version. Without this understanding of the title pages, it would hardly be possible to supply reasonable answers to these questions. Paragrammatic constructs appear neither spontaneously nor by chance. The more elements there are in a paragram (letters and numbers), the less the probability of its being coincidental. This unavoidably leads to the conclusion that the hypothetically reconstructed title page, proposed above, most probably really existed and that the author of the paragram could only have been Johann Sebastian Bach himself.

Notes

1 This chapter is also published in *Min-ad: Israel Studies in Musicology Online* 12 (2014): http://www.biu.ac.il/hu/mu/min-ad/, with the kind permission of Ashgate Publishing.
2 Hofmann, *NBA KB* VIII/2, p. 23; Bergel, *Bachs letzte Fuge*; Schleuning, *Johann Sebastian Bach's 'Kunst der Fuge*; Mikhail Semenovich Druskin, *Iogann Sebastian Bakh* (Moscow, 1982); Jacques Chailley (ed.), *L'Art de la fugue de J.S. Bach. Étude critique des sources: remise en ordre du plan, analyse de l'œuvre, au-delà des notes*, vol. 1 (Paris, 1971).
3 'Wenn wir auch nicht sicher wissen, ob der Titel "Kunst der Fuge" von Bach selber herstammt ... ' Philipp Spitta, *Johann Sebastian Bach*, vol. 2 (Leipzig, 1880), p. 678.
4 The title page has an additional inscription, 'in eigenhändiger Partitur', written in parentheses and located about an inch lower than the figure shown here. This inscription was added decades later, after the death of C.P.E. Bach but prior to 1824, by one of the subsequent owners of the manuscript, Georg Poelchau (1773–1836).
5 The question mark in square brackets marks an unclear sign, which will be discussed later.
6 Christoph Wolff identified the title as 'inscribed by Johann Christoph Friedrich Bach'. Wolff, *Bach: Essays*, p. 267–68. However, Klaus Hofmann classified the title as written 'von unbekannter Hand'. Hofmann, *NBA KB* VIII/2, p. 48.
7 The [Die] in square brackets was written by C.P.E. Bach. See Hofmann, *NBA KB* VIII/2, p. 48.
8 Wolff, *Bach: Essays*, p. 271.
9 *BD* I/81, pp. 148–9; *NBR*, no. 240, pp. 224–5.
10 Bergel, *Bachs letzte Fuge*, p. 57; Schleuning, *Johann Sebastian Bachs 'Kunst der Fuge'*, p. 179.
11 The concept of paragram is used here as defined in Ruth Tatlow's fundamental PhD dissertation 'LUSUS POETICUS VEL MUSICUS, Johann Sebastian Bach: The Baroque Paragram and Friedrich Smend's Theory of a Musical Number Alphabet' (London: King's College, 1987) and in her book *Bach and the Riddle of the Number Alphabet* (Cambridge, 1991). She expands on these ideas in several of her later articles, such as 'Collections, bars and numbers: Analytical coincidence or Bach's design?' in Ruth Tatlow (ed.), *Understanding Bach*, 2 (2007): pp. 37–58, and 'Bach's Parallel Proportions and the Qualities of the Authentic Bachian Collection', in Reinmar Emans & Martin Geck (eds.), *Bach oder Nicht Bach: Bericht über das 5. Dortmunder Bach-Symposion* (Dortmund, 2009), pp. 135–55.
12 Georg Philipp Harsdörfer, *Poetischer Trichter, Die Teutsche Dicht- und Reimkunst ohne Behuf der Lateinischen Sprache*. Dritter Theil (Nürnberg, 1653), p. 72. Harsdörfer (1607–58) was a poet and scholar, the author of 50 volumes of poetry and other works and a member of several literary societies, one of which he founded.
13 Yoshitake Kobayashi, 'Zur Chronologie', p. 70.
14 For example, the full title of *The Well-Tempered Clavier* reads: *Das Wohltemperirte Clavier. oder Præludia, und Fugen durch alle Tone und Semitonia, so wohl tertiam majorem oder Ut Re Mi anlan/gend, als auch tertiam minorem oder Re Mi Fa betreffend. Zum Nutzen und Gebrauch der Lehrbegierigen Musicalischen Jugend, als auch derer in diesem studio schon habil seyenden besonderem Zeitvertreib auffgesetzet und verfertiget von Johann Sebastian Bach. p.t: Hochfürstlich Anhalt-Cöthenischen Capel-Meistern und Directore derer Camer Musiquen. Anno 1722* [The Well-Tempered Clavier // or // Preludes and Fugues / through all the tones and semitones / both as regards the tertia major or Ut Re Mi / and as concerns the tertia minor or Re Mi Fa / For the Use and Profit of Musical Youth Desirous of Learning / as well as for the Pastime of those Already Skilled in this Study / drawn up and written by Johann Sebastian Bach / p.t: Capellmeister to His Serene Highness the Prince of Anhalt-Cöthen, / and Director of / His Chamber Music / Anno 1722].

188   *Part V: Toward a new interpretation of* The Art of Fugue

15   Friedrich Smend, *Edition of the B minor Mass by J.S. Bach*, NBA KB II/1 (Kassel, 1956), p. 333; Robin A. Leaver, 'Number Associations in the Structure of Bach's CREDO, BWV 232', *BACH*, 3 (1976): p. 17; Anthony Newman, *Bach and the Baroque: European Source Materials from the Baroque and Early Classical Periods, with Special Emphasis on the Music of J.S. Bach* (Stuyvesant, NY, 2nd edn 1995), p. 196.
16   Wolff, *Bach: Essays*, p. 267.
17   Schleuning, *Johann Sebastian Bach's 'Kunst der Fuge'*, p. 179.
18   Hofmann, *NBA KB* VIII/2, p. 23.
19   The capital C was used to mark truncated words especially in eighteenth century epistolary and formal etiquette, which was largely based on French. The term is also used to mark a cut in music or for the abbreviation of neumes. The author thanks Olga Blyoskina for this information.
20   The original letter is kept at the Niedersächs Staatsarchiv, Bückeburg (Shelfmark F2 Nr. 2642).
21   All three letters to Breitkopf are kept at the archive of Breitkopf und Härtel.
22   Although the last letter in the word *Fuge* may remind one of the letter 'a' in modern Latin script, here the whole inscription is performed in Gothic cursive, where it is definitely an 'e'.
23   A similar occurrence is found in Bach's composition *Musikalisches Opfer* (BWV 1079). Bach never used the term 'ricercar' for his fugues, while this term served as a synonym for 'fugue' in Germany of the seventeenth and eighteenth centuries. The only time Bach did so was when he needed to work with words, such as to compose an acrostic, as in 'Regis Iussu Cantio Et Reliqua Canonica Arte Resoluta'. It is clear that the word 'fugue' did not fit that task. See Anatoly Milka, *Muzykal'noe prinoshenie I.S. Bakha: k rekonstruktsii i interpretatsii* [J.S. Bach's *Musical Offering*: toward a reconstruction and interpretation] (Moscow, 1999), pp. 177–92; Milka, *Iskusstvo fugi' I.S. Bakha: k rekonstruktsii i interpretatsii* [J.S. Bach's *The Art of Fugue*: toward a reconstruction and interpretation] (Moscow, 2009), pp. 397–400.
24   The word 'durch' before the composer's name carries a nuance of formality and high literary style, where official solemnity had to be highlighted. Bach used it only in cases that had to do with members of royal families or some special municipal event. Even in such rare instances, the word appeared only in the printed title pages. One example is Cantata BWV 71, composed in 1708 for the election of the magistrate of Mühlhausen in Thuringia; another example is in the *Drama per Musica*, BWV 214, composed for the birthday of Maria Josepha, the Queen of Poland and the Court Princess of Saxony, on December 8, 1733.
25   Olga Kurtch presented this analysis in her 'Ot pomet kopiistov', pp. 79–81.

16 *Contrapunctur 5*

The title of the fifth piece in the Original Edition looks rather strange, ending with an 'r' and thus spelled 'contrapunctur' rather than 'contrapunctus'. This odd ending has always unanimously been interpreted as a simple misprint, and therefore corrected in practically all the work's editions. Some publishers mark it as an engraver's error while others correct it without any additional comment, regarding it as an obvious typo. We believe that this peculiarity calls for a deeper inquiry.

Fugue IV in the Autograph

The Autograph has a particularity quite typical of Bach's manuscripts. While looking at the pages of fugue IV, which became *Contrapunctur 5* in the Original Edition,[1] a certain puzzling visual effect is created, similar to that of an ambigram. The two pages of the spread are rastered practically without margins in the middle part, so that the staves almost seem to continue from page to page without interruption. Thus, one way of looking at it allows the perception of a large format in landscape set up, made up of the entire spread, while another reading sees the spread as made up of two separate pages, each in portrait set up (Figure 16.1).

There are grounds to suspect that Bach himself, too, might have perceived such spreads as one landscape page. For example, the score of the Cantata BWV 75 (*Die Elenden sollen essen*) suggests such a view. Here, too, the raster reaches the middle of the spread, not leaving any margins, so that several staves of both pages seem synchronised, continuing from one page to the other. Here, too, the spread can be perceived either as one landscape page or as two portrait pages. In this case, Bach chose the first option. Clearly, this perception was an afterthought, since the spread was not planned ahead for such a layout: the staves are badly synchronised, worse even than in the autograph. A similar situation can be seen in the autograph of the Mass in B minor, in the movements Patrem omnipotentem (pp. 104–5), Et resurrexit (pp. 116–21), Et ascendit (pp. 121–31) and Et expecto (pp. 140–9). Remarkably, in all these cases Bach does not write clefs or key signatures on the right page of the spread, perceiving the score as one large landscape layout.

Is there a connection between these 'ambigrammatic' layouts and the composer's fondness of paragrammatic puzzles? Possibly. Bach represented his name by two numerical symbols—14, which was the sum of the numerical values of his name's letters, and 41, the numerical value of 'J.S. Bach'. It just so happens that when the autograph of fugue IV is read as if the score is written in landscape layout, following the two top systems of the spread's two pages as if they were one consecutive system, its 14th bar is, in fact, bar 41 of the fugue, read conventionally (Figure 16.2). Thus, the horizontal and vertical coordinates of this score, carrying the

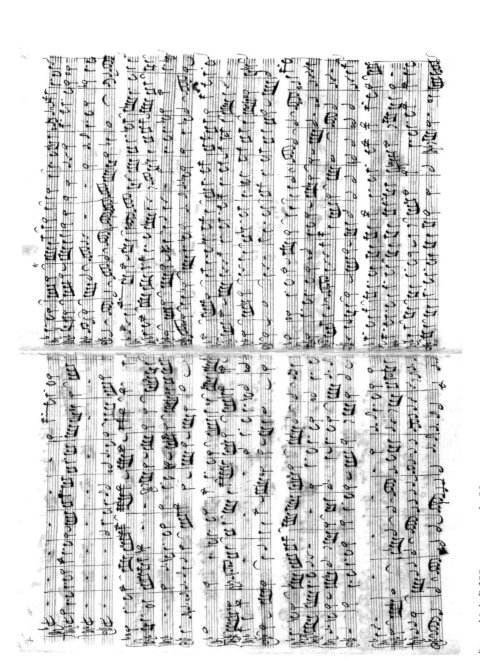

Figure 16.1 P 200: page spread of fugue IV.

Figure 16.2 P 200: fugue IV, 14 notes in bar 41/41; the four notes in the treble spell B-A-C-H.

192 Part V: Toward a new interpretation of The Art of Fugue

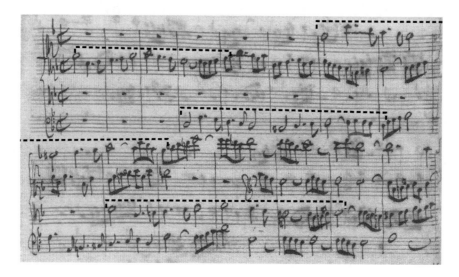

Figure 16.3 P 200: fugue IV, the theme, presented in all parts, consists of 14 notes.

indicators 14 and 41, intersect at one point represented by one and the same bar.[2] Could this be a coincidence?

This fugue is special, because the main theme of the collection appears here for the first time in a melodic version with additional passing notes that fill up the gaps between the original half notes, which are now dotted quarter notes. This variant of the theme consists of 14 notes, thus keeping with the symbolic number (Figure 16.3). Moreover, bar 14/41 includes 14 notes, too. Further, the top staff of this bar spells the name B-A-C-H.[3] Further yet, framed by bar lines, the inscription spells 'B-A-C-H C', marking Bach's name and his professional position (Bach, C[antor]).

The way in which Bach's name is displayed in this fugue follows the symbolic principle of *multiplicatio*:[4]

- The number of notes in the fugue's theme is 14.
- The bar number, when the Autograph score is read across the spread, is 14.
- The bar number, when the Autograph score is read in the traditional way, is 41.
- The number of notes in bar 14/41 is 14.
- The letter names of the first notes in the top part of bar 14/41 spell B-A-C-H (the numerical value of which is 14).

While each one of these phenomena could, perhaps, be regarded as coincidental, it does seem in this case there are simply too many signs, accumulated on one spot, to be considered as created by chance.

Contrapunctur 5 in the Original Edition

The same piece in the Original Edition of *The Art of Fugue* acquired a new title and also a different look (Figure 16.4).

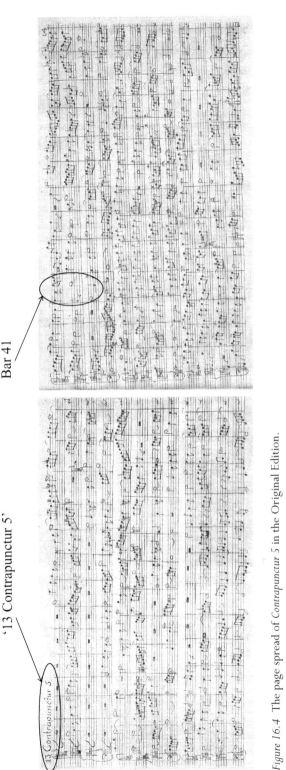

Figure 16.4 The page spread of *Contrapunctur 5* in the Original Edition.

194   Part V: Toward a new interpretation of The Art of Fugue

The difference in layout is the most noticeable. While the Autograph's layout is portrait, the Original Edition's is landscape. Also, unlike in the Autograph, the margins of the Original Edition pages are noticeable (20 mm) and the staves of the spread's two sides do not coincide, thus preventing the perception of the staves as continuous throughout the page spread. The number of bars on the top staff is 13, obliterating the equivalence of bars 14 and 41. The multiplicatio signs of Bach's name are now valid only inside bar 41: the number of the bar (14 in retrograde), 14 notes in the bar and the B-A-C-H (C) motif.

However, the landscape layout may have provided Bach with other venues to create signifiers that point at his own name. He did that by combining existing numbers in the layout and numerical values of letters and by introducing an intentional *lapsus linguare*, a standard mark for the existence of hidden information.[5] It was Bach who prepared the engraver copy of this page. Given the slow handwriting and careful alignment of the title, regarding the 'r' at the end of the word as a typo is rather unconvincing; even if it were so, the composer would have corrected it at the proofreading stage, just as he did in the case of the Canon in Augmentation.[6] The word 'contrapunctur', thus, is clearly written intentionally just so.

There could be ways to read this allegedly misspelled title, taking into account the intentionality behind it, for example—in yet another 'numbers and letters' game.[7] It is possible that Bach consulted two methods of numerical equivalents of the Latin alphabet: the 'natural' and the 'trigonal' systems (Tables 16.1 and 16.2).[8]

Table 16.1 The 'natural' numerological system

A	B	C	D	E	F	G	H	I J	K	L	M
1	2	3	4	5	6	7	8	9	10	11	12
N	O	P	Q	R	S	T	U V	W	X	Y	Z
13	14	15	16	17	18	19	20	21	22	23	24

Table 16.2 The 'trigonal' numerological system

A	B	C	D	E	F	G	H	I J
1	3	6	10	15	21	28	36	45
K	L	M	N	O	P	Q	R	S
55	66	78	91	105	120	136	153	171
T	U V	W	X	Y	Z			
190	210	231	253	276	300			

The title of this contrapunctus renders significant information when read in any of these systems. According to the 'natural' numerological system, the numerical value of the word 'contrapunctur' is 174 (Table 16.3).

The word 'contrapunctur', composed of 13 letters, is completely and accurately aligned with the page number—13 and with the serial number of the piece—5 (see Figure 16.4).

Table 16.3 Value of 'contrapunctur' in the natural numerological system

C	O	N	T	R	A	P	U	N	C	T	U	R		
3	14	13	19	17	1	15	20	13	3	19	20	17	=	174

The first stave of the piece comprises 13 bars, pointing at a possible *multiplicatio* of the number 13. This is telling, since 13 could be interpreted as a '14 minus one' just as the letter 'r' could be interpreted as 's minus one'. Further, the number 13 can be also interpreted as two digits, 1 and 3. These readings, combined, may render the following suprising result, which would be possible only with the letter 'r' at the end of the title word (Table 16.4).

Table 16.4 Numerological interpretation of the fifth fugue's title

Digits of the page number (1 and 3)	4	
Number of letters in the word 'contrapunctur'	13	
Numerical value of the letters in the word	174	
The serial number of the piece	5	
In total	196	$= 14^2$

Further, the word 'contrapunctur' can be read using another system, the 'trigonal'. According to that system, the numerical value of the word 'contrapunctur' is 1526. Beyond the fact that this number can be divided by 14, the sum of its digits (1 + 5 + 2 + 6) renders 14, too (Table 16.5).

Table 16.5 Value of 'contrapunctur' in the trigonal numerological system

C	O	N	T	R	A	P	U	N	C	T	U	R		
6	105	91	190	153	1	120	210	91	6	190	210	153	=	1526

In any of the above readings of the title according to different numerological systems, a meaningful result could be achieved only once the last letter of 'contrapunctus' is replaced by the one that is 'one less', just like the 13 bars in the first stave are 'one less' than the number of bars leading to the significant bar in the Autograph, number 14/41. Regardless of layout, Bach found ways to signify his name through his music composition and notation.

Notes

1 Fugue IV from the Autograph was replaced by the new *Contrapunctus 4* that was composed for the Third Version (see Chapter 10), and therefore was 'pushed forward' to become the fifth piece in the cycle: *Contrapunctur 5*.
2 Olga Kurtch, 'Ot pomet kopiistov', p. 82.
3 Ibid. Bach marked the same 'monogram' in the closing section of the Canon in Augmentation from the Canonic Variations BWV 769a, bars 39–40 (four bars before the end, middle staff, bass clef).
4 The principle of *multiplicatio*, a basic technique in symbolisation systems, is expressed by a simultaneous—or frequent—appearance of signs, all pointing at one intended signified.

For example, a grouping of a sharpened note, a musical motif of a cross (such as, coincidentally, is the name BACH) and the numerical symbol of four, would point by multiplication at one signified: the Cross.

5 *Lapsus linguare* is an intentional error inserted into an otherwise correct context. Such an error draws attention to itself and to its location within a given text; its appearance in unlikely instances, such as an engraved stone, a title or a printed book cover discloses its intentionality.
6 The Canon in Augmentation is discussed in Chapter 17.
7 This and the following revelations belong to the editor, Esti Sheinberg, whom I deeply thank for strengthening my hypothesis and valuable contribution in general.
8 In the natural system, each letter is assigned a number in consecutive order, that is, a = 1 to z = 24 (the letters 'I' and 'J' are considered as one letter and thus both equivalent to one number, and so are the letters 'U' and 'V'. In the trigonal system, the advance in value is applied to the *differences* between the numbers assigned to letters, that is: a = 1; b = 3(= 1 + 2); c = 6(= 3 + 3); d = 10(= 6 + 4); e = 15(= 10 + 5), and so on.

17 Myths about the Canon in Augmentation

The Art of Fugue studies have rendered a mass of interpretations and explanations, some of which seem quite plausible, while others are rather improbable. Sometimes, however, theories that sound quite convincing crumble once confronted with the facts. Such was, for example, a general view that *The Art of Fugue* was not written for a specific instrument but as an abstract musical study, maybe even just 'music for the eyes'. This assumption generated numerous arrangements for various ensembles, from one or two claviers and organ to chamber ensemble and even to a full orchestra. This perception was predominant until the very end of the twentieth century, with the publication of the document in which Carl Philipp Emanuel, who published the work, stated:[1] 'Es [*Die Kunst der Fuge*—A.M.] ist aber dennoch alles zu gleicher Zeit zum Gebrauch des Claviers und der Orgel ausdrücklich eingerichtet'.[2]

In other cases, though, theories that seemed at first improbable prove to be grounded in reality, in spite of their unlikelihood. Two persistent myths relate to one of the four canons in *The Art of Fugue*. This canon is referred to, in Bach studies, as Canon in Augmentation, Canon in Inversion or Canon in Augmentation and Inversion. J.S. Bach himself changed its title several times. Other elements in it were changed, too: its form, its musical material and the musical notation.

The first myth: The print and its source

Attempting to connect the print to an assumed source, certain studies of *The Art of Fugue* juxtapose this canon's first page, as it is printed in the Original Edition, to the engraver copy (*Abklatschvorlage*), which is the first page of P 200/1–1, to demonstrate their direct correspondence (Figures 17.1 and 17.2).[3]

Thus, Richard Koprowski presents both images and writes:

> The result of their [the sheets of the engraver copy—A.M.] transfer to the print can be seen in pages 48–50 of the first edition. … Clearly these pages preserve, to a large extent, the handwriting characteristics of the manuscript sheets. Herein lies the importance of this engraving process for the musicologist because, by comparing pages 48–50 with the rest of the original print, it is possible to determine other pages for which Bach also prepared the *Abklatschvorlagen*.[4]

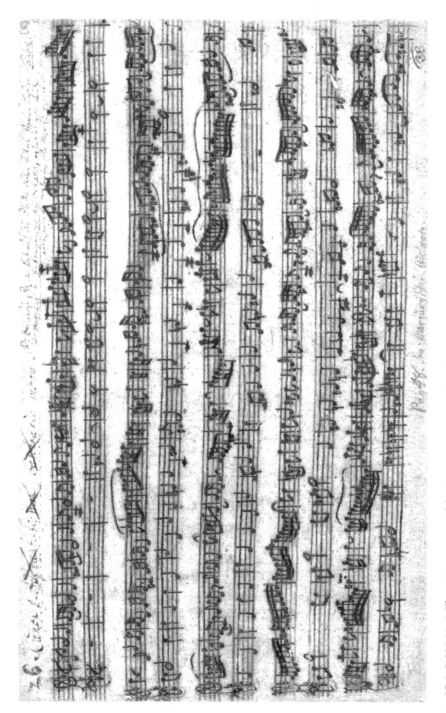

Figure 17.1 P 200/1–1: The engraver copy of the Canon in Augmentation, first page.

Figure 17.2 *Canon per Augmentationem in Contrario Motu*: page 48, Original Edition.

This type of comparison is typical of almost all the studies in which this topic is discussed in one way or another.[5] Unfortunately, none of these studies provides examples from any other work by Bach (or from any other composer's work) to corroborate the thesis explaining the quasi-facsimile similarity between the printout and the engraver copy of this canon.

It is generally assumed that engraver copies, just like the original manuscript materials, were usually returned to the composer.[6] This assumption, however, relies on the familiar precedent of the engraver copy of the Canon in Augmentation that had been returned to Bach. This leaves grounds for doubt whether this was indeed the normal practice.

Once the engraver copy had reached the engraver's workshop, it would first be oiled (usually with linseed oil), with the purpose that the text, mirrored, would be clearly seen through the back of the paper. Then it would be overlaid on the copper plate, which normally would be oiled, too. Following that, a master engraver would mark with his engraving needle through the mirrored image, the image that was to be printed on the copper plate. This procedure would be performed with great accuracy, preserving handwriting features of the person who prepared the engraver copy.

Since the paper used for this purpose was thin (in order to achieve better transparency) and friable (allowing the oil to be better absorbed), it was difficult to keep an engraver copy once it had been used: at that stage it looked more like refuse, suitable at best as burning fuel, rather than a manuscript worth keeping. Thus, normally, engraver copies were not returned to the composers. The lack of other examples of this kind is therefore unsurprising. The preserved engraver copy of this Canon in Augmentation is a unique case, having no equivalent in Bach's contemporary praxis. The copy would never be sent back to him unless there were some special circumstances calling for such an exceptional action.

Since the engraver performed the copy with great care and accuracy when transferring the musical text from the engraver copy to the copper plate, going over the mirrored image with his engraving needle, the measurements of elements on the engraver copy and the printed page should absolutely coincide. It is true that a comparison between Bach's engraver copy and its printout in the Original Edition discloses clear dependence and that the visual impression it renders is of an extremely close similarity. Nevertheless, a closer inspection reveals discrepancies in two excerpts, cropped off the two pages in question, both showing bars 23–25 and the top staff of bars 31–33 (Figure 17.3).

Evidently, the images do not match. For example, the second bar line in the middle staff quite accurately corresponds, in the engraver copy, to the bar line of the upper voice; its lower end is directed toward the slurred eighth note 'e' at the beginning of bar 33. In the Original Edition, however, this bar line forms an angle with the bar line of the top voice, while in respect to the lower voice it points toward the sharp sign before 'c', falling on the beginning of the last quarter note in bar 32. The difference is more than 1.5 cm. Additionally, the natural sign in the middle staff is directed, in P 200/1–1, to the 'b♮' on the bottom staff, almost in the centre of bar 33, while in the edition the same natural sign is directed toward the second eighth note 'd' of the same bar. Here, the difference is about 0.5 cm. Such mismatches prove that the print of the edition could not be engraved from P 200/1–1 as its engraver copy. The undeniable outcome of this comparison is that the Canon in Augmentation, as it appears in the Original Edition of *The Art of Fugue* was printed from another engraver copy, albeit also prepared by J.S. Bach himself.

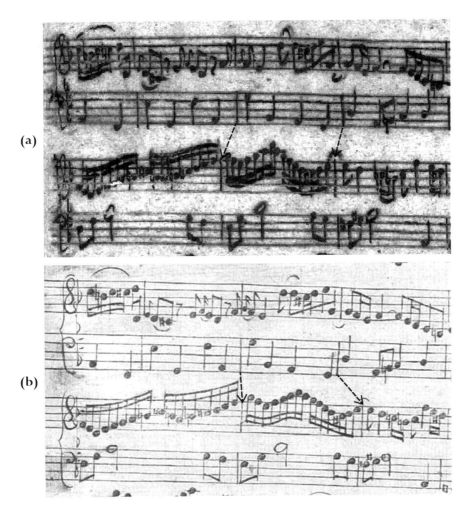

Figure 17.3 Canon in Augmentation, bars 23–25 and 31–33: comparison. (a): P 200/1–1; (b): in the Original Edition, page 48. The dashed arrows show clear discrepancies in bar lines alignment.

There are two more and quite remarkable facts. First, the Canon in Augmentation page carries no ornamentation in the Original Edition, while P 200/1–1 has a vignette at the end of its second page. The engraver transferred all the other vignettes scrupulously and with great care. On the other hand, the Original Edition does show a new vignette at the end of this canon, an ornament that does not appear on the engraver copy.

The fact that all three sheets of this engraver copy *are* oiled means that the engraver started to prepare them for the engraving process. Nevertheless, for some reason, he did not go ahead with the engraving. The copies were returned from Zella, where the engraver lived and worked, to Bach in Leipzig.

Other marks on these sheets are puzzling, too. Klaus Hofmann, for example, comments on traces made by a pencil that, in his opinion, were used to transfer the image onto the copper

202 Part V: Toward a new interpretation of The Art of Fugue

plate.[7] Yet, the transfer was performed on a mirror image. Therefore, if a pencil was used to transfer the musical text onto the copper plate, as Hofmann suggests, its traces should appear on the back of the sheet. Nevertheless, there are no pencil traces on the verso of any of the three sheets; all these marks appear on the recto side, meaning that they were not used for such a transfer.[8] This information indicates a peculiar course of events, according to which the engraver received his copy, oiled it in preparation for transfer to the copper plates, but did not proceed, sending it instead back to Bach. What could be the reason for such action?

A possible solution to this puzzle may be offered. Careful measurement of the pages of P 200/1–1 and their comparison with pages 48–50 of the Original Edition show that the distances between the top line of the top staff and the bottom line of the bottom staff (not including the empty staves on the third sheet) present a consistent difference: in all cases the smaller bar is in the Original Edition (Table 17.1).

Table 17.1 Comparison of score sizes of the Canon in Augmentation in P 200/1–1 and in the Original Edition

Page of supplement 1	Page in the Original Edition	Top to bottom distance in supplement 1	Top to bottom distance in the Original Edition
1	48	17.5 cm	17.1 cm
2	49	18.3 cm	17.4 cm
3	50	14.1 cm	13.6 cm

The fact that the engraver copies (in P 200) of all three pages of the Canon in Augmentation were vertically larger than the print in the Original Edition point, probably, to the reason for the copies being sent back to the composer: the sheets simply did not fit with Schübler's copper plates. Preparing to transfer the musical text, the engraver oiled and then positioned the engraver copy over the copper plate. At this point he discovered that the copy was larger than his plates. He therefore had to stop the process and, before leaving any needle marks of transfer to copper plates, he sent the pages back for recopy. Following the engraver's request, Bach reduced slightly the distances between the staves (as can be seen in Figure 17.3), thus diminishing the vertical axis of the copy to make it fit the plate.

This interpretation explains why P 200/1–1, while being *an* engraver copy of the Canon in Augmentation, does not match the print of the same work in the Original Edition: it is not *the* engraver copy that served for this print; Bach had to reproduce a new one from scratch. This also explains why only one engraver copy of this cycle was preserved: it was the only one that, unlike the usual practice, was ever returned to the composer.

The second myth: The versions of the Canon in Augmentation

Some scholars consider that the Canons in Augmentation xii and xv in P 200, the canon in P 200/1–1 and the *Canon per Augmentationem in Contrario Motu*, printed on pages 48–50 in the Original Edition are all one and the same piece, albeit in various versions.[9]

Indeed, it often happened, and certainly in Bach's oeuvre, that a particular work was composed in different versions. For example, the Invention in C Major, BWV 772, exists as

BWV 772a, where the theme's skips of thirds are filled up by steps in triplets. Several versions of larger works by Bach exist, too, such as the Canonic Variations (manuscript and printed versions) or even on a larger scale: the St John Passion. There are various types of differences: while the above example of the Invention BWV 772a is based on variation technique, other variants add or subtract parts of their original material, ranging from a few bars to whole sections. For example, several contrapuncti in the Original Edition differ from their presentation in the Autograph by the addition of bars at the end of a fugue without, actually, changing its form.[10] On the other hand, several bars added to the beginning of fugue VI of the Autograph led to a completely new version, presented as *Contrapunctus 10* in the Original Edition (BWV 1080/10 and 1080/10a), thus changing its very structure (the original simple fugue, with consistent countersubject, became a double fugue). The new variant, however, kept the music material of the original, thus allowing the classification of both compositions as two versions of one single work. To conclude, regardless of their diversity, the musical material in all the above versions of one composition basically remained the same.

Such cases need to be differentiated from instances in which a new composition is created on the basis of another work's theme. Fugue BWV 574, for example, is based on a theme by Giovanni Legrenzi. Nevertheless, it is not regarded as a version of Legrenzi's composition, but as a new, independent unit, composed by Bach. Another example is provided by the 13 compositions that comprise the *Musical Offering*: two ricercari, 10 canons and the sonata. While all are based on one theme ('the King's theme'), they are not considered to be versions of one another, but 13 independent compositions.

The criteria for this classification need to be clarified. Why is it that studies of *The Art of Fugue* regard certain fugues that share the same theme as versions and not as independent pieces?

The Canon in Augmentation provides a good case for discussion. It appears four times within the materials of *The Art of Fugue*:

- On pages 32–3 in the main body of P 200, numbered XII
- On pages 38–9 in the main body of P 200, numbered XV
- On P 200/1–1 (the engraver copy)
- On pages 48–50 of the Original Edition

The canon appears in these three sources under *five* different titles:

- The version numbered XII in P 200 is titled *Canon in Hypodiateßeron al roversio e per augmentationem, Perpetuum* [canon at the lower fourth in inversion and augmentation, perpetual]. The canon appears here in both decrypted and cryptic forms—but the title appears only on page 33, above the cryptic presentation.
- The version numbered XV in P 200 is titled *Canon al roverscio et per augmentationem* [Canon in Inversion and Augmentation]. This version of the canon appears later in the Autograph, on pages 38–9 and is numbered XV. Unlike the previous one, this canon is only presented in a decrypted form.
- The title *Canon per Augment. in Contrapuncto all octava* [Canon in Augmentation, in counterpoint at an octave] is positioned on the first sheet of the engraver copy (P 200/1–1). It appears in Johann Christoph Friedrich's *Nota Bene*.

204   Part V: Toward a new interpretation of The Art of Fugue

- On the same sheet, though, appears another title for this canon: *Canon p. Augmentationem contrario motu* [Canon in Augmentation and Inversion]. This title was written either by Johann Sebastian or by Christoph Friedrich.
- The title *Canon per Augmentationem in Contrario Motu* [Canon in Augmentation and Inversion] is the final title variant for this canon. It appears on page 48 of the Original Edition, right above the beginning of the piece.

Studies of *The Art of Fugue* regard these four instances as versions of one and the same canon. Indeed, the music of the last three pieces is, to a great extent, the same, permitting their interpretation as versions of one canon.[11] However, the first two variants (canons XII and XV in P 200) share only the proposta and the composition technique: both are canons in augmentation and inversion. Beyond that, however, they differ; the first is a perpetual canon while the second has an ending. Moreover, their musical material, after the first proposta and its reproduction in the risposta, is entirely different. Therefore, although composed on the same proposta, these two canons are different in type and in their music, in the same way that the 10 separate canons of the *Musical Offering* are written on one theme, although these, remarkably, had never been considered to be variants of the same canon but were rather looked upon as independent pieces.

The differences between the music materials of canons XII and XV can be observed through a careful comparison of their opening bars (Figure 17.4).

Figure 17.4   P 200: first bars in canons XII and XV.

The two canons are written on the same two-bar proposta. However, the beginnings of the counterpoint lines of the risposta (in augmentation; bars 3–6) are clearly different. Beyond this difference, there are studies that attempt one more additional version, replacing the sixteenth notes in bars 3–4 of canon XII with the thirty-second notes that Bach sketched in, while accepting that with this editing the pieces cease to be canons because their musical material is not repeated later in the risposta (Example 17.1).[12]

Example 17.1 Canon in Augmentation, variants of the first countersubject (bars 3–6); top stave: canon XII; middle stave: corrections inserted in canon XII; bottom stave: canon XV.

As the pieces develop, their dissimilarity becomes even more obvious. In bars 10–12, for example, finding identical points becomes difficult; clearly these are now two different canons (Example 17.2). The presence of two different canons on the same theme indicates that Bach discontinued the correction of canon XII and embarked on a new composition: canon XV, on the same proposta.[13] Not only the musical material, but the very structure of the canon changed in this process: instead of a perpetual canon (as canon XII is in both its decrypted and cryptic forms), Bach composed the bipartite canon XV, which is not perpetual.

The new canon is presented in its decrypted form, omitting the cryptic presentation. The reason for this choice may be found through an analysis of the cycle's structure, as well as a close inspection of the course of events that took place between the composition of canon XII and that of canon XV.

When canon XII was composed, *The Art of Fugue*'s structure was the one presented in Scheme 7.1, where it concluded the set of ordered pieces in one coherent composition, which was the First Version.[14] Its cohesion was determined by the fact that it encompassed 14 pieces organised in seven pairs.[15] Moreover, the first decrypted canon is positioned as number 10, while the last one occupies position 14.[16] Remarkably, a canon in augmentation, as a rule, is positioned last (among the canons) in all of Bach's cycles.[17]

Still, one cannot ignore the fact that the two pairs of canons, located on positions 9–10 and 13–14, consist each of just one canon in two presentations: cryptic and decrypted. It is unlikely that Bach did not notice this, since he decided, in the Second Version, to present each of the two canons just in their decrypted form. This cut left the composition with 12 pieces,

Example 17.2 Canon in Augmentation XII and XV, comparison of bars 10–12; different materials suggest two separate compositions.

two short of the desired number 14. The pair of mirror fugues (XIII and XIV in the Autograph), placed in positions 12 and 13, were then added, to complete the required number of pieces in the cycle, thus creating the Second Version of *The Art of Fugue*. There, still, the last position was kept for the Canon in Augmentation (Scheme 8.1).[18]

In the First Version (Scheme 7.1), the two canons IX and XII were each presented in two ways: cryptic and decrypted. Canon IX shows first in cryptic form, while canon XII is first decrypted. This presentation agrees with Bach's characteristic principle of contrast, here opposing the order in which the two possible presentations are inverted for the two canons (which formed a pair, albeit not juxtaposed). On the other hand, in Scheme 8.1, which represents the Second Version of *The Art of Fugue*, canon IX appears only in its decrypted presentation. This is indicated by the fact that Bach wrote the Canon in Augmentation (xv) only in decrypted form: the cryptic version of canon IX was not needed anymore.

This analysis clarifies certain peculiarities of the Autograph P 200. It reasons the presence of the two variants of the Canon in Augmentation and Inversion and also the appearance of the second variant, marked xv, only in a decrypted presentation. It also explains the allegedly deficient coherence of the Autograph.[19]

This means that two finalised versions of *The Art of Fugue* are present in P 200. The First Version (Scheme 7.1) was sealed by canon XII and rendered each of the canons IX and XII in both cryptic and decrypted presentations, relating to them as pairs. The Second Version (Scheme 8.1) dropped the cryptic versions, added two mirror fugues (XIII and XIV) and *replaced* canon XII with canon XV.

It is to be concluded, then, that the main body of the Autograph P 200 is neither a preliminary draft of *The Art of Fugue*, lacking a clear compositional structure, nor *just* an early version of this cycle, as it is often viewed, but actually two early versions, encompassed in one manuscript and representing two separate structures of *The Art of Fugue*, each complete and coherent in its own right.

Notes

1 Carl Philipp Emanuel Bach's announcement for subscriptions of *The Art of Fugue*, published in the *Critische Nachrichten aus dem Reiche der Gelehrsamkeit* (Berlin, May 7, 1751).
2 [Nevertheless, everything has at the same time been arranged for use at the harpsichord [*clavier*] or organ.] Wilhelmi, 'Carl Philipp Emanuel Bachs *Avertissement*', p. 102. Translated in *NBR*, no. 281, p. 257.
3 Here the first page of the engraver copy is compared with the printout of the Canon's first page in the Original Edition. Wolfgang Wiemer compares the last stave of the second page, and Richard Koprowski—the third page. Wiemer, 'Johann Heinrich Schübler', p. 93; Koprowski, 'Bach "Fingerprints"', pp. 61–7.
4 Koprowski, 'Bach "Fingerprints"', pp. 63–4.
5 See, for example, Tessmer, *NBA KB* IV/4, pp. 12–13; Wiemer, *Die wiederhergestellte Ordnung*, pp. 10 and 78–9.
6 See Wolff, *Bach: Essays on his Life and Music*, p. 270.
7 Hofmann, *NBA KB* VIII/2, p. 49. These faint traces (and the fact that the sheets were oiled) cannot be detected in a facsimile but only when holding the original Autograph.
8 Professor Hans-Joachim Schulze assumes that these are traces of pre-marking in the score, and I am grateful for the opportunity to discuss this matter with him. Indeed, a close examination of the original—P 200/1–1—shows that the ink used for writing the musical text was applied to paper over the pencil lines and not vice versa.
9 Baker, 'Bach's Revisions', pp. 67–71.
10 This happened, for example, in the cases of fugue I in the Autograph and *Contrapunctus 1* in the Original Edition, fugue II and *Contrapunctus 3*, and fugue III and *Contrapunctus 2*.
11 The existing incongruities between the versions are minor, because all three versions are not only composed on the same theme, but also have the same form of a bipartite finite canon and share the same musical material that is stated after the theme. The main difference is in the rhythmic writing that presents double values in the second and third variants.
12 Kopchevskiy, for example, sees in Bach's correction of these bars the source of Canon 15 (Kopchevskiy's numeration), which he regards as a version of Canon XII, in a decrypted form. See Nikolay Aleksandrovich Kopchevskiy: *"Iskusstvo fugi" I.S. Bakha* [J.S.Bach's *The Art of Fugue*] (Moscow, 1974), pp. 110–11.

208 *Part V: Toward a new interpretation of* The Art of Fugue

13 For a detailed discussion of this process see Chapter 8.
14 See Chapter 7.
15 On the function of pairing in Bach's works see Yuzhak, 'O prodvigayushchey' pp. 9–35; Anatoly Milka, 'K kompozitsionnoi funktsii BWV 870–93' [On the Compositional Function of BWV 870–93], in Anatoly Milka, (ed.) *Bakhovskie Chtenia 3: Khorosho Temperirovannyi Klavir*, vol. 2, [Bach Reading 3: The Well-Tempered Clavier, vol. 2] (St Petersburg, 1996), pp. 9–17.
16 Here Bach echoes old traditions concerning the number 10, which represented the *concept of canon* in its ancient philosophical meaning as a *basic principle* (for example, in Pythagorean philosophy, the 10 elements of the *tetractys*). The association of the number with the biblical Ten Commandments is a later cultural phenomenon.
17 It is interesting to look at Bach's copy of the canons' sequence from Zarlino's essay *Le istitutioni harmoniche* (Venice, 1558). Prepared for pedagogic purposes, the canons are ordered in ascending degrees of complexity. Seeing Zarlino's series as incomplete, Bach added a canon in augmentation at the very end of this cycle, and gave it the title *Canon / a3. Per / Augmentationem / Incerti / Autoris* [Three-part canon in augmentation: included by the author]. Werbeck, 'Bach und der Kontrapunkt', pp. 67–95.
18 At this point Bach introduced the new variant of this canon, numbered xv in the Autograph. By this, the former variant (xii in the Autograph), was downgraded to the status of a draft. Canon xii, thus, belonged only to the First Version and was not to be included in the Second Version of *The Art of Fugue*.
19 The Autograph P 200 was considered, for a long time, just as an early draft for *The Art of Fugue*.

18 The autograph of the last fugue

An unfinished copy?[1]

The last piece in *The Art of Fugue* is the one marked in the Original Edition as *Fuga a 3 Soggetti*.

Was that also Bach's last composition? Furthermore, was the whole cycle, called *The Art of Fugue*, Bach's last composition? The person whose acquaintance with the subject matter was considered totally reliable did answer this question. Johann Sebastian Bach's obituary was written by Carl Philipp Emanuel and Johann Friedrich Agricola.[2] In this document, which includes one of Bach's earliest biographies, it is unambiguously stated: 'Die Kunst der Fuge. Diese ist das letzte Werk des Verfassers ...'.[3]

Nevertheless, and despite the credibility of this source, the information issued in the obituary was decisively rejected by scholars in the 1980s and 1990s. At the musicological conference dedicated to Bach's 300th anniversary (Leipzig, 1985), Yoshitake Kobayashi presented results of a handwriting analysis in Bach's manuscripts from the composer's last years. The data of Kobayashi's analysis led to major revisions in the dating of many of Bach's compositions, including *The Art of Fugue*. Particularly dramatic was the scholar's conclusion that 'Nunmehr ist nicht die Kunst der Fuge, sondern die h-Moll-Messe als Bachs Opus ultimum anzusehen'.[4] Kobayashi repeated this statement in his major study,[5] for which he used diplomatics.[6]

Kobayashi's results looked so convincing that in the following (1990) international Bachakademie summer meeting in Stuttgart, a book calling the Mass in B minor Bach's 'Opus ultimum', was issued.[7] The book's title implies a universal acceptance of the status of the Mass in B minor as Bach's last opus. This was, indeed, the general impression: a year after Kobayashi's publication, Christoph Wolff declared that 'we must take leave of the time-honored idea that *The Art of Fugue* was Bach's "swan song"'.[8] Yet, there are substantial reasons, grounded in Bach's manuscripts and various other documents, to doubt this premise.

Documents

The most important source is the preserved handwritten fragment of the quadruple fugue. To clarify, however, what the fugue was as a whole, it is essential to understand its structure and position within the entire cycle and to juxtapose its autograph with available documents that reflect the publication process of *The Art of Fugue*. Several sources, beyond the musical materials, are needed for this undertaking. Listed in chronological order, these are:

- Carl Philipp Emanuel Bach's advertisement of subscriptions for *The Art of Fugue* in the *Critische Nachrichten aus dem Reiche der Gelehrsamkeit*, published in Berlin, on May 7, 1751[9]

210   *Part V: Toward a new interpretation of* The Art of Fugue

- C.P.E. Bach's notice ('*Nachricht*') on the verso of the title page in the Original Edition, offered for sale on September 29, 1751 (Figure 18.1)[10]
- Friedrich Wilhelm Marpurg's preface ('*Vorbericht*') to the second edition of *The Art of Fugue* (written probably in February or March 1752; the edition was offered for sale on April 2, 1752)
- Philipp Emanuel and Johann Agricola's description in the obituary of the 'unfinished' fugue's peculiarities (published in 1754)[11]
- C.P.E. Bach's *NB* on the last page of the 'unfinished' fugue's autograph (written after 1780)

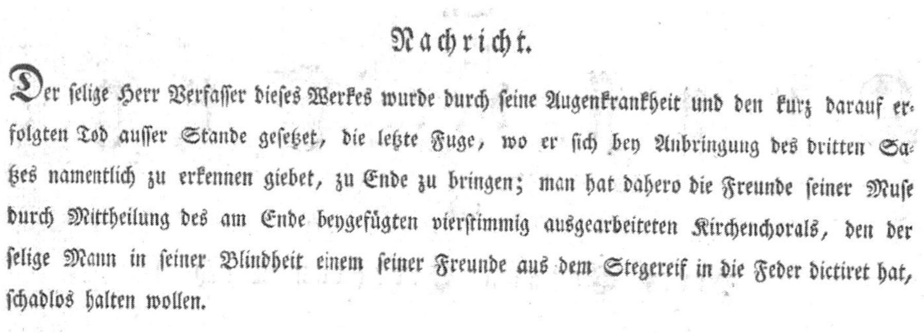

Nachricht.

Der selige Herr Verfasser dieses Werkes wurde durch seine Augenkrankheit und den kurz darauf erfolgten Tod ausser Stande gesetzet, die letzte Fuge, wo er sich bey Anbringung des dritten Satzes namentlich zu erkennen giebet, zu Ende zu bringen; man hat dahero die Freunde seiner Muse durch Mittheilung des am Ende beygefügten vierstimmig ausgearbeiteten Kirchenchorals, den der selige Mann in seiner Blindheit einem seiner Freunde aus dem Stegereif in die Feder dictiret hat, schadlos halten wollen.

Figure 18.1 C.P.E. Bach's notice on the verso of the Original Edition's title page.

Excerpts from these documents, related to the completion of the 'last' fugue and of *The Art of Fugue* in general are compiled here following their chronological order:

- From Carl Philipp Emanuel's advertisement (Berlin, May 7, 1751):

    Es ist aber dennoch alles zu gleicher Zeit zum Gebrauch des Claviers und der Orgel ausdrücklich eingerichtet. Die letzten Stück sind zwey Fugen für zwey unterschiedene Claviere oder Flügel, und eine Fuge mit drey Sätzen, wo der Verfasser bey Anbringung des dritten Satzes einen Namen Bach ausgeführet hat. Den Beschluß macht ein Anhang von einem vierstimmig ausgearbeiteten Kirchen-Choral, den der seelige Verfasser in seinem letzten Tagen, da er schon des Gesichtes beraubet war, einem seiner Freunde in die Feder dictiret hat.

    [Nevertheless, everything has at the same time been arranged for use at the harpsichord or organ. The last pieces are two fugues for two keyboard instruments and a fugue with three themes, in which the author, writing the third theme, has displayed his name *Bach*. The conclusion is made with an appendix of a four-part church hymn, which the late author, during his last days, already deprived of his eyesight, dictated to the pen of a friend.][12]

- From Carl Philipp Emanuel's notice on the verso of the Original Edition's title page:

    Der selige Herr Verfasser dieses Werkes wurde durch seine Augenkrankheit und den kurz darauf erfolgten Tod ausser Stande gesetzet, die letzte Fuge, wo er sich bey

Anbringung des dritten Satzes namentlich zu erkennen giebet, zu ende zu bringen; man hat dahero die Freunde seiner Muse durch Mittheilung des am Ende beygefügten vierstimmig ausgearbeiteten Kirchenchorals, den der selige Mann in seiner Blindheit einem seiner Freunde aus dem Stegereif in die Feder dictiret hat, schadlos halten wollen.

[The late author of this work was prevented by his disease of the eyes, and by his death, which followed shortly upon it, from bringing the last fugue, in which at the entrance of the third subject he mentions himself by name [through the notes BACH, that is, B♭-A-C-B♮], to conclusion; accordingly it was wished to compensate the friends of his muse by including the four-part church chorale added at the end, which the deceased man in his blindness dictated on the spur of the moment to the pen of a friend.][13]

- From Marpurg's preface to the second Original Edition (1752):

    Es ist nichts mehr zu bedauern, als daß selbiger durch seine Augen-Krankheit, und den kurz darauf erfolgten Tod außer Stande gesetzet worden, es selbst zu endigen und gemein zu machen. Er wurde von demselben mitten unter der Ausarbeitung seiner letzten Fuge, wo er sich bey Anbringung des dritten Satzes nahmentlich zu erkennen giebet, überraschet. Man hat indessen Ursache, sich zu schmeicheln, daß der zugefügte vierstimmig ausgearbeitete Kirchenchoral, der seelige Mann in seiner Blindheit einem seiner Freunde aus dem Stegereif in die Feder dictiret hat, diesen Mangel ersetzen, und die Freunde seiner Muse schadlos halten wird.

    [Nothing could be more regrettable than that, through his eye disease, and his death shortly thereafter, he was prevented from finishing and publishing the work himself. His illness surprised him in the midst of the working out of the last fugue, in which, with the introduction of the third subject, he identifies himself by name. But we are proud to think that the four-voiced chorale fantasy added here, which the deceased in his blindness dictated ex tempore to one of his friends, will make up for this lack, and compensate the friends of his Muse.][14]

- From C.P.E. Bach and Agricola's obituary, published in 1754 (Figure 18.2):

    Die Kunst der Fuge. Diese ist das letzte Werk des Verfassers, welches alle Arten der Contrapuncte und Canonen, über einen eintzigen Hauptsatz enthält. Seine letzte Kranckheit, hat ihn verhindert, seinem Entwurfe nach, die vorletzte Fuge völlig zu Ende zu bringen, und die letzte, welche 4 Themata enthalten, und nachgehends in allen 4 Stimmen Note für Note umgekehret werden sollte, auszuarbeiten. Dieses Werk ist erst nach des seeligen Verfassers Tode ans Licht getreten.

    [*The Art of the* [sic] *Fugue*. This is the last work of the author, which contains all sorts of counterpoints and canons, on a single principal subject. His last illness prevented him from completing his project of bringing the next-to-the-last fugue to completion and working out the last one, which was to contain four themes and to have been afterward inverted note for note in all four voices. This work saw the light of day only after the death of the late author.][15]

> 8) Die Kunſt der Fuge. Dieſe iſt das letzte Werk des Verfaſſers, welches alle Arten der Contrapuncte und Canonen, über einen einzigen Hauptſatz enthält. Seine letzte Kranckheit, hat ihn verhindert, ſeinem Entwurfe nach, die vorletzte Fuge völlig zu Ende zu bringen, und die letzte, welche 4 Themata enthalten, und nachgehends in allen 4 Stimmen Note für Note umgekehret werden ſollte, auszuarbeiten. Dieſes Werk iſt erſt nach des ſeeligen Verfaſſers Tode ans Licht getreten.

Figure 18.2 The paragraph in the obituary describing *The Art of Fugue*.

- Carl Philipp Emanuel's note (written after 1780) on the last page of P 200/1–3 (the 'unfinished' fugue):

  > NB. Ueber dieser Fuge, wo der Name BACH im Contrasubject angebracht worden, ist der Verfasser gestorben.
  >
  > [NB. While working on this fugue, in which the Name BACH appears in the countersubject, the author died.][16]

Even a superficial glance at these documents reveals some remarkable similarities among the three first documents. There is general agreement that the first two documents (the advertisement of the subscription and the preface to the 1751 edition) could have been written only by Emanuel.[17] The text of the third document (*Vorbericht*, 1752), although written by Marpurg, considerably depends on the first two (see Table 18.1, text in bold letters). Finally, the last two documents, too, are traced back to Emanuel.

Thus, although Marpurg is named the author of the 1752 preface and Johann Friedrich Agricola, J.S. Bach's student, might have contributed to the obituary, all five sources lead back to the same person—Carl Philipp Emanuel Bach. If this is correct, there should be no contradictions between the documents concerning the conclusion of the whole cycle in general, particularly concerning the last fugue.

Nevertheless, there are significant—and quite essential—incongruities between the documents, reflecting the changes in C.P.E. Bach's perception of the ways in which *The Art of Fugue* remained unfinished.

According to the first three documents, Emanuel was initially convinced that only *one* fugue remained unfinished, the one that should be the last in the cycle. This fugue appears in the Original Edition as the unfinished *Fuga a 3 Soggetti*, the fugue on three themes, the last of which was the B-A-C-H theme.

Table 18.1 Text comparison: the advertisement, the notice on the first edition and the preface to the second edition

Avertissement, May 7, 1751	*Nachricht*, 1751	*Vorbericht*, 1752
	Der seelige Herr Verfasser dieses Werkes wurde **durch seine Augenkrankheit und den kurz darauf erfolgten Tod ausser Stande gesetzet**	Es ist nichts mehr zu bedauern, als daß selbiger **durch seine Augen-Krankheit, und den kurz darauf erfolgten Tod außer Stande gesetzet**
Die letzten Stück sind zwey Fugen für zwey unterschiedene Claviere oder Flügel, und eine Fuge mit drey Sätzen, wo der Verfasser **bey Anbringung des dritten Satzes** einen Namen Bach ausgeführet hat. Den Beschluß macht ein Anhang	die **letzte Fuge, wo er sich bey Anbringung des dritten Satzes namentlich zu erkennen giebet,** zu Ende zu bringen; man hat dahero die Freunde seiner Muse durch Mittheilung des am Ende beygefügten **vierstimmig ausgearbeiteten Kirchenchorals,**	Worden, es selbst zu endigen und gemein zu machen. Er wurde von demselben mitten unter der ausarbeitung seiner **letzten Fuge, wo er sich bey Anbringung des dritten Satzes namentlich zu erkennen giebet,** überraschet.
Von einem **vierstimmig ausgearbeiteten Kirchen-Choral, den der seelige** Verfasser in seinem letzten Tagen, da er schon des Gesichtes beraubet war,	den der seelige Mann in seiner Blindheit	Man hat indessen Ursache, sich zu schmeicheln, daß der zugefügte **vierstimmig ausgearbeitete Kirchenchoral,** der seelige Mann in seiner Blindheit
einem seiner Freunde **in die Feder dictiret hat.**	**einem seiner Freunde aus dem Stegereif in die Feder dictiret hat** schadlos halten wollen.	**einem seiner Freunde aus dem Stegereif in die Feder dictiret hat,** diesen Mangel ersetzen, und die Freunde seiner Muse schadlos halten wird.

However, the excerpt from the obituary disagrees not only with perceptions about Bach's last days, as they are established in Bach studies, but also with other documents that were issued by Emanuel himself.

The text of the obituary implies that it is no later than the beginning of 1754 (more probably even earlier)[18] that Emanuel became aware that *in fact there were two unfinished fugues*: one 'penultimate' ('die vorletzte Fuge'), and another one 'last' ('und die letzte'). The essay

214   Part V: Toward a new interpretation of The Art of Fugue

specifies that the 'penultimate' was the *Fuga a 3 Soggetti*, while the 'last' was another fugue, one that had not been mentioned in previous documents. That last fugue was not on three but on four subjects.

The discrepancy between the 1751 announcement of the subscription and the obituary, published in 1754, shows that something must have changed Emanuel's perception of the intended content of *The Art of Fugue*. It is clear that his 1754 view of the work drastically differs from the one presented in his first and second editions, three and two years earlier, respectively.

This new perception of the cycle's ending could have been changed only by new information which Emanuel must have considered to be fully reliable. Who was his source?

Philipp Emanuel's informant

The competent informant, whom Emanuel could completely trust, was a person who watched the process of the last fugue's composition and perhaps even participated in the process in one way or another. Theoretically, it could be any member of the Bach family who was present at the composer's house when this process took place. The materials related to the last fugue show that one of Bach's younger sons, Johann Christoph Friedrich, who at that time was 17 and a half years old, was indeed deeply involved in this composition, and traces of his contribution as copyist and corrector are visible in the Autograph. However, he left Leipzig in the very last days of December 1749 for a new position at Bückeburg.

Christoph Friedrich's close involvement with *The Art of Fugue*'s composition process schooled him in fugue writing. It is not a coincidence that it was he, of all Bach's sons, who chose to follow his father's tradition in the field of fugue up to its highest degree. His own obituary states: 'Die Fuge war sein Element. Hier zeigte er sich jedesmal in seiner wahren Bachischen Gestalt'.[19] Charles Burney wrote that Christoph Friedrich was 'regarded as the greatest fugist, and most learned professor in Germany'.[20]

When and how could Christoph Friedrich convey to Philipp Emanuel important information about the concluding fugue (and further, about two closure fugues rather than one)? The only personal contact between Friedrich and Emanuel could take place in Bückeburg, at the end of July 1751, during the Prussian King Frederick II's visit to bestow upon Wilhelm, the Count of Schaumburg-Lippe-Bückeburg, the Order of the Great Prussian Eagle for military merits.[21] Christoph Friedrich left his father's home, probably shortly after Christmas 1749, to serve as musician in that court. Emanuel was part of the King's entourage and thus could have met his brother and learn new information, hitherto unavailable to him, about *The Art of Fugue*. Thus, by the end of July or, at the latest, the beginning of August 1751, C.P.E. Bach could have gained reliable information about the finalising particulars of *The Art of Fugue*, realising that Friedrich could tell his brother about the last fugue of the cycle only as it stood by the time of his departure from Leipzig to Bückeburg, that is, before January 1750.

This means that the new information about the existence of two closing fugues could have been introduced into the obituary only after the two brothers had met in July 1751. This news, with specific additional features concerning the last fugue, was sent to Mizler for publication in his *Musikalische Bibliothek* (albeit published only three years later). What did this new communication consist of?

The new information

The style of the paragraph that describes *The Art of Fugue* in the obituary differs from the rest of that text. It uses contemporary professional terminology, the meaning of which may be missed by the modern reader. The central sentence in this paragraph (quoted above in full, also in Figure 18.2) states:

> Seine letzte Kranckheit, hat ihn verhindert, seinem Entwurfe nach, die vorletzte Fuge völlig zu Ende zu bringen, und die letzte, welche 4 Themata enthalten, und nachgehends in allen 4 Stimmen Note für Note umgekehret werden sollte, auszuarbeiten.
>
> [His last illness prevented him from completing his project of bringing the penultimate fugue to completion and working out the last one, which was to contain four themes and afterwards to be inverted note for note in all four voices.][22]

This description may seem peculiar or even inarticulate, unless it is seen within the context of eighteenth-century fugue theory and, more specifically, of mirror fugues and their paradoxes.

The paradoxes of mirror fugues

This type of fugue has one curious characteristic. Each mirror fugue is, in fact, two fugues, thus creating what could be perceived as a numerical paradox. The two fugues that make for one mirror fugue are written usually one above the other within one brace, thus highlighting their mutual kinship and exposing how the lower system originates in the top one. The first, *Contrapunctus 12*, is a four-voice mirror fugue, and *Contrapunctus 13* is a three-voice one. Each one of the above is actually two fugues: *recta* and *inversa*. The Autograph score of the four-voice fugue presents its components separated by a row of short double strokes (Figure 18.3):

Figure 18.3 P 200/1–1: the opening of the four-part mirror fugue (XIII).

216 Part V: Toward a new interpretation of The Art of Fugue

The fugue at the bottom of the braced system, copied in inverse counterpoint, mirrors the top one. The initial combination (written at the top) is the *fuga recta* and its derivative—the *fuga inversa*. Hence, while composing the *fuga recta*, one should keep in mind that its material will be inverted, and once the initial combination is done, the composer has in mind its derivatives, too.[23] The remaining task is their realisation: writing them out, which in the musical theory of Bach's times was termed *elaboratio*, *evolutio*, or *Ausarbeitung*. Clearly, such operation does not require the same intellectual effort that was needed for the creation of the initial combination: the author knows the result ahead of its being written down.

One case, however, deserves special attention, in spite of being seemingly obvious. For a mirror fugue, one should first compose the whole *fuga recta*, and only afterwards invert all its parts, thus creating its mirror, the *fuga inversa*.

The paragraph in the obituary about *The Art of Fugue* is now clearer. Taking into account the paradox of mirror fugues and the terminological specificity of *Ausarbeitung*, *Note für Note*, *nachgehends*, and the like, the description of Bach's actions, implied in the obituary's paragraph about *The Art of Fugue*, becomes transparent.[24] Moreover, it is now apparent that the fugue described by Philipp Emanuel was the quadruple mirror fugue; Bach did not finalise the *fuga recta*, hence he could not elaborate upon (*Ausarbeiten*) its inversion—the *fuga inversa*. Bach intended to end *The Art of Fugue* precisely as it is described in the obituary, with the quadruple mirror fugue. The set of two fugues that Emanuel described as the penultimate and the last are in fact the one mirror fugue that was to conclude of *The Art of Fugue*.

What are the four subjects?

As Gustav Nottebohm showed already in 1881,[25] the answer to this question is quite simple. Since the last piece is a mirror fugue, then both the penultimate and the last fugue (the *fuga recta* and the *fuga inversa*) use the same set of four themes. Three are known: they appear in the Original Edition, as the 'unfinished' fugue, under the title *Fuga a 3 Soggetti*.

The fourth theme is not difficult to figure out: the obituary mentions that the whole cycle is composed 'über einen eintzigen Hauptsatz' [on a single principal subject] which is precisely the theme missing in the autograph of the 'unfinished' fugue. Bach could not have finished the cycle with this fugue without this particular theme.

Nottebohm showed that the three themes on which the *Fuga a 3 Soggetti* is written indeed combine well with the main theme of the cycle (see Example 18.1). It is hard to imagine that

Example 18.1 Nottebohm's combination of themes.

such a combination could exist just by coincidence. When combining contrapuntal materials Bach always strived to achieve a texture in which each theme would be easily identified, clearly heard and not intermingle with the others. In this respect, the high correlation of the main theme of the cycle with each one of the other themes and also of the whole construction in general, is evident.

However, the combination could sound even better if the main theme were presented not in its original form, which includes 12 notes, but in its more elaborate presentation, which consists of 14 notes (Example 18.2):

Example 18.2 Combination of themes using the 14 notes version of the main theme.

In such a form, the first motive of the cycle's main theme (in the alto) creates imitational correspondence with the first theme of the *Fuga a 3 Soggetti* (in the bass), the latter presenting the first four notes in an augmented imitation. The result of inverting this combination, in the *fuga inversa* (Example 18.3) sounds no less natural than the one of the *fuga recta*, strongly suggesting that Bach had already planned it during the composition process. Thus, although not proven beyond doubt, Nottebohm's hypothesis that Bach planned the simultaneous statement of the four subjects in the last fugue seems quite convincing.

Example 18.3 The hypothetical *fuga inversa*.

218   *Part V: Toward a new interpretation of* The Art of Fugue

For a long time, the thesis according to which J.S. Bach intended to end the cycle with the fugue on these four themes, implying that the simultaneous combination of the four themes should appear at the end of the 'Unfinished' *Fuga a 3 Soggetti*, remained undisputed. In 2008, however, Gregory Butler challenged this conception, rejecting ideas he formerly supported and offering instead two sensational assertions:[26] the first was that Bach had never planned to include the *Fuga a 3 Soggetti* in *The Art of Fugue*.[27] The second, that Nottebohm's contrapuntal combination is inadequate. Butler presented several arguments to support these claims:

- Emanuel did not regard this fugue as composed on the cycle's principal theme, since in his announcement of the subscription to the Original Edition[28] this fugue is grouped with the mirror fugue for two claviers and the arrangement of the chorale—pieces that do not belong to the cycle, listing them after his discussion of the fugues that are 'composed upon *one and the same principal theme*' (Butler's emphasis).
- The autograph paper on which the *Fuga a 3 Soggetti* is inscribed, its watermarks and handwriting all relate to the very last period of Bach's life, too late, in Butler's opinion, for the time in which the composer worked on *The Art of Fugue*.
- Unlike the rest of the cycle, the *Fuga a 3 Soggetti* is written in keyboard score.
- 'The principal subject of the *Art of Fugue* is uncomfortably close in its formulation to the first subject' [of the *Fuga a 3 Soggetti*—A.M.].[29]
- The main subject's 'supposed combination with the three subjects of this fugue is far from convincing, contrapuntally'.[30]
- Concluding the work with the group of four canons would be more congruent with Bach's *modus operandi*.

From the above, Butler infers that 'despite the fact that there is not a shred of evidence that this work belongs in the collection, and much that argues against this assumption, Bach scholars are unwilling to give it up, and so the myth endures'.[31] In lieu of this 'myth', he offers his own alternative interpretation:

- The piece under discussion had to be a triple fugue, just as its title indicates: *Fuga a 3 Soggetti*.
- The *Fuga a 3 Soggetti* was prepared by Bach for print as his due contribution to the Society of Musical Sciences for the year 1750, and not for *The Art of Fugue*.
- The autograph of the fugue (P 200/1–3) is a clean engraver copy (*Abklatschvorlage*).
- The *Fuga a 3 Soggetti* was completed at that particular time because Bach intended to take advantage of the opportunity, sending it to print together with *The Art of Fugue*.[32]

Butler does not explain his claim that the combination of the four themes is 'far from convincing, contrapuntally.' In fact, the good combination of the fugue's three themes with the main theme of the cycle actually suggests that this fugue *does* belong to *The Art of Fugue*. The high compatibility of rhythm, melody and harmony in the joint statement of all four themes meets all criteria of normative counterpoint. On the other hand, though, Butler's argument here relies on two typical mistakes that circulate in Bach studies. The first is that the resemblance between *The Art of Fugue*'s principal subject and the first subject of the *Fuga a 3 Soggetti* is '*uncomfortably close* in its formulation' [my emphasis—A.M.]. This claim, valid only for the 14-note version of the main theme, ignores that the relation between these two parts is a contrapuntally adequate imitation in augmentation (see Example 18.2). This emphasises the themes' compatibility as well as the innate coherence of the entire combination, an absolutely typical feature of Bach's compositional style. The second mistake is the claim that Nottebohm's combinations of the four themes are impossible to perform on a keyboard.[33] While Nottebohm's goal was to show the theme's contrapuntal compatibility rather than the possibility of performance, it is clear that all of his combinations can easily be performed on an organ.

Butler's reliance on the fugue's presentation in keyboard score, unlike the open score in which the rest of the cycle is written, to reinforce his claim that the *Fuga a 3 Soggetti* does not belong to *The Art of Fugue* is unconvincing. A similar case exists in the *Musical Offering*, where the six-part ricercar appears in both open and keyboard scores. Never was this fact presented as an argument claiming that this ricercar does not belong to that cycle. Indeed, the *Fuga a 3 Soggetti* appears in Philipp Emanuel's announcement among the last pieces that are unrelated to the cycle. However, since all these pieces are eventually included in the Original Edition, it is hard to accept this as a valid argument.

Butler highlights the long period of time that separates the composition of the main corpus of P 200 and P 200/1–3 and dates the *Fuga a 3 Soggetti* at the very end of the composer's life. This is quite an indefinite period, which requires a more precise chronological perspective. The manuscript is dated as written between August 1748 and October 1749,[34] and the main body of P 200 as completed during 1746.[35] Bach, however, continued to work on *The Art of Fugue* during 1747 until August 1748, with several intermittent breaks, which occurred naturally.[36] This specific time gap coincides with the period of approximately one year between the first and the second versions of *The Art of Fugue*. During this time Bach worked on the composition of the Mass in B minor, making it comparable to other events that took place during the composition process of *The Art of Fugue*. This timetable can hardly support an assumption claiming the *Fuga a 3 Soggetti* to be chronologically unconnected to *The Art of Fugue*.

Why does Bach's autograph of the *Fuga a 3 Soggetti* (P 200/1–3) end on bar 239?

It is often considered that *The Art of Fugue* remained unfinished, the widespread notion being that the composer had not succeeded in completing it. The manuscript of the last Contrapunctus (BWV 1080/19 in Schmieder's Catalogue)[37] seems abruptly cut off on bar 239, at the point where the final section of the fugue should normally appear. While this seems to exclude any doubts on this account it may nevertheless be worthwhile to consider whether the break in this bar simply means that the fugue is unfinished, or whether this fact may have some additional meaning.

There are several scholars who question the prevalent notion and consider the possibility that the fugue had been completed.[38] Christoph Wolff writes: 'The last fugue was not left unfinished as it appears today and, in fact, *The Art of Fugue* must have been a nearly completed work when Bach died'.[39] The author also offers an explanation as to why the piece stopped at this particular place, confirming that the fugue was finished and the stop was not coincidental.[40] Stating that Bach did not intend to continue the process of composition, he presents three propositions:

- The autograph under consideration is a 'composition manuscript', that is, a manuscript created during and through the process of composition.[41]
- The composition of a quadruple fugue should start from some draft fragment (which Wolff named 'fragment x'), in which all four themes are stated together. This fragment had to exist in reality, but eventually was lost.[42]
- Bach did not intend to continue writing after bar 239,[43] because it had to be followed by the closing part of the fugue, built (in a normative fugue fashion) as a sequence of joint statements. The next step would be, therefore, writing it down, using fragment x as a model and intercalating the voices in various combinations. It was thus unnecessary to continue the composition: the rest of it would be derived from said fragment x.[44]

There is no reason to deny that prior to composing a quadruple fugue, some preliminary work has to be done. The purpose of such work is to provide options for simultaneous combinations of all of the themes. Without such preparation work the composition of a multi-theme fugue is simply impossible.[45] Moreover, it makes perfect sense that such a combination did exist as a draft on paper.

Wolff's assumption that Bach did not intend to continue the manuscript after bar 239 seems further substantiated by the fact that the bottom part of the fifth and last page of the autograph is so carelessly lined that it is impossible to continue writing on it. The sheet had been so spoiled that if Bach nonetheless decided to write on it, he had in mind only a few bars, needing just the top part of the page.[46]

Nevertheless, Wolff's explanation for the cut at bar 239, according to which the rest of the fugue was already imparted in fragment x and was therefore unnecessary here,[47] is yet not convincing enough. First, there could be more than one reason for the cut (other reasons will be suggested below). Second, and more important: the existence of fragment x does not necessarily imply that the fugue was completed; this fragment could provide a basis for many variants that would function as the composition's closure. If the fugue had not been explicitly written down to its end (at least as a draft), a whole process of composing, albeit simplified by Bach's well-prepared fragment x, was still to be implemented. After all, the closure of a multi-theme fugue may contain any number of statements and various episodes or none at all. It is impossible, thus, to determine the closure—or the actual length—of a specific fugue based solely on one fragment x, even if its existence is highly plausible. The exclusive reliance on such a possibility does not provide enough grounds to conclude that the last fugue 'was not left unfinished', or, moreover, that the entire *Art of Fugue* had been completed.

While the question of whether this fugue was completed or not remains open, it is closely connected with another important starting point: the nature and the function of this particular autograph. The widely accepted assumption, shared by most scholars, is that the autograph is a composition manuscript. This point, however, is not so obvious and requires further consideration.

A composition manuscript or an engraver copy?

Indeed, the manuscript does look like a composition copy. It would suffice to look at its fifth page (Figure 18.4) in order to confirm this impression.

The first thing that one may notice in this page is its messiness: the handwritten notes—note stems flung carelessly in various angles, smears and expanding ink stains—suggest quick writing. The musical content on this page is drafty, too: each one of the four voices ends on a different point. Indeed, all this points at a composition process abruptly interrupted. The inscription made by Carl Philipp Emanuel, 'Ueber dieser Fuge ... ist der Verfasser gestorben' [Over this fugue... the author died] only reinforces this impression. How else could one interpret the given manuscript, if not as one created in the process of composition?

If, however, the autograph in its whole is critically analysed, some facts surface which might puzzle supporters of the 'compositional draft' theory. For example, the paper's quality, the handwriting's features and the specific corrections of the autograph's first page (Figure 18.5) show traits that would hardly fit the notion of a composition manuscript.

All of these elements deserve closer examination.

The paper

The paper of this manuscript is thin and porous. Such paper was used for engraver copies (*Abklatschvorlagen*). It had to be porous in order to better absorb the oil varnish and thin, to allow the mirrored text to be better seen in the verso after the oiling. Examples of Bach's *compositional* manuscripts written on paper of this kind have never been seen and as of today are unknown.

Still in agreement with traditional engraver copies, the music text is written only on the recto of each sheet; all verso sides were left blank. The bulk of evidence showing that Bach did his best to save on the high cost of paper makes such uncharacteristically prodigal use of paper for a draft highly unlikely.[48] The list of errata prepared by Carl Philipp Emanuel after his father's death and written on the verso of the fifth sheet only confirm this impression. In addition, his other son, Johann Christoph Friedrich mentions some 'new conception' ['... und einen andern Grund Plan'] that his father implemented in the last version of *The Art of Fugue*. The paper, therefore, supports the view of the discussed manuscript as an engraver copy rather than as a compositional draft.

The handwriting

The handwriting on the first page of the manuscript is very tidy. The writing pace is slow, as when meticulous attention is paid to calligraphy; the notes are large, particularly the note heads which are here larger than usual. Similar examples in Bach's scores exist exclusively in engraver copies and in most fair manuscripts (sometimes intended as gifts) but never in composition manuscripts.

The polyphonic writing is rhythmically aligned. This would be fairly impossible in draft, particularly when composing polyphonic music, let alone one rich in imitations and complex counterpoint combinations.

The rastering of the first four pages was performed with a ruler. Bach had stave-lined with a ruler only engraver and gift copies, but never his composition manuscripts. The fifth sheet, however, looks different. It is rastered by hand with no use of a ruler.

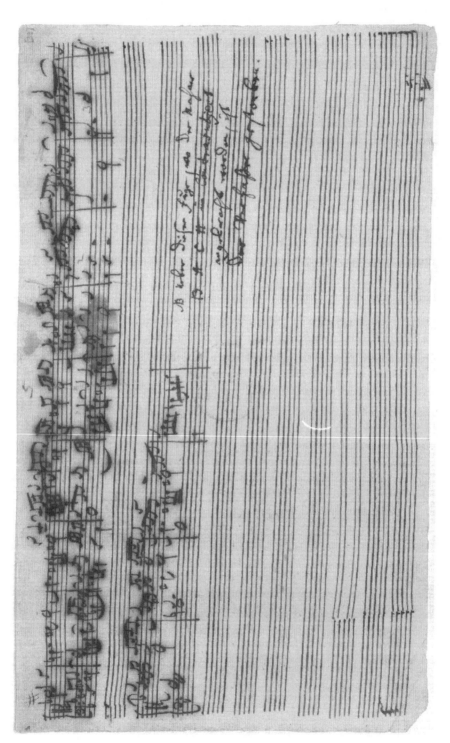

Figure 18.4 P 200/1–3: The last page of the 'unfinished' fugue (bars 227–239).

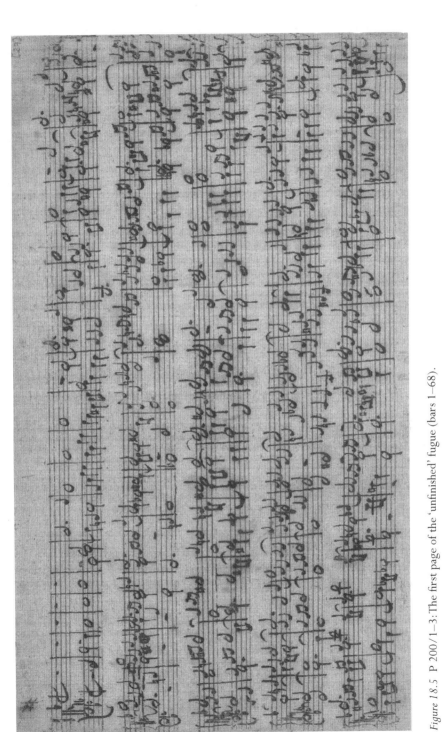

Figure 18.5 P 200/1–3: The first page of the 'unfinished' fugue (bars 1–68).

224   *Part V: Toward a new interpretation of* The Art of Fugue

Some scholars believe that the four first pages of the fugue were on leftovers of paper that remained unused after Bach finished the four canons, because Bach used here the same kind of paper, and these pages were similarly lined: five two-stave systems on each page.[49] Judging by the Original Edition of 1751, however, we see that Bach prepared the engraver copies of the canons himself, which means that he knew precisely how much room he needed to write them down and the amount of paper this would require. Taking into account that Bach always minimised his use of paper, the hypothesis that he prepared four additional pages without being sure that he would fill them up seems improbable.

Thus, not only the peculiarities of the paper, but also the characteristics of the note writing on the first four pages contradict the appearance of Bach's composition manuscripts. On the other hand, they reinforce the argumentation for the first four pages to be interpreted as engraver copies.

Corrections and amendments

In many cases the kind of corrections on a page allows detection of the circumstances under which they have been performed: during the composition or the copying, after the composition or after the copying. Not focusing now on the specific features of Bach's corrections (which are meticulously researched and classified in the two-volume study by Robert L. Marshall),[50] I will only bring examples of the corrections that are relevant for the present discussion.

The first correction appears at the very first page of the manuscript (Figure 18.5, bars 19–20). It is difficult to establish what exactly was written in bar 19 before the correction. However, it can be clearly seen that the previous writing had been scraped off with a knife,[51] the stave lines accurately restored and the new musical text written on them. The new note writing was performed carefully, keeping the calligraphic style before and after this point. Why, all of a sudden, would Bach care so much about calligraphy in a composition manuscript? He never did so in composition manuscripts, and not even in many fair copies, as, for example, in the main body of P 200.[52] Once an error was noticed, or when Bach changed his mind right after he wrote something down, he would usually insert the correction above or, if that was impossible, simply strike out what should be corrected and continue to compose or to copy further on the same stave. Examples of this practice can be seen in other autograph manuscripts, for example, in the Confiteor section from the Mass in B minor, BWV 232, where whole bars are crossed out and the correction written below the system.[53] This is exactly the type of amendment that appears on the second page of P 200/1–3. Its appearance—quite messy, with multiple corrections—points at an entirely contradictory conclusion, suggesting that this is, actually, a composition manuscript (Figure 18.6).

Two bars—113 and 114—were crossed out and three bars indicated to be inserted instead. Note that the correction, in German organ tablature, is written at the bottom margin of the page.

Our attempt to reconstruct the process of this correction starts with the notes that were originally written in bars 109–15 (Figure 18.7).

The musical text seems fairly typical, except for two questionable points that are not quite attuned to Bach's style. The first point is the absence of a subdominant before the dominant–tonic closing cadenza in bars 113–14; the second is the melodic motion of the bass in bars 112–13, which is atypical for Bach when preparing a dominant in cadenzas. Such motion

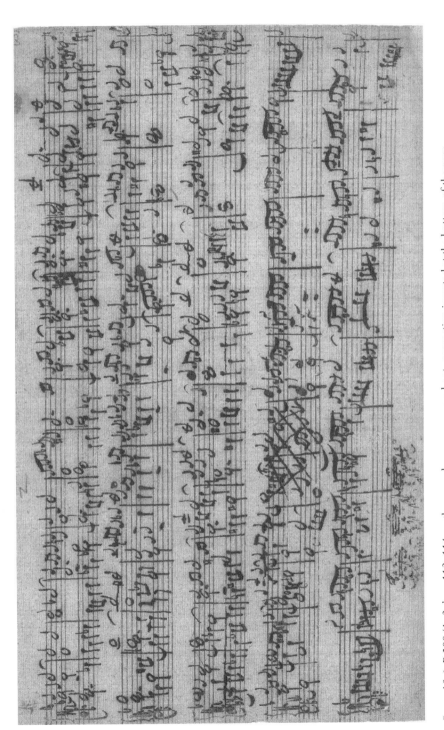

Figure 18.6 P 200/1–3: bars 113–114 on the second page are crossed out, correction inserted at the bottom of the page.

226 Part V: Toward a new interpretation of The Art of Fugue

Figure 18.7 P 200/1–3: bars 109–115 (top system) and their correction (bottom page margin, below the bottom system).

cannot be found anywhere in the entire *Art of Fugue*. The coincidence of these two uncharacteristic gestures may suggest that one bar, presenting the subdominant degree, was missed. Such proposition is supported by Bach's own correction (Example 18.4).

Example 18.4 P 200/1–3: correction in the 'unfinished fugue'. Top: bars 111–115, before the correction; bottom: bars 111–116 (with the additional bar), after the correction.

Clearly, Bach did not notice the mistake on the spot. If he had discovered it on time (that is, immediately after writing the following bar, in this case, bar 114 or even bars 113–14), and if this were indeed a composition manuscript, he would most probably have acted like he did in similar cases: either write the correction above the already written bars or cross out the incorrect bar(s) and continue his writing thereafter. This analysis indicates, then, that Bach made the corrections while copying and not in the process of composition.

A whole complex of factors—the quality of paper, the style of musical graphics and the character of corrections—conveys that the writing of these pages took place not in the process of composition but while copying. Moreover, many other signs suggest that this was not intended just as a copy, but rather as a copy for engraving.

This first conclusion deduced from the analysis of the first four sheets of the autograph is, then, that this is an engraver copy on which a mistake was found, requiring a correct copy to be written on a new page. The fifth sheet of P 200/1–3 (Figure 18.4), however, presents a completely different picture.

The fifth sheet of P 200/1–3

As mentioned earlier, this last sheet looks significantly different from the other ones in this supplement: its format and the sort of paper differ from the first four pages; there are many stains, making the page look quite messy; the writing speed is higher, the notes are smaller than on the previous pages, and the handwriting does not manifest any intention of calligraphic writing. Finally, the staves are rastered by hand and quite negligently, to the point that music cannot be written on the bottom staves. On the other hand, the musical text is absolutely clear, and furthermore all proportions of the musical alignment are carefully kept, enhancing the clarity of the musical text.

Consequently, it is quite safe to state that all the characteristics of the fifth page reflect Bach's striving to achieve one single goal: readability.[54] All the rest does not seem to be essential. A manuscript of this kind would usually be given to a copyist; it only needed to be clear, to minimise the chances of copyist errors.

What could be the reason for this difference between the first four pages and the fifth one, which looks as if it belonged to another manuscript? What change of intentions could it reflect?

In our view, the discussed autograph reflects quite an unusual process of copying, during which *the relation of the composer to this manuscript had changed*, which leads to a second and more accurate conclusion concerning P 200/1–3: while the first page is, indeed, an engraver copy, the fifth (and last) one is just a plain copy, intended for a copyist who would prepare of it an engraver copy.

The situation is quite unusual, and we cannot but be curious *why* it emerged. Other circumstances accompanying this story are equally intriguing. For what did Bach need an engraver copy? Why did he need a plain copy? And, why did he abandon the initial idea in the process of preparing the manuscript?

The purpose of the engraver copy is unequivocally clear: Bach intended to send this fugue to print. Note, however, that the fugue is written on a two-stave system (clavier version), while all the other contrapuncti of *The Art of Fugue* are written in *open score*. This is crucial, because this version could not be used for the publication of *The Art of Fugue*. Hence the purpose of this two-stave variant of the fugue is utterly unclear. It was mainly this discrepancy that drew the attention of Gregory Butler, who concluded that Bach did not intend to include this fugue in *The Art of Fugue*.[55] The facts, however, suggest another interpretation.

228   Part V: Toward a new interpretation of The Art of Fugue

The *Fuga a 3 Soggetti* in the context of Bach's social life

The period between March 21, 1749, and the beginning of March 1750 is a meaningful time in Bach's life: on March 21, 1750 he would celebrate his 65th birthday. This age had special significance for a member of the Society of Musical Sciences,[56] to which Bach had belonged since 1747. According to the constitution of the Society, each member had to make an annual contribution of an original work. To create a work was not enough: it should be published. The members who reached the age of 65 were assigned to the category of *pro emerito* and were released from the obligation of this annual contribution, as well as from the annual membership fee.[57]

Bach's contribution for 1747 appears in the portrait made by Elias Gottlob Hausmann (1746), in which the composer holds the score of the six-part triple canon. In this form, however, it can be considered as a 'legitimate' publication only conditionally. In reality, it had been published in Mizler's *Musikalische Bibliothek*. In 1748 Bach most probably contributed the *Einige canonische Veraenderungen über das Weynacht-Lied: Vom Himmel hoch, da komm ich her*, BWV 769. The piece was engraved by Balthasar Schmid[58] and printed in Nüremberg.

The year 1749 was supposed to be the last time that Bach would be expected to contribute to the Society. From 1750 on, he would become one of the *pro emeriti* and be released from this obligation. However, looking through the works he composed in 1749 (as far as the preserved manuscripts allow), one cannot attest to any particular piece as fitting this purpose. The only one that meets the criteria is *The Art of Fugue*. Indeed, the hypothesis that the composer could use it for this purpose is quite popular among Bach scholars and most categorically fostered by Hans Gunter Hoke.[59] His principal arguments are based on the facts that *The Art of Fugue* completely met the requirements of the annual contribution and that in 1750 Bach turned 65. Accepting Hoke's argumentation, we would like to draw attention to some details that are important for the present discussion, but were not addressed in his work.

One of the peculiarities of the Society of Musical Sciences was that it worked by correspondence; even the title of its constitution includes the words '*correspondirenden Societät*'.[60] There was a particular 'packet' that circulated among its members through the post service. The packet contained various materials: information on current events, discussions of works composed by the Society's members, the works themselves (including those that had been considered as their annual contributions (in case they were not published in the *MMB*). Mizler's letter from September 1, 1747, from Końskie (Poland) to the Society member Meinrad Spieß from the Irsee Monastery gives us an idea about the size of the material that the envelope could contain.[61] The piece Bach mentioned was obviously the six-part ricercar from the *Musical Offering*. The size of its printed copy is seven pages on four sheets. As already mentioned, Bach's contribution to the Society in 1748 was the *Einige canonische Veraenderungen über das Weynacht-Lied: Vom Himmel hoch, da komm' ich her*, BWV 769. Its size in print was six pages on four sheets. It is plausible, therefore, that the size of a contribution within four sheets was considered optimal for these contributions, and Bach took every step to fit into this. In the case of BWV 769, for example, the first, second and third variations present the canon's risposta in a cryptic form (while even in the autograph of this work it is written in full). Else, for a full presentation, Bach would need 18 more staves, which would exceed the four sheet required format (printing the end of his music on the back cover of an edition would not have been considered *bon ton*). Further, it is clear that in this edition Bach strove to avoid a page turn in the course of any single variation. Were the canon of the first two variations not cryptic, the fifth (last) variation would have a page turn in the middle of its third canon. Encrypting certain parts allowed Bach to provide the performer with a comfortable reading, to save a whole page and to fit the composition into the desirable format of four sheets.

The Original Edition of *The Art of Fugue* is large (70 pages) and weighty. Clearly, its dimensions would not allow fitting into the Society's packet. However, if only the *Fuga a 3 Soggetti* were submitted, and not as a score but in clavier format, presenting only the *fuga recta*, its size and weight would perfectly fit the Society's 'packet'. Indeed, as calculation shows, the size of the *fuga recta* of the last piece of *The Art of Fugue* would require nine pages if written in open score[62] and even less if written in a clavier reduction. For comparison: the six-part ricercar from the *Musical Offering* is seven pages long in open score and only four pages in clavier reduction.[63] Bearing in mind that after bar 239 of the last fugue there were still approximately 90 bars of music to be written, and judging by the density of writing in P 200/1–3, this would take less than two pages that should be added to the existing four. In other words, the completed fugue in clavier layout would be about six pages long. Including the title page and the empty verso of the last sheet would render four sheets, the exact format of materials hitherto sent to the Society's mail. Considering the likelihood of such a sequence of events, Bach's intention to publish this fugue in clavier layout for Mizler's Society seems quite feasible: at least in size it fully corresponds to the format of the Society's 'packet'. Our third conclusion, thus, is that Bach was preparing the engraver copy in order to publish it in clavier layout as his creative contribution to the Society of Musical Sciences for 1749.

Why, however, would Bach desert the idea of making this engraver copy and, during the course of his work, switch to the preparation of a plain copy?

The first four pages of the fugue exhibit characteristics that prove Bach's diligent concern for calligraphic quality, which was a necessary condition for an engraver copy. However, the bar missed in the process of copying and the subsequent correction spoiled the second page, forcing Bach to abandon his original plan.

In its clavier version the fugue could not be added to *The Art of Fugue*: for that Bach would need to prepare an engraver open score of this fugue. At this stage, however, he was physically too weak to do it himself and, besides, he realised that his calligraphic efforts would not match the required quality anymore. The next step would be to use the service of an engraver, for whom a plain and easily readable copy would be provided. It is highly likely that this is exactly what happened. Failing to prepare the engraver copy on his own, Bach simply decided to use these five pages as copies for a copyist.

Bach had to copy these pages from some draft. As mentioned earlier, prior to composing a quadruple fugue one should have a thoroughly checked combination of all the four themes in one common statement. Only following this procedure, other sections based on each of the themes could be written.[64] It is in such sections that most of the corrections, so typical of a composition manuscript, can be found, particularly in the contrapuntal constructs characteristic of fugues. An analysis of the preserved part of the P 200/1–3 indeed presents such structures in high density. The draft of this fugue surely was brimming with corrections, making it hardly readable. While the composer was able to understand it, a copyist would most probably find it absolutely undecipherable. On the other hand, the closing section of the fugue had to be built upon the previously prepared joint statement of all of the themes. It is very likely, then, that this particular section of the fugue's draft was clear enough to provide a reference for an engraver copy.[65] It was unnecessary, therefore, to copy it yet again, particularly considering its size—about 90 bars—and the fact that Bach was enduring, by then, serious difficulties with his vision.

Our fourth conclusion, therefore, is that there are grounds to assume that Bach wrote the first four pages of the P 200/1–3 as an engraver copy, while the 12 remaining bars, written on the fifth page, were a fair draft intended for a copyist.

Our main (and last) conclusion, however, is that based on our interpretation of the data found in the analysis of P 200/1–3 there is reason to contemplate *The Art of Fugue* as *a completed composition*. Consequently, it might have been published by Bach himself, were he still alive, rather than by his sons, which would have been possible if not for the unfortunate visit of the guest celebrity, the oculist John Taylor, in Leipzig.

The fate of the copies

What happened to the copies of this fugue, the one for clavier and the second in score layout?

The clavier layout copy

There are still no traces of the copy intended for submission to the Society of Musical Sciences. For the time being it can only be regarded as Bach's *intention*, deduced from the P 200/1–3. It is highly probable that it was never actually created, but incompletely preserved only in this autograph. This would mean that Bach's duties for the Society of Musical Sciences for the year 1749 were not fulfilled. It is unlikely that Bach put himself in an awkward position versus his colleagues, violating the constitution of the Society. However, the eighth clause of the Society's constitution specifies special conditions, among which health problems are considered. According to this clause, only a prolonged illness of a Society's member can justify missing the presentation of an annual contribution: 'Wer es unterlässet, liefert zur Casse 1 Rth. und entschuldiget nichts, als langwierige Krankheit'.[66] Indeed, this is exactly what happened to Bach.

The open score copy

We would hardly know anything about the existence of this engraver copy, except for the copyist's mistake.[67] The additional pagination that Bach used in the second part of *The Art of Fugue* allows us to delineate the number of pages reserved by the composer for the quadruple fugue. The copyist tried to save one page, writing the musical text of the fugue more thriftily than the composer had planned. Subsequently, Bach had to exchange the position of several pieces within the cycle. The traces of this story can be found in another autograph, which could serve as topic for another discussion.[68] Here, however, the most important point is that the engraver copy of the score for the edition of *The Art of Fugue* was executed by the copyist to whom Bach handed the following materials: five pages of P 200/1–3 (four written as engraver copies and one as a fair draft) and the end of the (now lost) draft in which the text was clearly legible, because it was based on the (now lost) composition fragment x.[69]

Notes

1 The chapter was formerly published in Russian as an article: Anatoly Milka, 'O sud'be poslednego vznosa I.S. Bakha v "Obshchestvo muzykal'nykh nauk"' [On the fate of J.S. Bach's last contribution to the Society of Musical Sciences], in A. Dolinin, I. Dorochenkov, L. Kovnatskaya and N. Mazur (eds.), *(Ne)Muzykal'noe prinoshenie ili Allegro Affettuoso* [(Non)-Musical Offering or Allegro Affettuoso]: Collection in Honor of Boris Katz toward his 65th Anniversary (St Petersburg, 2013), pp. 7–21. Also in German, Anatoly Milka, 'Warum endet die Fuga a 3 Soggetti BWV 1080/19 in Takt 239?', *BJ* 100 (2014): pp. 11–26.
2 The obituary was first published in *MMB* IV (1754): pp. 158–76; reprinted in *BD* III/666, pp. 80–93; translated to English in *NBR*, no. 306, pp. 295–307.
3 [*The Art of The Fugue*. This is the last work of the author …] *MMB* IV (1754): p. 168; *BD* III/666, p. 86; *NBR*, no. 306, p. 304.
4 [From now on it is not *The Art of Fugue*, but the Mass in B minor that should be regarded Bach's *opus ultimum*.] Yoshitake Kobayashi, 'Bemerkungen zur Spätschrift', p. 462.
5 Yoshitake Kobayashi, 'Zur Chronologie', p. 66.
6 See Chapter 4, note 9.
7 Ulrich Prinz (Ed.), *Johann Sebastian Bach: Messe H-Moll: 'Opus ultimum', BWV 232 – Vorträge der Meisterkurse und Sommerakademien J.S. Bach, 1980, 1983 und 1989* (Stuttgart, 1990). For particular interest in this volume see Robert L. Marshall, 'Bachs H-moll-Messe: Zur Quellensituation und Überlieferung', pp. 48–67. Hans-Joachim Schulze, 'J.S. Bachs Missa h-Moll BWV 232-I. Die Dresdener Widmungsstimmen von 1733: Entstehung und Überlieferung', pp. 84–102, and Yoshitake Kobayashi, 'Bachs Spätwerke: Versuch einer Korrektur des Bach-Bildes', pp. 132–50.
8 Wolff, *Bach: Essays*, p. 27.
9 Wilhelmi, 'Avertissement', pp. 101–5; *BD* V/C 638a, pp. 182–3; *NBR*, no. 281, pp. 256–8.
10 *BD* III/645, pp. 12–13.
11 Editor's note: in Bach literature, this essay is usually referred to as the 'obituary'. To avoid confusion, this term is kept here, too. This, however, is not the original title of Philipp Emanuel and Agricola's essay. The obituary was published as the third part of the 'Denkmal dreyer verstorbenen Mitglieder der Societät der Musikalischen Wissenschafften' [Memorial for three deceased members of the Society of Musical Sciences], *MMB* IV, (1754): pp. 129–76. The part honouring J.S. Bach, written by C.P.E. Bach and Johann Agricola, is the third among these, starting on p. 158. The title *Denkmal*, suggests a 'memorial essay' rather than 'obituary' (which in German would appear as *Nekrolog*, *Nachruf* or *Todesanzeige*). The word '*Nekrolog*' does appear however, for the first time in relation to this particular essay, in *BD* III/666, p. 80, in a very short introduction to the text, probably following the late eighteenth-century tradition of lengthy obituary writings (indeed titled '*Nekrolog*'). However, the late date – four years after J.S. Bach's death (although its first draft might have been written earlier – see note 17), its sheer length and the character of its content imply a memorial essay rather than an obituary.
12 See note 8, above.
13 *Die Kunst der Fuge*, Original Edition, (Leipzig, 1751); reprinted in *BD* III/645, pp. 12–13; translated in *NBR*, no. 284, pp. 259–60.
14 Friedrich Wilhelm Marpurg, *Die Kunst der Fuge durch Herrn Johann Sebastian Bach, ehemahligen Capellmeister und Musikdirector zu Leipzig*. Vorbericht, in der Leipziger Östermesse, 1752. Reprinted in *BD* III/648, p. 15; translated in *NBR*, no. 374, p. 376.
15 *MMB* IV (1754): p. 168; reprinted in *BD* III/666, p. 86; translated in *NBR*, no. 306, p. 304.
16 Also in *BD* III/631, p. 3; translated in *NBR*, no. 285, p. 260.

17 A second advertisement of subscriptions was issued a month later, on June 1, 1751 in the *Leipzig newspapers*. Its style reveals that Emanuel wrote that one, too.

18 According to Mizler, C.P.E. Bach's first version of this essay might have been written as early as the end of 1750 (see *NBR*, no. 306, p. 297, note 28). However, it is more than likely that in the time between 1750 and 1754, when the essay was published, it went through several corrections and additions.

19 [Fugue was his element. Here he showed himself each time in his true Bachian shape.] Adolf Heinrich Friedrich Schlichtegrol, *Nekrolog auf das Jahr 1795* (Gotha, 1797), pp. 268–84, quote from p. 281; See Peter Wollny, 'Johann Christoph Friedrich Bach und die Teilung des Väterlichen Erbes', *BJ* 87 (2001): p. 67.

20 Charles Burney, *The Present State of Music in Germany, the Netherlands, and United Provinces, or, the Journal of a Tour through Those Countries, Undertaken to Collect Materials for a General History of Music*. By Charles Burney, Mus. D., in Two Volumes (vol. 2, London, 1773), p. 323; reprinted in *BD* III/777, p. 249.

21 Ernst Suchalla (ed.), *Carl Philipp Emanuel Bach: Briefe und Dokumente: kritische Gesamtausgabe*, vol. 1 (Göttingen, 1994), documents 3–5, pp. 9–13.

22 See note 13.

23 It is a norm in the composition process of complex counterpoint that the initial idea must include its derivatives, and careful thought must be given to the peculiarities of various counterpoint types, because each type carries and implies a set of its own limitations.

24 For relevant eighteenth-century German terminology see, for example, Johann Gottfried Walther, *Musicalisches Lexicon oder Musicalische Bibliothec* (Leipzig, 1732), p. 180; Johann Mattheson, *Kern melodischer Wissenschaft* (Hamburg, 1737), p. 137 and his *Der volkommene Capellmeister* (Hamburg, 1739), p. 383; Mainard Spiess, *Tractatus Musicus Compositorio-Practicus* (Augsburg, 1745), p. 134; Wilhelm Marpurg, *Abhandlung von der Fuge* (Leipzig, 1753), p. 10.

25 Martin Gustav Nottebohm, 'J.S. Bach's letzte Fuge', *Musik-Welt*, 20 (March 1881): p. 234.

26 Gregory Butler, 'Scribes', pp. 111–24.

27 'One of the most persistent myths surrounding *The Art of Fugue* is that the collection was to be crowned with a quadruple fugue, the "incorrectly" titled *Fuga a 3 Soggetti* that survives in autograph form.' Ibid. pp. 116–17.

28 Butler mistakenly relates this announcement to the *second* edition (ibid.); however this announcement is dated May 7, 1751, more than four months before the *first* edition's publication. Emanuel's announcement concerning the second edition merely informed the availability of its copies for the subscribers.

29 Ibid.

30 Ibid. p. 117.

31 Ibid.

32 Ibid. pp. 117–18.

33 Butler relies here on Christoph Wolff's opinion. Ibid. p. 122, note 24.

34 Kobayashi, 'Zur Chronologie', p. 62.

35 Ibid.

36 Ibid.

37 Wolfgang Schmieder, *Thematisch-systematisches Verzeichnis der musikalischen Werke von Johann Sebastian Bach* (Leipzig, 1961), p. 609; Alfred Dürr and Yoshitake Kobayashi, *Bach-Werke-Verzeichnis* (Wiesbaden, 1998), p. 445.

38 Christoph Wolff, 'The Last Fugue: Unfinished?' in *Current Musicology*, 19 (1975): pp. 71–7, reprinted in Wolff, *Bach: Essays on His Life and Music*, pp. 259–64.

39 Wolff, 'The Last Fugue', p. 76.

40 Ibid.

41 Not all scholars interpret Wolff's conclusion in this way. Gregory Butler, being convinced that Wolff considers the given autograph to be a fair copy, writes in reference to p. 72 in Wolff's article: 'both the status of this source as *fair copy* and also physical evidence in the source itself led Wolff to the conclusion that the work had been completed by Bach' (Butler, 'Scribes', p. 122, note 27; emphasis added). Butler's interpretation, however, is incorrect: Wolff does not consider this manuscript to be a fair copy. On the contrary, he describes it as a compositional manuscript: '...*Beilage* 3 represents the composition manuscript ...' (Wolff, 'The Last Fugue', p. 73); see also next note.

42 '... The combinatorial section of the Quadruple Fugue in a manuscript (hereafter designated fragment x) that originally belonged together with *Beilage* 3, but is now lost'. Ibid. p. 74.

43 '... Bach obviously had never planned to fill the sheet from top to bottom, in other words that he stopped writing deliberately at m. 239'. Ibid. p. 71.

44 '... He [Bach – A. M.] stopped at m. 239 ... because the continuation of the piece was already written down elsewhere, namely in fragment x'. Ibid. p. 74.

45 '... Bach had no choice but to start with the combinations of the four themes before writing the opening sections of the fugue'. Ibid. p. 74.

46 'Surely he used the last page only because he needed a sheet of music paper for just a few bars; since he never wasted paper, such a piece could serve his purpose'. Ibid. p. 72.

47 See note 45.

48 Scholars often pointed at this fact. See, for example: Wolff, 'The Last Fugue', pp. 72–3; Butler, 'Scribes', p. 122; Hofmann, *NBA KB* VIII/2, p. 82.

49 See for example: Wolff, 'The Last Fugue', p. 73.

50 Robert Lewis Marshall, *The Compositional Process of J.S. Bach: A Study of the Autograph Scores of the Vocal Works*. Princeton, 1972, two volumes. See also: Tatiana Shabalina, *Rukopisi I.S. Bakha: klyuchi k tainam tvorchestva* [J.S. Bach's manuscripts: keys to the mysteries of his work] (St Petersburg, 1999), pp. 118–28.

51 About Bach's use of the scraping knife for corrections in his scores see: Yoshitake Kobayashi, 'Bachs Notenpapier und Notenschrift', in Susanne Spannaus et al. (eds), *Thüringer Landesausstellung*, vol. 1 (Erfurt, 2000), p. 427.

52 'The main portion of the autograph – referred to as P 200, after its call number – represents a fair copy'. Wolff, *Bach: Essays*, p. 268.

53 Autograph D–B Mus. ms. Bach P 180 in the Staatsbibliothek zu Berlin – Preußischer Kulturbesitz; see correction in bars 140–42.

54 Wolff, 'The Last Fugue', p. 72.

55 '... as I have argued, the *Fuga a 3 Soggetti* was never to have been included in the collection [*The Art of Fugue* – A.M.]'. Butler, 'Scribes' p. 118.

56 See Chapter 1.

57 'Wenn ein Mitglied 65 Jahr alt ist, so ist er für verdient (*pro emerito*) zu halten, und von Arbeiten frey, und nur zu einem freywilligen Beytrage zur Casse verbunden ...' *MMB*, III/2 (1746): pp. 355–6.

58 Schmid was probably one of Bach's former students. He also took part in the edition of *Clavierübung III*.

59 Hans Gunter Hoke, *Zu Johann Sebastian Bachs 'Die Kunst der Fuge'* (Leipzig, 1974), pp. 14–15.

60 'Gesetze der correspondirenden Societät der musikalischen Wissenschaften in Deutschland.' *MMB* III/2 (1746): p. 348.

61 See Chapter 1, p. 10.

62 The calculation is based on the fact that there are two additional paginations in P 200/1–1. Their analysis shows that in the final stage of the work on *The Art of Fugue* the interchanging of canons took place. This interchanging enables the calculation of the number of pages that Bach reserved for the

last fugue (*recta* and *inversa*). Since this fugue, like the two previous, was a mirrored one and had the structure of *rectus* + *inversus*, it appears that Bach reserved for it 18 pages in total, that is, nine pages for each section. See also Milka, *Iskusstvo fugi*, pp. 186–91; Milka, 'Zur Datierung', pp. 53–68.

63 There is an autograph of two-stave version of the six-part ricercar from the *Musical Offering* (P 226). It takes four pages.

64 Usually it is the exposition of the first theme, followed by the expositions of the second and of the third themes. These sections are obligatory. However, after the expositions free sections may follow, which is exactly the case in this fugue. Here, the exposition of the fourth theme is absent, because in this particular fugue it is used as cantus firmus.

65 If Christoph Wolff considers fragment x to be a ready 'combinatorial section' of the fugue, then the section based on it must be at least clear.

66 [The one who will not fulfil this, should pay one Reichsthaler, and, only long illness can serve as a justification.] *MBB* III/2, p. 350.

67 As Peter Wollny established, Bach's main copyist then was his pupil Johann Nathanael Bammler. Wollny, 'Neue Bach-Funde', p. 44. For more information about the error of this copyist see in Milka, 'Zur Datierung', pp. 65–7.

68 Milka, *Iskusstvo fugi*, pp. 174–90 please see detailed analysis and description in Chapter 11.

69 Unfortunately, these materials are lost, but signs of their existence are present in the Autograph and in the Original Edition of *The Art of Fugue*.

19 'Over this fugue …'

Philipp Emanuel's inscription on the last page of the autograph of the 'unfinished' fugue is familiar to all Bach scholars (Figure 19.1; see also Figure 18.4):

Figure 19.1 P 200/1 3: C.P.E. Bach's inscription on the last page.

It reads: '*Ueber dieser Fuge, wo der Nahme BACH im Contrasubject angebracht worden, ist der Verfaßer gestorben*'.[1]

This text puzzles music lovers and, perhaps even more so, professional musicians. In view of the known details about Bach's inability to compose music in the last months of his life, a certain metaphorical quality of this inscription is apparent, thus leading to a simple acceptance of its existence, without looking for any actual relation to historical facts.

Indeed, the situation described in the inscription is absolutely unrealistic, because between March 31 (the day of Bach's eye surgery) and July 28 (the day of his death) of 1750, a period that encompasses almost four months, Bach was completely blind and could neither read nor write. Thus, he could not die while working on this fugue. Realising the discrepancy between this inscription and the facts of the composer's biography, scholars keep trying to understand its real meaning. Consequently, translations such as 'while working on this fugue…'.[2] (presenting the work on the fugue as a process, thus indefinitely stretching the period of time), although similar to the German 'ueber dieser Fuge', still sound slightly softer. Such attempts, however, do not really solve the puzzle. There are quite a few other, non-literal interpretations of the text, but none convincingly explain its meaning.

236   *Part V: Toward a new interpretation of* The Art of Fugue

Assuming that Philipp Emanuel was completely aware of the content of his inscription, we propose to interpret the text literally. Clearly, the autograph of the 'unfinished' fugue, traditionally dated between August 1748 and October 1749, is the focal point of our inquiry.³ The date was established by Yoshitake Kobayashi, who based his assessment on the peculiarities of Bach's handwriting at that particular period and on the particular traits of the paper on which the fugue is written. As we remember, however, in another part of his study, Kobayashi stated: 'Spätestens ab Ende Oktober 1749, als Bach eine Quittung im Zusammenhang mit dem Nathanischen Legat von seinem Sohn Johann Christian schreiben ließ [Dok. I, Nr. 143], leistete er, vermutlich bedingt durch die Behinderung des Sehvermögens, keine Schreibarbeit mehr'.⁴ It means that the discussed period could be even longer than six months. And if Kobayashi's dating is correct, then from the moment that 'the name BACH as a countersubject' was introduced into the 'unfinished' fugue, until the moment in which 'the author died', elapsed no less than 10 months and maybe even as long as two years. Philipp Emanuel's inscription, however, clearly states that both events occurred at the very same moment. Since such an occurrence could not have taken place in reality, Emanuel's statement is clearly false. Was it an unconscious oversight, or was Emanuel himself misinformed?

If the latter, it would mean that the son was completely clueless about the state of his father's health during the last years of his life: the deterioration of his eyesight, the surgery and his inability to write. Nevertheless, in the obituary, first written in 1751, Emanuel describes the circumstances of these events in detail. This means that he wrote the inscription on the fugue's last page while being aware of the factual circumstances around his father's death, which would make his *Nota Bene* even more perplexing. Most baffling of all, however, is the assertion, based on Emanuel's handwriting, that his inscription was written sometime in the 1780s, that is, more than a quarter of a century after Johann Sebastian Bach's death.

Had the inscription been written soon after his father's death, it might have been judged as a natural surge of emotional outpouring; a gap of 30 years, though, is strange and requires a more exacting explanation of special, perhaps more complex, contextual circumstances. In 1768, 18 years after his father's death, Emanuel's life changed dramatically. In that year he moved from Berlin to Hamburg, after accepting the position of the City's Music Director and the Kantor in the Johanneum academy.⁵ Carl Philipp Emanuel found himself in an absolutely new situation. Instead of the royal capital he now resided in a free Hanseatic city, and instead of abiding by Berlin's pedantic royal court etiquette rules, he enjoyed a more relaxed atmosphere of camaraderie among equals. The instrumental music of the Prussian court was replaced by church music, mostly vocal and choral (although composition of clavier music continued). His circle of friends was quite similar to that of Berlin: mostly artists, sculptors, poets, writers, philosophers and clerics, although there were not so many musicians. The social and financial standings of these creative personalities in the Hanseatic Hamburg, however, were unlike those of the imperial capital. Even a pastor in Hamburg carried other parish callings than a pastor in Berlin and also enjoyed a different social status.

Like his father's house in Leipzig, Emanuel's Hamburg home was a hub for artists and thinkers. The atmosphere was created not just by the visitors' personalities, but also by the ideas that stirred the European society during the last four decades of the eighteenth century, the dominant opinions, typical for educated society, and the popular topics and themes for discussion. Among Emanuel's circle of friends were the poets and literati Friedrich Gottlieb Klopstock, Johann Wilhelm Ludwig Gleim, Johann Heinrich Voss, Heinrich Wilhelm von Gerstenberg, Heinrich Christian Boie, Gotthold Ephraim Lessing and Christoph Daniel Ebeling;[6] the scientist and historian Johann Albert Heinrich Reimarus; the pastor Christoph Christian Sturm and the painter Andreas Stöttrup. Most of these belonged to the *Sturm und Drang* literary movement that rebelled against the French neo-classical style of the enlightenment aristocracy.[7]

Fed up with the strenuous and poorly paid service at the court of Frederick II, Philipp Emanuel welcomed the long awaited opportunity to start a new life elsewhere. The *Sturm und Drang* movement agreed with his own worldview; his compositions included quite a few in genres that were popular among the *Sturm und Drang* artists whose texts he set to music. He composed spiritual songs ('geistliche Gesänge') and songs in popular styles, spiritual odes and a melodeclamation.[8]

The aesthetic ideals and values enhanced by the *Sturm und Drang* artists—intuition, subjective views and insight—differed significantly from the enlightenment's professed rational clarity and balance and took precedence over them. Inexplicable feelings of transcendental entities were perceived as deeper and more meaningful than down to earth reasoning and rational inquiries. The *Sturm und Drang* art world was imbued with creatures of fantasy taken from ancient myths, German fairy tales and the romantic imagination of poets, playwrights and artists. Night, with its typical attributes, became the favourite time for the narrative: dreams, moonlight, nightingale song, mysterious rustlings and appearances of forest and pond spirits. Favourite topics were death as an unavoidable closure of mystery tales, bloody thrillers involving murder of family members but also stories about life-saving bloodline ties.

The magic power attributed to the *name* of a person (or a spirit) and its ritual inscription or utterance played a particular role in this cultural milieu. In this regard, *Carls Name*, a poem by Christian Friedrich Daniel Schubart, of which an excerpt is presented here, is telling:

> Ich muß sagen—laut muß ich sagen
> Was ihr verschweigt.
> C A R L S Name flammte heut
> Mit Sternengold geschrieben
> Am Olymp—Der Name C A R L S ! !—
> Hah! mit welcher Wonne sprech ich ihn aus,
> Deinen Namen, C A R L ! !—
> (Pause.)
> Zwar wird schon dein Name
> An beeden Polen genennt:—
> C a t h a r i n a s weltenstürzender Name
> Schlingt sich um ihn!—
> J o s e p h s Name—das Erstaunen der Völker—
> Schlingt sich um ihn!—
> Wodan F r i e d r i c h s Name—des Einzigen!
> Des Unerreichten!!—
> Schlingt sich um ihn![9]

238   Part V: Toward a new interpretation of The Art of Fugue

In the course of this short excerpt of 15 lines, the word *Name* [*Name*] appears seven (!) times, clearly showing that *a name* is a key concept for the poet. All the proper names are emphasised by expanded spacing, and the name Carl is spelled entirely in capital letters. A Name is endowed with qualities such as blazing [*flammte*], world overthrowing [*weltensturzender*], uttered with rapture [*mit welcher Wonne sprech ich ihn aus*] and inscribed in stars' gold [*mit Sternengold geschrieben*]. Not just the inscription but also the pronunciation of the Name is a required action of the poet: 'I have to say and I should say loud … Carl's name is blazing today' [*Ich muß sagen—laut muß ich sagen … Carls Name flammte heut…*]. Finally, with regard to perception of Name: it is hard to find such an abundance of proper names in any poetic style except for the *Sturm und Drang*—where names appear even in the titles of poems.

Throughout the second half of the eighteenth century there was a significant increase of interest in ancient Greek literature. This affected the kind of motifs that appeared in *Sturm und Drang* topics, many of which were focused on family relations. Against the background of horror scenes replete with of parricides, matricides and infanticides, the close relationship between father and son looked particularly gratifying. A typical example of this type is the legend in verse, *Das wunderthätige Crucifix* [The Miraculous Crucifix], by C.F.D. Schubart, where a deceased father protects his living son, who seeks his father's guidance. The motive of mutual self-sacrifice is clearly seen. In our context it is significant to note that the names of the spouses, pious and loyal to each other, are *Sebastian* and *Anna*. It may also be significant to note that the main focus of the poem quoted above is on *Carl*.

The period's imaginative world of poetic reference was greatly influenced by the renewed interest in classical culture in general, inspired by ongoing excavations in Herculaneum and Pompeii. Johann Joachim Winckelmann, the leading scholar of antiquity and a friend of Emanuel's, introduced the results of these studies to the European educated society. Representatives of the *Sturm und Drang* embraced the newly found literary and poetic treasures, contributing significantly to new translations of Greek poetry and drama. Subsequently, both content and poetic forms of this literary corpus were adopted and incorporated into the contemporary fashionable poetic styles.

Stories involving the Sphinx and its riddles gained particular popularity. Death awaited the traveller who answered wrongly the riddles, and death awaited the Sphinx if its riddles were solved. The very name *Sphinx* posed mystery, and its uttering would lead to the Sphinx's death. The stories reached beyond the unique Oedipus myth, reincarnating into narratives related to the excavations themselves. For example, the account according to which death overtakes the scholar who, when deciphering an ancient manuscript, utters aloud the newly found magic incantation, or the written name of a deity.

The wave of mysticism that swept through Europe in the eighteenth century was not limited to Greek mythology. A great part of it was inspired by the Masonic movement that was popular at that time, particularly among the educated circles of society. An old friend of Philipp Emanuel was Gotthold Ephraim Lessing, with whom he was acquainted from his Berlin years. His *Ernst and Falk: Dialogues for Freemasons*, written between 1776 and 1778, discuss the political and ethical issues that concerned members of the Masonic order.[10] Many of Emanuel's acquaintances and friends in both Berlin and Hamburg (including Lessing) were Freemasons. It is hard to assert whether Emanuel was a Freemason himself, but his work does relate to Masonic ideas, states of mind and mystic rituals. His *Twelve Masonic Songs* were published in 1788 and appear in two anthologies.[11]

Within this setting, the composition circumstances of *The Art of Fugue* and the death of his idolised father gained a mystical tinge in Emanuel's mind: the great composer who, while writing his last opus, inscribes his own name, encoding it into his music, and as soon as this mystical procedure is completed, the pen drops off the artist's hand, concluding his life's journey. The picture is of Bach parting this world not as a sick and infirm old man in his deathbed, but—as befits an outstanding person and a great musician—in the moment of his greatest inspiration, the conclusion of his opus magnum. How could one resist posing such a picture for posterity? 'Ueber dieser Fuge, wo der Nahme BACH im Contrasubject angebracht worden, ist der Verfasser gestorben'—this was a far more appropriate description.

Regardless of the excitement such possibility incurs, the simple way of describing what happened is that the beauty of the pictured idea was favoured over the actual facts. It sometimes happens with creative people.

Notes

1 [Over this fugue, where the name BACH is stated in the countersubject, the author died.]
2 *NBR*, no. 285, p. 260.
3 Kobayashi, 'Zur Chronologie', pp. 62 and 70.
4 [At the very latest, occurred by the end of October 1749, when Bach's receipt concerning the Nathan Bequest (Nathanischen Legat) was written by his son Johann Christian (Doc. 1, No. 143) most likely, due to deterioration of vision, he could no more perform any writing work.] Ibid. p. 25.
5 In this, Philipp Emanuel echoed the life change of his father, who moved from Cöthen to Leipzig, replacing the position of the court Kapellmeister with that of the Leipzig Music Director.
6 Ebeling also translated to German Charles Burney's *The Present State of Music in France and Italy* (London, 1771), published as *Carl Burney's der Musik Doctors Tagebuch einer musikalischen Reise durch Frankreich und Italien* (Hamburg, 1772) and *The Present State of Music in Germany, the Netherlands, and United Provinces London* (London, 1773), published as *Carl Burney's der Musik Doctors Tagebuch seiner Musikalischen Reisen* (Hamburg, 1773).
7 *Sturm und Drang* was a literary and artistic movement in Germany during the 1760s–1780s, named after one of Friedrich Maximilian Klinger's dramatic plays. Several of its representatives belonged to Emanuel's close circle, while with others he had intensive correspondence.
8 These works were published not only as individual songs but also as collections of vocal works published during the composer's lifetime and issued in several editions (for example: Herrn Christoph Christian Sturms / Hauptpastors an der Hauptkirche St Petri und Scholarchen in Hamburg / Geistliche Gesänge / mit / Melodien zum Singen bey dem Claviere / vom Herrn Kapellmeister Carl Philipp Emanuel Bach / Musikdirektor in Hamburg (Hamburg, 1780), the cover of the latter publication illustrated by Andreas Stöttrup.
9 'CARLS Name / gefeyert von der deutschen Schaubühne zu Stuttgart. / am 4. Nov. 1784', in *Christian Friedrich Daniel Schubart sämtliche Gedichte*, vol. 2 (Stuttgart, 1786), pp. 29–30.
10 Gotthold Ephraim Lessing, *Ernst und Falk: Gespräche für Freymäurer* (1776–1778), in his *Theologiekritischen und Ästhetischen Schriften*, vol. 5 (München, 1970). Translated to English by Hugh Barr Nisbet in *Gotthold Ephraim Lessing, Philosophical and Theological Writings* (Cambridge, 2005).
11 *Freymauer-Lieder mit ganz neuen Melodien von den Herren Capellmeistern Bach* (Copenhagen, 1788); *Allgemeines Liederbuch für Freymaurer*, vol. III (Copenhagen, 1788).

20 Revelation (instead of an Epilogue)

The third and fourth versions of *The Art of Fugue*, planned after the composition of the *Musical Offering* (and possibly also after the Canonic Variations on the Christmas Chorale *Vom Himmel Hoch*, roughly after 1747/1748), show that J.S. Bach changed the conception of his work. Christoph Friedrich, who witnessed and participated in the process, clearly indicated the existence of 'einen andern Grund Plan.' This *other* plan, as Bach's ensuing actions show, was radically different from the composition's previous two versions, abandoning the former principle of pair-organisation.[1] The new *Art of Fugue*, as presented in Chapter 10, was based on the following model (Scheme 20.1):

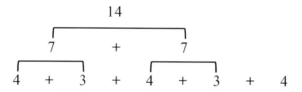

Scheme 20.1 The numerical structure of *The Art of Fugue*.

While the framework of the cycle is clear, its significance is not entirely so. This particular model hid a message that was encoded in a numerological symbolic system that is neither verbal nor musical. Within this system and in this particular composition, the number 14 was the organising principle and the single factor that determined the number of fugues regarded as contrapuncti. Expressing the sum of the numerical value of the letters in Bach's name, it carries a unifying meaning that defines each one of its elements and also its distinctiveness as a whole, joining two groups of seven contrapuncti each.

While the significance of number seven in Christian symbolic systems is multifaceted, given the multiplicity of its meanings in both Old and New Testaments, its particular substructure, where each half of seven fugues is represented by the specific combination of four and three, may provide more determined results.

In seventeenth- and eighteenth-century German studies (for example, in the works of Leibniz) the number seven is always interpreted as a combination of two components: four (as a symbolic representation of the world's material aspects) and three (in a variety of meanings of the word *Geist*—spirit), thus read as a symbol of inspiration and of the spirit's infiltration into substance.[2]

Such interpretation indeed may reflect the idea of spirituality imbued in *The Art of Fugue*. However, the division of the 14 units, which comprise the core of the work, into two groups of seven, is not the only peculiarity of the cycle's numerical construction. Each of these groups is further internally subdivided, in both cases, into four works followed by three. Given Bach's meticulous attention to numerical details, the fact that the internal units are twice positioned as four and three (rather than three and four) calls for some scrutiny.

Bach's intellectual environment and personal interests played a significant part in his approach to musical composition. His involvement with the Society of Musical Sciences, founded in 1738 by his student and friend Lorenz Mizler, substantially affected his musical, scientific and pedagogical principles and preferences.[3] Despite the fact that Bach was officially initiated into the Society only in 1747, he had socialised with its members and closely followed its discussions and activities since the moment of its establishment.

Bach's interest in literary and scholarly works increased significantly during these years. He copied musical and theoretical resources and acquired newly published books, as well as older ones, in book auctions.[4] Poetry collections of authors with whom Bach collaborated and from which he chose texts for his compositions often demonstrate the poetic technique of paragrams in which Bach was keenly interested. The musical part of his library included, among others, the theoretical works of Angelo Berardi, Johann Joseph Fux, Johann Mattheson, Johann David Heinichen and Johann Gottfried Walther. His collection of theological books shows that he was interested not only in dogmatic, but also in polemical writings, in particular those devoted to non-canonical interpretations of the scriptures, including studies discussing techniques of Kabbalah.[5] It is not by coincidence that Bach purchased books that address philosophical and existential issues. As often happens in one's later years, he became keenly interested in these questions and looked for answers in the books he read. Among these, Caspar Heunisch's *Haupt-Schlüssel über die hohe Offenbahrung S. Johannis* [The principal key to the St John's Revelation], listed in the inventory of Bach's estate as *Heinischii Offenbahrung Joh.*, calls for particular attention in its explanation of each and every number found in this scripture.[6]

The presence of this book in Bach's library was not coincidental. It seems that the St John Revelation occupied a special place in his mind and artistic output. In his cantatas Bach quoted this source more than 160 times, a remarkable number when compared with the 62 quotes from the Gospel according to St Mark, or with the 72 quotes from the book of Ecclesiastes.[7]

The core of the St John Revelation

Within the 22 chapters of the *Book of Revelations*, chapters 4–11 occupy a special place. The most discussed in theological and philosophical treatises, these chapters have been the subject of many works of art, too. In Lutheran sources, they are often presented in a bipartite structure: *Das Buch mit den sieben Siegeln* (chapters 4–7, 'The Book with the Seven Seals') and *Die sieben Posaunen* (chapters 8–11, 'The Seven Trumpets').[8]

The first group, which includes four chapters, consists of seven episodes, each relating the opening of one of the book's seven seals. The episodes are again subdivided into two groups of four and three episodes, respectively: the first four episodes describe the four riders of the apocalypse, and the remaining three episodes describe calamities: the martyrs under the Altar, the Lamb's Wrath, and Silence.

242   Part V: Toward a new interpretation of The Art of Fugue

The second group consists of seven episodes, too, respective of the seven angels that blow their trumpets. The subdivision here is similar: four natural disasters (hail and fire, earthquake, water pollution and eclipses) are followed by three woes (torture, plague and war). This division is highlighted by the verse that follows the four disasters with a triple exclamation: 'And I beheld, and heard an angel flying through the midst of heaven, saying with a loud voice, Woe, woe, woe, to the inhabiters of the earth by reason of the other voices of the trumpet of the three angels, which are yet to sound!'[9]

Bach could have identified this structure in the Revelation, and then again, as it was presented by Heunisch in his book. It can clearly be seen that this structure is echoed in *The Art of Fugue* in its new guise (Scheme 20.1). The scheme, however, shows an additional group of four works, the four canons, beyond and above the 14 contrapuncti. This additional group may relate, too, to the central part of the *Book of Revelation*.

The four figures of the Apocalypse

The Glorification of the Divine on His Throne, described at the beginning of chapter four of the *Revelation*, just before the opening of the seven seals, has been a favourite subject of artists throughout Christian history. Its particular presentations are diverse, but most of them comply with a composition similar to the engraving from the 1488 edition of Johannes Nider's book *Vier und zwanzig guldin Harfen* (24 Golden Harps).[10] The engraving shows, around the central figure, four small drawings of the 'four celestial images'.[11] The *Revelation* in Luther's Bible, owned by Bach, says:

> Und die erste Gestalt war gleich einem Löwen, und die zweite Gestalt war gleich einem Stier, und die dritte Gestalt hatte ein Antlitz wie ein Mensch, und die vierte Gestalt war gleich einem fliegenden Adler.
>
> [And the first beast was like a lion, and the second beast like a calf, and the third beast had a face as a man, and the fourth beast was like a flying eagle.][12]

In art depictions, these figures are virtually never lined up, but rather spread over the surface. Their description in the scripture agrees with such presentation, portraying the creatures as 'in der Mitte am Thron und um den Thron' [in the midst of the throne, and round about the throne].[13] Moreover, while in many illustrations of the scene they are distributed over the four corners of a rectangle, the particular position of each image is not fixed (compare Figures 20.1 and 20.2).

In the Revelation story, before the Lamb opens the first seal, the four celestial images partake in the glorification of God:

> Und da es das Buch nahm, da fielen die vier Tiere und die vierundzwanzig Ältesten nieder vor dem Lamm und hatten ein jeglicher Harfen und goldene Schalen voll Räuchwerk, das sind die Gebete der Heiligen, / und sangen ein neues Lied und sprachen: Du bist würdig, zu nehmen das Buch und aufzutun seine Siegel; denn du bist erwürget und hast uns Gott erkauft mit deinem Blut aus allerlei Geschlecht und Zunge und Volk und Heiden / und hast uns unserm Gott zu Königen und Priestern gemacht, und wir werden

Figure 20.1 The Astronomical Clock in Marienkirche, Lübeck. The four corners show the four figures of the Apocalypse. Enlarged details: Top left — the eagle, symbol of St John; top right — the angel, symbol of St Matthew; bottom left — the winged lion, symbol of St Mark; bottom right — the bull, symbol of St Luke.[14]

Könige sein auf Erden. ... Und die vier Tiere sprachen: Amen! Und die vierundzwanzig Ältesten fielen nieder und beteten an den, der da lebt von Ewigkeit zu Ewigkeit.

[And when he had taken the book, the four beasts and four and twenty elders fell down before the Lamb, having every one of them harps, and golden vials full of odours, which are the prayers of saints. And they sung a new song, saying, Thou art worthy to take the book, and to open the seals thereof: for thou wast slain, and hast redeemed us to God by thy blood out of every kindred, and tongue, and people, and nation; And hast made us unto our God kings and priests: and we shall reign on the earth. ... And the four beasts said, Amen. And the four and twenty elders fell down and worshipped him that liveth for ever and ever.][15]

Since the fourth century, the four celestial figures became increasingly associated with the four evangelists. For instance, between the sixteenth and eighteenth centuries they often appear on grave slabs, particularly in the main Protestant areas of Flanders, North Germany and Demark;[16] The common composition is showing them encircled and distributed over the four corners of the slab.

In Germany, these four figures were sometimes expressed emblematically through other media, including through musical emblems. In such compositions, four perpetual two-part canons were composed. Echoing the circular idea of being 'in the midst of the throne and round about the throne,' these perpetual canons are traditionally inscribed in cryptic form and on a stave drawn as a circle.[17] A typical example is the canon *clama ne cesses* from the 1618 edition of Adam Gumpelzhaimer's *Compendium musicae* (Figure 20.2). In this interpretation, the series of four two-part canons is associated with the four figures of the Revelation. Each one of the four celestial figures is placed within a circle formed by one two-part canon.[18] Here, too, they are not arranged in a line but rather in a two-dimensional distribution over the illustration's area.

Bach's work during his last period includes several such sets of four two-part canons positioned as a section within a cycle. Beyond *The Art of Fugue*, they also appear in the *Clavierübung III* (four duets), in the *Musical Offering* and in the Canonic Variations (four thematic canons in both cycles).[19] The appearance of such canon sets within these cycles often puzzled scholars, performers and publishers, who were unsure how to position them: in the beginning of the cycle, in its middle or in its conclusion? What should be the internal order of these canons? Editors tended to locate them at the end of the work. However, the canons, usually, did not possess the sound and character needed for an effective closure of a cycle. While both performers and publishers may find this fact somewhat frustrating, the nonlinear character of this four-canons set renders the question of their order meaningless.

It would suffice to look at the engraving of Gumpelzhaimer's canon (Figure 20.2) to realise the complexity of this question, which is applicable to such sets of four canons in *The Art of Fugue*, the *Clavierübung III*, the thematic canons in the *Musical Offering* and the Canonic Variations: their positioning at the end of these cycles is a matter of convention. Four musical canons cannot be located 'at the corners' of a cycle or 'around' it, as it can be done in pictorial presentations or literary descriptions. Indeed, as is shown in the analysis of P 200 and the Original Edition, Bach defined the position of the canons in the same way as in the other comparable works: 'at the end by convention.'

Figure 20.2 The canon *Clama ne Cesses* from the *Compendium musicae* by Adam Gumpelzhaimer (Augsburg, 1611).

The comparison reveals the parallelism of *numerical structures* of chapters 4–11 in St John's *Revelation* and the final version of *The Art of Fugue*. However, it would be a distortion (or even vulgarisation) to regard *The Art of Fugue* as a musical equivalent of the *Revelation*, or perceive the four two-part canons as a musical depiction of its four creatures (or, for that matter, of the four Gospels). The significance of the detected structural correspondence is more akin to numerological word relations that indicate a hermeneutic comment rather than a lexical identity obviously impossible. In this sense, these two great works can be observed as not only two parts of a paragram, the related parts of which go beyond numerical equivalence (which in this case is 14), but *two numbers that share the same structure* (seven and seven, each made out of four and three) and therefore, by allusion, *echo* similar meanings.

In the same way, the life circumstances of two great human beings may comment on each other in their life paragram. At the end of his life journey, St John was granted a revelation

246   *Part V: Toward a new interpretation of* The Art of Fugue

about the future of the world. It could just be that Johann Sebastian Bach, in his later years, was granted a revelation of the subject to which he devoted himself, *The Art of Fugue*. Whether by divine coincidence, a Jungian synchronicity of a 'common psyche' or a simple human design, the affinity between these two works is a subject about which one might feel compelled to keep thinking. And rethinking.

Notes

1 However, Bach's principle of gradual increase (*Steigerungsprinzip*) in the complexity of contrapuntal techniques remained intact, as did the general organising factor that determined the number of 14 fugues.
2 See, for example: Caspar Heunisch, *Haupt-Schlüssel über die hohe Offenbahrung S. Johannis* (Schleusingen, 1684), pp. 26–31; Johann Jacob Schmidt, *Biblischer Mathematicus, oder Erläuterung der Heil: Schrift aus den Mathematischen Wissenschaften: Der Arithmetic, Geometrie, Static, Architectur, Astronomie, Horographie und Optic* (Zullichau, 1736), pp. 14–18; Ludwig Prautzsch, *Vor deinen Thron tret ich hiermit: Figuren und Symbole in den letzten Werken Johann Sebastian Bachs* (Stuttgart, 1980), p. 12; Erich Bergel, *Bachs letzte Fuge: Die 'Kunst der Fuge', ein zyklisches Werk: Entstehungsgeschichte, Erstausgabe, Ordnungsprinzipien* (Bonn, 1985), pp. 147–8.
3 In a letter to Johann Nikolaus Forkel from January 13, 1775, Philipp Emanuel writes that his father taught his pupils to omit 'all the dry species of counterpoint that are given in Fux and others' (*NBR*, no. 395, p. 399; 'In der Composition gieng er gleich an das Nützliche mit seinen Scholaren, mit Hinweglaßung aller der trockenen Arten von Contrapuncten, wie sie in Fuxen u. andern stehen.' *BD* III/803, p. 289). This description quite matches Bach's principles as they were *prior to the mid-1730s*, when Emanuel left his paternal home, never to return. Therefore he was probably unaware of the changes in Bach's views during the late 1730s and thereafter, when Bach recommended Mizler to translate Johann Joseph Fux's treatise from Latin into German in order to make it more accessible to music students. Further, Bach probably copied Angelo Berardi's *Documenti armonici* (1687), which by that time became a bibliographic rarity. He also explored the technique of strict style counterpoint by copying stile antico works, especially by Giovanni Palestrina.
4 A receipt from mid-September 1742 confirms Bach's purchase of theological literature for the amount of 10 thalers in a Leipzig auction (*BD* I/123, p. 199).
5 In this regard, it is appropriate to specify, for example, Johann Müller's book that was in Bach's library, *Judaismus oder Jüdenthum, das ist: Außführlicher Bericht von des Jüdischen Volckes Unglauben, Blindheit und Verstockung: Darinne Sie wider die Prophetischen Weissagungen von der Zukunfft, Person und Ampt Messiae, insonderheit wider des Herrn Jesu von Nazareth wahre Gottheit … mit grossem Ernst und Eifer straiten* (Hamburg, 1644).
6 The importance of numerological exegesis is apparent in the full title of the book: *Haupt-Schlüssel über die hohe Offenbahrung S. Johannis welcher durch Erklärung aller und jeder Zahlen, die darinnen vorkommen und eine gewisse Zeit bedeuten zu dem eigentlichen und richtigen Verstand Oeffnung thut* (Schleusingen, 1684). A new edition of this book, by Thomas Wilhelmi, with contributions by Christoph Trautman and Walter Blankenburg, was published as part of the international workshop of theological Bach research in Schlüchtern, Hessen (Basel, 1981).
7 Ulrich Meyer, *Biblical quotation and allusion in the cantata libretti of Johann Sebastian Bach* (Lanham, Maryland, 1997), pp. 215–16.
8 *Die Offenbarung des Johannes. Die Bibel. Nach der Übersetzung Martin Luthers. Das Neue Testament* (Stuttgart, 1985), p. 289.
9 *Revelation* 8:13, *King James Bible* Authorised Version, Cambridge University Edition (1985).
10 The image can be seen on the website of Munich's Digital Library Centre (Münchener digitalisierungs Zentrum, Digitale Bibliothek (http://daten.digitale-sammlungen.de/~db/0005/bsb00054285/images/index.html?id=00054285&groesser=&fip=193.174.98.30&no=&seite=5).

There are many similar depictions of this scene of which the following are just a few examples: Ninth century: the frontpiece of the book of Revelations in the Bible of San Paolo Fuori le Mura, in Rome; thirteenth century: the stone carving over the west portal of the Angers Cathedral, in France; fifteenth century: Albrecht Dürer's 1497–98 woodcut of *The Revelation of St John, 13: The Adoration of the Lamb and the Hymn of the Chosen* (at the Staatliche Kunsthalle, Karlsruhe), and many more.

11 In Luther's translation, 'vier himmlische Gestalten' (*Revelation* 4:6).
12 Luther's Bible (*Revelation* 4:7); English: *King James Bible*.
13 Ibid. 4:6. English: *King James Bible*.
14 Photograph taken by A.P. Milka (2006). The clock is a 1961 reconstruction of the sixteenth-century clock that was destroyed in 1942.
15 *Revelation* 5:8–10 and 5:14. English: *King James Bible*.
16 These areas have a considerably common cultural background, being heavily involved in the Eighty Years' and Thirty Years' Wars as well as united by the economic interest in the trade of linen and wool for all Europe.
17 Editor's note: presenting each of these four figures in a circle does echo the *Revelation* description, but is also, probably, related to the *Merkavah* vision in the book of Ezekiel, to which the *Revelation* alludes poetically. The element of a circle is far more evident there: 'Now as I beheld the living creatures, behold one wheel upon the earth by the living creatures, with his four faces. The appearance of the wheels and their work was like unto the colour of a beryl: and they four had one likeness: and their appearance and their work was as it were a wheel in the middle of a wheel'. (Ezekiel 1:15–16); English translation: ibid. The music emblem borrowed this principle to create two identical circular parts moving within the one-staff wheel of the canon.
18 The inscription at the bottom of the engraving states: eight voices for the four evangelists (*Quatuor Evangeliste 8 vocii*).
19 In the Canonic Variations all four thematic canons appear in one variation; the printed version of the composition has this variation as the closing one, while in the manuscript copy it occupies a centre position.

Bibliography

Manuscript sources

Berlin, Staatsbibliothek zu Berlin – Preußischer Kulturbesitz.
D-B Mus. ms. [autogr.] Bach P 200 and P 200/1 (BWV 1080).
D-B Mus. ms. Bach P 66 (BWV 75).
D-B Mus. ms. Bach P 65 (BWV 195, späteste Fassung).
D-B Mus. ms. Bach St 76 (BWV 210).
D-B Mus. ms. Bach P 180 (BWV 232).
D-B Mus. ms. Bach St 110, Faszikel 1 (BWV 245, 2. Fassung).
D-B Mus. ms. Bach P 32 (BWV 248).

Printed primary sources

Bach, Johann Sebastian, *Die Kunst der Fuge* (Leipzig, 1751) [Original Edition].
Bach-Dokumente, Hrsg. v. Bach-Archive Leipzig (Supplement zu: Johann Sebastian Bach Neue Ausgabe sämtlicher Werke):
    BD I *Schriftstücke von der Hand Johann Sebastian Bachs. Kritische Gesamtausgabe*, eds. Werner Neumann and Hans-Joachim Schulze (Kassel: Bärenreiter; Leipzig: VEB Deutscher Verlag für Musik, 1963).
    BD II *Fremdschriftliche und gedruckte Dokumente zur Lebensgeschichte Johann Sebastian Bachs, 1685–1750. Kritische Gesamtausgabe*, eds. Werner Neumann and Hans-Joachim Schulze (Kassel: Bärenreiter; Leipzig: VEB Deutscher Verlag für Musik, 1969).
    BD III *Dokumente zum Nachwirken Johann Sebastian Bachs, 1750–1800*, ed. Hans-Joachim Schulze (Kassel: Bärenreiter; Leipzig: VEB Deutscher Verlag für Musik, 1972).
    BD V *Dokumente zu Leben, Werk, Nachwirken Johann Sebastian Bachs, 1685–1800*, eds. Hans-Joachim Schulze and Andreas Glöckner (Kassel: Bärenreiter, 2007).
The New Bach Reader: A Life of Johann Sebastian Bach in Letters and Documents, eds. Hans T. David and Arthur Mendel, revised and enlarged by Christoph Wolff (New York: W.W. Norton, 1998).
Die Bibel, Nach der Übersetzung Martin Luthers. Das Neue Testament (Stuttgart: Deutsche Bibelgesellschaft, 1985).
Revelation, King James Bible, Authorised Version, Cambridge University Edition (1985).
Algarotti, Francesco, *Saggio sopra l'Architettura* (Venice: Graziosi, 1784; originally published in Bologna, 1756).
Bach, Johann Christoph, 'Eingabe an der Rat der Stadt Schweinfurt, Eisenach, 4. 10. 1686', *BJ* 85 (1999): pp. 198–9.
Berardi, Angelo, *Documenti Armonici* (Bologna: G. Monti, 1687).
Brosses, Charles de, *Le Président De Brosses en Italie: Lettres Familières écrites d'Italie en 1739 et 1740 par Charles de Brosses*. Quatrième édition authentique d'après les manuscrits annotée et précédée d'une étude biographique par R. Colomb (Paris, 1885).

Burney, Charles, *The Present State of Music in Germany, the Netherlands, and United Provinces, or, the Journal of a Tour*, in Two Volumes, vol. 2 (London: Becket & Co. Strand, 1773); translated to German by Christoph Daniel Ebeling as *Carl Burney's der Musik Doctors Tagebuch seiner Musikalischen Reisen* (Hamburg: Bode, 1773).

Burney, Charles, *Dr. Karl Burney's Nachricht von Georg Friedrich Händel's Lebensumständen und der ihm zu London im Mai und Jun. 1784 angestellten Gedachtnißeyer* (Berlin: Nicolai, 1785).

Cappelli, Adriano, *Dizionario di abbreviature latine ed italiani*, Sesta edizione (Milano: Hoepli, 1961).

Carl Philipp Emanuel Bach: Briefe und Dokumente, vol. 1, ed. Ernst Suchalla, (Göttingen: Vandenhoeck & Ruprecht, 1994).

Euler, Leonhard, *Tentamen novae theoriae musicae ex certissimis harmoniae principiis dilucide expositae* (Petersburg: Academy of Sciences, 1739).

Fux, Johann Joseph, *Gradus ad Parnassum, sive manuductio ad compositionem musicae regularem...* (Viennae: Joannis Petri van Ghelen, 1725).

Fux, Johann Joseph, *Gradvs ad Parnassvm oder Anführung zur Regelmäßigen Musikalischen Composition* [translated to German by Lorenz Mizler von Kolof] (Leipzig: Mizlerischer Bücherverlag, 1742).

Harsdörfer, Georg Philipp, *Poetischer Trichter, Die Teutsche Dicht- und Reimkunst ohne Behuf der Lateinischen Sprache* (Nürnberg: Wolfgang Endter, 1653).

Henning, Johann, *Cabbalologia, i.e. Brevis Institutio de Cabbala cùm Veterum Rabbinorum judicâ, tùm Poëtarum Paragrammaticâ, Artis Cabbalistico-Poëticae* (Lipsiae: Calvisius, 1683).

Heunisch, Caspar, *Haupt-Schlüssel über die hohe Offenbahrung S. Johannis* (Schleusingen: Sebastian Göbel, 1684).

Iamblichus, *De Vita Pythagorica liber*, Graece et Germanice, edidit, transtulit, praefatus est M. von Albrecht (Zürich: Artemis Verlag, 1963).

Kircher, Athanasius, *Musurgia universalis sive ars magna consoni et dissoni in X. Libros digesta.* (Rome: Haeredum Francisci Corbelletti, 1650).

Kirnberger, Johann Philipp, *Die Kunst des Reinen Satzes in der Musik: aus sicheren Grundsätzen hergeleitet und mit deutlichen Beyspielen erläutert* (Berlin: Decker und Hartung, 1771).

Leibniz, Gottfried Wilhelm von, *Disputatio Metaphysica de Principio Individui* (Lipsiae: Henningi Coleri, 1663).

Leibniz, Gottfried Wilhelm von, *Dissertatio de arte combinatoria* (Lipsiae: apud Joh. Simon Fickium et Joh. Polycarp. Seuboldum, Literis Spörelianis, 1666).

Lessing, Gotthold Ephraim, *Ernst und Falk: Gespräche für Freymäurer (1776–1778)*, in his *Theologiekritischen und Ästhetischen Schriften. Werke*. Ed. Herbert G. Göpfert. Band 5 (München: Carl Hanser Verlag, 1970). Translated to English in Gotthold Ephraim Lessing, *Philosophical and Theological Writings*, transl. and ed. Hugh Barr Nisbet (Cambridge: Cambridge University Press, 2005).

Marpurg, Friedrich Wilhelm, *Abhandlung von der Fuge nach dem Grundsätzen und Exempeln der besten deutschen und ausländischen Meister* (Berlin: Kühnel, 1753–54).

Marpurg, Friedrich Wilhelm, *Historisch-Kritische Beyträge zur Aufnahme der Musik* (Berlin: Schützens Witwe, 1754).

Mattheson, Johann, *Kern Melodischer Wissenschaft* (Hamburg: Christian Herold, 1737).

Mattheson, Johann, *Philologisches Tresespiel* (Hamburg: Martini, 1752).

Mattheson, Johann, *Der vollkommene Capellmeister* (Hamburg: Christian Herold, 1739). Tanslation to English: Ernest C. Harriss, *Johann Mattheson's Der volkommene Capellmeister: A Revised Translation with Critical Commentary* (Ann Arbor: UMI Research Press, 1981).

Mizler von Kolof, Lorenz Christoph, *Neu eröffnete musikalische Bibliothek, oder Gründliche Nachricht nebst unpartheyischem Urtheil von musikalischen Schriften und Büchern*, 4 vols. [*MMB*] (Leipzig, 1736–54). Vol. I: Part 1 (1736); Parts 2 and 3 (1737); Parts 4–6 (1738)—six parts republished together in 1739; vol. II: Parts 1 and 2 (1740); Part 3 (1742); Part 4 (1743)—four parts republished together in 1743; vol. III: Parts 1 and 2 (1746); Part 3 (1747); Part 4 (1752)—four parts republished together in 1752; vol. IV: Part 1 (1754).

Mizler, von Kolof, Lorenz Christoph, 'Tentamen novae theoriae musicae, das ist: Versuch einer neuen theoretischen Music, aus untrüglichen Gründen der Harmonie deutlich vorgetragen von Leonhard Euler, Petersburg 1739', in *Zuverlässige Nachrichten von dem gegenwärtigen Zustande, Veränderung und Wachstum der Wissenschaften* (Leipzig, 1741), pp. 722–51.

Müller, Johann, *Judaismus oder Jüdenthumb, das ist: Außführlicher Bericht von des Jüdischen Volckes Unglauben, Blindheit und Verstockung: Darinne Sie wider die Prophetischen Weissagungen von der Zukunfft, Person und Ampt Messiae, insonderheit wider des Herrn Jesu von Nazareth wahre Gottheit … mit grossem Ernst und Eifer straiten* (Hamburg: Härtel, 1644).

Olearius, Johannes, *Biblische Erklärung darinnen nechst dem allgemeinen Haupt-Schlüssel der gantzen heiligen Schrifft*, 5 vols. (Leipzig: Tarnoven, 1678–81).

Picander [Henrici, Christian Friedrich], *Ernst-Schertzhaffte und satyrische Gedichte*, 5 vols (Leipzig: Boetius, 1727–51).

Psellus, Michael, 'Des Psellus vollständiger kurzer Inbegriff der Musik', *MMB* III/2 (1746): pp. 171–200.

Quinctiliani, M. Fabii [Marcus Fabius] *De Institutione Oratoria. Libri duodecim collatione codicis Gothani et Iensonianae editionis aliorumque librorum ac perpetuo commentario illustrati a Io. Matthia Gesnero* (Gottingae: Abram Vandenhoeck, 1738).

Schlichtegrol, Adolf Heinrich Friedrich, *Nekrolog auf das Jahr 1795* (Gotha: Julius Perthes, 1798).

Schmidt, Johann Jacob, *Biblischer Mathematicus oder Erläuterung der Heil: Schrift aus den Mathematischen Wissenschaften: Der Arithmetic, Geometrie, Static, Architectur, Astronomie, Horographie und Optic* (Züllichau: Gottlob Benjamin Frommann, 1736).

Schubart, Christian Friedrich Daniel, 'CARLS Name / gefeiert von der deutschen Schaubühne zu Stuttgart. / am 4. Nov. 1784.' in *Christian Friedrich Daniel Schubart sämtliche Gedichte. Von ihm selbst herausgegeben*. vol.2 (Stuttgart: der Buchdruckerei der Herzoglichen Hohen Carlsschule, 1786), pp. 29–30.

Spiess, Mainard, *Tractatus Musicus Compositorio-Practicus* (Augsburg: Johann Jakob Lotters seel. Erben, 1745).

Verzeichniß des musikalischen Nachlasses des H. Capellmeisters Carl Philipp Emanuel Bach (Hamburg: Gottfried Friedrich Schniebes, 1790).

Walther, Johann Gottfried, *Musicalisches Lexicon oder Musicalische Bibliothec* (Leipzig: Wolfgang Deer, 1732).

Werckmeister, Andreas, *Erweiterte und verbesserte Orgel-Probe* (Quedlinburg: Calvisius, 1698).

Zarlino, Gioseffo, *Le istitutioni harmoniche* (Venice, 1558).

Secondary sources

Ammann, Robert, *Die Handschrift der Künstler* (Bern: Huber, 1953).

Baker, Thomas, 'Bach's Revisions in the Augmentation Canon', *Current Musicology*, 19 (1975): pp. 67–71.

Beißwenger, Kirsten, *Johann Sebastian Bachs Notenbibliothek*, Catalogus musicus, vol. 13 (Kassel: Bärenreiter, 1992).

Bergel, Erich, *Bachs letzte Fuge: Die "Kunst der Fuge," ein zyklisches Werk: Entstehungsgeschichte, Erstausgabe, Ordnungsprinzipien* (Bonn: Brockhaus, 1980).

Busoni, Ferruccio, *Choral-Vorspiel und Fuge über ein Bachsches Fragment: der Fantasia contrappuntistica* (Leipzig: Breitkopf & Härtel, 1912).

Butler, Gregory, *Bach's Clavier-Übung III: The Making of a Print, with a Companion Study of the Canonic Variations on Von Himmel hoch BWV 769* (Durham, NC: Duke University Press, 1990).

Butler, Gregory, 'Ordering problems in J.S. Bach's *Art of Fugue* resolved', *The Musical Quarterly*, 69/1 (1983): pp. 44–61.

Butler, Gregory, 'Scribes, engravers and notational styles: The final disposition of Bach's *Art of Fugue*', in *About Bach*, ed. Gregory G. Butler, George B. Stauffer and Mary Dalton Greer (Urbana and Chicago: University of Illinois Press, 2008), pp. 111–23.

Butler, Gregory G., '*Der vollkommene Capellmeister* as a stimulus to J.S. Bach's late fugal writing', in *New Mattheson Studies*, ed. George J. Buelow and Hans Joachim Marx (Cambridge: Cambridge University Press, 1983), pp. 293–305.

Caligiuri, Michael P. and Mohammed, Linton A., *The Neuroscience of Handwriting: Applications for Forensic Document Examination* (Boca Raton: CRC Press, 2012).

Chailley, Jacques (ed.), *L'Art de la fugue de J.S. Bach. Étude critique des sources: remise en ordre du plan, analyse de l'oeuvre, au-delà des notes*, vol. 1 (Paris: Alfonse Leduc, 1971).

Clark, Stephen L., *The Letters of C.P.E. Bach* (Oxford: Clarendon Press, 1997).

Dadelsen, Georg von, *Beiträge zur Chronologie derWerke Johann Sebastian Bachs*. Tübinger Bach-Studien, vols. 4–5 (Trossingen: Hohner-Verlag, 1958).

Dehn, Siegfried Wilhelm, 'Ueber einige Theils noch ungedruckte, Theils durch den Druck bereits veröffentliche musikalische Manuskripte von Johann Sebastian Bach, welche sich in der musikalischen Abteilung der König. Bibliothek zu Berlin befinden', *Cäcilia*, 24 (1845): pp. 17–24.

Dequevauviller, Vincent, *'L'art de la fugue', un problème algébrique: étude sur les caractéristiques numériques et les raisons de l'inachèvement de la dernière oeuvre de Jean-Sébastien Bach* (Paris: Association pour la Connaissance de la Musique Ancienne, 1998).

Dirksen, Pieter, *Studien zur Kunst der Fuge von Joh. Seb. Bach: Untersuchungen zur Entstehungsgeschichte, Struktur und Aufführungspraxis* (Wilhelmshaven: Florian Noetzel Verlag, 1994).

Druskin, Mikhail Semenovich, *Iogann Sebastian Bakh* (Moscow: Muzyka, 1982).

Dürr, Alfred, 'Neue Forschungen zu Bachs "Kunst der Fuge"', *Die Musikforschung*, 32/2 (1979): pp. 153–8.

Dürr, Alfred, Yoshitake Kobayashi and Kirsten Beißwenger (eds.), *Bach-Werke-Verzeichnis: Kleine Ausgabe (BWV2a), nach der vonWolfgang Schmieder vorgelegten 2. Ausgabe* (Wiesbaden: Breitkopf & Härtel, 1998).

Ferguson, Michael, *Bach Ferguson. Contrapunctus XIV. A completion of J.S. Bach's Unfinished Quadruple Fugue from The Art of Fugue*. Musical score (St Paul, Minnesota: Holbrook & Associates, 2nd edn 1990).

Forkel, Johann Nikolaus, *Ueber J.S. Bachs Leben, Kunst und Kunstwerke: für patriotische Verehrer echter musikalischer Kunst… Mit Bachs Bildniß und Kupfertafeln* (Leipzig, 1802). Translated to English by Charles Sanford Terry as *Johann Sebastian Bach: His Life, Art andWork* (New York: Harcourt, Brace and Howe, 1920).

Fuller-Maitland, J.A., 'A set of Bach's proof sheets', *Sammelbände der Internationalen Musikgesellschaft*, II/4 (August 1900): pp. 643–50.

Göncz, Zoltán, 'Reconstruction of the Final Contrapunctus of *The Art of Fugue*', *International Journal of Musicology*, 5 (1995): pp. 25–93, and 6 (1996): pp. 103–19.

Graeser, Wolfgang, 'Bachs Kunst der Fuge', *BJ* 21 (1924): pp. 1–104.

Hauptmann, Maurice, *Erläuterungen zu Joh. Sebastian Bach's Kunst der Fuge* (Leipzig: Peters, 1841).

Helm, Ernest Eugene, *Music at the Court of Frederick the Great* (Norman: University of Oklahoma Press, 1960).

Hindemith, Paul, *Johann Sebastian Bach. Heritage and Obligation* (London: Oxford University Press, 1952), translated to Norwegian as *Johann Sebastian Bach. Arv og forpliktelse* (Oslo: Det norske studentersamfund, 1954).

Hofmann, Klaus, *Bach, Johann Sebastian, Die Kunst der Fuge (BWV 1080)*, NBA VIII/2.1–2.2 and NBA KB VIII/2 (Kassel: Bärenreiter, 1995 and 1996).

Hoke, Hans Gunter, *Zu Johann Sebastian Bachs 'Die Kunst der Fuge'* (Leipzig: Deutscher Verlag für Musik, 1974).

Hoke, Hans Gunter, 'Zur Handschrift Mus. ms. autogr. Bach P 200 der Deutschen Staatsbibliothek Berlin', in *Johann Sebastian Bach, Die Kunst der Fuge BWV 1080: Autograph, Originaldruck*, Faksimile-Reihe Bachscher Werke und Schriftstücke, vol. 14, ed. H.G. Hoke (Leipzig: VEB Deutscher Verlag für Musik, 1979).

Katz, Boris, 'O kul'turologicheskikh aspektakh analiza', *Sovetskaya muzyka*, 1 (1978): pp. 37–40.

Kellner, Herbert, *Die Kunst der Fuga [i.e. Fuge]: how incomplete is the fuga a 3 sogetti [sic]? (BWV 1080/19, Contrapunctus 14)* (Darmstadt: H.A. Kellner, 2002).

Kinsky, Georg, *Die Originalausgaben derWerke Johann Sebastian Bachs* (Wien: H. Reichner, 1937).

Klaiber, Roswitha, and Reinhard Ludewig, 'Zur schriftpsychologischen und medizinischen Interpretation der Autographen von Johann Sebastian Bach', *Zeitschrift für Schriftpsychologie und Schriftvergleichung*, 1 (2000): pp. 2–21.

Klotz, Hans, *Die Orgelchoräle aus der Leipziger Originalhandschrift*, NBA KB IV/2 (Kassel: Bärenreiter, 1957).

Kobayashi, Yoshitake, 'Bachs Notenpapier und Notenschrift', in *Der junge Bach: 'weil er nicht aufzuhalten … '. Begleitbuch*, Thüringer Landesausstellung, vol. 1, ed. Reinmar Emans (Erfurt: Predigerkirche; Sebald Sachsendruck Plauen, 2000), pp. 413–27.

Kobayashi, Yoshitake, 'Bemerkungen zur Spätschrift Johann Sebastian Bachs', in *Bericht über die wissenschaftliche Konferenz zum V. Internationalen Bachfest der DDR in Verbindung mit dem 60. Bachfest der Neuen Bachgesellschaft Leipzig, 25–27 März 1985*, ed. W. Hoffmann and A. Schneiderheinze (Leipzig: Deutscher Verlag für Musik, 1988), pp. 457–63.

Kobayashi, Yoshitake, 'Zur Chronologie der Spätwerke Johann Sebastian Bachs: Kompositions- und Aufführungstätigkeit von 1736 bis 1750', *BJ* 74 (1988): pp. 7–72.

Kolneder, Walter, 'Die Datierung des Erstdruckes der Kunst der Fuge', *Musikforschung*, 30/3 (1977): pp. 329–32.

Kopchevskiy, Nikolay Aleksandrovich, *"Iskusstvo fugi" I.S. Bakha* [J.S.Bach's *The Art of Fugue*] (Moscow: Muzyka, 1974).

Koprowski, Richard, 'Bach "Fingerprints" in the engraving of the Original Edition', in 'Bach's "Art of Fugue": An examination of the sources', seminar report. *Current Musicology*, 19 (1975): pp. 61–7.

Kranemann, Detlev, 'Johann Sebastian Bachs Krankheit und Todesursache: Versuch einer Deutung,' *BJ* 76 (1990): pp. 53–64.

Kulukundis, Elias N., 'Die Versteigerung von C.P.E. Bachs musikalischem Nachlaß im Jahre 1805', *BJ* 81 (1995): pp. 145–76.

Kurtch, Olga, 'Ot pomet kopiistov – k strukture tsikla Iskusstvo fugi' [From scribes' annotations to the structure of *The Art of Fugue*], in *Vtorye Bakhovskie chtenia: 'Iskusstvo fugi'*, ed. Anatoly Milka (St. Petersburg: SPbGK, 1993), pp. 76–93.

Leaver, Robin A., *Bachs theologische Bibliothek* (Neuhausen-Stuttgart: Hänssler-Verlag, 1983).

Leaver, Robin A., 'Number associations in the structure of Bach's CREDO, BWV 232', *BACH*, 7/3 (1976): pp. 17–24.

Lee, Douglas A. 'Nichelmann, Christoph', in *Grove Music Online* (updated and revised February 6, 2012).

Ludewig, Reinhard, 'Zur Interpretation ausgewählter Schriftveränderungen', *Zeitschrift für Menschenkunde*, 63 (1999): pp. 2–16.

Ludewig, Reinhardt, *Johann Sebastian Bach im Spiegel der Medizin: Persönlichkeit, Krankheiten, Operationen, Ärzte, Tod, Reliquien, Denkmäler und Ruhestätten des Thomaskantors* (Grimma: Edition Wæchterpappel, 2000).

MacDonogh, Giles, *Frederick the Great: a Life in Deed and Letters* (New York: St. Martin's Griffin, 2000).

Marshall, Robert Lewis, *The Compositional Process of J. S. Bach: A Study of the Autograph Scores of the Vocal Works*, 2 vols (Princeton: Princeton University Press, 1972).

Marshall, Robert Lewis, 'The Nathan Bequest: Payment receipts in the hand of Johann Sebastian Bach, 1746 to 1748 (With a fragment for the year 1749 in the hand of his son)', *Moldenhauer Archives at the Library of Congress* http://memory.loc.gov/ammem/collections/moldenhauer/2428108.pdf (accessed January 26, 2015).

Melamed, Daniel R., 'Bach und Palestrina – Einige praktische Probleme I', *BJ* 89 (2003): pp. 221–4.

Meyer, Ulrich, *Biblical Quotation and Allusion in the Cantata Libretti of Johann Sebastian Bach* (Lanham, MD: Scarecrow Press, 1997).

Milka, Anatoly, 'Bakhovskie "shestërki": Printsip organizatsii bakhovskikh sbornikov v kontekste osobennostei barokko' [Bach's 'cycles of six': the organisation principle of Bach's collections in the context of baroque characteristics], in *Muzykal'naya kommunikatsia* [Musical Communication], series Problemy muzykoznaniya, vol. 8, ed. Vyacheslav Kartsovnik (St Petersburg: Compozitor, 1996), pp. 220–38.

Milka, Anatoly, 'Inventsiya – tak chto zhe eto takoe?' [An invention – what is it?], in Anatoly Milka and Tatiana Shabalina (eds), *Zanimatel'naya Bakhiana*, vol. 1 (St Petersburg: Compozitor, 2001) pp. 87–116.

Milka, Anatoly, *Iskusstvo fugi I.S. Bakha: k rekonstruktsii i interpretatsii* [Bach's *The Art of Fugue*: toward a Reconstruction and Interpretation] (St Petersburg: Compozitor, 2009).

Milka, Anatoly, 'K kompozitsionnoy funktsii BWV 870–93' [On the compositional function of BWV 870–93], in *Bakhovskie Chtenia 3: Khorosho Temperirovannyi Klavir*, vol. 2 [Bach Reading 3: *The Well-Tempered Clavier*, vol. 2], ed. Anatoly Milka (St Petersburg: SPbGK, 1996), pp. 9–17.

Milka, Anatoly, *Muzykal'noye prinoshenie I.S. Bakha: K rekonstruktsii i interpretatsii* [J.S. Bach's *Musical Offering*: toward a Reconstruction and Interpretation] (Moscow: Muzyka, 1999).

Milka, Anatoly, 'O sud'be poslednego vznosa I.S. Bakha v "Obshchestvo muzykal'nykh nauk"' [On the fate of J.S. Bach's last contribution to the Society of Musical Sciences], in *(Ne)Muzykal'noe prinoshenie ili Allegro Affettuoso* [(Non)-musical Offering or Allegro Affettuoso]: Collection in Honor of Boris Katz toward his 65th Anniversary, ed. A. Dolinin, I. Dorochenkov, L. Kovnatskaya and N. Mazur (St Petersburg, 2013), pp. 7–21.

Milka, Anatoly, 'Warum endet die Fuga a 3 Soggetti BWV 1080/19 in Takt 239?', *BJ* 100 (2014): pp. 11–26.

Milka, Anatoly, 'Zur Datierung der H-Moll Messe und der Kunst der Fuge', *BJ* 96 (2010): pp. 53–68.

Milsom, John, *Christ Church Library Music Catalogue* (http://library.chch.ox.ac.uk/music/).

Newman, Anthony, *Bach and the Baroque: European Source Materials from the Baroque and Early Classical Periods, with Special Emphasis on the Music of J.S. Bach* (Stuyvesant, NY: Pendragon Press, 2nd edn, 1995).

Newman, William S., 'Emanuel Bach's autobiography', *The Musical Quarterly*, 51/2 (1965): pp. 363–72.

Nottebohm, Martin Gustav, 'J.S. Bach's letzte Fuge', *Musik-Welt*, 20 (1881): pp. 232–46.

Perrez, Thomas, 'Graphologische Aspekte der morbiden und prämorbiden Parkinsonschrift', *Zeitschrift für Menschenkunde*, 1 (1995): pp. 245–56.

Plamenac, Dragan, 'New light on the last years of Carl Philipp Emanuel Bach', *The Musical Quarterly*, 35/4 (1949): pp. 565–87.

Prautzsch, Ludwig, *Vor deinen Thron tret ich hiermit: Figuren und Symbole in den letzten Werken Johann Sebastian Bachs* (Stuttgart: Hänssler, 1980).

Prinz, Ulrich (ed.), *Johann Sebastian Bach, Messe h-Moll: 'Opus ultimum', BWV 232. Vorträge der Meisterkurse und Sommerakademien J.S. Bach, 1980, 1983 und 1989* (Stuttgart: Internationale Bachakademie, 1990).

Rotter, Günther, 'London gegen Bückeburg: fünf zu drei? Ein Bach-Portrait und zwei Komponisten', *Musica*, 44/4 (1990): pp. 83–6.

Rust, Wilhelm, *Bach-Gesellschaft Ausgabe*, Band 25/1: *Die Kunst der Fuge* (Leipzig: Breitkopf & Härtel, 1878).

Shabalina, Tatiana, *Rukopisi I.S. Bakha: klyuchi k tainam tvorchestva* [J. S. Bach's manuscripts: the keys to mysteries of his creative works] (St Petersburg: Muzyka, 1999).

Schleuning, Peter, *Johann Sebastian Bachs 'Kunst der Fuge'* (München: Deutscher Taschenbuch Verlag; Kassel: Bärenreiter, 1993).

Schmidt, Gabriele; Kästner, Ingrid and Ludewig, Reinhard, 'Medizinisch-graphologischer Beitrag zum Einfluß der visuellen und kinästhetischen Kontrolle auf die Schreibhandlung', *Zeitschrift für Menschenkunde*, 1 (1995): pp. 219–44.

Schmieder, Wolfgang (ed.), *Thematisch-systematisches Verzeichnis der musikalischen Werke von Johann Sebastian Bach. Bach-Werke-Verzeichnis (BWV)*, 2nd rev. and enl. edn (Wiesbaden: Breitkopf & Härtel, 1990).

Schneider, Max, 'Das sogenannte Orgelkonzert d-moll von Wilhelm Friedemann Bach', *BJ* 8 (1911): pp. 23–6.

Schulenberg, David, *The Keyboard Music of J.S. Bach* (New York: Taylor & Francis, 2nd edn 2006).

Schumann, Robert, 'Ueber einige muthmaßlich corrumpirte Stellen in Bach'schen, Mozart'schen und Beethoven'schen Werken', *Neue Zeitschrift für Musik*, 38 (1841): pp. 149–51.

Schwebsch, Erich, *Joh. Seb. Bach und die Kunst der Fuge* (Stuttgart: Orient-Occident-Verlag, 1931).

Smend, Friedrich, 'Bachs Kanonwerk über Vom Himmel hoch da komm ich her', *BJ* 30 (1933): pp. 1–29.

Smend, Friedrich, *Missa; Symbolum Nicenum; Sanctus; Ossana, Benedictus, Agnus Dei et Dona Nobis Pacem (später genannt 'Messe in h-Moll')*, NBA KB II/1 (Kassel: Bärenreiter, 1956).

Spitta, Philipp, *Johann Sebastian Bach*, vol. 2 (Leipzig: Breitkopf & Härtel, 1880). English translation in Philipp Spitta, *Johann Sebastian Bach: his Work and Influence on the Music of Germany, 1685–1750*, translated by Clara Bell and J.A. Fuller-Maitland, vol. 3 (London: Novello, 1899).

Tatlow, Ruth, *Bach and the Riddle of the Number Alphabet* (Cambridge: Cambridge University Press, 1991).
Tatlow, Ruth, 'Bach's Parallel Proportions and the Qualities of the Authentic Bachian Collection,' in *Bach oder Nicht Bach: Bericht über das 5. Dortmunder Bach-Symposion*, ed. Reinmar Emans & Martin Geck (Dortmund: Klangfarben, 2009), pp. 135–55.
Tatlow, Ruth, 'Collections, Bars and Numbers: Analytical Coincidence or Bach's design?', *Understanding Bach*, 2 (2007): pp. 37–58.
Tatlow, Ruth, 'J.S. Bach and the Baroque Paragram: A Reappraisal of Friedrich Smend's Number Alphabet Theory', *Music and Letters*, 70/2 (1989): pp. 191–205.
Tatlow, Ruth, 'LUSUS POETICUS VEL MUSICUS, Johann Sebastian Bach: The Baroque Paragram and Friedrich Smend's Theory of a Musical Number Alphabet' (PhD dissertation. London: King's College, 1987).
Tessmer, Manfred, *Dritter Teil der Klavierübung*, NBA KB IV/4 (Kassel: Bärenreiter, 1974).
Walcha, Helmut, 'Weiterführung und Beendigung der Schlußfuge', in *Johann Sebastian Bach: Die Kunst der Fuge – Übertragung für Orgel von Helmut Walcha* (Frankfurt am Main: C.F. Peters, 1967), pp. 129–32.
Weiss, Wisso, and Yoshitake Kobayashi, *Katalog der Wasserzeichen in Bachs Originalhandschriften*, NBA IX/1–2 (Kassel: Bärenreiter, 1985).
Werbeck, Walter, 'Bach und der Kontrapunkt – Neue Manuskript-Funde', *BJ* 89 (2003): pp. 67–95.
Wiemer, Wolfgang, 'Johann Heinrich Schübler, der Stecher der Kunst der Fuge', *BJ* 65 (1979): pp. 75–95.
Wiemer, Wolfgang, *Die wiederhergestellte Ordnung in Johann Sebastian Bachs Kunst der Fuge: Untersuchungen am Originaldruck* (Wiesbaden: Breitkopf & Härtel, 1977; 2nd edn 1986).
Wiemer, Wolfgang, 'Zur Datierung des Erstdrucks der Kunst der Fuge', *Musikforschung*, 31/2 (1978): pp. 181–5.
Wiermann, Barbara, 'Bach und Palestrina – einige praktische Probleme II', *BJ* 89 (2003): pp. 225–7.
Wiermann, Barbara 'Bach und Palestrina – Neue Quellen aus Johann Sebastian Bachs Notenbibliothek', *BJ* 88 (2002): pp. 9–25.
Wilhelmi, Thomas, 'Carl Philipp Emanuel Bachs *Avertissement* über den Druck der Kunst der Fuge', *BJ* 78 (1992): pp. 101–5.
Wolff, Christoph, *Bach: Essays on his Life and Music* (Cambridge, MA: Harvard University Press, 1991).
Wolff, Christoph, '"Et incarnatus" and "Crucifixus": The earliest and the latest settings of Bach's B-Minor Mass', in *Eighteenth-Century Music in Theory and Practice: Essays in Honor of Alfred Mann*, ed. Mary Ann Parker (Stuyvesant, NY: Pendragon Press, 1994), pp. 1–17.
Wolff, Christoph, *Johann Sebastian Bach: The Learned Musician* (New York: W.W. Norton; Oxford: Oxford University Press, 2000).
Wolff, Christoph, *Johann Sebastian Bachs Klavierübung: Kommentar zur Faksimile-Ausgabe* (Leipzig; Dresden: Edition Peters, 1984).
Wolff, Christoph, *Kanons. Musikalisches Opfer*, NBA KB VIII/1 (Kassel: Bärenreiter, 1976).
Wolff, Christoph, 'The Last Fugue: Unfinished?', *Current Musicology*, 19 (1975): pp. 71–7; republished in Christoph Wolff, *Bach: Essays on His Life and Music* (Cambridge, MA: Harvard University Press, 1991), pp. 259–64.
Wolff, Christoph, 'Die Originaldrucke Johann Sebastian Bachs: Einführung und Verzeichnis', in *Die Nürnberger Drucke von J.S. und C.P.E. Bach: Katalog der Ausstellung*, ed. Willi Wörthmüller (Nürnberg: Neue Bach-Gesellschaft, 1973), pp. 15–20.
Wolff, Christoph, 'Die Rastrierungen in den Originalhandschriften Joh. Seb. Bachs und ihre Bedeutung für die diplomatische Quellenkritik', in *Festschrift für Friedrich Smend zum 70. Geburtstag: dargebracht von Freunden und Schülern* (Berlin: Verlag Merseburger, 1963).
Wolff, Christoph, *Der stile antico in der Musik J. S. Bachs: Studien zu Bachs Spätwerk*, Beihefte zum Archiv für Musikwissenschaft, vol. 6 (Wiesbaden: Steiner, 1968).
Wolff, Christoph, 'Zur Kunst der Fuge', *Musica*, 33 (1979): pp. 288–9.
Wollny, Peter, 'Johann Christoph Friedrich Bach und die Teilung des Väterlichen Erbes', *BJ* 87 (2001): pp. 55–70.

Wollny, Peter, 'Neue Bach-Funde', *BJ* 83 (1997): pp. 7–50.
Wollny, Peter, 'Ein Quellenfund in Kiew: Unbekannte Kontrapunktstudien von Johann Sebastian und Wilhelm Friedemann Bach', in *Bach in Leipzig – Bach und Leipzig: Konferenzbericht Leipzig*, Leipziger Beiträge zur Bach-Forschung, vol. 5, ed. Ulrich Leisinger (Hildesheim: Georg Olms Verlag, 2002), pp. 275–87.
Yankus, Alla Irmenovna, 'Predvaritel'naya rabota nad fugoy v rukopisyakh Anny Amalii Prusskoy: sistema I.F. Kirnbergera' [Preliminary work over fugues in manuscripts by the Princess Anna Amalia of Prussia: the method of J.P. Kirnberger], in *Rabota nad fugoy: metod i shkola I.S. Bakha: Materialy Vos'mykh Bakhovskikh chteniy 20–27 aprelya 2006 goda* [Working on fugues: the Method and School of J.S. Bach: Materials from the Eighth Bach Reading, April 20–27, 2006], ed. Anatoly P. Milka and Kira I. Yuzhak (St Petersburg: SPbGK, 2008) pp. 120–62.
Yuzhak, Kira, 'O prodvigayushchey i svertyvayushchey tendentsiakh v Iskusstve fugi: "Alio Modo" i parnost' vysshego poryadka', [Expanding and contracting tendencies in *The Art of Fuge*: "Alio Modo" and the pairing of the highest order], in *Polifoniya i kontrapunkt*. vol. 1, K. Yuzhak, (St Petersburg: SPbGK, 2006), pp. 165–94.
Zegers, Richard H.C., 'The eyes of Johann Sebastian Bach', *Archives of Ophtamology*, 123/10 (2005): pp. 1427–30.

Index

Abklatschvorlage (see engraver copy)
Avertissement (also advertisement) 23, 148, 159, 168n, 170n, 207, 209–10, 212–13, 231n, 232n
Agricola, Johann Friedrich 8, 31n, 33n, 57, 58, 147, 159n, 209, 210, 211, 212, 231n
Algarotti, Francesco 152–3, 160n; *Saggio sopra l'Architectura* 152–3
Altnickol, Johann Christoph 8, 37, 58, 127n, 147, 159n, 175, 177, 181
Amalia, Prussian Princess 160n
Archimedes 13, 17n
Argens, Jean-Baptiste de Boyer, Marquis d' 152
Aristotle 13, 17n
Arnstadt 124

B-A-C-H 191, 192, 194, 212
Bach, Anna Magdalena 57, 58, 64n, 159n
Bach, Carl Philipp Emanuel i, 2, 8, 13n, 14n, 15n, 18, 21–2, 23n, 30, 31n, 33n, 37–8, 47, 49, 53n, 54n, 57–8, 61–2, 63n, 64n, 65n, 115, 128n, 142, 147 60, 162–71, 175, 182–3, 187n, 197, 207n, 209–214, 216, 218–9, 221, 231n, 232n, 235–39, 246n; *Versuch über die wahre Art das Clavier zu spielen* 64n; *Twelve Masonic Songs* 239
Bach, Christina Dorothea 6
Bach, Ernestus Andreas 7
Bach, Gottfried Heinrich 6
Bach, Johann August Abraham 6
Bach, Johann Christian 6–7, 29, 236, 239n
Bach, Johann Christoph Friedrich (the son) 30, 37, 48, 56–7, 64n, 119–22, 124–5, 127n, 135, 139, 147, 149, 154–5, 157, 160n, 169–170, 171n, 175, 180, 182, 187n, 203–4, 214, 221, 232n, 240
Bach, Johann Christoph (the uncle) 27, 31n; *Lieber Herr Gott, weck uns auf* 27
Bach, Johann Elias 28, 32n
Bach, Johann Sebastian; Vocal; Cantatas; BWV 12, *Weinen, Klagen, Sorgen, Zagen* 69; BWV 36, *Schwingt freudig euch Empor* 8; BWV 36a, [*Steigt freudig in die Luft*] 8; BWV 36b, *Die Freude reget sich* 8; BWV 36c, *Schwingt freudig euch empor* 8; BWV 69, *Lobe den Herrn, meine Seele* 27; BWV 71, [*Gott ist mein König*] 188n; BWV 75, *Die Elenden sollen essen* 189; BWV 195, *Dem Gerechten muss das Licht* 27, 32n; BWV 198, [*Laß, Fürstin, laß noch einen Strahl*] 7; BWV 205, *Der zufriedengestellte Aeolus* 8; BWV 207, *Vereinigte Zwietracht der wechselnden Saiten* 8; BWV 210, [*O holder Tag, erwünschte Zeit*] 25, 26; BWV 214, [*Tönet ihr Pauken! Erschallet, Trompeten*] 188n; BWV Anh. 13b, [*Wilkommen! Ihr herrschenden Götter der Erde*] 7; BWV Anh. 18, *Froher Tag, verlangte Stunden* 6; BWV Anh. 196, [*Auf, süß entzückende Gewalt*] 7; Mass, Magnificat and Passions; BWV 232, Mass in B minor 13, 27–9, 32n, 33n, 69–70, 78n, 86n, 87n, 108n, 179–80, 189, 209, 219, 224, 231n; BWV 243 and BWV 243a, *Magnificat in D* 69; BWV 245, St John Passion 27, 32n, 69, 203; Organ music; BWV 525–530, Trio sonatas 64n5, 159n; BWV 574, *Fuge in c* 203; BWV 669–689; BWV 802–805; BWV 552; *Clavierübung III* 70–78, 87n, 100n, 107, 115, 124–5, 156–7, 159n, 160n, 161n, 170n, 233n, 244; BWV 769, 769a, Canonic

Index

Variations (*Einige canonische Veraenderungen über das Weynacht-Lied: Vom Himmel hoch, da komm ich her*) 78n, 86n, 87n, 107, 127n, 195n, 203, 228, 240, 244, 247n; Clavier music; BWV 772–801, *Auffrichtige Anleitung* (Inventions and Sinfonias) 18, 31n, 69, 86n, 107, 115, 179, 202–3; BWV 831, BWV 971; *Clavierübung II* 122; BWV 846–869, BWV 870–803, *The Well Tempered Clavier* 18, 86n, 115, 179, 187n; *The Well Tempered Clavier II* 13; BWV 924–932, *Clavier-Büchlein vor Wilhelm Friedemann Bach* 69, 149; BWV 988, Goldberg Variations (*Aria mit verschiedenen Veränderungen*) 23n, 86n, 87n, 100n, 107, 127n; Chamber music; BWV 1005/2, Sonata for violin solo in C 143n; Canons, *Musical Offering*; BWV 1076, Triple canon 22, 228; BWV 1077, Double canon 22, 25–7; BWV 1079, *Musical Offering* 13, 55n, 56–7, 64n, 86n, 87n, 100n, 115, 124, 127n, 153, 188n, 203–4, 219, 228–9, 234n, 240, 244; BWV 1087, *Fourteen Canons* 22, 23n, 86n, 87n
Bach, Johanna Karolina 6
Bach, Wilhelm Friedemann 8, 15n, 58, 101n, 147, 149–50, 159n; *Sonata for clavier in E-flat major* 64n
Baker, Thomas 101n, 207n
Bammler, Johann Nathanael 25, 28–9, 32n, 142, 143n, 234n
Baudis, Gottfried Leonhard 7
Baudis, Magdalena Sybilla 7
Beach, David 15n
Beißwenger, Kirsten 11, 16n, 23n
Benda, Franz 153
Benda Georg Anton 153
Berardi, Angelo 11, 80, 86n, 127n, 241, 246n; *Documenti armonici* 11, 86n, 127n, 246n
Bergel, Erich 139, 143n, 187n, 246n
Berlin 22, 57–8, 153–4 159n, 209, 228, 236, 238
Berlin Royal Library (*Staatsbibliothek zu Berlin*) xix, xxi, 10, 11, 23n, 32n, 33n, 37, 39, 53n, 54n, 55n, 115–6, 125, 127n, 160n, 170, 171n, 233n
Blankenburg, Walter 246n
Blyoskina, Olga N. 188n
Boie, Heinrich Christian 237
Bohse, August, (*Letzte Liebes- und Heldengedichte*) 9

Bokemeyer, Heinrich 17n
Borman, Theodor Benedict 31n
Bouhier, Jean 151, 160n
Breitkopf (the publishing company) 57–8
Breitkopf, Johann Gottlob Immanuel 180, 188n
Brosses, Charles de, (*Lettres sur l'etat actuel de la ville souterraine d'Herculee et sur les causes de son ensevelissement sous les ruines du Vesuve*) 151–2, 160n
Bückeburg 30, 139, 149, 154–5, 157, 169, 180, 182, 188n, 214
Bümler, Heinrich 17n
Burney, Charles 150, 160n, 214, 232n, 239n
Busoni, Ferruccio 139, 143n
Butler, Gregory 2n, 64n, 72, 78n, 109n, 124, 128n, 133, 135, 137, 142n, 143n, 156–7, 160n, 161n, 170n, 218–9, 227, 232n, 233n

Cabbala (*see* Kabbalah)
Calvisius, Sethus (*Melopoeia*) 11
Cöthen 5, 159n, 187n, 239n

Dadelsen, Georg von 25, 32n
David, Hans Theodor 14n, 148
Dehn, Siegfried Wilhelm xxi, 43, 46–9, 54n, 55n, 148, 170, 171n
Dequevauviller, Vincent 137, 143n
Dresden 7, 15n
Dürer, Albrecht 247n
Dürr, Alfred 26–7, 32n, 132, 137, 143n, 232n

Ebeling, Christoph Daniel 237, 239n
Eisenach 27, 31n
Engraver copy 49, 56, 58, 64n, 106, 121–2, 124–5, 128n, 132–3, 135, 137, 139, 141–2, 143n, 155–6, 158, 160n, 161n, 165–7, 170, 194, 197–8, 200–203, 207n, 218, 221, 224, 227, 229–230
Ernesti, Johann August 6
Ernesti, Johann Heinrich 6
Ernesti, Regina Maria 6
Eschenburg, Johann Joachim 150
Espagne, Franz 46–9, 55n
Eulenburg 29
Euler, Leonhard 11, 16n, 23n, 160n; *Tentamen nouae theoriae musicae ex certissimis harmoniae principiis dilucide* 11, 23n
Ezekiel, Vision of the Chariot 246–7n

Fasch, Johann Friedrich (Church Cantata) 128n
Ferguson, Michael 139, 143n
Flemming, Joachim Friedrich von 7
Forkel, Johann Nicolaus 13n, 63n, 159n, 246n
Frankfurt-an-der-Oder 15n
Frederick II (The Great) 10, 16n, 57, 86n, 149–55, 160n, 214, 237
Frescobaldi, Girolamo Alessandro (*Fiori musicali*) 11
Friedländer, Emil Gottlieb 43–4, 46–9, 54n, 55n
Fulde, Johann Gottfried 22
Fuller-Maitland, John Alexander 122, 124, 126n
Fux, Johann Joseph 11, 13–14n, 19–20, 23n, 241, 246n; *Gradus ad Parnassum* 11, 19–21, 23n, 127n

Gerstenberg, Heinrich Wilhelm von 237
Gesner, Elizabeth Karitas 6
Gesner, Johann Matthias 6, 8, 14n
Gleim, Johann Wilhelm Ludwig 237
Gluck, Christoph Willibald 28
Göncz, Zoltán 139, 143n
Göttingen 6
Gottsched, Johann Christoph 7
Graeser, Wolfgang 139, 143n, 148
Graun, Carl Heinrich 153
Gumpelzhaimer, Adam, (*Compendium musicae*) 244–5

Halle 149, 159n
Hamburg 54n, 72, 73, 236, 238, 239n
Handel, Georg Friedrich 150
Hanover 15n
Harsdörfer, Georg Philipp, (*Poetischer Trichter*) 177, 187n
Hartmann 128n, 170
Hauptmann, Maurice 148, 159n
Hausmann, Elias Gottlieb 22, 228
Hebenstreit, Christina Dorothea 6
Hebenstreit, Johann Christian 6, 14n
Heinichen, Johann David 241
Henning, Johann (*Cabbalologia*) 9, 21n
Henrici, Christian Friedrich (Picander) 9, 15n; *Ernst-, Schertzhaffte und Satyrische Gedichte* 9
Herculaneum 151–52, 238
Hessen 73
Heunisch, Caspar (*Haupt-Schlüssel über die hohe Offenbahrung S. Johannis*) 241, 242, 246n

Hofmann, Klaus 52, 54n, 55n, 57–8, 63n, 64n, 65n, 97, 100, 101n, 109n, 116, 127n, 143n, 159n, 180, 187n, 188n, 201–202, 207n, 233n
Hoke, Hans Gunter 18, 22n, 46–7, 55n, 228, 233n
Holle, Adam Heinrich 72

Iamblichus from Cochide (*De Vita Pythagorica liber*) 16n
Irsee Abbey near Kaufbeuren 10

Jung, Carl 246

Kabbalah 9, 15n, 16n, 241
Karlsruhe 247n
Kellner, Herbert 137, 143n
Kepler, Johannes (*Harmonices mundi*) 11
Kinsky, Georg 57, 64n
Kircher, Athanasius, (*Musurgia universalis sive ars magna consoni et dissoni in X. libros digesta*) 11–12, 16n
Kirnberger, Johann Philipp 8, 160n; *Die Kunst Des Reinen Satzes In Der Musik: Aus Sicheren Grundsätzen Hergeleitet Und Mit Deutlichen Beyspielen Erläutert* 8
Klinger, Friedrich Maximilian 239n
Klopstock, Friedrich Gottlieb 237
Knittel, Caspar (*Via Regia Ad Omnes Scientias et Artes*) 9
Knobelsdorff, Georg Wenzeslaus von 151–3
Kobayashi, Yoshitake 22n, 29–30, 33n, 39, 54n, 55n, 187n, 209, 231n, 232n, 233n, 236, 239n
Kolneder, Walter 63n, 64n
Kolof, Lorenz Christoph Mizler von (*See* Mizler)
Końskie (Poland) 10, 228
Kopchevskiy, Nikolay Alexandrovich 207n
Kopfermann, Albert 46–9, 55n
Koprowski, Richard 64n, 197, 207n
Kortte, Gottlieb 7–8
Kuhnau, Johann 5–6, 14n; *De juribus circa musicos ecclesiasticos* 14n
Kurtch, Olga 109n, 188n, 195n

Leaver, Robin 16n, 180, 188n
Legrenzi, Giovanni 203
Leibniz, Gottfried Wilhelm 9, 12, 15n, 240; *Disputatio Metaphysica de Principio Individui* 15n; *Dissertatio de arte combinatoria* 12, 15n; *Monadology* 9

260 Index

Leipzig xxi, xxii, 5–10, 13, 30, 57–9, 63n, 65n, 72–3, 101n, 124, 142, 149, 159n, 161n, 176–7, 182–3, 201, 214, 230, 231n, 232n, 236, 239n, 246n
Leipzig University 5–9, 14n, 15n
Lessing, Gotthold Ephraim 153–4, 237–8, 239n; *Ernst and Falk Conversations for Freemasons* 239n; *Laocoon (Laokoon oder Uber die Grenzen der Malerei und Poesie* 154
Lippold, Viera xxi
Löscher, Valentine Ernst (*Unschuldige Nachrichten von Alten und Neuen Theologischen Sachen*) 9
Ludwig, Ernest 73
Ludewig, Reinhard 25, 27, 31n, 32n
Ludovici, Christian 6
Luther, Martin 9, 241–2, 246n, 247n

Marchand, Louis 7
Maria Josepha of Austria 188n
Marpurg, Friedrich Wilhelm 18, 21, 22n, 23n, 59, 65n, 161n, 168, 210–12, 231n, 232n
Marshall, Robert Lewis 29, 33n, 224, 231n, 233n
Maskov, Johann Jacob 7
Mattheson, Johann 18, 22n, 72–3, 77, 78n, 86n, 127n, 170n, 232n, 241; *Der vollkommene Capellmeister* 72–3, 78n, 86n, 127n; *Die wolklingende Fingersprache* 72; *Philologisches Tresespiel* 22n, 170n, 171n
Maupertuis, Pierre-Louis de 152, 160n
Menz, Johann Friedrich 7, 14n
Menzel, Adolph von 160n
Meyerbeer, Giacomo 54n
Mieth, Johann Christoph (*Das ABC: cum notis variorum*; *Das Einmahl Eins: cum notis variorum*) 9
Mittag, Johann Gottfried, (*Leben und Thaten Friedrich August III*) 9
Mizler, Lorenz Christoph 8, 10–11, 13, 14n, 17n, 19–20, 23n, 72–3, 86n, 170, 214, 228–9, 232n, 241, 246n; 'Dissertatio quod musica ars sit pars eruditionis philosophicae' (*Quod musica scientia sit pars eruditionis philosophicae*) 8, 11; *Musikalische Bibliothek* 8, 10–12, 14n, 16n, 72–3, 170, 214, 228; Society of Musical Sciences 9–13, 16n, 17n, 18–9, 22, 23n, 72–73, 109n, 218, 228–230, 231n, 241
Müller, August Friedrich 7, 8

Müller, Johann, (*Judaismus Oder Jüdenthumb…*) 16n, 246n
Musikalische Bibliothek (see Mizler)

Newman, Anthony 180, 188n
Nichelmann, Christoph 8, 14n, 15n; *Die Melodie nach ihrem Wesen sowohl, als nach ihren Eigenschaften* 8
Nider, Johannes, (*Twenty Four Golden Harps*) 242
Niedt, Friedrich Erhardt, (*Musicalische Handleitung*) 11
Nottebohm, Martin Gustav 148, 168n, 216–9, 232n
Numerology (see also paragram) 83, 86n, 97, 194, 195, 240, 245, 246n
Nuremberg 124, 228

Obituary 30, 31n, 33n, 170, 171n, 209–216, 231n, 236
Olearius, Johannes, (*Biblische Erklärung*) 9, 15n
Palestrina, Giovanni 11, 16n, 23n, 246n; *Ecce sacerdos magnus* 11; *Missa sine nomine* 11
Paragram (see also numerology) 9, 13, 15n, 177–187, 189, 241, 245
Pesne, Antoine 151, 153
Picander, (see Henrici)
Poelchau, Georg Johann Daniel 37–8, 47–8, 53n, 55n, 187n
Pompeii 238
Potsdam 149, 168n
Propp, Vladimir, (*Morphology of Folk Tale*) xxii
Psellus, Michael 11, 16n
Pythagoras 11–3, 16n, 17n, 208n

Quantz, Johann Joachim 153, 160n
Quintilianus, Marcus Fabius, (*De Institutione Oratoria…*) 8

Rastration 47, 49–53, 55n, 79, 85, 86, 100, 102, 109n, 116, 143n, 189, 221, 227
Reimarus, Johann Albert Heinrich 237
Riccio, Teodoro 7
Riemer, Johann, (*Über-Reicher Schatz-Meister Aller hohen Standes und Burgerlichen Freud- und Leid-Complimente*) 9
Rivinus, Andreas Florens 7–8

Rivinus, Johann Florens 7
Rome 247n
Rust, Wilhelm 148, 171n

St John 241, 243, 245
Sanssouci 151–4, 160n
Saxony 5, 188n
Schaller, Christian Friedrich 28
Schaumburg-Lippe, Wilhelm 154, 180–81, 214
Schleuning, Peter 128n, 180, 187n, 188n
Schmid, Balthasar 228, 233n
Schmieder, Wolfgang 22, 219, 232n
Schröter, Christoph Gottlieb 17n, 30
Schubart, Christian Friedrich Daniel ('CARLS Name') 237–8, 239n
Schübler, Johann Heinrich 56–8, 64n, 125, 128n, 142, 156, 161n, 202
Schudt, Johann Jacob, (*Jüdische Merckwürdigkeiten*) 9
Schulenberg, David 77n, 127n, 159n
Schulze, Hans-Joachim xxi, 207n, 231n
Schumann, Robert 115, 148, 159n
Schweinfurt 31n
Schwenke, Christian Friedrich Gottlieb 38, 47, 49, 54n
Siber, Urban Gottfried 6
Smend, Friedrich 15n, 78n, 180, 187n, 188n
Society of Musical Sciences (*see* Mizler)
Socrates 13, 17n
Spieß, Meinrad 10, 228
Spitta, Philipp 109n, 110–11, 115, 126n, 127n, 148, 175, 187n
Stöttrup, Andreas 237, 239n
Sturm, Christoph Christian 237, 239n
Sturm und Drang 237–8, 239n
Stuttgart 209, 239n

Tatlow, Ruth 15n, 187n
Taylor, John 30, 142, 230
Telemann Georg Philipp 17n
Teller, Romanus 6–7
Terpander of Antissa 13, 17n
Tessmer, Manfred 124, 128n, 161n, 207n
Thomaskirche 5–8
Thomasschule 5–8, 14n
Thomassius, Christian 15n
Thym, Jurgen 15n

Tosi, Pier Francesco (*Opinioni de' cantori antichi e moderni*) 8
Trautman, Christoph 246n

Vienna 128n, 161n
Vivaldi, Antonio, [Concerto in D minor, Bach's copy (BWV 596)] 159n
Voltaire, (François–Marie Arouet) 152, 160n
Voss, Johann Heinrich 237

Walcha, Helmut 139, 143n
Walther, Johann Gottfried 11, 232n, 241; *Musicalisches Lexicon* 11, 232n
Wasserzeichen (also watermarks, WZ) 39, 42, 47, 54n, 55n, 64n, 84, 85, 86, 218
Weimar 7
Weise, Christian 9; *Curieuse Fragen über die Logica* 9, 15n
Weiss, Christian the Elder 6–7
Weiss, Christian the Younger 6
Werckmeister, Andreas 11, 16n; *Orgel-Probe* 11
Wiemer, Wolfgang 64n, 128n, 132–3, 135, 143n, 207n
Wiermann, Barbara 16n, 19, 23n
Wilhelm Ernst, Duke of Saxe-Weimar 7
Wilhelmi, Thomas 23n, 170n, 207n, 231n, 246n
Winckelmann, Johann Joachim 238
Winckler, Johann Heinrich 6
Wolle, Christoph 6–7
Wolff, Christian 15n
Wolff, Christoph xxi, 11, 13n, 14n, 15n, 16n, 17n, 18, 22n, 23n, 27, 29, 32n, 33n, 55n, 58, 63n, 64n, 65n, 78n, 125, 127n, 128n, 143n, 155, 159n, 160n, 161n, 180, 187n, 188n, 207n, 209, 219–20, 231n, 232n, 233n, 234n
Wollny, Peter xxi, 29, 31n, 32n, 33n, 101n, 143n, 232n, 234n

Yankus, Alla Irmenovna xxii, 160n
Yuzhak, Kira Iosifovna xxii, 109n, 160n, 208n

Zarlino, Gioseffo, (*Le Istitutioni harmoniche*) 11, 208n
Zella, Thuringia, (Zella-Mehlis) 56–8, 64n, 124, 201
Zielińska, Teresa 32n